DISSENT

Explorations in the History of American Radicalism

DISSENT

Explorations in the History of
AMERICAN RADICALISM

edited by

Alfred F. Young

NORTHERN ILLINOIS UNIVERSITY PRESS

DeKalb

Second printing, 1969

Standard Book Number 87580–502–7
Library of Congress Card Number 68–57389
Copyright © 1968 by Northern Illinois University Press
DeKalb, Illinois 60115

Preface

This book is an outgrowth of a series of four lectures at Northern Illinois University in the 1966–67 academic year by Staughton Lynd, Carl Degler, Martin Duberman, and Howard Zinn on the theme "Dissent in American History." To round out the theme for publication, it seemed desirable to invite other scholars to contribute additional essays. The sole criterion for inviting lecturers and essayists was whether they were engaged in a scholarly exploration of a significant subject that is related to the general theme. No effort was made to "touch all bases," to impose a unifying focus or framework, or to choose historians of a particular point of view.

Most of the essays are either a "progress report" on scholarship under way or an interpretation of recently completed work. Some offer fresh perceptions of familiar subjects. A few deal with subjects long neglected even by students of American radicalism. Some try to apply the approaches of English scholars to American movements. The essays at the end of the volume grapple with contemporary history, hopefully proving that the historian can contribute to an understanding of events in motion.

"We historians," one of the contributors has written elsewhere, "are everlastingly loquacious as to how the approach of this or that past historian was influenced by the times in which he lived. When it comes to our own history, however, that of course is objective. Why? This seems to me," Staughton Lynd continues, "a ridiculous intellectual schizophrenia. We are no better men than were our predecessors in the craft and without doubt are every bit as much culture-bound in our history as were they. Why be ashamed to admit this?" *

Most of the contributors to this volume probably would not "be ashamed to admit" that contemporary dissent has in-

* From Staughton Lynd, "Wearing Two Hats: Historian and Peace Activist," a paper delivered at the American Historical Association Convention, Toronto, December, 1967.

fluenced their inquiry into the dissent of the past. Although they may not share Staughton Lynd's point of view, some might agree with him that "if history, like a mountain, can be viewed from many different sides, all equally 'objective,' the historian's personal experience may legitimately suggest to him new passes and valleys which are really there." The headnotes will enable the reader to judge each essay in the context of the writer's "personal experience" and scholarly interests. The essays, we hope, will show him parts of the mountain he had not seen before and will do what all good scholarship should do: stimulate further explorations.

The essays by Staughton Lynd, Martin Duberman, and Jesse Lemisch, by agreement with the authors, appeared in print elsewhere before this volume was ready for publication. The essays by Herbert Gutman and Kenneth McNaught are reprinted from scholarly journals. I gratefully acknowledge the cooperation of these journals and publishers in allowing joint publication. It is a pleasure, also, to acknowledge a generous grant from Northern Illinois University that made the lectures and essays possible, and to express appreciation to the Lecture Committee and to my colleagues in the Department of History for their suggestions on authors and topics.

Alfred F. Young

DeKalb, Illinois
April, 1968

Contents

DISSENT

Explorations in the History of American Radicalism

Freedom Now: The Intellectual Origins of American Radicalism

Staughton Lynd

Staughton Lynd began his explorations in the history of American radicalism at Columbia University in 1959 while working on a master's thesis which was later published as *Anti-Federalism in Dutchess County, New York: A Study in Democracy and Class Conflict in the Revolutionary Era* (Chicago, 1962). Initially sympathetic to Charles Beard, Lynd writes that he did not expect "to be driven beyond Beard, to lay greater stress than he did upon city artisans, upon slavery, upon the role of ideas." His doctoral dissertation, adding the New York City artisans to upstate tenant farmers, revealed another group Beard had not accounted for. Between 1961 and 1964, while teaching at Spelman College (a Negro women's college in Atlanta), Lynd comments that he "became more conscious of the degree to which American historiography leaves the Negro out." Several essays on Beard, Frederick Jackson Turner and slavery, and the Constitution's compromises with slavery followed. They are collected with his New York essays in *Class Conflict, Slavery, and the United States Constitution* (Indianapolis, 1968).

Lynd also explored the tradition of nonviolent social activism that lay at the core of his own Quaker commitment. He edited *Nonviolence in America: A Documentary History* (Indianapolis, 1966), completing the introduction while directing the Freedom Schools project in Mississippi, and reading proof while enroute to North Vietnam for his since-famous visit. The essay that follows is part of a larger study under the same title exploring the intellectual roots of the radical tradition. He probes the intuitive ethical individualism he finds embedded in the Declaration of Independence.

From 1964 through 1966 Staughton Lynd was a member of the department of history at Yale University. In 1968 he taught at Chicago State College after academic opinion forced its Board of Governors to reverse their earlier decision to reject him because of his "public activities." Administrations at four other universities in Illinois have thwarted the efforts of their history departments to appoint him; at this writing he is jobless.

A version of this essay appears in the Introduction and Chapters 1 and 2 of *Intellectual Origins of American Radicalism*, by Staughton Lynd. © 1968 by Staughton Lynd. Used by permission of publisher, Pantheon Books, a Division of Random House, Inc.

Americans have made two revolutions, in 1776–83 and in 1861–65. Both were "bourgeois" revolutions; the first preserved inherited property as it destroyed inherited government; the second preserved and enhanced property in factories and railroads as it abolished property in man.[1] Nevertheless, it is quite wrong to suppose that the American Revolution and Civil War had no "ideology . . . capable of being made universal."[2] To energize and explain these upheavals, the men who made them created a revolutionary intellectual tradition. They addressed to the opinion of mankind the dramatic proposition that all men are created equal, possessing natural liberties, which, if they can ever be taken away, cannot be justly taken away without consent. As Tom Paine observed, the American Revolution was unique precisely in being "a revolution in the principles and practice of governments" and not "merely a separation from England."[3] That is why those principles have been echoed by revolutionaries the world over from that day to this (most recently by the Vietnamese, whose 1945 declaration of independence begins with the words "All men are created equal").

Because they expressed the aspiration of different social groups that were united only on behalf of independence, the words of the American Revolution meant many things to many men. Abolitionists, as they built a new revolutionary movement against chattel slavery, drew selectively on the intellectual resources of the past, clarifying and interpreting the resources to suit their own needs. The American revolutionary tradition, as described in this essay, is the tradition that culminated in abolitionism: a tradition based on the more radical readings of the Declaration of Independence, which traced its intellectual ancestry more to Paine and Richard Price than to Harrington and Locke.

Of necessity, however, all variants of the revolutionary tradition defended the right of revolution. During the century 1760–1860 the right of revolution was justified by presidents as well as by prophets, by politicians in power as well as by radicals out of power. "Revolutionary ground should be occupied," stated the address of the Executive Committee of the American Anti-Slavery Society in 1844, which continued: "Up, then, with the banner of revolution!" [4] But this only rephrased more flamboyantly what the Declaration of Independence termed the people's right "to alter or to abolish" the governments they created. And Abraham Lincoln's first inaugural address asserted:

> This country, with its institutions, belongs to the people who inhabit it. Whenever they shall grow weary of the existing government, they can exercise their constitutional right of amending it, or their revolutionary right to dismember or overthrow it.

I

For all its ambiguities, the preamble to the Declaration of Independence is the single most concentrated expression of the revolutionary intellectual tradition. Without significant exception, subsequent variants of American radicalism have taken the Declaration as their point of departure and have claimed to be true versions of the spirit of '76. Jefferson developed the philosophy of the document he had drafted in the direction of states' rights and the defense of southern sectionalism, but in doing this he continued to invoke the Declaration of Independence—as did the very language of South Carolina's Declaration of the Causes of Secession in 1860. Northern radicalism also traced its lineage to Carpenters' Hall. On July 4, 1826, the day Jefferson and John Adams died, Robert Owen delivered a "declaration of mental independence" that comprised secularism, equality of the sexes, and common ownership of property. These ideas inspired one current of Jacksonian dissent. But William Lloyd Garrison, anything but secular, and intensely anti-Jacksonian, also adopted the rhetoric of the Declaration in drafting the manifestoes of the American Anti-Slavery Society in 1833 and the New England Non-Resistance Society in 1838. Lincoln referred to the Declaration of Independence as the "standard maxim for a free society" and compared its role as a spiritual regulator to that of the Biblical injunction "Be ye perfect." [5] The Radical Republicans—Charles Sumner, for example—maintained that the Declaration was part of the United States Constitution, or if it was not it should at once be made so.

After the Civil War the glittering generalities of the Declaration retained their potency, and American radicalism continued to present itself as their fulfillment. "The reform I have proposed," wrote Henry George in *Progress and Poverty,*

is but the carrying out in letter and spirit of the truth enunciated
in the Declaration of Independence. . . . They who look upon Liberty as having accomplished her mission when she has abolished
hereditary privileges and given men the ballot . . . have not seen
her real grandeur. . . . We cannot go on prating of the inalienable
rights of man and then denying the inalienable right to the bounty
of the Creator.[6]

When Julian West awoke in Edward Bellamy's *Looking Backward*,
Doctor Leete's explanation of the new society used similar terms. "In
a word," he said, "the people of the United States concluded to assume the conduct of their own business, just as one hundred odd
years before they had assumed the conduct of their own government,
organizing now for industrial purposes on precisely the same grounds
that they had then organized for political purposes." [7] Henry Dema-
rest Lloyd invoked the analogy of the American Revolution in *Wealth
against Commonwealth,* declaring:

> Myriads of experiments to get the substance of liberty out of
> the forms of tyranny, to believe in princes, to trust good men to do
> good as kings, have taught the inexorable lesson that, in the econ-
> omy of nature, form and substance must move together. . . . Iden-
> tical is the lesson we are learning with regard to industrial power
> and property.

"Liberty recast the old forms of government into the Republic,"
Lloyd concluded, "and it must remould our institutions of wealth
into the Commonwealth." [8]

In the twentieth century it has been no different. Both the NAACP
and SNCC derive from W. E. B. Du Bois' seminal essay "Of Booker T.
Washington and Others," which ended with an appeal to "those great
words which the Sons of the Fathers would fain forget": the preamble
to the Declaration of Independence. Similarly, Patrick Henry "was
one of my first heroes," stated Eugene Debs, "and my passion for his
eloquent and burning defiance of King George inspired the first speech
I ever attempted in public." Among the French and American revolutionaries who inspired Debs, Tom Paine "towered above them all." [9]

During the New Deal and World War II it was voguish among
radicals to identify their various causes with the alleged "tradition
of Jefferson, Jackson, and Lincoln." The New Left of the 1950's and

1960's, despite its oft-described sense of alienation and its quarrel with the intellectual habits of the previous generation, also uses the Revolution as a touchstone. Thus in November, 1965, Carl Oglesby, then the president of Students for a Democratic Society, asked an antiwar demonstration that had gathered at the Washington Monument to imagine what Thomas Jefferson or Thomas Paine would say to President Johnson and McGeorge Bundy about the war in Vietnam. Thus in August, 1966, when the House Un-American Activities Committee subpoenaed several antiwar activists, the head of the Free University of New York issued a statement invoking the spirit of the Green Mountain Boys, and the chairman of the Berkeley Vietnam Day Committee appeared in the hearing chamber in the uniform of an officer of George Washington's army.

For almost two hundred years American radicals have traced their intellectual origins to the Declaration of Independence and to the revolution it justified. Much as—with or without the help of therapists—all of us occasionally look back to our individual pasts to find strength for new beginnings, so—with or without the help of historians —Americans who wish to change their present society have used the past as a source for forgotten alternatives. The Revolution-cum-Declaration serves us as a means toward reviving that "frequent recurrence to fundamental principles" that the Virginia Bill of Rights advised.

II

The preamble to the Declaration of Independence made its case in universal terms. It appealed not to the British constitution but to nature and nature's God. It spoke not of the rights of Englishmen known to lawyers but of rights of man self-evident to all. These qualities led an earlier generation of historians to regard the Declaration as the product of French revolutionary philosophy.

Since the publication in 1922 of Becker's *Declaration of Independence,* historians have been content to ascribe its intellectual origins to John Locke; as Becker put it, "Jefferson copied Locke." [10] The recent scholarship of Bernard Bailyn and others adds the corollary that Americans often copied not Locke himself but English publicists of the early eighteenth century who had made Locke accessible in popularized form. Among these publicists the names most often mentioned are John Trenchard and Thomas Gordon, joint authors of *Cato's Letters,* which appeared in the English press between 1720 and 1723.[11]

A different perspective arises from recognition that halfway through the eighteenth century, as Becker himself stressed, a pervasive intellectual crisis occurred that was based on the perception that Locke's theory of knowledge contradicted his political philosophy.[12] In the preamble to the Declaration of Independence, those phrases justifying revolution that Jefferson took from Locke's *Second Treatise of Government* logically depended on the prior statement that held it to be "self-evident" (or, in an earlier draft, "sacred and undeniable") that men were born equally possessed of inalienable natural rights. Although in the *Second Treatise* Locke referred to a law of nature "writ in the hearts of mankind" and to natural rights that "cease not" in society, in the *Essay Concerning Human Understanding* he maintained, as Becker paraphrased him, that "God has not . . . stamped upon the minds of all men certain intuitively perceived intellectual and moral ideas."[13] He simultaneously advocated a political philosophy of liberation and a psychology that seemed to deny the possibility of human freedom.

According to Locke's theory of psychology, ideas were derived from experience as man was stimulated by pain and pleasure to repeat some actions and to eschew others. But if man was endowed by his Creator with a mind that was no more than a blank page, what happened to self-evident inalienable rights? and to a theory of revolution that presumed the existence of those rights? Impressions written by experience upon the *tabula rasa* of the mind could, presumably, be erased by new experience in the future. Convictions that had been shaped by a particular environment would change if the environment were altered. Reformers required, in Becker's words, "a fulcrum in Nature for moving the existing order; . . . they had to demonstrate that 'life, liberty, and the pursuit of happiness' were according to Nature and the will of God, whereas tyranny and cruelty and the taking of property without consent were not."[14] Locke's theory of environmental psychology, however, semed to assert that ideas of right and wrong were no different from ideas of hot and cold.

The dilemma that Locke thus bequeathed to his disciples may be compared to our twentieth-century discussion of what Marx "really meant." Locke, like Marx, had provided the most vigorous rationale for social change, which no reformer wished altogether to discard.

But Locke, like Marx, also brilliantly explained how circumstances created the convictions in the name of which change was demanded. A twentieth-century version of the resulting impasse, by Edward Thompson of the English New Left, runs as follows:

> Men had abandoned human agency. They could not hold back change; but change went with the shuffling gait of circumstance. It did not stem from the operation of human consciousness and will upon circumstance. Events seemed to will men, not men events. For meaning can be given to history only in the quarrel between "ought" and "is." [15]

Eighteenth-century materialism led to the identical dead end. As Basil Willey paraphrased Holbach: "Our errors *cannot* be 'natural,' are not what Nature intended; yet there is nothing which Nature has not produced, nothing which does not fall within the 'domain of causality.'" Or, as Ernst Cassirer put the problem, "How does the necessity and immutability of the concept of law agree with the proposition that every idea is derived from the senses and that, accordingly, it can possess no other and no higher significance than the various sense experiences on which it is based?" [16]

Stimulated as much by Locke's environmental psychology as by the economic determinism of James Harrington, English political philosophy in the eighteenth century turned away from the natural rights philosophy and toward a social science that was characterized by ethical relativism and pragmatic accommodation to existing reality. Although this generalization probably applies most fully to such conservatives as David Hume—in Peter Gay's phrase "the complete modern pagan"—it also applies to such opposition ideologues as Trenchard and Gordon. In the belief (following Harrington) that "the first Principle of all Power is Property; and every Man will have his Share of it in Proportion as he enjoys Property," the authors of *Cato's Letters* concluded that "the great Secret in Politicks is, nicely to watch and observe this Fluctuation and Change of natural Power, and to adjust the political to it." Because property in England was unequally distributed, a republican government was impossible: "The Phantome of a Commonwealth must vanish, and never appear again but in disordered Brains." [17]

Such sophisticated skepticism was no doubt less characteristic of the American colonies, a young and hopeful society, but, as Alan

Heimert maintains, in America too the rationalist "Liberal" clergy tended toward "restricting the Christian pilgrimage to a methodical adjustment to the given norms of existence." "The starting point of Liberal doctrine was the 'objective realities' of the 'present state' of human existence," Heimert continues. For the Liberal, according to Heimert, happiness "came through accommodation to the environment in which man had been placed." [18]

In the more secular discourse of the Revolutionary era a persistent strain of American thinking continued to restrict the vision of the possible to what the existing economic realities appeared to permit. All the Founding Fathers—Jefferson as well as Hamilton, Madison along with John Adams—shared a deep-seated fatalism about the ultimate instability of republican government. In Douglass Adair's words, "the Fathers' scientific reading of history committed them and their contemporaries in varying degrees of rigidity to a species of *political determinism.*" [19] In fact, as Adair adds, their determinism was fundamentally economic, for it followed from Harringtonian assumptions about the relation of property and power. Moreover, Jefferson and others of his generation tended to fall back on the argument from economic realism to explain their inability to put an end to chattel slavery. Hence abolitionism, as David B. Davis suggests, was in part an insistence that active human will could overcome the objective conditions that to the Fathers appeared inalterable.[20]

Up to this point in my discussion the relativism and fatalism of Locke's psychology have been counterposed to the natural rights philosophy of the *Second Treatise.* A careful reading shows, however, that Locke's environmental psychology seriously weakened his apologia or justification for revolt. Thus, for Locke, the law that God has written on men's hearts turns out to be similar to Hobbes' instinct of self-preservation, "that great law of nature, 'Whoso sheddeth man's blood, by man shall his blood be shed.'" [21] Quoting Locke's subsequent assertion that "however strange it may seem, the law-maker hath nothing to do with moral virtues and vices," Leo Strauss concludes that, even in the *Second Treatise,* Locke did not subscribe to a law of nature in the traditional normative sense.[22]

Throughout his writings Locke systematically segregated things sacred from things secular, allowing freedom of conscience to religion only after carefully barring it from all interference in secular society. Locke either invoked the traditional morality to win acceptance for a theory based upon hard self-interest, or ignored the traditional morality entirely. The former is exemplified by the chapter on property in the *Second Treatise*, which begins with the observation that God has given the earth to "mankind in common" and ends by rationalizing the unlimited accumulation of wealth. An illustration of the latter is the society envisioned by the Fundamental Constitutions of South Carolina (drafted or at least transcribed by Locke), which gave its citizens broad religious liberty together with "absolute power and authority" over their Negro slaves.

Property, not life or liberty, was the basis of Locke's whole system. According to his *Second Treatise,* a man can justly kill a thief who threatens only his property, and an officer who may not take a penny from a soldier's pocket can justly order the soldier's execution.[23] As Sheldon S. Wolin observes, Locke made conscience into a safeguard for property by conceiving it as "an internalized expression of external rules rather than the externalized expression of internal convictions." Locke, in Wolin's words, "ushered in a new social world where men, no longer able to communicate on the basis of a common interior life, were reduced to knowing each other solely from the outside." This meant that

> man had become estranged from man, which corresponds exactly with Locke's terse description of the human condition where individual consciences are strangers to each other: 'no particular man can know the existence of any other being, but only when, by actual operating upon him, it makes itself perceived by him.' Man becomes conscious of his fellows only when he and they collide; conflict and friction are thus the sources of man's awareness of man.[24]

Therefore the neo-Lockeans of the eighteenth century, like the neo-Marxists of the twentieth, were obliged to reintroduce the ethical dimension by insisting on the reality of the good and on man's ability to recognize it, by defending the intuitions of the heart against the paralyzing analyses of the mind. "It was necessary," wrote Becker, "to execute a strategic retreat from the advanced position occupied by abstract reason, from the notion that nature has 'no more regard to good above ill than to heat above cold.'" Thus, Becker went on, "the innate ideas which Locke had so politely dismissed by way of the hall door had to be surreptitiously brought back again through the kitchen window." [25]

The image is an apt one, for the energizing of Locke's doctrines in the third quarter of the eighteenth century was associated with a new emphasis on the political capacity of the common man.

III

James Burgh, Richard Price, Joseph Priestley, John Wilkes, John Cartwright, Granville Sharp, Catherine Macaulay, and Thomas Paine were the English radicals who—as Morley says of Rousseau—"converted the blank practice of the political *philosophes* into a deadly affair of ball and shell." [26] Not all of them were Dissenters; Sharp, for instance, was an Anglican, and some of the group, such as Wilkes, were hardly religious. Their characteristic type, however, was a preacher in a Nonconformist chapel (Price) or a teacher in a Nonconformist private school (Burgh), and, as a group, their impact was to add to Locke's natural rights philosophy the "moral significance, severity and urgency" of which Heimert speaks.[27] From 1750 through the period of the American Revolution they wrote books and pamphlets that expounded the doctrine of a natural law, made by God. evident to every man, and congruent with the best parts of the traditional law of England, but superior to any law or government that was arbitrary or unjust. When, on the brink of open rebellion, Americans needed an intellectual resource more potent that the concept of the rights of Englishmen in order to justify actions so obviously seditious as the Boston Tea Party, they turned to the rights-of-man-teaching of their staunchest English supporters.[28]

The influence of the Dissenters (as we shall term them) on American Revolutionary thought is generally recognized. Reprints of the Dissenters' works "appeared everywhere in the colonies." Their pamphlets and letters "were read avidly, circulated, published and republished, in America." It was they, rather than British Whigs such as Burke, whose thought corresponded to the thought of those called Whigs in America. The Dissenters in England and the rebellious colonists in America brought about, through the exchange of pamphlets, a transatlantic radicalization that "gave both parties . . . a feeling of strength and pushed them toward an ever more radical view of existing authority." [29]

The extent of the Dissenters' influence can be measured in many ways. Perhaps the Dissenters' most important reprint in the colonies was James Burgh's three-volume *Political Disquisitions,* published in London in 1774 and in Philadelphia in 1775. The work was praised by Revolutionary leaders so diverse as Jefferson, John Adams, and John Dickinson (who owned two sets). Indeed, "the subscription list for Burgh's *Disquisitions* reads like a 'Who's Who in the American Revolution.'" [30] *Political Disquisitions,* like *Common Sense,* also is said to have had "a widespread influence . . . upon the common folk," for example in the town meetings of western Massachusetts.[31] Very likely the next most influential work was Richard Price's *Observations on the Nature of Civil Liberty,* published early in 1776 in London (at about the same time *Common Sense* appeared in Philadelphia) and reprinted the same year in Boston, New York, Charleston, and (two printings) Philadelphia, as well as in the Hartford and Boston newspapers.

Earlier, and more pervasive, was the impact of John Wilkes. His writings were reprinted in New York, Philadelphia, and Boston in 1763, and his complete works in New York in 1768. But it was, of course, Wilkes' actions—his arrest for seditious libel, his flight to France, his return to England and successive reelections by Middlesex County in the face of Parliament's refusal to seat him—that attracted most attention. The press in America was "[so] full of his trials, tribulations, and speeches . . . that one may go to almost any issue of any newspaper between 1763–1775 and read of John Wilkes." [32] His very name was a popular toast among all classes. Babies were named for him. The Boston Sons of Liberty began a correspondence with him in 1768, and South Carolina patriots sent him 1,500 pounds of turtles. Thirty years ago, an American recalled in 1802, a handkerchief or snuffbox was "hardly saleable, unless it exhibited the patriotic motto of 'Wilkes and Liberty,'" and anyone who questioned Wilkes' patriotism could expect a broken head as a result. The agitation on behalf of Wilkes in England paralleled resistance in the colonies. Wilkes' papers were seized in 1763, under a general warrant like the one protested by Otis in 1761, and rioters were shot down in London in 1768, as would happen in Boston in 1770.[33]

A web of personal relationships between the English Dissenters and colonial radicals complemented the written word. Catherine Macaulay sent her "more ardent pamphlets" to Dickinson; Priestley forwarded Price's *Observations on Civil Liberty* to Franklin; and Granville Sharp and Anthony Benezet exchanged pamphlets on slavery. After the outbreak of hostilities, when Price's position in England became difficult, the American commissioners in Paris invited him to become a United States citizen. He later became a member of the American Academy of Arts and Sciences and the American Philosophical Society. Benjamin Franklin, the American leader who was most influenced by the Dissenters, was closely associated with Price, Burgh, and Priestley in the Honest Whig Club of London, which met regularly at least as early as 1764 and continued until after the Revolutionary War, and in which, according to James Boswell, "much was said . . . against Parliament." [34] Benjamin Rush classically illustrates the influence of personal contact. As an American student in England during the 1760's, Rush attended Catherine Macaulay's salon, where he met James Burgh, and he dined with John Wilkes in King's Bench prison. Back in America, Rush received books and pamphlets from Edward Dilly, a publisher of radical books, and he corresponded with Mrs. Macaulay, her brother Alderman Sawbridge, Granville Sharp, and Price. When Priestley came to the United States in the 1790's he and Rush at once became fast friends.[35]

Although the extent of Dissenters' influence upon America is well understood, the nature of the influence is not. Far from simply elaborating the characteristic themes of the opposition ideologues of the previous generation, the Dissenters reached beyond Trenchard and Gordon, even beyond Locke, back to the "religious republicans" of the 1640's and 1650's. This meant, in part, that whereas the early-eighteenth-century commonwealth men explicitly disavowed republicanism, the Dissenters inclined toward it; indeed, Catherine Macaulay praised the Levellers' "Agreement of the People," [36] and Paine called George III a "royal brute." More broadly, the ascendancy of Dissenting radicalism represented a return to an essentially religious outlook. Locke, Harrington, and their popularizers wrote as rational analysts, almost as social scientists, whose vision of what might be was sensibly limited by recognition of what was. The standpoint of the Dissenters was the experienced reality of conscience, and their tone tended to be personal and prophetic. For them the great secular truths were "self-evident" in the same sense as the truths of religion, which is to say they were intuitively accessible to average men.

The Dissenters clarified their quarrel with an environmental psychology in their first major works. James Burgh's *The Dignity of Human Nature,* published in 1754, was well enough known in America eighty years later for Thoreau to borrow it from the Harvard library. Burgh's thesis, that "a self-evident truth is not collected, or deduced, but intuitively perceived," held equal force for truth of all kinds inasmuch as "moral truth is in no respect naturally more vague or precarious than mathematical truth." [37]

Richard Price's *A Review of the Principal Questions and Difficulties in Morals,* published in 1758, was a more substantial work than Burgh's. William Ellery Channing credited Price's *Review* for his lifelong emancipation from Locke's psychology,[38] and in the twentieth century it has enjoyed a revival among philosophers of the school of G. E. Moore. Price, however, posed the same problem as Burgh, whether "*right* and *wrong,* or *moral good* and *evil,* signify somewhat *really true* of actions, and not merely *sensations*"; and he gave the same answer: a man can intuitively tell that an action is good "in much the same sense [that he can say] of an object of sight, that it is *coloured,* or of an object of taste, that it is *sweet.*" [39]

Price preferred not to repudiate Locke directly. As much as he admired Locke's excellent essay on understanding, Price said, he found it was not "sufficiently clear or explicit." If Locke meant merely that sensation and reflection furnished all the "subjects, materials, and occasions of knowledge," that was well enough, but if he meant they were "the sources of all our ideas, as he so often calls them," then he was in error. The mind, Price held, has a faculty of perception that can give rise to new ideas that are "not received immediately from the aforesaid springs: . . . the power within us that *understands; the Intuition* of the mind." [40]

Price was in fact talking about a faculty very much akin to the Quakers' "inner light." This faculty, however, was not a "moral sense," for Price rejected the theories associated with that term because they were variants of the environmentalism that reduced man to a machine-like recorder of pains and pleasures. Price conceived the perception of moral truth as an intellectual function, and to describe its operation he resorted to some remarkable metaphors. It is the "eye of the mind," the "innate light," to   which we owe "our belief of all self-evident truths, . . . our moral ideas, and whatever else we discover without making use of any process of reasoning." Sense "lies prostrate under its object" and "must therefore remain a stranger to the objects"; it "sees only the outside of things." Reason, however, "looks downward upon things" and "acquaints itself with their natures." Failing to make this distinction, Locke had offered a definition of the good as action in conformity to some rule or law that, said Price, cannot discriminate between a thing that is right because it is the will of God and a thing that is "right" because it conforms to "the decrees of the magistrate, or the fashion of the country." Locke did not admit this, however, and Price remarked that Locke "was strangely embarrassed, and inconsistent in his notions on this, as well as some other subjects." But Price himself was in search of a ground for moral truth that—in his word—"transcends" the sense impressions man derives from the particular society in which he is born.[41]

In morals as in mathematics, the Dissenter's intuition perceived a natural order made by nature's God. His radicalism, as Harry Hayden Clark says of Paine, was "an attempt to re-establish in politics and religion a lost harmony with this uniform, immutable, universal and eternal law and order, and to modify or overthrow whatever traditional institutions have obscured this order."[42] For Trenchard and Gordon, as for Locke, the threat of papism was so vivid that they sought to place limits on the pretensions of men who, in the name of religion, tried to interfere with the affairs of secular society. The radical Dissenters, on the other hand, reverted to what Professors Haller and Woodhouse term the "confusion" between the law of nature and the law of God that was characteristic of the commonwealth men of the 1640's—a belief better understood as the conviction that nature and nature's God speak with a single voice.[43] Just as John Lilburne in the space of two pamphlet pages cited the English chronicles, the Petition of Right, half a dozen medieval statutes, Coke's *Institutes*, divers speeches in the Long Parliament, Psalms, Romans, and Deuteronomy as equally appropriate authorities for a political argument (the footnote "see the 36 Edw. 3, 15, and 1 Cor. 14. 7, 11, 16, 19, 23" suggests the tone of the whole), or as Gerrard Winstanley, urging the common ownership of land, argued successively from "natural experience," "the old Scriptures," and "the practice of Kings," so John Cartwright asserted that "the law of God and the law of the land *are all one*," and Granville Sharp in tract after tract maintained that statute law must conform to the "eternal Laws of God (which . . . Civilians commonly call 'the *Laws of Nature*')."[44]

Locke's teaching left men isolated from each other and passive recipients of sensory experience, separated, as it were, from the kingdom of God both without and within. The search to overcome this state of alienation discovered no solid resting place until it reached theorists who were inspired by the radical Reformation—who, in the words of David Brion Davis, shifted "the locus of fundamental value from external authority to internal impulse." [45] The close congruity between this principle and the doctrine of Burgh or Price explains why Priestley turned back to the sixteenth-century Unitarian, Faustus Socinius; why the most frequently quoted authority in the moral philosophy of Price was the seventeenth-century Platonist, Ralph Cudworth; why, in America, when Benjamin Rush converted to a belief in universal salvation he found sustenance in the writings of Oliver Cromwell's chaplain; and why, when John Woolman decided not to pay war taxes, he strengthened himself by thinking of John Huss.[46] According to the Dissenters' most searching analyst,

> one great principle lay at the center of all that the Dissenters thought and wrote, linking them spiritually with the storms and stress of the seventeenth century. That principle was the natural right to freedom of conscience.[47]

But what made the thought of the Dissenters politically revolutionary was that, having restored conscience to the center of man's experience, they generalized and secularized it. They insisted, that is, that all forms of traditional authority should submit to the judgment of that inner light or intuition which all men shared. In the words of Anthony Lincoln, "Dissenting radicalism was a vital movement in the history of political philosophy because it revealed the process by which Christian liberties could be transformed into the Rights of Man. That process was psychological. . . . Once men have taken the short step of investigation from the spiritual privileges of the Christian to the spiritual composition of the understanding, the transformation into Natural Rights is achieved." [48]

This forward step also was a step backward to the un-Lockean thesis of the sixteenth-century treatise, "Doctor and Student" ("a favorite of Jefferson's," [49] as of Lilburne, Cartwright, and Sharp), that there is a law

> written in the heart of every man, teaching him what is to bee

done, and what is to be fled: and because it is written in the heart, therefore it may not bee put away . . . and therefore against this law, prescription, statute, nor custome may not prevaile.[50]

Commenting on the tendency of Locke and those who came after him to let nature come between themselves and God, Becker alludes to the seventeenth-century English sectaries who justified resistance by "natural law, which was that right reason or inner light of conscience which God had given to men for their guidance." [51] It was precisely that inner light to which the Dissenters recurred. Its reliability in all things was their essential teaching. Conscience, relegated by Locke to the periphery of a society based on property, became the critic of all social orders.

IV

The difference between Locke's conception of the law of nature and the conception of his Dissenting quasi-disciples appears most clearly in response to the question: To whom is natural law "self-evident"? As Sheldon Wolin says, "the roots of the divergence between the liberal and the radical democratic traditions lie in their contrasting faiths concerning the ability of the human mind to fathom reality and to translate the results into practical actions." [52]

Locke believed that knowledge of the law of nature was accessible only to a minority of gentlemen, and that "the greatest part of mankind want [lack the necessary] leisure or capacity" for this.[53] Similarly, Harrington expressed the opinion that "your mechanics, till they have first feathered their nests, like the fowls of the air whose whole employment is to seek their food, are so busied in their private concernments that they have neither leisure to study the public nor are safely to be trusted with it because a man is not faithfully embarked in this kind of ship if he have no share in the freight." [54]

Locke sought to make sure that, if political participation presupposed leisure, the poor would be kept at work. In 1697, in conformity with his view that unemployment was caused by "nothing else but the relaxation of discipline and corruption of manners," he recommended a poor law that, among other things, deplored the fact that the labor of the children of the poor "is generally lost to the public till they are twelve or fourteen years old." He therefore provided that all children over the age of three in families on relief should attend "working schools," which would ensure that they would be "from infancy . . . inured to work." Bread, he recommended, should be given to the children at their "school" in lieu of money so that their parents would not waste a monetary stipend on drink. "And to this may be also added, without any trouble, in cold weather, if it be thought needful, a little warm water-gruel; for the same fire that warms the room may be made use of to boil a pot of it." [55] Here Locke anticipated the view of his popularizers, Trenchard and Gordon, who (says Pocock) "in their vehement and repeated objections to Church of England charity schools . . . want the children of the poor left in the servant class where they belong." [56]

The Dissenting radicals found their way slowly to faith in the common man's ability to know. Burgh, in his *Dignity of Human Nature*, observed that although all truths were "alike certain," they were not all "alike obvious," moral truth being as clear as mathematical truth only to "superior minds" that were "fitted for receiving and examining it." [57] Introducing his lectures on history in 1765, Priestley disclaimed any wish of "teaching politics to low mechanics and manufacturers," a remark his subsequent editor regretted.[58]

But as the American Revolution drew near the Dissenters' faith in the capacity of the poor for knowledge grew, together with their insistence that the poor should vote. Thus in 1775 Wilkes told Parliament that "the meanest mechanic, the poorest peasant and day-labourer" had rights that were affected by the laws, which, accordingly "the mass of the people" should have some share in making.[59] Burgh in his *Political Disquisitions,* republished that same year in Philadelphia, rejected "the commonly received doctrine, that servants, and those who receive alms, have no right to vote for members of parliament, [because thereby] an immense multitude of the people are utterly deprived of all power in determining who shall be the protectors of their lives, their personal liberty, their little property." [60] In keeping with this political doctrine, John Cartwright's *Legislative Rights of the Commonalty Vindicated* (1776) espoused the epistemological theory that "common sense" brought natural law within the reach of the "laboring mechanic and the peasant." [61]

It was an enduring controversy. Burke would later denounce Price for his "mechanic philosophy" and maintain that the state suffers oppression if hair-dressers or working tallow-chandlers "either individually or collectively, are permitted to rule." [62] By then the friends of Franklin, whose father *was* a working tallow-chandler, and of Paine, whose father made corsets, were committed to Paine's great affirmation that

> there is existing in man, a mass of sense lying in a dormant state, and which, unless something excites it to action, will descend with him, in that condition, to the grave. . . . The construction of government ought to be such as to bring forward, by a quiet and regular operation, all that extent of capacity which never fails to appear in revolution.[63]

In this way a belief in equality became associated with a belief in intuitively self-evident moral truth.

Perfectibility, of society as well as man, followed from what Priestley describes as his first heresy: questioning the doctrine of man's fall and his innate evilness.[64] The words with which Rousseau began *Emile*, "All is well when it leaves the hands of the Creator of things," were echoed during the American Revolution by Price, who affirmed that equality was a right with which men came "from the hands of their Maker," and by Paine, who said that the revolutionary constitution of Pennsylvania considered men "as they came from their maker's hands." [65] In 1787 Price, in a sermon titled "The Evidence for a Future Period of Improvement in the State of Mankind," quoted the words of Condorcet: "Let us be cautious not to despair of the human race." [66]

Thus it happened that by the time the Declaration of Independence was drafted the belief once more was current that natural rights depend neither on precedent nor rational demonstration but are, as Jefferson put it, "rights of human nature" that are evident to every man. Perhaps the most striking formulation of this thought before the writing of the preamble to the Declaration was in Cartwright's *American Independence*, which was printed in 1774 in London and republished in Philadelphia in 1776. "It is a capital error in the reasonings of several writers on this subject," Cartwright said,

> that they consider the liberty of mankind in the same light as an estate or chattel, and go about to prove or disprove their right to it, by the letter of grants and charters, by custom and usage, and by municipal statute. Hence we are told that these men have a right to more, those to less, and some to none at all. But the title

> to the liberty of mankind is not established on such rotten founda-
> tions. 'Tis not among mouldy parchments, or in the cobwebs of a
> casuist's brain, we are to look for it; it is the immediate gift
> of God.

Cartwright concluded that liberty "is not derived from any one, but it is original in every one; it is inherent and unalienable." [67]

v

What is an "inalienable" right? Locke simultaneously affirmed that ideas are not "innate" ("in-born," from the Latin *natus*, "born") but that rights are "natural"; that is (according to Webster's International Dictionary), "existing or characteristic from birth; innate; inborn." To add to the confusion, Locke distinguished between natural rights that upon entering society a man "wholly gives up" [68] and natural rights that "cease not" even in society. Nor did he adequately clarify whether those rights that cease not may be exercised by individuals, or merely constitute (as it were) the stock on behalf of which authorized representatives act by proxy.[69]

If rights were viewed as property, inalienability might mean only that a man must consent to what is done with them. Pitt, moving the withdrawal of British troops from Boston in 1775, used the term in this sense when he asserted that a British subject's property was "invariably inalienable, without his own consent." [70] Thus defined, inalienability did not exclude the permanent transfer of a right from the original owner to a delegated purchaser or donee. David B. Davis comments that

> as Rousseau shrewdly observed, Pufendorf had argued that a man
> might alienate his liberty just as he transferred his property by
> contract; and Grotius had said that since individuals could alienate
> their liberty by becoming slaves, a whole people could do the same,
> and become the subjects of a king.

"Here, then," Davis concludes, "was the fatal flaw in the traditional theories of natural rights." [71]

The consequences were quite different if inalienability was defined by analogy to conscience. Liberty of conscience, wrote Francis Hutcheson in his *System of Moral Philosophy*, "is not only an essential but an unalienable branch [of natural liberty]."

This right appears from the very constitution of the rational mind which can assent or dissent solely according to the evidence presented, and naturally desires knowledge. The same considerations shew this right to be unalienable: it cannot be subjected to the will of another.[72]

When rights were termed "unalienable" in this sense, it did not mean that they could not be transferred without consent but that their nature made them untransferrable.

This proposition was peculiarly congenial to Dissenting radicalism, because freedom of conscience was inseparable from moral agency. When this conception was transferred to the secular sphere, conflict was inevitable between inalienability thus defined and any understanding of rights that stressed their surrender when men joined society or that regarded them as powers not personally exercised but delegated to trustees.

The statesmanship of the American Revolution, however, tended to reserve absolute inalienability for the life of the mind (or, even more narrowly, for religious conscience) and to leave actions of every kind subject to state regulation. This becomes evident if one examines the bills of rights of the constitutions created by all but two of the thirteen original states. One finds that the adjective "inalienable" was repeatedly applied to two kinds of rights: the right of conscience and the right of revolution.

"All men," said the 1776 constitutions of North Carolina and Pennsylvania, "have a natural and unalienable right to worship Almighty God according to the dictates of their own consciences." Although almost every constitution provided for religious freedom, almost every provision was coupled with a clause that protected the state from disturbance undertaken in the name of religion. ". . . *Provided*, that nothing herein contained shall be construed to exempt preachers of treasonable or seditious discourses, from legal trial and punishment" (North Carolina). ". . . Unless, under colour of religion, any man shall disturb the good order, peace or safety of the State, or shall infringe the laws of morality, or injure others, in their natural, civil, or religious rights" (Maryland). ". . . *Provided*, That the liberty of conscience, hereby granted, shall not be so construed as to excuse acts of licentiousness, or justify practices inconsistent with the peace or safety of this State" (New York). ". . . provided it be not repugnant to the peace and safety of the State" (Georgia). ". . . provided he doth not disturb the public peace" (Massachusetts).

The inalienable right of revolution, on the other hand, was available only to majorities. It was "the people" (in Maryland and Massachusetts), "the community" (in Pennsylvania), and, more precisely, "a majority of the community" (in Virginia) that alone could alter, reform, or abolish government. The literature of the Revolution, as Thad Tate has written, "described resistance as a right exercised only by decision of the community, never on the initiative of the individuals." [73]

Both definitions of inalienability severely limited the individual's scope of action. For some Dissenting radicals, however, self-determination had become the very definition of freedom. Richard Price, in particular, implicitly challenged the Lockean assumptions of the state constitutions, and, later, of the federal constitution.

Price believed not only that man was capable of intuitively telling good from evil but also that he had free will to choose how to act. Speaking to an audience of children in 1766, Price voiced his doctrine in the simplest terms. Everyone knows, he said, that the soul is active. "Every one feels that he has a power of self-motion, that he can begin action or cease from action as he pleases, and that he has an absolute command over his thoughts and determinations." [74] The principle of what he termed "Spontaneity, or Self-determination, which constitutes us Agents," became the basis of Price's political thought.

In his *Observations on the Nature of Civil Liberty*, the principal English defense of the American Revolution, Price argued that physical, moral, religious, and civil liberty were aspects of "liberty in general," linked together by "one general idea, that runs through them all; I mean, the idea of Self-direction, or Self-government." Liberty, "natural and unalienable," therefore was the opposite of slavery, or of submission to forces outside oneself.

> Without Physical Liberty, man would be a machine acted upon by mechanical springs, having no principle of motion in himself, or command over events; and, therefore, incapable of all merit and demerit. Without Moral Liberty, he is a wicked and detestable being, subject to the tyranny of base lusts, and the sport of every vile appetite. And without Religious and Civil Liberty he is a poor and

abject animal, without rights, without property, and without a conscience, bending his neck to the yoke, and crouching to the will of
every silly creature who has the insolence to pretend to authority
over him.[75]

The consequences of this position for Americans were largely reserved for the nineteenth century—when it turned out that it made
some difference whether one said slavery was wrong because every
man has a natural right to the possession of his own body or because
every man has a natural right freely to determine his own destiny.
The first kind of right was alienable: thus Locke neatly derived
slavery from capture in war and the forfeiture of life to the con-
queror, who might rightfully have killed the captive.[76] But the second kind of right, what Price called "that power of self-determination
which all agents, as such, possess," [77] was inalienable as long as man
remained man. Like the mind's quest for religious truth, from which
it was derived, self-determination was not a claim to self-ownership
that might be acquired and surrendered but an inextricable aspect of
the activity of being human.

Under heavy criticism for his defiant criticism of his own government in time of war, Price insisted that his principles were "the same
as those taught by Mr. Locke, and all the writers on Civil Liberty
who have been hitherto most admired in this country." [78] But Price
differed from Locke "in certain cardinal aspects: in his psychological
beliefs and in the purpose of his work." If in expressing his philosophy
"he sometimes fell into the prevailing terminology of property, it was
because he felt that moral self-determination was the most precious
property a man could possess." [79]

Where Price most obviously went beyond Locke was in his extension of Priestley's concept that the individual retains some natural
rights in society to the conclusion: "In every free state every man is
his own Legislator." This phrase, Price remarked in his subsequent
Additional Observations, "has been much exclaimed against, and oc-
casioned no small part of the opposition which has been made to the
principles advanced in the *Observations on Civil Liberty*." [80]

Price responded to this criticism ambiguously. On the one hand
he said he meant that "every independent agent in a free state ought
to have a share in the government of it." On the other hand Price said
that, with various limitations, he accepted the charge that the liberty

for which he pleaded was "a right or power in every one to act as he likes without restraint."[81]

In the characteristic manner of Dissenting thought, Price built his case on an analogy to religion. All men have "the same unalienable right" to religious liberty, he said, provided only that "no one has a right to such a use of it as shall take it from others." This reasoning "is equally applicable to the Liberty of man in his *civil* capacity." Citing Priestley's "Essay on Government," Price said that it "may be accommodated to all I have said on this subject, by only giving some less general name to that which Dr. Priestley calls *civil* liberty." In fact, however, Priestley still took it for granted that, in joining society, men must "voluntarily resign some part of their natural liberty," but in Price's account the idea of the surrender of natural rights has disappeared. It was more than a change in terminology. Price no longer spoke of the specific natural liberties (religion and education) that society might not infringe; he referred simply to "liberty" in general. "Just government, therefore, does not *infringe* liberty, but *establish* it. —It does not *take away* the rights of mankind, but *protect* and *confirm* them." In this and in similar passages Price seemed to be saying that all natural liberty is inalienable. For Price, a government constructed on any other plan represented

> the folly of *giving up* liberty in order to *maintain* Liberty; and, in the very act of endeavouring to secure the most valuable rights, to arm a body of enemies with power to destroy them.[82]

In sum, then, Dissenting political philosophy, in its culmination in the *Observations* and *Additional Observations* of Richard Price, shifted the burden of proof from the individual who sought to preserve control over his own actions to the state, which claimed the right to regulate them. As Halévy observed, this amounted to abolishing the social contract.

> it may be held that men formed the original pact in order to guarantee a certain number of pre-existing natural rights. This is the sense in which Price and Cartwright tend to interpret Locke's theory. But, in this case, . . . what is the point of the mediation of the contract? When men have adopted a position of legitimate insurrection, what is the point of saying that they are rising because the contract which should have guaranteed their rights has been

violated, instead of saying, more simply, that they are rising because their rights have been violated? [83]

The Declaration of Independence, too, made the purpose of government "to secure these rights," and said not one word about rights
given up. Nor does this seem to have been an oversight. A different
spirit was reflected at the Constitutional Convention of 1787, when
one of the working papers of the Committee of Detail observed: "We
are not working on the natural rights of men not yet gathered into
society, but upon those rights modified by society." [84] In contrast,
writing to Frances W. Gilmer after his retirement from the presidency, Jefferson declared:

> Our legislators are not sufficiently apprized of the rightful limits of
> their power; that their true office is to declare and enforce only our
> natural rights and duties, and to take none of them from us. . . .
> The idea is quite unfounded, that on entering into society we give
> up any natural rights.[85]

This doctrine of natural rights put property in considerable jeop-
ardy. Jefferson not only repudiated inherited political power but on
occasion even argued that the earth, too, belonged to the living generation. According to Vernon L. Parrington, it was his belief that the
human rights of life and liberty are more valuable than the rights of
property that led Jefferson, in the preamble, to reject the word "property" and speak of "the pursuit of happiness." [86]

Julian P. Boyd, the magnificent editor of Jefferson, seeks to refute
Parrington with the argument that "the pursuit of happiness" was a
conventional phrase that Locke himself had used "at least three times,
though not in a political context." [87] But whether or not there was significance in Jefferson's use of "pursuit of happiness," there may have
been significance in his failure to use the word "property." Early in
the French Revolution, when Lafayette showed Jefferson a draft of the
Declaration of the Rights of Man and Citizens, Jefferson struck the
word "property" from the rights that had been itemized by Lafayette
and in its place put "the power to dispose of his person and the
fruits of his industry, and of all his faculties." [88] These rights or
powers, we may assume Jefferson believed, were natural; property
was only a social convention. In a letter he wrote after he left the
presidency, Jefferson explicitly denied that property was a natural
right.[89]

Nevertheless, Parrington and the Progressive historians generally exaggerate the extent to which the Declaration, or its author, or the revolution it rationalized, frontally attacked the rights of property. Jefferson's reforms dealt only with the edges of society, both in space and in time: with the West, and with the law of inheritance. He prided himself that his well-known reforms in Virginia involved no violence and "no deprivation of natural right, but rather an enlargement of it." [90] When Jefferson returned to the United States from France, his words about the rights of the living generation—contrary to what he had clearly signified in revolutionary France—avoided justifying the seizure of accumulated wealth without compensation. Instead, he made the more innocuous affirmations that every generation can rewrite its political constitution and that no legislature should create debts that its children will have to repay. It was left for Lincoln, not Jefferson, to confiscate—without compensation—$2 billion worth of slaves.

The most precise formulation of the relationship between human rights and property rights in the Declaration of Independence was suggested by James Madison. Writing to James Brown of Kentucky in 1788, Madison said that when the Declaration was drafted "the two classes of rights were so little discriminated, that a provision for the rights of persons was supposed to include of itself those of property; and it was natural to infer, from the tendency of republican laws, that these different interests would be more and more identified." But experience had shown, Madison said, that "in all populous countries the smaller part only can be interested in preserving the rights of property." He therefore recommended the creation of a separate legislative chamber, a senate, to protect the rights of property.[91]

John Adams had always believed in this, and at the same time that Madison was writing to Brown he was saying it again, at length, in his *Defense of the Constitutions of the United States.* His new exposition was prompted by the same pressures Madison felt: from the debtor democracy of the mid-1780's and, in particular, Shays' Rebellion. Thus in November, 1786, John Adams wrote to John Jay:

> The just complaints of the people of real grievances ought never to be discouraged and even their imaginary grievances may be treated with too great severity. But when a cry is set up for the abolition of debts, equal division of property, and the abolition of

senates and governors, it is time for every honest man to consider his situation.

Adams, ironically, in a letter to Richard Price, traced these dangerous doctrines to Price's fellow radicals. I wrote my book, said Adams, because

> it appeared to me that my countrymen were running wild and into danger from a too ardent and inconsiderate pursuit of erroneous opinions of government which have been propagated among them by some of their ill-informed favorites and by various writings which were very popular among them, such as the pamphlet called *Common Sense,* for one example among many others, particularly Mrs. Macaulay's *History,* Mr. Burgh's *Political Disquisitions,* Mr. Turgot's *Letters.*" [92]

Thus the ideology of the American Revolution contained a latent tension between a political philosophy built on property and a political philosphy built on conscience. Indeed, only conventional familiarity leads us to consider the logic of the Declaration's preamble as a seamless web. It was necessarily ambiguous, reflecting the composite character of the Revolution as a social movement. Both capitalist *and* democratic, the Revolution drew support from many disparate social groups: southern slaveholders as well as northern merchants, poor tenant farmers and artisans as well as men of wealth. The Revolution's manifesto had to speak to and for all of them. The Declaration could no more counterpose property rights and human rights than its framers could permit their coalition for the single goal of independence to degenerate into a squabble between rich and poor. A portion of Jefferson's draft that too visibly exposed the contradictions in the coalition and the ambiguity of its ideology—that is, his condemnation of the slave trade—had to be excised. Yet implicit in the few sentences of the Declaration's preamble were very different visions of the future. After the success of the Revolution, still more after the adoption of the Constitution, the coalition broke down and the ambiguity had to be confronted.

VI

The transition from eighteenth- to nineteenth-century radicalism can be illustrated by the case of Unitarian minister William Ellery

Channing. Born in 1780, Channing grew up in Newport, Rhode Island. His grandfather was a signer of the Declaration of Independence; George Washington once slept at the Channings' home; and Channing himself was present at the Rhode Island convention that ratified the United States Constitution. The pastors of the First and the Second Congregational Churches, which his family attended, were Stephen Hopkins, a pioneer abolitionist, but also an expositor of Calvinist orthodoxy, and William Patten, who in 1795 published *Christianity, The True Religion* in reply to Paine's *Appeal to Reason*. At Harvard, according to his classmate, Joseph Story, Channing studied Locke's essay on human understanding and Bishop Watson's apologia for the Bible, which the Harvard Corporation placed in the hands of every student. As a senior at Harvard, Channing instigated an address that supported President John Adams in his cold war with revolutionary France. In brief, if there was a conservative factor that failed to influence Channing's youth it has not been recorded.

But Channing, while at Harvard, chanced on Richard Price's *Review of Morals*, and Price, Channing wrote two years before his death, "saved me from Locke's philosophy. He gave me the doctrine of ideas, and during my life I have written the words Love, Right, etc., with a capital. That book profoundly moulded my philosophy into the form it has always retained." During two seminal years as a tutor in Richmond, Virginia, Channing also read Rousseau and Godwin. His emergent radicalism, as he expounded it in letters to friends from Virginia, contained three cardinal ideas:

> 1. I am convinced that virtue and benevolence are natural to man, [for the] principle of benevolence, sympathy or humanity is . . . strongly impressed on the heart by God himself.
>
> 2. You evidently go upon the supposition [Channing wrote to one of his correspondents] that the circumstances of our lives are decided by Heaven. I believe they are decided by ourselves. Man is the artificer of his own fortune.
>
> 3. I find avarice the great bar to all my schemes, and I do not hesitate to assert that the human race will never be happier than at present till the establishment of a community of property.

Thus enunciating the characteristic Dissenting axioms of the natural goodness of man and of free will, and—in an extreme form—the equally characteristic corollary that human rights come before property rights, the young prophet ended: "I fear you will say I am crazy. No, no, ———." [93]

[1] The relationship between the American Revolution and the Civil War is explored in my *Class Conflict, Slavery, and the United States Constitution: Ten Essays* (New York and Indianapolis, 1967). It was Beard who suggested that the Civil War was the "second American revolution."

[2] Carl Degler, "The American Past: An Unsuspected Obstacle in Foreign Affairs," *American Scholar*, 32 (1962–63): 207.

[3] *Rights of Man* (part 2), in *The Complete Writings of Thomas Paine*, ed. Philip Foner (New York, 1945), I: 354.

[4] *The Liberator*, May 31, 1844.

[5] In speeches of June 26, 1857, and July 10, 1858, quoted in Harry V. Jaffa, *Crisis of the House Divided* (Garden City, N.Y., 1959), p. 316.

[6] Henry George, *Progress and Poverty* (New York, 1881), pp. 490–91, 496.

[7] *Looking Backward, 2000–1887* (Boston, 1941), pp. 41–42.

[8] New York, 1894, p. 517.

[9] *Labor and Freedom. The Voice and Pen of Eugene V. Debs* (St. Louis, 1916), pp. 16–17.

[10] See Carl L. Becker, *The Declaration of Independence* (New York, 1922), pp. 27–28, 79.

[11] The three most important books on this subject are Clinton G. Rossiter's *Seedtime of the Republic* (New York, 1953), which first made the point that the colonists read "Cato" more than Locke; Caroline Robbins' *The Eighteenth-Century Commonwealthman* (Cambridge, 1959), which portrayed Cato's predecessors and successors in England; and Barnard Bailyn's *The Ideological Origins of the American Revolution* (Cambridge, Mass., 1967).

[12] Glanced at in Becker's *Declaration of Independence*, pp. 57–61, this internal contradiction in the thought of Locke and in the entire Enlightenment became the central theme of Becker's *The Heavenly City of the Eighteenth Century Philosophers* (New Haven and London, 1932), pp. 66–70 and *passim*.

[13] *Second Treatise of Government*, sec. 11 and 135; *Declaration of Independence*, p. 56.

[14] *Declaration of Independence*, p. 60.

[15] See Edward P. Thompson, "Outside the Whale," in *Out of Apathy* (London, 1960), p. 184.

[16] Basil Willey, *The Eighteenth Century Background* (London, 1940), p. 157; Ernst Cassirer, *The Philosophy of the Enlightenment*, trans. Koelln and Pettigrove (Princeton, 1951), p. 244.

[17] *Cato's Letters; Or, Essays on Liberty Civil and Religious, And Other Important Subjects,* 3d ed. (London, 1733), 3: 151, 162. Russell Smith commented, in *Harrington and His Oceana* ([Cambridge, 1914], p. 146): "They concluded (with a sentiment typical of the age) 'we can preserve Liberty by no other establishment than what we have.'" For such sentiments, see *Cato's Letters,* 1: liii–liv.

[18] *Religion and the American Mind* (Cambridge, Mass., 1966), p. 46.

[19] "The Use of History by the Founding Fathers," unpublished paper. See also my "Beard, Jefferson, and the Tree of Liberty," in *Class Conflict, Slavery, and the United States Constitution,* pp. 247–69.

[20] "The Emergence of Immediatism in British and American Antislavery Thought," *Mississippi Valley Historical Review,* 49 (1962): 209–30.

[21] *Second Treatise,* sec. 11.

[22] *Natural Right and History* (Chicago, 1953), p. 212 n. *et seq.*

[23] Secs. 18 and 139.

[24] *Politics and Vision* (Boston, 1960), pp. 338, 340.

[25] *The Heavenly City,* pp. 86–87.

[26] Quoted in Willey, *Eighteenth Century Background,* p. 208.

[27] *Religion and The American Mind,* 17.

[28] Rossiter remarks in *Seedtime* (p. 360): "Not until the argument shifted away from English rights and over to natural justice did Price and Priestley influence American minds."

[29] *Idem*; Bailyn, *Ideological Origins,* pp. 132–33; Robert R. Palmer, *The Age of the Democratic Revolution: A Political History of Europe and America, 1760–1800* (Princeton, 1959), 1: 179; Oscar and Mary Handlin, "James Burgh and American Revolutionary Theory," *Massachusetts Historical Society Proceedings,* 73 (1961): 52.

[30] H. Trevor Colbourn, "John Dickinson, Historical Revolutionary," *Pennsylvania Magazine of History and Biography,* 83 (1959): 285.

[31] Handlin and Handlin, "James Burgh," p. 38.

[32] Rossiter, *Seedtime,* p. 527. On the close relation between Wilkes and the Nonconformists, Anthony Lincoln quotes the contemporary comment: "Round the standard of 'Wilkes and Liberty' the nonconformists flocked in crowds. . . . A Dissenter and a Wilkite were synonymous terms" (*Some Political and Social Ideas of English Dissent, 1763–1800* [Cambridge, 1938], p. 26).

[33] Ezra Sampson, *Sham Patriot Unmasked, Or, An Exposition of the Fatally Successful Arts of Demagogues* (New York, 1802), pp. 8–9; Horace Bleakley, *Life of John Wilkes* (London, New York, and Toronto, 1917), pp. 243–44; O. A. Sherrard, *A Life of John Wilkes* (London, 1930), pp. 270–71; Pauline Maier, "John Wilkes and American Disillusionment with Britain," *William and Mary Quarterly,* 20 (1963): 373–95.

[34] J. P Agnew, "Richard Price and the American Revolution" (Ph.D. diss., University of Illinois, 1949), pp. 9–10; Nicholas Hans, "Franklin, Jefferson, and the English Radicals at the End of the Eighteenth Century," *Proceedings of the American Philosophical Society*, 98 (1954): 407, 410, 416, 418–21; Verner W. Crane, "The Club of Honest Whigs: Friends of Science and Liberty," *William and Mary Quarterly*, 3d ser., 23 (1966): 210–33.

[35] *The Autobiography of Benjamin Rush*, ed. George W. Corner (Princeton, 1948), pp. 60–62, 229–31; Colbourn, "Dickinson," p. 284 n.

[36] *The History of England from the Accession of James I to the Elevation of the House of Hanover* (London, 1772), 5: 7–9. Cf. with Robert Molesworth's definition of "commonwealthman" (with which Caroline Robbins begins her study): We are not "*Haters* of *Kingly* Government," we believe in "the true old *Gothick Constitution*, under the Three Estates of King (or Queen), Lords and Commons" (preface to Francois Hotman's *Franco-Gallia*, 2nd ed. [London, 1738], in Robbins, *Eighteenth-Century Commonwealthman*, p. 3).

[37] James Burgh, *The Dignity of Human Nature* (London, 1754), pp. 171, 178; for Thoreau, see Kenneth W. Cameron, *Emerson the Essayist* (Raleigh, N.C., 1945), 2:193.

[38] See Section VI, below.

[39] Richard Price, *A Review of the Principal Questions and Difficulties in Morals* (London, 1758), pp. v, 13.

[40] *Ibid.* pp. 18–19.

[41] *Ibid.*, pp. 22–23, 63–64, 466; see also Joseph Priestley, "Of the Resemblance between the Doctrine of Common Sense and the Principles of Dr. Price's Review of the Questions and Difficulties in Morals," in *The Works of Joseph Priestley*, ed. J. T. Rutt (Hackney, Eng. 1821), 3: 146–151.

[42] Harry Hayden Clark, "An Historical Interpretation of Thomas Paine's Religion," *University of California Chronicle*, 35 (1933): 60. Robert R. Palmer, in his "Tom Paine: Victim of the Rights of Man" (*Pennsylvania Magazine of History and Biography* [66 (1942): 164], agrees with Clark: "He [Paine] believed in a fundamental natural harmony, an underlying peaceableness of society which the influence of governments disrupted."

[43] See *The Leveller Tracts*, ed. William Haller and Godfried Davies (New York, 1944), pp. 3, 43, 45; A. S. P. Woodhouse, *Puritanism and Liberty* (London, 1938), p. 93.

[44] "The earnest Petition Of many Free-born People Of This Nation," in *The Leveller Tracts*, pp. 108–109; "The Law of Freedom in a Platform," in *The Works Of Gerrard Winstanley*, ed. George H. Sabine (New York, 1941), pp. 520 ff.; John Cartwright, *The Legislative Rights of the Com-*

monalty Vindicated; Or, Take Your Choice! (London, 1777), p. 65 n.; Granville Sharp, *A Declaration of the People's Natural Right to a Share in The Legislature* . . . (London, 1774), p. xxiii.

[45] *The Problem of Slavery in Western Culture* (Ithaca, N.Y. 1966), p. 229. Woodhouse observes that the Levellers' Agreements of the People derived from the concept of the church as a voluntary covenant "first found among the Anabaptists of Germany" (*Puritanism and Liberty*, p. 72); see also George H. Williams, *The Radical Reformation* (London, 1962), p. xxviii. More broadly, Ernst Troeltsch called the Anabaptists the "fathers of the rights of man" (in Gustav Salander, *Vom Werden der Menschenrechte* [Leipzig, 1926], p. 84). The passage of Continental Anabaptist ideas to England is described by Rufus Jones in his *Studies in Mystical Religion* ([London, 1909], chap. 17–20), and is stressed by Roland H. Bainton in his "The Left Wing of the Reformation" (*Journal of Religion,* 21 [1941]: 134). Lilburne believed himself to be in the tradition of "John Hus in Bohemia, Jerom of Prague, John Wickliff in England, the Martyrs in Queen Maryes days, the Hugonots or Protestants in France, the Gues in the Low-Countrys: all not only esteemed Hereticks by the Church, but rebels and traytors to their several States and Princes" ("The Just Defense of John Lilburn," in *The Leveller Tracts,* p. 452). Lilburne, like Fox, "began as a proselyte of the Baptists" (*ibid.,* p. 40, and *Leveller Manifestoes of the Puritan Revolution,* ed. Don M. Wolfe [New York and London, 1944], p. 3; *George Fox, An Autobiography,* ed. Rufus M. Jones [Philadelphia, 1903–6], 1: 18).

[46] The role of Cudworth and other Platonists in handing on, through Shaftesbury, a world outlook that was antagonistic to Locke's environmentalism is described by Davis in *Problem of Slavery,* pp. 348 ff., and by Ernst Cassirer, *The Platonic Renaissance in England,* trans. Pettigrove (Austin, Texas, 1953), esp. pp. 191–195. For Rush and Jeremiah White, see the former's *Autobiography,* pp. 163–64; for Woolman and Huss, see *The Journal and Essays of John Woolman,* ed. Amelia M. Gummere (New York, 1922), pp. 204–5.

[47] Lincoln, *English Dissent,* pp. 10–11.

[48] *Ibid.* p. 269. The thesis that the rights of man represented a secularization of religious rights of conscience is also argued in an almost forgotten little book by Georg Jellinek, *The Declaration of the Rights of Man and of Citizens,* trans. Max Farrand (New York, 1901).

[49] Rossiter, *Seedtime,* p. 357.

[50] Quoted in *The Leveller Tracts,* p. 42. See also Woodhouse, *Puritanism and Liberty,* pp. 71 n., 89.

[51] Becker, *Declaration of Independence,* p. 34.

[52] *Politics and Vision,* p. 297.

[53] "The Reasonableness of Christianity," in *The Works of John Locke* (London, 1794), 6: 146, and quoted in Strauss, *Natural Right and History*, p. 225.

[54] "The Commonwealth of Oceana," in *The Political Writings of James Harrington*, ed. Charles Blitzer (Indianapolis and New York, 1955), p. 135.

[55] Quoted in H. R. Fox Bourne, *The Life of John Locke* (London, 1876), 2: 378, 383, 384. See also Locke's "Some Considerations of the Consequences of the Lowering of Interest" (1691): "The labourers, living generally but from hand to mouth . . . may well enough carry on their part, if they have but money enough to buy victuals, cloaths, and tools" (*The Works of John Locke in Four Volumes* [London, 1768], 2: 16).

[56] J. G. A. Pocock, "Machiavelli, Harrington, and English Political Ideologies in the Eighteenth Century," *William and Mary Quarterly*, 3d ser., 22 (1965): 575.

[57] P. 178.

[58] "Lectures on History and General Policy," in *Works*, 24: 23 and 23 n.

[59] *The Speeches of John Wilkes* (London, 1777), 2: 107.

[60] James Burgh, *Political Disquisitions* (London, 1774), 1: 37.

[61] Pp. 67–68.

[62] Edmund Burke, *Reflections on the Revolution in France* (London, 1790), pp. 115, 73.

[63] *Rights of Man* (part 2), in *Complete Writings of Paine*, 1: 368.

[64] Priestley's assertion (in 1768) that "the human species . . . is capable of . . . unbounded improvement" and that "the progress of the species [is] towards perfection" (in "Essay on Government," *Works*, 22: 8) has often been considered the first expression of perfectionism in Anglo-American political philosophy.

[65] Price, *Additional Observations on the Nature and Value of Civil Liberty*, 3d ed. (London, 1778), p. 22; Paine, "Address to the People of Pennsylvania," in *Complete Writings of Paine*, 2: 285.

[66] London, 1787, p. 51 n.

[67] John Cartwright, *American Independence, The Interest and Glory of Great Britain* (Philadelphia, 1776), pp. 32–33.

[68] *Second Treatise*, sec. 130.

[69] Locke's lack of concern over safeguarding minority rights once individuals have entered society is emphasized by Willmoore Kendall, *John Locke and the Doctrine of Majority-Rule* (Urbana, Ill., 1941), and by C. B. Macpherson, *The Political Theory of Possessive Individualism* (Oxford, 1962).

[70] Quoted in J. W. Gough, *Fundamental Law in English Constitutional History* (Oxford, 1955), p. 195.

[71] *Problem of Slavery*, p. 413.

[72] London, 1755, 1: 257, 295. Hutcheson first distinguished alienable from inalienable rights in his *Inquiry into the Original of Our Ideas of Beauty and Virtue* ([London, 1725], p. 261), in which he said that the "marks" of an inalienable right are (*a*) that it is not within our natural power to transfer the right, and/or (*b*) that the transfer would serve no "valuable purpose."

[73] Thad W. Tate, "The Social Contract in America, 1774–1787: Revolutionary Theory as a Conservative Instrument," *William and Mary Quarterly*, 3d ser., 22 (1965): 378.

[74] Richard Price, *The Nature and Dignity of the Human Soul* (London, 1766), p. 4. There may be connection between Priestley's somewhat less absolute insistence on individual liberties and the fact that, in contrast to Price, he was a philosophical determinist. The two friends debated the matter in *A Free Discussion of the Doctrines of Materialism, and Philosophical Necessity, In a Correspondence between Dr. Price and Dr. Priestley* (London, 1778). It also is of some interest that Anthony Collins (1676–1729), from whom Priestley said he first learned of philosophical materialism, and who inspired the youthful Franklin's *Dissertation on Liberty and Necessity, Pleasure and Pain* (London, 1725), is thought to have been a collaborator of Trenchard and Gordon, who were attacked for their determinism in John Jackson, *A Defense of Human Liberty, In Answer to the Principal Arguments Which Have Been Alleged Against It; And Particularly to Cato's Letters on That Subject* . . . (London, 1725).

[75] Price, *Observations on the Nature of Civil Liberty, The Principles of Government, And the Justice and Policy of the War with America*, 8th ed. (London, 1778), pp. 1–3.

[76] *Second Treatise*, sec. 22–24. Leslie Stephen comments: "Locke could reconcile slavery to his theories; Rousseau declares that the words 'slavery' and 'right' are contradictory and mutually exclusive" (*History of English Thought in the Eighteenth Century*, 3d ed. [reprinted in New York, 1949], 2: 125 n.).

[77] *Additional Observations*, p. 2.

[78] In the Preface to the 5th edition of *Additional Observations*.

[79] Lincoln, *English Dissent*, pp. 114–15. Price's work, as Lincoln adds, "reveals the extent to which the theories of Locke had become a technique, a political text capable of sustaining any gloss, and yet certain, from its familiarity, to excite attention" (*ibid.*, p. 148).

[80] *Additional Observations*, pp. 6, 10.

[81] *Ibid.*, pp. 10, 10–11.

[82] *Ibid.*, pp. 11–14, 17. The quotation from Priestley is in "Essay On Government," *Works*, 22: 10; see also *ibid.*, 22: 12: "It is a man's civil

liberty which is originally in full force, and part of which he sacrifices when he enters into a state of society; and political liberty is that which he may, or may not acquire in the compensation he receives for it."

[83] Elie Halévy, *The Growth of Philosophical Radicalism* (London, 1928), p. 138.

[84] *The Records of the Federal Convention of 1787,* ed. Max Farrand (New Haven, London, and Oxford, 1911), 2: 137.

[85] June 7, 1816, in *The Works of Thomas Jefferson,* ed. Paul L. Ford (New York, 1904-5), 10: 32.

[86] *Main Currents in American Thought* (New York, 1927), 1: 343–44.

[87] *The Declaration of Independence: The Evolution of the Text* (Princeton, 1945), pp. 3–5, 5 n. Blackstone, as a matter of fact, used the term "happiness" to mean "self-love" and "pursuit of happiness" to describe the quest for individual, material interest.

[88] Dumas Malone, *Jefferson and the Rights of Man* (Boston, 1951), p. 223; see also *The Papers of Thomas Jefferson,* ed. Julian P. Boyd (Princeton, 1958), 15: 230–33.

[89] ". . . It is a moot question whether the origin of any kind of property is derived from nature at all. . . . It is agreed by those who have seriously considered the subject, that no individual has, of natural right, a separate property in an acre of land, for instance. By an universal law, indeed, whatever, whether fixed or movable, belongs to all men equally and in common, is the property for the moment of him who occupies it; but when he relinquishes the occupation, the property goes with it" (Jefferson to Isaac M'Pherson, August 13, 1813, in *Writings,* ed. H. A. Washington [Washington, D.C., 1854], 6: 180).

[90] *Autobiography,* in *Works of Thomas Jefferson,* 1: 58, 78.

[91] October, 1788, in *Letters and other Writings of James Madison,* ed. William C. Rives (Philadelphia, 1865), 1: 187–88.

[92] Quoted in Page Smith, *John Adams* (Garden City, N.Y., 1962), 2: 690, 691.

[93] *Memoirs of William Ellery Channing,* 5th ed. (Boston, 1851), esp. 101–2, 109–15.

The Radicalism of the Inarticulate: Merchant Seamen in the Politics of Revolutionary America

Jesse Lemisch

The scholarship of non-Americans—of George Rudé on "the crowd" and of Edward P. Thompson and Eric Hobsbawm on the "sub-political" and "pre-political" behavior of the peasants, workers, and "primitive rebels"—has given impetus to similar research in American history. Here Jesse Lemisch probes the political behavior of American seamen in the era of the American Revolution and finds that it was "purposeful" and radical. In doing this he breaks the stereotype of "jolly jack tar," an image remarkably similar to that of the "happy Negro" under slavery. At the same time, he provides evidence of a cause of the Revolution that has been frequently mentioned but rarely documented: the impressment of seamen.

This essay is part of a larger study that follows the seamen from the late colonial era through the Revolution. Lemisch suggested his over-all approach to the period in "The American Revolution Seen from the Bottom Up" (in Barton Bernstein, ed., *Towards a New Past: Dissenting Essays in American History* [New York, 1968]). He has edited *Benjamin Franklin: The Autobiography and Other Writings* (New York, 1961).

Lemisch received his doctorate from Yale, and for the past four years has conducted courses at the University of Chicago on "the crowd" and "the inarticulate" in American history. He is presently a visiting member of the Department of History at Northwestern University.

This essay also appears in the *William and Mary Quarterly*, 3d ser., vol. 25, no. 3 (July, 1968), under the title "Jack Tar in the Streets: Merchant Seamen in the Politics of Revolutionary America." © Jesse Lemisch. A grant and a fellowship from the American Council of Learned Societies aided his research.

Here comes Jack Tar, his bowed legs bracing him as if the very Broadway beneath his feet might begin to pitch and roll.[1] In his dress he is, in the words of a superior, "very nasty and negligent," his black stockings ragged, his long, baggy trousers tarred to make them waterproof.[2] Bred in "that very shambles of language," the merchant marine, he is foul-mouthed, his talk alien and suspect.[3] He is Jolly Jack, a bull in a china shop, always, in his words, "for a Short Life and a Merry one," and, in the concurring words of his superiors, "concerned only for the present . . . incapable of thinking of, or inattentive to, future welfare," "like froward Childeren not knowing how to judge for themselves."[4]

Clothes don't make the man, nor does language; surely we can do better than these stereotypes. Few have tried. Maritime history, as it has been written, has had as little to do with the common seaman as business history has had to do with the laborer. In that *mischianza* of mystique and elitism, "seaman" has meant Sir Francis Drake, not Jack Tar; the focus has been on trade, exploration, the great navigators, but rarely on the men who sailed the ships.[5] Thus we know very little about Jack.

Samuel Eliot Morison is one of the few who have tried to portray the common seaman. In an influential anecdote in *The Maritime History of Massachusetts* Morison described a "frequent occurrence" in early New England. A farmer's boy, called by the smell or the sight of the sea, suddenly runs off; three years later he returns as a man, marries the hired girl, and lives "happily ever after." This experience, Morison tells us, was "typical of the Massachusetts merchant marine," where the "old salt" was almost non-existent and where there never was "a native deep-sea proletariat." The ships were sailed by wave after wave of "adventure-seeking boys," drawn by high wages and wanderlust. If they recovered, they took their earnings, married, and bought a farm; if not, these "young, ambitious seamen culled from the most active element of a pushing race" stayed on and rose to become masters in a merchant marine distinguished from its class-ridden European counterparts by easy mobility.[6]

I

There is much to support Morison's tableau. Even if the mystique of the sea has been no more than mystique, still it has existed and exerted a powerful force. Washington, Franklin, and thousands of others did suffer attacks of "sea fever."[7] Seamen were, as Morison says, young men, averaging in one sample slightly over twenty-four, with many like John Paul Jones, who went to sea at thirteen, and even some who went at eight.[8] Many of them "hove in hard at the Hause-hole"[9] and became masters of their own vessels; later, while their sons and grandsons added to their wealth, they retired, perhaps to their farms, and wrote proud histories of their successes.[10] Some, like Nicholas Biddle, found the navy a better outlet for their ambitions than the merchant service.[11] Others, following Morison's pattern, quit the sea early and turned to farming.[12] For many there was mobility between generations and between trades.[13] Seamen and landsmen might be distinct classes in Europe, but in America men such as Albert Gallatin, who knew both the Old World and the New, found no "material distinction."[14] So Jack Tar seems to have been simply the landsman gone to sea, indistinguishable from his fellows ashore, and, together with them, on his way to prosperity.

If the seaman was a clean young farm-boy on the make—and likely to succeed—why was Josiah Franklin so apprehensive lest young Benjamin "break loose and go to sea"? Why did Josiah fight his son's "strong inclination to go to sea" by frantically trying to make of him a joiner, a bricklayer, a turner, a brazier, a tallow-chandler, a cutler, a printer—anything, so long as it would keep him on land?[15] Why did Washington's uncle suggest that young George would better became a planter or even an apprentice to a tinker, while explicitly urging that he not become a seaman?[16]

"All masters of vessels are warned not to harbor, conceal, or employ him, as they will answer for it, as the law directs."[17] To a fleeing apprentice, dissatisfied with the "bondage" of work ashore,[18] to a runaway slave, the sea might appear the only real shelter. Men with no experience at sea tried to pass for seamen, and before long discovered that they had indeed become seamen. Others *were* seamen, apprenticed in one vessel and fled to another. Still others, deserted soldiers, bail-jumpers, thieves, and murderers, had gotten into trouble with the law.[19] And others went to sea entirely unwillingly, originally impressed—perhaps from jail—into the navy, or tricked into the merchant service by crimps.[20] These were the floaters who drifted and slipped their moorings, the eventual suicides, the men whose wives— if they had wives—ran off with other men; the beneficiaries in their wills—when they left wills—were innkeepers.[21] Hitherto, argued a proponent of a United States navy in 1782, the merchant marine had been "the resource of necessity, accident or indulgence."[22]

The merchant marine was a place full of forces beyond the seaman's control: death and disease, storms, and fluctuations in employment. Indeed, the lack of "old salts" in Morison's merchant marine might reflect a somber irony: was the average seaman young because mobility rapidly brought him to another trade or because seamen died young?[23] A man in jail, said Dr. Johnson, was at least safe from drowning, and he had more room, better food, and better company. The Quaker John Woolman was one of the few sensitive enough to see that if the "poor bewildered sailors" drank and cursed, the fault lay not so much in themselves as in their harsh environment and the greed of employers. Nor was the way up through the hawse-hole so easy as Morison asserts. That the few succeeded tells us nothing of the many; only the successful left autobiographies.[24] Perhaps the sons of merchants and ship-masters made it, along with the captain's brother-in-law[25] and those who attended schools of navigation,[26] but what of the "poor lads bound apprentice" who troubled Woolman, those whose wages went to their masters? What of the seamen in Morison's own Boston who died too poor to pay taxes and who were a part of what James Henretta has called "the bottom" of Boston society?[27] What of those who went bankrupt with such frequency in

Rhode Island? [28] Why, at the other end of the colonies, did Washington's uncle warn that it would be "very difficult" to become master of a Virginia vessel and not worth trying? [29]

The presence of such men, fugitives and floaters, powerless in a tough environment, makes wanderlust appear an ironic parody of the motives which made at least some men go to sea. Catch the seaman when he is not pandering to your romanticism, said former seaman Frederick Law Olmstead a century later, and he will tell you that he hates the sight of blue water, he hates his ship, his officers, and his messmates—and he despises himself. Melville's Ishmael went to sea when he felt grim, hostile, and suicidal: "It is a way I have of driving off the spleen." No matter what we make of Ishmael, we cannot possibly make him into one of Morison's "adventure-seeking boys." Others, perhaps, but not Ishmael. The feelings of eighteenth-century Americans toward seafaring and seamen, and the evidence we have of the reasons men had for going to sea indicates that there were many like Ishmael in the colonial period, too, who left the land in flight and fear, outcasts, men with little hope of success ashore. These were dissenters from the American mood. Their goals differed from their fellows ashore; these were the rebels, the men who stayed on to become old salts.[30]

Admiralty law treated seamen in a special way, as "wards." Carl Ubbelohde says that seamen favored the colonial Vice Admiralty Courts as "particular tribunals in case of trouble," and Charles M. Andrews and Richard B. Morris agreed that these courts were "guardians of the rights of the seamen." The benefits of being classified as a "ward" are dubious, but, regardless of the quality of treatment which admiralty law accorded to seamen, it certainly does not follow that, all in all, the colonial seaman was well treated by the law. Indeed, if we broaden our scope to include colonial law generally, we find an extraordinarily harsh collection of laws, all justifying Olmsted's later claim that American seamen "are more wretched, and are governed more by threats of force than any other civilized laborers of the world." [31] There were laws providing for the whipping of disobedient seamen and in one case for their punishment as "seditious"; laws prohibiting seamen in port from leaving their vessels after sundown and from traveling on land without certificates of discharge from their last job; laws empowering "every free white person" to catch runaway seamen.[32] We find other laws that were less harsh, some seeming to protect the seaman: laws against extending credit to seamen and against arresting them for debt, and against entertaining them in taverns for more than one hour per day; laws against selling them liquor and prohibiting them from gambling with cards or dice; laws waiving imprisonment for seamen convicted of cursing; laws requiring masters to give discharge certificates to their seamen and laws prohibiting hiring without such certificates.[33] Finally, there were laws which clearly helped the seaman: laws requiring masters to provide "good and sufficient diet and accommodation" and providing for redress if the master refused or failed to do this; laws providing punishment for masters who "immoderately beat, wound, or maim" their seamen; laws providing that seamen's contracts be written.[34]

These harsh or, at best, paternalistic laws [35] add up to a structure whose purpose was to assure a ready supply of cheap, docile labor.[36] Obedience, both at sea and ashore, is the keystone.[37] Charles Beard at his most rigidly mechanistic would doubtless have found the Constitution merely mild stuff along side this blatantly one-sided class legislation. Today's historians of the "classless society" would do well to examine the preambles of these laws, written in a more candid age by legislatures for which, even by Robert Brown's evidence, most seamen could not vote.[38] Again and again these laws tried to inhibit acts of seamen which could do "prejudice to masters and owners of vessells" or constitute a "manifest detriment of . . . trade." [39] The seamen's interests were sacrificed to the merchants', and even the laws which seem friendly to the seaman benefited the master. Laws against giving credit, arresting, and suing were meant to keep seamen available rather than involved in a lawsuit or imprisoned; the certificates and written contracts sought to prevent desertion and to protect the master against what would today be called a strike; [40] the laws protecting seamen against immoderate punishment and requiring adequate food and accommodations were implicitly weak in that they required that dependents make open complaint against their superiors.[41] Sometimes this limitation is made explicit, as in a South Carolina law of 1751 whose stated purpose is "TO DISCOURAGE FRIVOLOUS AND VEXATIOUS ACTIONS AT LAW BEING BROUGHT BY SEAMEN AGAINST MASTERS AND COMMANDERS." [42]

Thus if we think of Jack Tar as jolly, childlike, irresponsible, and in many ways like the Negro stereotype, it is because he was treated like a child, a servant, and a slave. What the employer saw as the necessities of an authoritarian profession were written into law and confirmed by culture: the society that wanted Jack dependent made him that way, and then concluded that that was the way he really was.[43]

II

Constantly plagued by short complements, the Royal Navy attempted to solve its manning problems in America, as in England, by impressment.[44] Neil Stout has recently attributed these shortages to "death, illness, crime, and desertion," which were caused largely by rum and by the deliberate enticements of American merchants.[45] Rum and inveiglement certainly took a high toll, but to focus on these two causes of shortages is unfairly to shift the blame for impressment onto its victims. The navy itself caused shortages. Impressment, said Thomas Hutchinson, caused desertion, rather than the other way around.[46] Jack Tar had good reasons for avoiding the navy. It would, a young Virginian was warned, "cut him and staple him and use him like a Negro, or rather, like a dog." James Otis grieved at the loss of the "flower" of Massachusetts's youth "by ten thousands" to a service which treated them little better than "hewers of wood and drawers of water." Discipline was harsh and sometimes irrational, and punishments were cruel.[47] Water poured into sailors' beds, they went mad, and died of fevers and scurvy.[48] Sickness, Benjamin Franklin noted, was more common in the navy than in the merchant service and more frequently fatal.[49] In a fruitless attempt to prevent desertion, wages were withheld and men shunted about from ship to ship without being paid.[50] But the unpaid accumulation of even three or four years' back wages could not keep a man from running.[51] And why should it have? Privateering paid better in wartime, and wages were higher in the merchant service; even laborers ashore were better paid.[52] Thus Stout's claim that the navy was "forced" to press is only as accurate as the claim that the South was forced to enslave Negroes. Those whose sympathies lie with the thousands of victims of this barbaric practice—rather than with naval administrators— will see that the navy pressed because to be in the navy was in some sense to be a slave, and for this we must blame the slaveowners rather than the slaves.[53]

Impressment angered and frightened the seamen, but it pervaded and disrupted all society, giving other classes and groups cause to share a common grievance with the press-gang's more direct victims: just about everyone had a relative at sea.[54] Whole cities were crippled. A nighttime operation in New York in 1757 took in eight hundred men, the equivalent of more than one-quarter of the city's adult male population.[55] Impressment and the attendant shortage of men may have been a critical factor in the stagnancy of "the once cherished now depressed, once flourishing now sinking Town of Boston." [56] H.M.S. *Shirley's* log lists at least ninety-two men pressed off Boston in five months of 1745–1746; *Gramont* received seventy-three pressed men in New York in three days in 1758; *Arethusa* took thirty-one men in two days off Virginia in 1771.[57] Binges such as these left the communities where they occurred seriously harmed. Preachers' congregations took flight, and merchants complained loudly about the "many Thousands of Pounds of Damage." [58] "Kiss my arse, you dog," shouted the captain as he made off with their men, leaving vessels with their fires still burning, unmanned, finally to be wrecked.[59] They seized legislators and slaves, fishermen and servants.[60] Seamen took to the woods or fled town altogether, dreading the appearance of a man-of-war's boat (in the words of one) as a flock of sheep dreaded a wolf's appearance.[61] If they offered to work at all, they demanded inflated wages, and refused to sail to ports where there was danger of impressment.[62] "New York and Boston," Benjamin Franklin commented during the French and Indian War, "have so often found the Inconvenience of . . . Station Ships that they are very indifferent about having them: The Pressing of their Men and thereby disappointing Voyages, often hurting their Trade more than the Enemy hurts it." Even a ferryboat operator complained as people shunned the city during a press; food and fuel grew short and their prices rose.[63]

From the very beginning the history of impressment in America is a tale of venality, deceit, and vindictiveness. Captains kept deserters and dead men on ships' books, pocketing their provision allowances. In 1706 a captain pressed men and literally sold them to short-handed vessels. His midshipman learned the business so well that after his dismissal he became a veritable entrepreneur of impressment, setting up shop in a private sloop. Another commander waited until New York's governor was away to break a no-press agreement and when the governor returned he seriously considered firing on the Queen's ship.[64] In Boston in 1702, the lieutenant-governor *did* fire, responding to merchants' complaints. "Fire and be damn'd," shouted the impressing captain as the shots whistled through his sails. The merchants had complained that the press was illegal under 1697 instructions which required captains and commanders to apply to colonial governors for permission to press.[65] These instructions, a response to complaints of "irregular proceedings of the captains of some of our ships of war in the impressing of seamen," had clearly not put an end to irregularities.[66] In 1708 a Parliament fearful of the disruptive effect of impressment on trade, forbade the practice in America. In the sixty-seven years until the repeal (in 1775) of this Act for the Encouragement of the Trade to America, there was great disagreement as to its meaning and indeed as to its very existence. Did the Sixth of Anne, as the act was called, merely prohibit the navy from impressing and leave governors free to do so? At least one governor, feeling "pinioned" under the law, continued impressing while calling it "borrowing." [67] Was the act simply a wartime measure, which expired with the return of peace in 1713? [68] Regardless of the dispute, impressment continued, routine in its regularity but often spectacular in its effects.[69]

Boston was especially hard hit by impressment in the 1740's, with frequent incidents throughout the decade and major explosions in 1745 and 1747. Again and again the town meeting and the province's House of Representatives protested, drumming away at the same themes: impressment was harmful to maritime commerce and to the economic life of the city in general and illegal if not properly authorized.[70] In all this the seaman himself becomes all but invisible. The attitude toward him in the protests was at best neutral, and often sharply antagonistic. In 1747 the House of Representatives condemned the violent response of hundreds of seamen to a large-scale press as "a tumultuous riotous assembling of armed Seamen, Servants, Negroes, and others . . . tending to the Destruction of all Government and Order." While acknowledging that the people had reason to protest, the House chose to level *its* protest against "the most audacious Insult" to the governor, Council, and House. And the town meeting, that stronghold of democracy, offered its support to those who took "orderly" steps while expressing its "Abhorence of such Illegal Criminal Proceedings" as those undertaken by the seamen "and other persons of mean and Vile Condition." [71]

Protests such as these at the same time reflect both unity and division in colonial society. All kinds of Americans—both merchants and seamen—opposed impressment, but the town meeting and the House spoke for the merchant, not the seaman. They opposed impressment not for its effect on the seaman but for its effect on commerce. Thus their protests express antagonism to British policy at the same time that they express class division. These two themes continue and develop in American opposition to impressment in the three decades between the Knowles Riots of 1747 and the Declaration of Independence.

During the French and Indian War the navy competed with privateers for seamen.[72] Boston again protested against impressment, and then considered authorizing the governor to press, "provided said Men be impressed from inward-bound Vessels from Foreign Parts only, and that none of them be Inhabitants of this Province." [73] In 1760 New York's mayor had a naval captain arrested on the complaint of two shipmasters who claimed that he had welched on a deal to exchange two men he had pressed for two others they were willing to furnish.[74] With the return of peace in 1763, admirals and Americans alike had reason to suppose that there would be no more impressment.[75] But the Admiralty's plans for a large new American fleet required otherwise, and impressment began again in the spring of 1764 in New York, where a seven-week hot press was brought to a partial stop by the arrest of one of the two offending captains.[76] In the spring and summer a hunt for men between Maine and Virginia by four naval vessels brought violent responses, including the killing of a marine at New York, and another fort, at Newport, fired on another naval vessel.[77]

Along with the divisions there was a certain amount of unity. Seamen who fled after violently resisting impressment could not be found —probably because others sheltered them—and juries would not indict them. Captains were prevented from impressing by the threat of prosecution.[78] And in 1769 lawyer John Adams used the threat of displaying the statute book containing the Sixth of Anne to frighten a special court of Admiralty into declaring the killing of an impressing lieutenant justifiable homicide in necessary self-defense.[79]

There were two kinds of impressment incidents: those in which there was immediate self-defense against impressment, usually at sea, and those in which crowds ashore, consisting in large part of seamen, demonstrated generalized opposition to impressment. This is what the first kind of incident sounded like: a volley of musketry and the air full of langrage, grapeshot, round shot, hammered shot, double-headed shot, even rocks. "Come into the boat and be damned, you Sorry Son of a Whore or else Ile breake your head, and hold your tongue." Small arms, swords and cutlasses, blunderbusses, clubs and pistols, axes, harpoons, fishgigs, twelve-pounders, six-pounders, half-pounders. "You are a parsill of Raskills." Fired five shots to bring to a snow [a square-rigged vessel] from North Carolina, pressed four. "You have no right to impress me . . . If you step over that line . . . by the eternal God of Heaven, you are a dead man." "Aye, my lad, I have seen many a brave fellow before now." [80]

Here is hostility and bloodshed, a tradition of antagonism. From the beginning, impressment's most direct victims—the seamen—were its most active opponents. Bernard Bailyn's contention that "not a single murder resulted from the activities of the Revolutionary mobs in America" does not hold up if it is extended to cover resistance to impressment; there were murders on both sides. Perhaps the great bulk of incidents of this sort must remain forever invisible to the historian, for they often took place out of sight of friendly observers, and the only witness, the navy, kept records which are demonstrably biased and faulty, omitting the taking of thousands of men. [81] But even the visible records provide a great deal of information. This much we know without doubt: seamen did not go peacefully. Their violence was purposeful, and sometimes they were articulate. "I know who you are," said one, as reported by John Adams and supported by Thomas Hutchinson. "You are the lieutenant of a man-of-war, come with a press-gang to deprive me of my liberty. You have no right to impress me. I have retreated from you as far as I can. I can go no farther. I and my companions are determined to stand upon our defence. Stand off." [82] (It was difficult for Englishmen to fail to see impressment in such terms—even a sailor *doing* the pressing could feel shame over "*fighting* with honest sailors, to deprive them of their liberty.") [83]

Ashore, seamen and others demonstrated their opposition to impressment with the only weapon which the unrepresentative politics of the day offered them—riot. In Boston several thousand people responded to a nighttime impressment sweep of the harbor and docks with three days of rioting beginning in the early hours of November 17, 1747. Thomas Hutchinson reported that "the lower class were beyond measure enraged." Negroes, servants, and hundreds of seamen seized a naval lieutenant, assaulted a sheriff and put his deputy in the stocks, surrounded the governor's house, and stormed the Town House where the General Court was sitting. The rioters demanded the seizure of the impressing officers, the release of the men they had pressed, and execution of a death sentence which had been levied against a member of an earlier press-gang who had been convicted of murder. When the governor fled to Castle William—some called it "abdication"—Commodore Knowles threatened to put down what he called "arrant rebellion" by bombarding the town. The governor, who, for his part, thought the rioting a secret plot of the upper class, was happily surprised when the town meeting expressed its "Abhorence" of the seamen's riot.[84]

After the French and Indian War, press riots increased in frequency. Armed mobs of whites and Negroes repeatedly manhandled captains, officers, and crews, threatened their lives, and held them hostage for the men they had pressed. Mobs fired at pressing vessels and tried to board them; they threatened to burn one, and they regularly dragged ships' boats to the center of town for ceremonial bonfires. In Newport in June, 1765, five hundred seamen, boys, and Negroes rioted after five weeks of impressment. "Sensible" Newporters opposed impressment but nonetheless condemned this "Rabble." In Norfolk in 1767, Captain Jeremiah Morgan retreated, sword in hand, before a mob of armed whites and Negroes. "Good God," he wrote to the governor, "was your Honour and I to prosecute all the Rioters that attacked us belonging to Norfolk there would not be twenty left unhang'd belonging to the Toun." [85] According to Thomas Hutchinson, the *Liberty* riot in Boston in 1768 may have been as much against impressment as against the seizure of Hancock's sloop. *Romney* had pressed before June 10, and on that day three officers were forced by an angry crowd "arm'd with Stones" to release a man newly pressed from the Boston packet.[86] *Romney* pressed another man, and on June 14, after warding off "many wild and violent proposals," the town meeting petitioned the governor against both the seizure and impressment; the instructions to their representatives (written by John Adams) quoted the Sixth of Anne at length. On June 18 two councillors pleaded with the governor to procure the release of a man who had been pressed by *Romney* "as the peace of the Town seems in a great measure to depend upon it." [87]

There were other impressment riots: at New York in July of 1764 and July of 1765; [88] at Newport in July of 1764; [89] at Casco Bay,

Maine, in December 1764.[90] Incidents continued during the decade following, and impressment flowered on the very eve of the Revolution. Early in 1775 the practice began to be used in a frankly vindictive and political way—because a town had inconvenienced an admiral, or because a town supported the Continental Congress.[91] Impresses were ordered and took place from Maine to Virginia.[92] In September a bundle of press warrants arrived from the Admiralty, along with word of the repeal of the Sixth of Anne. What had been dubious was now legal. Up and down the coast, officers rejoiced and went to work.[93]

Long before 1765 Americans had developed beliefs about impressment, and they had expressed those beliefs in words and deeds. Impressment was bad for trade and it was illegal. It was, in the words of the Massachusetts House in 1720, "a great Breach on the Rights of His Majesties Subjects." In 1747 it was a violation of "the common Liberty of the Subject," and in 1754 "inconsistent with Civil Liberty, and the Natural Rights of Mankind." [94] Some felt, in 1757, that it was even "abhorrent to the English Constitution." [95] In fact, the claim that impressment was unconstitutional was wrong. (Even *Magna Charta* was no protection. *Nullus liber homo capiatur* did not apply to seamen.) [96] Impressment indicated to Benjamin Franklin "that the constitution is yet imperfect, since in so general a case it doth not secure liberty, but destroys it." "If impressing seamen is of right by common law in Britain," he also remarked, "slavery is then of right by common law there; there being no slavery worse than that sailors are subjected to." [97]

For Franklin, impressment was a symptom of inherent injustice in the British constitution. In *Common Sense* Tom Paine saw impressment as a reason for rejecting monarchy. In the Declaration of Independence Thomas Jefferson included impressment among the "Oppressions" of George III; later he likened the practice to the capture of Africans for slavery. Both practices "reduced [the victim] to . . . bondage by force, in flagrant violation of his own consent, and of his natural right in his own person." [98]

Despite all this, and all that went before, we have thought little of impressment as an element in explaining the conduct of the common man in the American Revolution.[99] Contemporaries knew better. John Adams felt that a tactical mistake by Thomas Hutchinson on the question of impressment in 1769 would have "accelerated the revolution.

. . . It would have spread a wider flame than Otis's ever did, or could have done." [100] But ten years later American seamen were being impressed by *American* officers. The United States Navy had no better solution for "public Necessities" than had the Royal Navy. Joseph Reed, President of Pennsylvania, complained to Congress of "Oppressions," and in so doing offered testimony to the role of *British* impressment in bringing on revolution. "We cannot help observing how similar this Conduct is to that of the British Officers during our Subjection to Great Britain and are persuaded it will have the same unhappy effects viz., an estrangement of the Affections of the People from the Authority under which they act which by an easy Progression will proceed to open Opposition to the immediate Actors and Bloodshed." [101]

Impressment had played a role in the estrangement of the American people from the British government. It had produced "Odium" against the navy, and even six-year-olds had not been too young to detest it.[102] The anger of thousands of victims did not vanish. Almost four decades after the Declaration of Independence an orator could arouse his audience by tapping a folk-memory of impressment by the same "haughty, cruel, and gasconading nation" which was once again trying to enslave free Americans.[103]

III

The seamen's conduct in the 1760's and 1770's makes more sense in the light of previous and continued impressment. What may have seemed irrational violence can now be seen as purposeful and radical. The pattern of rioting as political expression, established as a response to impressment, was adapted and broadened as a response to the Stamp Act.

In New York General Gage described the "insurrection" of October 31, 1765, and following as "composed of great numbers of Sailors." The seamen, he said, were "the only People who may be properly Stiled Mob," and estimates indicate that between a fifth and a fourth of New York's rioters were seamen. The disturbances began among the seamen—especially former privateersmen—on October 31. On November 1 they had marched in protest against the Stamp Act, led primarily by their former captains; later they rioted, led by no one but themselves Why? Because they had been duped by merchants, or, if not by merchants, then certainly by lawyers. So British officials believed—aroused by these men who meant to use them, the seamen themselves had nothing more than plunder on their minds. In fact, at that point in New York's rioting when the leaders lost control, the seamen, who were then in the center of town, in an area rich for plunder, chose instead to march in an orderly and disciplined way clear across town to do violence to the home and possessions of an English major whose provocative conduct had made him the obvious political enemy. Thus the "rioting" was very discriminating.[104]

Seamen and non-seamen alike joined to oppose the Stamp Act for many reasons,[105] but the seamen had two special grievances: impressment and the effect of England's new attitude toward colonial trade. To those discharged by the navy at the end of the war and those thrown out of work by the end of privateering were added perhaps twenty thousand more seamen (and fishermen) who were thought to be the direct victims of the post-1763 trade regulations.[106] This problem came to the fore in the weeks following November 1, 1765, when the Stamp Act went into effect. The strategy of opposition chosen by the colonial leadership was to cease all activities which required the use of stamps; thus maritime trade came to a halt in the cities.[107] Some said that this was a cowardly strategy; if the Americans opposed the Stamp Act, let them go on with business as usual, refusing outright to use the stamps.[108] The leaders' strategy was especially harmful to the seamen, who took the latter more radical position— otherwise the ships would not sail. And this time the seamen's radicalism triumphed over both colonial leadership and British officials. Within little more than a month the act had been largely nullified. Customs officers were allowing ships to sail without stamps, offering as the reason the fear that the seamen, "who are the people that are most dangerous on these occasions, as their whole dependance for a subsistence is upon Trade," would certainly "commit some terrible Mischief." Philadelphia's customs officers feared that the seamen would soon "compel" them to let ships pass without stamps. Customs officers at New York yielded when they heard that the seamen were about to have a meeting.[109]

Customs officers had worse luck on other days. Seamen battled them throughout the 1760's and 1770's. In October, 1769, a Philadelphia customs officer was attacked by a mob of seamen, who also tarred, feathered, and nearly drowned a man who had furnished him with information about illegally imported goods. A year later a New

Jersey customs officer who approached an incoming vessel in Delaware Bay had *his* boat boarded by armed seamen who threatened to murder him and came close to doing so. When the officer's son came to Philadelphia, he was similarly treated by a mob of seamen. There were one thousand seamen in Philadelphia at the time, and, according to the customers collector there, they were "always ready" to do such "mischief." [110] This old antagonism had been further politicized in 1768, when, under the American Board of Customs Commissioners, searchers began to break into sea chests and confiscate those items not covered by cockets, thus breaking an old custom of the sea which allowed seamen to import small items for their own profit. Oliver M. Dickerson has described this new "Invasion of Seamen's Rights" as a part of "customs racketeering" and a cause of animosity between seamen and customs officers.[111]

Many of these animosities flared in the Boston Massacre. What John Adams described as "a motley rabble of saucy boys, negroes and molattoes, Irish teagues and out landish jack tarrs," including twenty or thirty of the latter, armed with clubs and sticks, did battle with the soldiers. Their leader was Crispus Attucks, a mulatto seaman; he was shot to death in front of the Custom House.[112] One of the seamen's reasons for being there has been too little explored. The Massacre grew out of a fight between workers and off-duty soldiers at a ropewalk two days before.[113] That fight, in turn, grew out of the long-standing practice in the British army of allowing off-duty soldiers to take civilian employment. They did so, in Boston and elsewhere, often at wages which undercut those offered to Americans—including unemployed seamen who sought work ashore—by as much as fifty percent.[114] In hard times this led to intense competition for work, and the Boston Massacre was in part a product of this competition. Less well known is the Battle of Golden Hill, which arose from similar causes and took place in New York six weeks before. In January, 1770, a gang of seamen went from house to house and from dock to dock, using clubs to drive away the soldiers employed there and threatening anyone who might rehire them.[115] In the days of rioting which followed and which came to be called the Battle of Golden Hill, the only fatality was a seaman, although many other seamen were wounded in the attempt to take vengeance for the killing.[116] The antipathy between soldiers and seamen was so great, said John Adams, "that they fight as naturally when they meet, as the elephant and Rhinoceros." [117]

IV

To the wealthy Loyalist judge, Peter Oliver of Massachusetts, the common people were only "Rabble"—like the "Mobility of all Countries, perfect Machines, wound up by any Hand who might first take the Winch." The people were "duped," "deceived," and "deluded" by cynical leaders who could "turn the Minds of the great Vulgar." In other words, had they been less ignorant, Americans would have spurned their leaders, and there would have been no Revolution.[118] I have tested this generalization and found it unacceptable, at least in its application to colonial seamen. Obviously, the seamen did not cause the American Revolution. But neither were they simply irrational fellows who moved only when others manipulated them. I have attempted to show that the seaman had a mind of his own and genuine reasons to act, and that he did act—purposefully. The final test of this purposefulness must be the Revolution itself. Here we find situations in which the seamen were separated from those who might manipulate them and thrown into great physical danger; if they were manipulated or duped into rebellion, on their own we might expect them to have shown little understanding of or enthusiasm for the war.

To a surprising extent, American seamen remained Americans during the Revolution. Beaumarchais heard from an American in 1775 that seamen, fishermen, and harbor workers had become an "army of furious men, whose actions are all animated by a spirit of vengeance and hatred" against the English, who had destroyed their livelihood "and the liberty of their country." [119] The recent study of loyalist claimants by Wallace Brown confirms Oliver Dickerson's earlier contention that "the volumes dealing with loyalists and their claims discloses an amazing absence of names" of seamen. From a total of 2,786 loyalist claimants whose occupations are known, Brown found only 39, or 1.4 percent, who were seamen (or pilots). (It is possible to exclude fishermen and masters but not pilots from his figures.) In contrast, farmers numbered 49.1 percent, artisans 9.8 percent, merchants and shopkeepers 18.6 percent, professionals 9.1 percent, and officeholders 10.1 percent. Although, as Brown states, the poor may be underrepresented among the claimants, "the large number of claims by poor people, and even Negroes, suggests that this is not necessarily true." [120]

An especially revealing way of examining the seamen's loyalties under pressure is to follow them into British prisons.[121] Thousands of them were imprisoned in such places as the ship *Jersey*, anchored in New York harbor, and Mill and Forton prisons in England. Conditions were abominable. Administration was corrupt, and in America disease was rife and thousands died.[122] If physical discomfort was less in the English prisons than in *Jersey*, the totality of misery may have been as great with prisoners more distant from the war and poorly informed about the progress of the American cause. Lost in a no-man's land between British refusal to consider them prisoners of war and Washington's unwillingness in America to trade his trained soldiers for captured seamen, these men had limited opportunities for exchange. Trapped in this desperate situation, the men were offered a choice: they could defect and join the Royal Navy. To a striking extent the prisoners remained patriots,[123] and very self-consciously so. "Like brave men, they resisted, and swore that they would never lift a hand to do any thing on board of King George's ships." [124] The many who stayed understood the political significance of their choice, as well as the few who went. "What business had he to sell his Country, and go to the worst of Enemies?" [125] Instead of defecting they engaged in an active resistance movement. Although inexperienced in self-government and segregated from their captains, on their own these men experienced no great difficulties in organizing themselves into disciplined groups. "Notwithstanding they were located within the absolute dominions of his Britanic majesty," commented one, the men "adventured to form themselves into a republic, framed a constitution and enacted wholesome laws, with suitable penalties." [126] Organized, they resisted, celebrating the Fourth of July under British bayonets, burning their prisons, and escaping. Under intolerable conditions, seamen from all over the colonies discovered that they shared a common conception of the cause for which they fought.[127]

At the Constitutional Convention Benjamin Franklin spoke for the seamen:

> It is of great consequence that we shd. not depress the virtue and public spirit of our common people; of which they displayed a great deal during the war, and which contributed principally to the favorable issue of it. He related the honorable refusal of the American seamen who were carried in great numbers into the British

prisons during the war, to redeem themselves from misery or to seek their fortunes, by entering on board of the Ships of the Enemies to their Country; contrasting their patriotism with a contemporary instance in which the British seamen made prisoners by the Americans, readily entered on the ships of the latter on being promised a share of the prizes that might be made out of their own Country.[128]

Franklin spoke against limiting the franchise, *not* for broadening it: he praised the seamen, but with a hint of condescension, suggesting that it would be prudent to grant them a few privileges. A decade later a French traveler noticed that "except the laborer in ports, and the common sailor, everyone calls himself, and is called by others, a *gentleman*." [129] Government was still gentleman's government: more people were defined as gentlemen, but Jack Tar was not yet among them.

v

Bernard Bailyn has recently given needed illumination to our understanding of pre-Revolutionary crowd action. Bailyn has disagreed with Peter Oliver and with modern historians who have concurred in describing pre-Revolutionary rioters as mindless, passive, and manipulated: "Far from being empty vessels," rioters in the decade before the outbreak of fighting were "politically effective" and "shared actively the attitudes and fears" of their leaders; theirs was a 'fully fledged political movement'." [130] Thus it would seem that Bailyn has freed himself from the influential grasp of Gustave Le Bon,[131] but Bailyn stopped short of total rejection. Only in 1765, he says, was the colonial crowd "transformed" into a political phenomenon. Before that it was "conservative"—like crowds in seventeenth- and eighteenth-century England, aiming neither at social revolution nor at social reform, but only at immediate revenge. Impressment riots and other "demonstrations by transient sailors and dock workers," Bailyn says, expressed no "deep-lying social distress" but only a "diffuse and indeliberate antiauthoritarianism"; they were "ideologically inert." [132]

Other historians have seen the colonial seamen—and the rest of the lower class—as mindless and manipulated, both before and after 1765.[133] The seeming implication behind this is that the seamen who

demonstrated in colonial streets did so as much out of simple vindictiveness or undisciplined violence as out of love of liberty. Certainly such motivation would blend well with the traditional picture
of the seaman as rough and ready. For along with the stereotype of
Jolly Jack—and in part belying that stereotype—is bold and reckless
Jack, the exotic and violent.[134] Jack *was* violent; the conditions of his
existence were violent. Was his violence non-political? Sometimes.
The mob of seventy to eighty yelling, club-swinging, out-of-town seamen who tried to break up a Philadelphia election in 1742 had no
interest in the election; they had been bought off with money and
liquor.[135]

Other violence is not so clear-cut. Edward Thompson has seen the
fighting out of significant social conflict in eighteenth-century England
"in terms of Tyburn, the hulks and the Bridewells on the one hand;
and crime, riot, and mob action on the other." [136] Crime and violence
among eighteenth-century American seamen needs reexamination from
such a perspective. Does "mutiny" adequately describe the act of the
crew which seized *Black Prince*, re-named it *Liberty*, and chose their
course and a new captain by voting? What shall we call the conduct
of the 150 seamen who demanded higher wages by marching along
the streets of Philadelphia with clubs, unrigging vessels, and forcing
workmen ashore? If "mutiny" is often the captain's name for what we
have come to call a "strike," perhaps we might also detect some significance broader than mere criminality in the seamen's frequent as-
saults on captains and thefts from them.[137] Is it not in some sense a
political act for a seaman to tear off the mast a copy of a law which
says that disobedient seamen will be punished as "seditious"?

Impressment meant the loss of freedom, both personal and economic, and sometimes the loss of life. The seaman who defended himself against impressment felt that he was fighting to defend his
"liberty," and he justified his resistance on grounds of "right." [138] It is
in the concern for liberty and right that the seaman rises from vindictiveness to a somewhat more complex awareness that certain values
larger than himself exist and that he is the victim not only of cruelty
and hardship but also, in the light of those values, of injustice. The
riots ashore, whether they were against impressment, the Stamp Act,
or competition for work, express that same sense of injustice.
Thousands of men took positive and effective steps to demonstrate
their opposition to both acts and policies.

Two of England's most exciting historians have immensely broadened our knowledge of past and present by examining phenomena strikingly like the conduct and thought of the seamen in America. These historians have described such manifestations as "sub-political" or "pre-political," and one of them has urged that such movements be "seriously considered not simply as an unconnected series of individual curiosities, as footnotes to history, but as a phenomenon of general importance and considerable weight in modern history."[139]

When Jack Tar went to sea during the American Revolution, he fought, as he had for many years before, quite literally, to protect his life, liberty, and property. It might be extravagant to call the seamen's conduct and the sense of injustice which underlay it in any fully developed sense ideological or political; on the other hand, it makes little sense to describe their ideological content as zero. There are many worlds and much of human history in that vast area between ideology and inertness.

[1] His walk was sometimes described as a "waddle" (*New-York Gazette; or the Weekly Post-Boy*, September 3, 1759). Seamen were often called Jack Tar in England and in the colonies (e.g., *ibid.*, October 15, 1770). The term was used more or less interchangeably with "seaman," "sailor," and "mariner," with the latter frequently connoting "master" (as in Panel of Jurors [n.d.], New York Supreme Court, Pleadings P–2689, Office of County Clerk, Hall of Records, New York City, where seven of ten "mariners" are identifiable as captains by comparison with such sources as *The Burghers of New Amsterdam and the Freemen of New York, 1675–1866* [New York Historical Society, *Collections*, vol. 18 (New York, 1886)], *passim, New-York Gazette; or the Weekly Post-Boy, passim*; and the especially valuable list of privateer captains in Stuyvesant Fish, *The New York Privateers, 1756–1763* [New York, 1945], pp. 83–90). In this article "Jack Tar" is a merchant seaman, a "sailor" is in the Royal Navy, and a "mariner" is the captain of a merchant vessel. If a source calls a man a "mariner" or a "sailor," I have had to have evidence that he was in fact a merchant seaman before I would count him as one. For a useful discussion of terms, see "I.M.V.," "Note," *Mariner's Mirror*, 7 (1921): 351.

[2] George Balfour, "Memorandum," *Mariner's Mirror*, 8 (1922): 248. For the seaman's dress, see *Abstracts of Wills on File in the Surrogate's Office, City of New York* (New York Historical Society *Collections*, vols. 25–41 [New York, 1893–1909]); *ibid.*, 6: 111; descriptions of dress scattered throughout Admiralty Group, Class 98, Piece 11–14, Public Record Office

(Hereafter cited as Adm. 98/11) *New York Gazette; Weekly Post-Boy*, December 10, 1759, October 14, December 16, 1762, November 3, 1763, March 6, June 26, 1766, October 1, 1767, January 29, 1770, July 6, 1772; Samuel Eliot Morison, *John Paul Jones* (Boston, 1959), p. 72. A pair of useful illustrations appears in *Mariner's Mirror*, 9 (1923): 128.

[3] J. R. Hutchinson, *The Press Gang, Afloat and Ashore* (New York 1910), p. 10. See *The Acts and Resolves . . . of the Province of Massachusetts Bay . . .* (Boston, 1869–1922), 3: 318–19, for an act of February 10, 1747, prescribing the stocks and whipping for seamen guilty of "profane cursing or swearing." For a landsman's version of some seamen's dialogue, see *New-York Gazette; Weekly Post-Boy*, December 10, 1767.

[4] Robert E. Peabody, "The Naval Career of Captain John Manley of Marblehead," Essex Institute *Historical Collections*, 45 (1909): 25; Ralph D. Paine, *The Ships and Sailors of Old Salem* (New York, 1909), p. 23; John Cremer, *Ramblin' Jack . . .*, ed. R. Reynell Bellamy (London, 1936), pp. 38–39; Congressman Edward Livingston, April 10, 1798, United States Congress, *Debates and Proceedings in the Congress of the United States . . .* (Washington, D.C., 1834–56), 5th Cong., 2d sess., p. 1388. (Hereafter cited as *Annals of Congress*); Colvill to Admiralty, November 12, 1765 (Adm. 1/482).

[5] The bibliography is endless; a typical recent instance is Edmund O. Sawyer, *America's Sea Saga: Tales of Ships and Their Stalwart Skippers Who Paced Behind the Mizzen* (New York, 1962), Foreword, p. 185 ("a tale of unending courage" by a retired lieutenant colonel who now lives in Hollywood where he "plays an active role in the relentless crusade against the Communist conspiracy"). Although there is much of use in *American Neptune,* the magazine's definition of maritime history has been too genteel, dwelling too often on such matters as ship design and construction, yachting, reminiscences, and model-building. On the other hand, even the WPA Writer's Program neglected the seamen in *Boston Looks Seaward* (Boston, 1941) and *A Maritime History of New York* (Garden City, N.Y., 1941).

[6] Samuel Eliot Morison, *The Maritime History of Massachusetts* (Boston, 1921), pp. 105–7, 111; see also Morison, *John Paul Jones*, pp. 22–23.

[7] Mason L. Weems, *The Life of Washington,* ed. Marcus Cunliffe (Cambridge, Mass., 1962), pp. xxxv, 27; Douglas S. Freeman, *George Washington* (New York, 1948–57), 1: 190–99; Jesse Lemisch, ed., *Benjamin Franklin: The Autobiography and Other Writings* (New York, 1961), p. 23. Elmo Paul Hohman, *Seamen Ashore* (New Haven, 1952), p. 217, calls this kind of motivation "positive"; see *ibid.* for "negative" motives.

[8] Morison, *John Paul Jones*, p. 11; sixty-one American seamen of ascertainable age who are listed in *Muster Rolls of New York Provincial Troops:*

1755–1764 (NYHS *Collections,* vol. 24 [New York, 1892], *passim*) average 24.3 years; Cremer, *Ramblin' Jack,* ed. Bellamy, p. 38.

⁹ The phrase appears in Cremer, *Ramblin' Jack,* ed. Bellamy, pp. 31–32, and in Morison, *Maritime History,* p. 107.

¹⁰ See, for example, Mary Barney, ed., *A Biographical Memoir of the Late Commodore Joshua Barney* (Boston, 1832); Thomas Dring, *Recollections of the Jersey Prison-Ship,* ed. Albert G. Greene (Providence, 1829); Ebenezer Fox, *The Adventures of Ebenezer Fox in the Revolutionary War* (Boston, 1847 [?]); Christopher Hawkins, *The Adventures of Christopher Hawkins* ed. Charles I. Bushnell (New York, 1864); Paine, *Ships and Sailors of Salem,* pp. 100, 117–19; James A. Henretta, "Economic Development and Social Structure in Colonial Boston," *William and Mary Quarterly,* 3d ser., 22 (1965): 76.

¹¹ Joseph Galloway to Benjamin Franklin, April 23, 1771, in Franklin Papers, 3: 50, American Philosophical Society, Philadelphia.

¹² "In America . . . all sorts of people turn farmers—where no mechanic or artizan—sailor—soldier—servant, etc. but what, if they get money, take land, and turn farmers," in Harry J. Carman, ed., *American Husbandry* (New York, 1939), p. 124.

¹³ The sons of captains might find themselves apprenticed to gentlemen or to butchers or barbers as well as to other mariners; see, for example, *Burghers of New Amsterdam,* pp. 577–78, 617, 620; *Indentures of Apprentices, 1718–1727* (NYHS *Collections,* 42 [New York, 1910]: 122–23, 140, 142–43, 150, 155, 166, 169, 181, 188, 189, 193, 195).

¹⁴ Albert Gallatin, April 10, 1798, in *Annals of Congress,* 5th Cong., 2d sess., p. 1392; J. Hector St. John de Crevecoeur, *Letters from an American Farmer* (New York, 1957), p. 122, has similar observations about American "sea-faring men," but he seems to be describing only whalers.

¹⁵ Lemisch, *Franklin,* pp. 23, 25–26. History apparently repeated itself in the next generation: Franklin's son, William, "left my house unknown to us all, and got on board a privateer, from whence I fetched him" (Benjamin Franklin to Jane Mecom [June [?], 1748], in Leonard W. Labaree *et al.,* eds., *The Papers of Benjamin Franklin* [New Haven, 1959—], 3: 303).

¹⁶ Freeman, *Washington,* 1: 198–99. For some other instances of opposition by families of young men who expressed the intention of going to sea, see Barney, ed., *Memoir,* pp. 3–4, and Fox, *Adventures,* pp. 29, 36, 40.

¹⁷ This is a composite of advertisements that appeared in almost every colonial newspaper; see, for example, *New-York Gazette; Weekly Post-Boy,* May 17, 24, 1764, June 27, 1765.

¹⁸ The term is used by Fox in *Adventures* (p. 18) in describing his situation in 1775. In an interesting passage on 17–19 he sees in the movement for independence a cause of a general "spirit of insubordination" among

American youth at the time. For another runaway, see Bushnell, *Adventures of Hawkins,* pp. 10, 60–61.

[19] See *New-York Gazette; Weekly Post-Boy,* September 3, December 10, 1759, October 14, December 16, 1762, July 21, October 6, November 3, 1763, March 29, May 10, 24, July 19, September 6, 20, 1764, April 4, 18, June 27, 1765, June 29, July 6, 1772; *New York Journal: or the General Advertiser,* May 13, 1773. For a Negro seaman, see log of *Hunter,* September 8, 1758 (Adm. 51/465). Some Negro seamen were free and some received their freedom as a reward for service in warships (Benjamin Quarles, *The Negro in the American Revolution* [Chapel Hill, 1961], p. 84; Robert McColley, *Slavery and Jeffersonian Virginia* [Urbana, 1964], p. 89). But Negroes also served at sea and in related maritime trades as part of their bondage, and were sometimes advertised as "brought up from his Infancy to the sea." See also William Waller Hening, *The Statutes at Large . . . of Virginia* (Richmond, 1809–23) 11: 404; *New-York Gazette; Weekly Post-Boy,* March 26, 1761, July 7, August 18, November 17, 1763; Samuel Hallet, in American Loyalists: Transcripts of the Commission of Enquiry into the Losses and Services of the American Loyalists . . . 1783–1790, 19: 207, New York Public Library; George William Edwards, *New York as an Eighteenth Century Municipality, 1731–1776* (New York, 1917), p. 178.

[20] For crimps, see Hutchinson, *Press-Gang,* pp. 48–49. Hohman, *Seamen Ashore,* pp. 273–74, dates the development of crimping in America from between 1830 and 1845, but there were crimps in Norfolk in 1767. See Captain Jeremiah Morgan to Governor Francis Fauquier, September 11, 1767, Adm. 1/2116 (Library of Congress transcript).

[21] *New-York Gazette; Weekly Post-Boy,* September 30, 1773; *The King v. Jane the Wife of Thomas Dun,* Indictment for Bigamy, filed October 26, 1763, New York Supreme Court, Pleadings K–41. Although no statistical conclusions are possible, to a surprising extent the beneficiaries in a sample of seamen's wills are not wives but rather brothers and sisters, friends and innkeepers (*Abstracts of Wills,* 6: 111, 226; 7: 12, 38, 148, 397; 8: 98; 11: 194.

[22] *Independent Chronicle* (Boston), September 5, 1782.

[23] For some reflections on mortality in the merchant marine, see Ralph Davis, *The Rise of the English Shipping Industry in the Seventeenth and Eighteenth Centuries* (London, 1962), p. 156. As late as the 1840's, Massachusetts seamen, with an average age at death of 42.47 years, died younger than farmers, clergymen, lawyers, physicians, blacksmiths, carpenters, merchants, and laborers. Only painters, fishermen, manufacturers, mechanics, and printers are listed as having shorter lives in Lemuel Shattuck, *et al., Report of the Sanitary Commission of Massachusetts, 1850* (Cambridge,

Mass., 1948), p. 87. For unemployment, see *New York Journal: or the General Advertiser*, October 5, 1775; Thomas Paine, *The Complete Writings*, ed. Philip S. Foner (New York, 1945), 1: 33. In addition, a kind of unemployment is built into the profession: a seaman ashore is generally unemployed (See Hohman, *Seamen Ashore*, p. 209).

24 Quoted in Davis, *Rise of English Shipping*, p. 154; John Woolman, *The Journal of John Woolman and A Plea for the Poor* (New York, 1961), pp. 206, 192–93, 196. Morison, in *Maritime History* gives very little attention to the common seaman and much more to the "codfish aristocracy," which he clearly admires. For comments on elitism in the writings of Morison and other historians of early America, see Jesse Lemisch, "The American Revolution Seen from the Bottom Up," in Barton J. Bernstein, ed., *Towards a New Past: Dissenting Essays in American History* (New York, 1968), pp. 3–45.

25 Barney, ed., *Memoir*, p. 10. For the relative prospects of the sons of merchants and masters as opposed to others in the English merchant marine, see Davis, *Rise of English Shipping*, p. 117.

26 For such schools, see Boston Registry Department, *Records Relating to the Early History of Boston* (Boston, 1876–1909), 13: 2, 204; Carl Bridenbaugh, *Cities in Revolt* (New York, 1955), p. 377.

27 Woolman, *Journal*, p. 105; *Bethune* v. *Warner*, May 27, 1724, Admiralty Court, Boston, Minute Book 2 (1718–26), p. 177, Office of Clerk, Supreme Judicial Court, Suffolk County, Mass.; Boston Reg. Dept., *Records of Boston*, 14: 88–89, 94–95; Henretta, "Economic Development," p. 85; see also Jackson T. Main, *The Social Structure of Revolutionary America* (Princeton, 1965), p. 74.

28 Only three occupational groups exceeded "mariners" in the number of insolvency petitions filed with the Rhode Island legislature from 1756 to 1828; see Peter J. Coleman, "The Insolvent Debtor in Rhode Island, 1745–1828," *William and Mary Quarterly*, 3d ser., 22 (1965): 422n. Mr. Coleman has stated in conversation with the author that the "mariners" appear to have been predominantly common seamen.

29 Freeman, *Washington*, 1: 199.

30 Frederick Law Olmsted, *A Journey in the Back Country . . .* (New York, 1860), p. 287. Morison, in *Maritime History*, offers no evidence for the assertion that his anecdote of the adventurous farm boy is "typical" and that Massachusetts "has never had a native deep-sea proletariat." In the absence of such evidence and in light of the evidence offered above for the existence of a very different type, there is no basis for a claim that either group was "typical." My contention about the nature of the merchant marine is limited and negative: the presence of runaway slaves, thieves, and murderers—of fugitives and floaters—*in addition to* Morison's adventure-

seekers prevents any statement about typicality until we can offer quantitative evidence. Meanwhile, all that we can say is that both types existed and that it is misleading to view the colonial merchant marine as a homogeneous entity.

31 Carl Ubbelohde, *The Vice-Admiralty Courts and the American Revolution* (Chapel Hill, 1960), pp. 20, 159–60; Charles M. Andrews, introduction to Dorothy S. Towle, ed., *The Records of the Vice Admiralty Court of Rhode Island, 1716–1752* (Washington, D.C., 1936), p. 60; Richard B. Morris, *Government and Labor in Early America* (New York, 1946), pp. 232, 256; Olmsted, *Journey,* p. 287. Ubbelohde, Morris, and Andrews do not contend that the seaman was well treated by the law in an overall sense; Ubbelohde and Morris show that the seaman was treated better in vice admiralty courts than in courts of common law, but when the focus moves to colonial legislation the hostility of the law emerges as the central fact for the seaman.

32 Hening, *Statutes at Large,* 4:107–8; 6: 26; E. B. O'Callaghan, ed., *Laws and Ordinances of New Netherland, 1638–1674* (Albany, 1868), pp. 11–12. This law also prevented landsmen from going abroad vessels without authorization from the director of the West India Company. On June 13, 1647, two seamen convicted of tearing down a copy of this law (attached to their vessel's mainmast) were sentenced to be chained to a wheelbarrow and employed at hard labor, on bread and water, for three months. See I. N. P. Stokes, *The Iconography of Manhattan Island, 1498–1909* (New York, 1915–28), 4: 87; Thomas Cooper, ed., *The Statutes at Large of South Carolina* (Columbia, 1836–41), 3: 736.

33 See the laws cited in Morris, *Government and Labor,* p. 230, n. 2; *Minutes of the Common Council of the City of New York, 1675–1776* (New York, 1905), 1: 223, 372; *Acts and Resolves,* 1: 142, 560; 3: 318–19; 4: 73; James T. Mitchell and Henry Flanders, eds., *Statutes at Large of Pennsylvania from 1682 to 1801* (Harrisburg, 1890–1908), 2: 239–40; Albert S. Batchellor and Henry H. Metcalf, *Laws of New Hampshire* (Manchester, 1904–22), 1: 691; J Hammond Trumbull and C. J. Hoadly, eds., *The Public Records of the Colony of Connecticut (1636–1776)* (Hartford, 1850–90), 3: 54; *Charters and General Laws of the Colony and Province of Massachusetts* (Boston, 1814), p. 185; Cooper, ed., *Statutes of South Carolina,* 3: 735, 736; Hening, *Statutes of Virginia,* 4: 108–10; 6: 25, 28.

34 Hening, *Statutes of Virginia,* 4: 109–10; 6: 27. *Colonial Laws of New York from the Year 1664 to the Revolution* . . . (Albany, 1894–96), 4: 484–85; Morris, *Government and Labor,* p. 230, n 5 and 7.

35 Eugene T. Jackman, "Efforts Made before 1825 to Ameliorate the Lot of the American Seaman, with Emphasis on his Moral Regeneration"

(*American Neptune*, 24: [1964]: 109), describes legislation for seamen after the Revolution as "paternalistic." As late as 1897 the Supreme Court declared that "seamen are treated by Congress, as well as by the Parliament of Great Britain, as deficient in that full and intelligent responsibility for their acts which is accredited to ordinary adults" (Hohman, *Seamen Ashore*, p. 214).

[36] Morris (Government and Labor, p. 230) agrees with this statement in a somewhat more limited form.

[37] See the deposition of Commander Arthur Tough (in 1742) in Gertrude MacKinney, ed., *Pennsylvania Archives*, 8th ser. (Harrisburg, 1931–35), 4: 2993.

[38] Robert E. Brown, in *Middle-Class Democracy and the Revolution in Massachusetts, 1691–1780* ([Ithaca, 1955], pp. 27–30), acknowledges that the "city proletariat" constituted "the largest disfranchised group" and strongly implies that itinerant seamen could not vote. Even so, Brown has stated the case too optimistically. By including propertied captains under the ambiguous label "mariner," he has disguised the fact, legible in his own evidence, that the "mariners" who could vote were captains and the common seamen could not. See John Cary, "Statistical Method and the Brown Thesis on Colonial Democracy, with a Rebuttal by Robert E. Brown," *William and Mary Quarterly*, 3d ser., 20 (1963): 257. For Brown's acknowledgment of the error, see *ibid.*, p. 272. Arthur M. Schlesinger's *The Colonial Merchants and the American Revolution, 1763–1776* ([New York, 1918], p. 28) includes seamen in a list of those who were, "for the most part, unenfranchised." For an assertion that "sailors" could vote, based on evidence that *masters* could, compare Jacob R. Marcus, *Early American Jewry* (Philadelphia, 1953), 2: 231, and B. R. Carroll, ed., *Historical Collections of South Carolina* (New York, 1836), 2: 441.

[39] Trumbull and Hoadly, *Public Records of Connecticut*, 3: 54; Cooper ed., *Statutes of South Carolina*, 2: 54; 3: 735; for other legislation containing similar phrases, see Batchellor and Metcalf, *Laws of New Hampshire*, 1: 691; *Minutes of the Common Council of New York*, 1: 223; *Colonial Laws of New York*, 4: 483; Hening, *Statutes at Large*, 4: 107.

[40] For instance, *Colonial Laws of New York* (4: 484) (later disallowed) required a written contract in order to end such practices as this: "Very often when Ships and vessels come to be cleared out . . . the Seamen refuse to proceed with them without coming to new agreements for increasing their wages and many of them will Leave their Ships and Vessels and not proceed on their voyages which puts the owners of such ships and vessels to Great Trouble and Charges." The act also mentions subterfuges of seamen but fails to acknowledge the possibility that masters might also use

subterfuge. For a "mutiny" which clearly expressed a labor grievance, see below.

41 See the procedure for this in Hening, *Statutes at Large*, 4: 109–10; see also Morris, *Government and Labor*, p. 268.

42 Cooper, ed., *Statutes of South Carolina*, 3: 735.

43 For examples of the similarity between life at sea and life on the plantation, compare Morris, *Government and Labor*, pp. 230, 247, 256, 262, 274, and McColley, *Slavery and Jeffersonian Virginia*, p. 103. For Frederick Olmsted's comments on the similarity, based on his own experience at sea in 1843 and 1844, see *The Cotton Kingdom*, ed. Arthur M. Schlesinger (New York, 1953), p. 453. For the image of the seaman in literature, see Harold F. Watson, *The Sailor in English Fiction and Drama, 1550–1880* (New York, 1931), pp. 159–60 and *passim*.

44 For shortages which led to impressment, see, for example, Captain Thomas Miles to Admiralty, January 31, 1705/6 (Adm. 1/2093); Lord Cornbury to Lords of Trade, October 3, 1706 (E. B. O'Callaghan, ed., *Documents Relative to the Colonial History of the State of New York* [Albany, 1853–87], 4: 1183–85); Captain A. Forrest to Lieutenant Governor Spencer Phips, October 26, 1745 (Adm. 1/1782). For a detailed record of such shortages, see items headed "The State and Condition of His Majesty's Ships and Sloops" throughout Admirals' Dispatches (Adm. 1/480–86). For impressment in the colonies, see Neil R. Stout, "Manning the Royal Navy in North America, 1763–1775," *American Neptune*, 23 (1963): 174–85, and *idem*, "The Royal Navy in American Waters, 1760–1775," (Ph.D. dissertation, University of Wisconsin, 1962), pp. 359–95; R. Pares, "The Manning of the Navy in the West Indies, 1702–63," Royal Historical Society *Transactions*, 4th ser., 20 (1937): 31–60; Dora Mae Clark, "The Impressment of Seamen in the American Colonies," in *Essays in Colonial History Presented to Charles McLean Andrews by His Students* (New Haven, 1931), pp. 198–224; Jesse Lemisch, "Jack Tar vs. John Bull: The Role of New York's Seamen in Precipitating the Revolution" (Ph.D. dissertation, Yale University, 1962), pp. 12–51. Two useful accounts that deal primarily with impressment in England may be found in Hutchinson, *Press-Gang, passim*, and Daniel A. Baugh, *British Naval Administration in the Age of Walpole* (Princeton, 1965), pp. 147–240.

45 Stout, in "Manning the Royal Navy" (pp. 176–77), suggests the possibility of other causes when he notes that desertion was high "whatever the causes," but he mentions no cause other than rum and inveiglement. The admiralty made the seamen's "natural Levity" another possible reason for desertion (Admiralty to Governor Thomas on Impressments, 1743 [Pennsylvania Archives, 1st ser. (Philadelphia, 1852–56), 1: 639]). See

also Massachusetts Historical Society, *Journals of the House of Representatives of Massachusetts* (Boston, 1919——), 20: 84, 98; Colvill to Admiralty, August 8, 1765 (Adm. 1/482); Pares, "Manning the Navy," pp. 31, 33–34.

[46] Hutchinson to Richard Jackson, June 16, 1768, in G. G. Wolkins, "The Seizure of John Hancock's Sloop 'Liberty'," *Massachusetts Historical Society Proceedings*, 45 (1923): 283.

[47] Freeman, *Washington*, 1: 199; James Otis, *The Rights of the British Colonies Asserted and Proved* (Boston, 1764), in Bernard Bailyn, ed., *Pamphlets of the American Revolution, 1750–1776* (Cambridge, Mass., 1965), 1: 464. Flogging was universal and men received as many as 600 and 700 lashes (Covill to Admiralty, November 12, 1765 [Adm. 1/482]). For obscenity, the tongue was scraped with hoop-iron; there were punishments for smiling in the presence of an officer; and one captain put his sailors' heads in bags for trivial offenses (Hutchinson, *Press-Gang*, pp. 31–36). And, of course, the captain might go mad, as did Captain Robert Bond of *Gibraltar* (Admiral Gambier to Admiralty, October 10, 1771 [Adm. 1/483] and log of *Gibraltar*, February 10, 14, 1771 (Adm. 51/394).

[48] The log of *Arethusa* (December 28, 1771 [Adm. 51/59] and the petition of Jeremiah Raven (in fall of 1756), in Letters as to Admission of Pensioners to Greenwich Hospital, 1756–70 (Adm. 65/81) are excellent sources for the effects of service in the navy on health. See also the items headed "Weakly Account of Sick and Wounded Seamen" in Admirals' Dispatches (e.g., Admiral Gambier to Admiralty, May 6, June 10, July 20, 27, 1771 [Adm. 1/483], and November 9, 1771, August 29, 1772 [Adm. 1/484]).

[49] Remarks on Judge Foster's Argument in Favor of . . . Impressing Seamen, in Jared Sparks, ed., *The Works of Benjamin Franklin* (Boston, 1884), 2: 333 (Sparks gives this no date). John Bigelow, ed., *The Complete Works of Benjamin Franklin* ([New York, 1887–88], 4: 70), dates it 1767; Helen C. Boatfield of The Papers of Benjamin Franklin, Yale University, dates it post-1776.

[50] Pares, "Manning the Navy," pp. 31–38; Roland G. Usher, Jr., "Royal Navy Impressment during the American Revolution," *Mississippi Valley Historical Review*, 37 (1950–51): 686. At the time of the mutiny at the Nore, the crew of one ship had not been paid in fifteen years (Hutchinson, *Press-Gang*, p. 44).

[51] William Polhampton to Lords of Trade, March 6, 1711 (O'Callaghan, ed., *Documents Relative to the Colonial History of New York*, 5: 194). A seaman who deserted his ship would leave an R (for "run") written against his name in the ship's book; see Hutchinson, *Press-Gang* (p. 151) for a

song which urges seamen to flee the press-gang and "leave 'em an R in pawn!"

[52] Peter Warren to Admiralty, September 8, 1744 (Adm. 1/2654); William Polhampton to Lords of Trade, March 6, 1711 (O'Callaghan, ed., *Documents Relative to the Colonial History of New York,* 5:194); Admiralty to Thomas, 1743 (*Pennsylvania Archives,* 1st ser., 1: 638–39); Morris, *Government and Labor,* pp. 247–48. The navy's most imaginative response to the problem was sporadic and abortive attempts to limit the wages given to merchant seamen, but the inviting differential remained. When the navy offered bounties for enlistment, this merely served to induce additional desertions by men who could pick up a month's pay simply by signing up (Pares, "Manning the Navy," pp. 33–34; Hutchinson, *Press-Gang,* pp. 22, 48–49; Remarks on Judge Foster's Argument, Sparks, ed., *Works of Franklin,* 2: 333; *New-York Gazette; Weekly Post-Boy,* March 31, April 21, 1755, March 11, 1771).

[53] Stout, "Manning the Royal Navy," p. 182. England abolished the press-gang in 1833 (see Hutchinson, *Press-Gang,* p. 311). Parliament abolished slavery in the British colonies in the same year.

[54] At least in Pennsylvania and New Jersey, according to the *Independent Chronicle* (Boston), September 5, 1782.

[55] Three thousand men participated in this massive operation, and three or four hundred of those seized were released. See Lord Loudoun to Pitt, May 30, 1757, in Gertrude S. Kimball, ed., *Correspondence of William Pitt* (New York, 1906), 1: 69; Paul L. Ford, ed., *The Journals of Hugh Gaine, Printer* (New York, 1902), 2: 8–9; entries for May 20, 1757, *The Montresor Journals* (NYHS *Collections* [1882]): 150–51; Benjamin Cutter, *History of the Cutter Family of New England* (Boston, 1871), p. 67; Evarts B. Greene and Virginia D. Harrington, *American Population before the Federal Census of 1790* (New York, 1932), p. 101 (1756 census).

[56] Boston is so described in a petition of the town meeting to the House of Representatives, March 11, 1745/46 Massachusetts *House Journals,* 22: 204). This petition is but one of many attributing the depletion of Boston's population in part to impressment. For a table indicating a downward trend in Boston's population after 1743 see Stuart Bruchey, ed., *The Colonial Merchant: Sources and Readings* (New York, 1966), p. 11. I am indebted to Joel Shufro, a graduate student at the University of Chicago, for the suggestion of a connection between impressment and the decline of Boston.

[57] Log of *Shirley,* December 25, 1745–May 17, 1746 (Adm. 51/4341); log of *Gramont,* April 25–27, 1758 (Adm. 51/413); log of *Arethusa,* March 19–20, 1771 (Adm. 51/59). *Shirley's* haul was not mentioned in the *Boston Evening Post* or in the records of any American governmental body.

Here is but one instance in which the serious grievance of ninety-two Americans has previously gone unnoticed. Such grievances were nonetheless real and played a causal role despite their invisibility to historians. On the other hand, overdependence on British sources is apt to be extremely misleading. Either because of sloppiness or because of the clouded legality of impressment, official records seem more often to ignore the practice or to distort it than to complement information from American sources. Admiral Charles Hardy neglected to mention the massive press in New York in 1757 in his correspondence with the admiralty (see May–June, 1757, Adm. 1/481). The absence of impressment in *Triton's Prize's* log in 1706 (Adm. 51/1014) is contradicted in Lord Cornbury to Lords of Trade, October 3, 1706 (O'Callaghan, ed., *Documents Relative to the Colonial History of New York*, 4: 1183–85). Sometimes logs show what seems to be purposeful distortion: *Diana* whose log of April 15, 1758 (Adm. 51/4162), reveals only that she "saluted with 9 guns" but *Prince of Orange*, a privateer, in fact pressed her hands (*Montresor Journal*, p. 152). In another instance, *St. John* "received on board a Boat Load of Ballast" (log of July 16, 1764 [Adm. 51/3961]), which seems in fact to have consisted of hogs, sheep, and poultry stolen from the people of Martha's Vineyard (see *Newport Mercury*, July 23, 1764). See also n. 69 below.

[58] *Boston Evening Post*, September 3, 1739, and July 6, 1741.

[59] See depositions of Nathaniel Holmes, July 18, 1702, and John Gullison, July 17, 1702, in Lieutenant Governor Thomas Povey to Lords Commissioners for Trade and Plantations, July 20, 1702 (Colonial Office Group, Class 5, Piece 862, Public Record Office, hereafter cited as C.O. 5/862); *Boston Evening Post*, December 14, 1747; *New-York Gazette; Weekly Post-Boy*, January 14, 1771.

[60] Peter Woodbery and John Tomson to Governor William Phips, July 1, 2, 1692 (C.O. 5/751); James and Drinker to (?), October 29, 1756 (James and Drinker Letterbook 1, Historical Society of Pennsylvania, Philadelphia); *Boston Evening Post*, December 9, 1745; *Massachusetts House Journals*, 2: 300–1, and 33, pt. 2: 433; *New-York Gazette; Weekly Post-Boy*, July 12, 1764.

[61] *Massachusetts House Journals*, 35: 267; William Shirley to Gideon Wanton, June 6, 1745 (Charles H. Lincoln, ed., *Correspondence of William Shirley* [New York, 1912], 1: 227); Colden to Lords of Trade, August 30, 1760, O'Callaghan, ed., *Documents Relative to the Colonial History of New York*, 7: 446; Andrew Sherburne, *Memoirs of Andrew Sherburne* (Utica, 1828), p. 68.

[62] *Massachusetts House Journals*, 35: 267; James and Drinker to Nehemiah Champion, July 13, 1757 (James and Drinker Letterbook, 1: 145).

[63] Franklin to Joseph Galloway, April 7, 1759, Labaree *et al.*, eds., *Papers of Benjamin Franklin*, 8: 315–16; Morris, *Government and Labor*, p. 274; Colden to Lords of Trade, August 30, 1760, O'Callaghan, ed., *Documents Relative to the Colonial History of New York*, 7: 446; *Massachusetts House Journals*, 18: 202, 20: 84; Boston Registry Department, *Records of Boston*, 17: 125. See also Gerard G. Beekman to William Beekman, July 3, 1764 (Philip L. White, ed., *The Beekman Mercantile Papers, 1746–1799* [New York, 1956], 1: 469).

[64] William Polhampton to the Lords of Trade, March 6, 1711, Lord Cornbury to Lords of Trade, October 3, December 14, 1706 (O'Callaghan, ed., *Documents Relative to the Colonial History of New York*, 5: 194, 4: 1183–84, 1190–91). The captain later publicly declared that he hated the whole province and would not help a New York vessel in distress at sea if he met one (Lord Cornbury to Lords of Trade, July 1, 1708, *ibid.*, 5: 60). It seems increasingly to have become common practice to press after a public declaration that there would be no press; see, for example, *Boston Evening Post*, December 9, 23, 1745, and log of *Shirley*, December 25, 1745–May 17, 1746 (Adm. 51/4341).

[65] See Lieutenant Governor Thomas Povey to Lords Commissioners for Trade and Plantations, July 20, 1702 Memorial of Thomas Povey, July, 1702, and depositions of Nathaniel Holmes, July 18, 1702, John Arnold and John Roberts, July 18, 1702 (C.O. 5/862).

[66] For instructions to royal governors giving them sole power to press in their province, see Leonard W. Labaree, ed., *Royal Instructions to British Colonial Governors, 1670–1776* (New York, 1935), 1: 442–43, and Instructions for the Earl of Bellomont, August 31, 1697, Copy of . . . Lovelace's Instructions, n.d., in O'Callaghan, ed., *Documents Relative to the Colonial History of New York*, 4: 287; 5: 101. See also Clark, "Impressment of Seamen," in *Essays to Andrews*, pp. 202–5.

[67] *Calendar of Council Minutes, 1668–1783* (New York State Library *Bulletin 58* [March 1902]), pp. 229, 230); Stokes, *Iconography of Manhattan*, 4: 465, 973, 5: 99–101; Chief Justice . . . Opinion, June 30, 1709, Report of the Council, July 3, 1709 and Governor Hunter to Secretary St. John, September 12, 1711, in O'Callaghan, ed., *Documents Relative to the Colonial History of New York*, 5: 100, 102, 254–55.

[68] In 1716 the attorney general declared "I am of Opinion, that the whole American Act was intended . . . only for the War" (*Massachusetts Gazette* [Boston], June 17, 1768). Governor Shirley of Massachusetts agreed in 1747, despite the fact that along with other colonial governors, he was still instructed to enforce the Sixth of Anne and had indeed sworn to do so (see The Lords Justices to William Shirley, September 10, 1741, in Lincoln, ed., *Correspondence of Shirley*, 1: 74–76, and Stout, "Royal

Navy" p. 391). Twenty-two years later, Governor Hutchinson feared that John Adams might publicize the act. The admiralty continued to instruct American commanders to obey the act after Queen Anne's War (see, for example, Admiralty to Captain Balcher, March 9, 1714 [Adm. 2/48]), but ceased so to instruct them in 1723 (Clark "Impressment of Seamen," in *Essays to Andrews,* p. 211). Of course, the act's repeal in 1775 indicated that it had been on the books, if no place else, all that time.

[69] Stout's claim ("Royal Navy," p. 366) that the navy again began pressing only in 1723 again illustrates the dangers of over-reliance on British sources in such controversial matters. That the admiralty continued to instruct commanders not to press does not mean that they did not in fact press. *Shark* pressed in Boston in 1720 (*Massachusetts House Journals,* 2: 300–1), her log for October–November, 1720 (Adm. 51/892) contains no mention of the fact.

[70] See, for example, *Massachusetts House Journals,* 18: 202; 20: 98–99, 22: 76–77, 204–5.

[71] *Ibid.,* 24: 212; Boston Registry Department, *Records of Boston,* 14: 127. Bridenbaugh (*Cities in Revolt,* p. 117) sees the law for suppressing riots of 1751 as in part a response to the Knowles riots; he calls the law "brutal" even for its own day and a "triumph for the reactionaries."

[72] See, for example, Lord Loudoun to Pitt, March 10, May 30, 1757 (Kimball, ed., *Correspondence of Pitt,* 1: 19, 69); Lieutenant Governor De Lancey to Secretary Pitt, March 17, 1758 (O'Callaghan, ed., *Documents Relative to the Colonial History of New York,* 7: 343).

[73] *Massachusetts House Journals,* 33, pt. 2: 434; 34, pt. 1: 134; *Records of Boston,* 19: 96–97; log of *Hunter,* August 31, 1758 (Adm. 51/465). The council voted such authorization, but the house did not concur.

[74] Captain George Ant. Tonyn to Admiralty, March 1, 1760, depositions of Peter Vaile and Singleton Church, January, 15, 16, 1760 (Adm. 1/2588).

[75] Admiral Colvill's journal, March 19, 1764 (Adm. 50/4); Colvill to Admiralty, May 19, 1764 (Adm. 1/482); *New-York Gazette; Weekly Post-Boy,* July 18, 1765.

[76] Stout ("Royal Navy," pp. 72–73), citing Admiralty to Egremont, January 5, 1763 (State Papers Group, Class 42, Piece 43, Public Record Office, hereafter cited as S.P. 42/43); Captain Jno. Brown to Admiralty, May 16, 1764 (Adm. 1/1494); log of *Coventry,* March 31, 1764 (Adm. 51/213), indicates impressment on that date; cf. Stout, Royal Navy, 379, 393*n.*

[77] Admiral Colvill's journal, June 4, 1764 (Adm. 50/4); Colvill to Admiralty, June 18, 1764 (Adm. 1/482). On the violence at New York, see log of *Jamaica,* June 8, 1764 (Adm. 51/3874); *New-York Gazette; Weekly*

Post-Boy, July 12, 1764; Report of the Grand Jury, August 2, 1764, New York Supreme Court Minute Book (July 31–October 28, 1764), p. 7. On the violence at Newport, see log of *St. John,* July 10, 1764 (Adm. 51/3961); Captain Smith to Colvill, July 12, 1764, in Colvill to Admiralty, August 24, 1764 (Adm. 1/482); John Temple to Treasury, September 9, 1765 (Treasury Group, Class 1, Piece 442, Library of Congress transcript).

⁷⁸ *The King* v. *Osborn Greatrakes* and *The King* v. *Josiah Moore,* October 24, 28, 30, and November 11–17, 1760 (New York Supreme Court Minute Book [1756–61], pp. 1–6, 200, 209, 215); Henry B. Dawson, *The Sons of Liberty* in New York (New York, 1859), p. 53; *New-York Gazette; Weekly Post-Boy,* July 12, 1764; Report of Grand Jury, August 2, 1764 (New York Supreme Court Minute Book [July 31, 1764–October 28, 1767], p. 7); Colville to Admiralty, August 5, 1766 (Adm. 1/482).

⁷⁹ Charles Francis Adams, ed., *The Works of John Adams* (Boston, 1850–56), 2: 225*n.*–226*n.,* and "The Inadmissable Principles of the King of England's Proclamation of October 16, 1807, Considered" (1809), 9: 317–18; Thomas Hutchinson, *The History of the Colony and Province of Massachusetts Bay,* ed. Lawrence S. Mayo (Cambridge, Mass., 1936), 3: 167*n.*; log of *Rose,* April 22, 1769 (Adm. 51/804); Admiral Hood to Admiralty, May 5, 1769 (Adm. 1/483).

⁸⁰ *The King v. Ship Sampson,* Examination of Hugh Mode, pilot, taken August 19, 1760 (New York Supreme Court, Pleadings K–304); *New-York Gazette; Weekly Post-Boy,* May 1, 1758, August 7, 1760; Captain J. Hale to Admiralty, August 28, 1760 (Adm. 1/1895); William McCleverty to Admiralty, July 31, 1760 (Adm. 1/2172); Howard Thomas, *Marinus Willett* (Prospect, N.Y., 1954), pp. 3–4; depositions of John Gullison, July 17, 1702, Woodward Fay, July 17, 1702 (C.O. 5/862); log of *Magdelen,* April 6, 1771 (Adm. 51/3984), describing the loss during a press "by Accident" of a sword and musket—apparently a common accident. See also log of *Arethusa,* April 18, 1772 (Adm. 51/59); Weyman's *New-York Gazette,* August 25, 1760; Admiral Hood to Admiralty, May 5, 1769 (Adm. 1/483); paraphrase of log of Shirley, January 17, 1746 (Adm. 51/4341); "Inadmissable Principles" (1809), in Adams, *Works of Adams,* 9: 318.

⁸¹ Bailyn, ed., *Pamphlets,* 1: 581. Six Englishmen of varying ranks were killed while pressing in the 1760's. In addition to the incidents just discussed (in which a lieutenant of marines was murdered on June 8, 1764, while pressing at New York and in which John Adams' clients-to-be, accused of murdering a lieutenant off Cape Ann on April 22, 1769, got off with justifiable homicide in self-defense), four sailors were shot to death at New York on August 18, 1760 (Cadwallader Colden to Lords of Trade, August 30, 1760, in O'Callaghan, ed., *Documents Relative to Colonial History of New York,* 7: 446; *The King v. Osborn Greatrakes* and the King

v. *Josiah Moore*, October 24, 28, 30, November 11–17, 1760, in New York Supreme Court Minute Book [1756–61], pp. 1–16, 200, 209, 215; *The King v. Ship Sampson*, Examination of Hugh Mode, pilot taken August 19, 1760, New York Supreme Court, Pleadings K-304; Captain J. Hale to Admiralty, August 28, 1760 [Adm. 1/1895]; Weyman's *New-York Gazette*, August 25, 1760; Dawson, *Sons of Liberty*, pp. 51–54). Governor Cadwallader Colden called the last incident murder, but the jury refused to indict. For some instances of Americans killed while resisting impressment, see deposition of William Thwing, Nathaniel Vaill, and Thomas Hals, July 15, 1702 (C.O. 5/862); Governor Hunter to Secretary St. John, September 12, 1711 (O'Callaghan, ed., *Documents*, 5: 254–55 [conviction of murder]); Bridenbaugh, *Cities in Revolt*, pp. 114–15; *New-York Gazette; Weekly Post-Boy*, August 7, 1760. There is every reason to suppose that this list is partial. See n. 57 above.

[82]"Inadmissable Principles" (*Works of Adams*, 9: 318) quotes Michael Corbet, commenting that Corbet displayed "the cool intrepidity of a Nelson, reasoned, remonstrated, and laid down the law with the precision of a Mansfield." Hutchinson (*History Massachusetts Bay*, 3: 167*n.*) notes that Corbet and his companions "swore they would die before they would be taken, and that they preferred death to slavery."

[83] "Inadmissable Principles," in *Works of Adams*, 9: 317–318.

[84] Hutchinson, *History of Massachusetts Bay*, 2: 330–31, 333; *Massachusetts House Journals*, 24: 212; Bridenbaugh, *Cities in Revolt*, pp. 115–17; *Records of Boston*, 14: 127. William Shirley to Lords of Trade, December 1, 1747 (*Correspondence of Shirley*, 1: 412–19), is the best single account; Shirley says that only the officers responded to his call for the militia.

[85] *Newport Mercury*, June 10, 1765; Captain Jeremiah Morgan to Governor Francis Fauquier, September 11, 1767 (Adam. 1/2116); log of *St. John*, July 10, 1764 (Adm. 51/3961); remarks of Thomas Hill, in Colvill to Admiralty, July 26, 1764, and January 12, September 21, 1765 (Adm. 1/482); log of *Maidstone*, June 5, 1765 (Adm. 51/3897); Captain Smith to Colvill, July 12, 1764, extract in Colvill to Admiralty, August 24, 1764 (Adm. 1/482); *New-York Gazette; Weekly Post-Boy*, July 12, 1764; Thomas Laugharne to Admiral Colvill, August 11, 1764, extract in Colvill to Admiralty, August 24, 1764 (Adm. 1/482); Stout's contention ("Manning the Royal Navy," p. 185), that "there is no recorded case of impressment on shore during the 1760's and 1770's, although the Navy did capture some deserters on land" is inaccurate. See Captain Jeremiah Morgan to Governor Francis Fauquier, September 11, 1767 (Adm. 1/2116), and *Pennsylvania Chronicle and Universal Advertiser* (Philadelphia), October 26, 1767.

[86] For impressment by *Romney,* see log for June 10, 1768 (Adm. 51/ 793). Oliver M. Dickerson, in *The Navigation Acts and the American Revolution* ([Philadelphia, 1951], p. 238), sees the riot as growing out of the seizure, and this has the support of most sources. Massachusetts Council to Governor Gage, October 27, 1768 (Bowdoin-Temple Papers, 1: 120, Massachusetts Historical Society); Admiral Hood to Admiralty, July 11, 1768 (Adm. 1/483); Hutchinson, *History of Massachusetts Bay,* 3: 136. On the other hand, Thomas Hutchinson also spoke of impressment as adding "more fewel to the great stock among us before (Massachusetts Historical Society *Proceedings, 1921–1922* (Boston, 1923), p. 283. Clark ("Impressment of Seamen," in *Essays to Andrews,* p. 219) describes the rioting as a response to impressment alone, by a mob "which seemed to be always ready to resent any infringement of American liberties." Dickerson (*Navigation Acts,* pp. 219–20) attributes the burning of a boat belonging to the customs collector to the mob's failure to locate *Romney's* press boat. In 1922, G. G. Wolkins ("Seizure of 'Liberty'," p. 250) speculated that "impressment of seamen, rather than the seizure of John Hancock's goods, was perhaps the genesis of what happened." L. Kinvin Wroth and Hiller B. Zobel (eds., *Legal Papers of John Adams* [Cambridge, Mass., 1965], 2: 179n.) summarize: "Boston's position was that the employment of the *Romney,* already despised for the impressment activities of her captain, brought on the riot of 10 June." The riot seems to have been caused by a combination of factors, among which impressment has been given too little attention.

[87] *Records of Boston,* 20: 296; Thomas Hutchinson, "State of the Disorders, Confusion, and Misgovernment, which have lately prevailed . . . in . . . Massachusetts," June 21, 1770 (C.O. 5/759, pt. 4); Report of Resolves Relating to Riot of June 10, June 14, 18, 1768, in James Bowdoin and Royall Tyler to Jno. Corner, June 18, 1768 (Bowdoin-Temple Papers, 1: 102, 104; *Massachusetts Gazette* (Boston) November 10, 1768. For Adams' authorship, see L. H. Butterfield *et al.,* eds., *Diary and Autobiography of John Adams* (New York, 1964), 3: 291 and *Works of Adams,* 3: 501.

[88] *New-York Gazette; Weekly Post-Boy,* July 12, 1764, July 18, 1765; Thos. Lagharne to Admiral Colvill, August 11, 1764, extract in Colvill to Admiralty, July 26, August 24, 1764 (Adm. 1/482); Weyman's *New-York Gazette,* July 18, 1765.

[89] Captain Smith to Colvill, July 12, 1764, extract in Colvill to Admiralty, August 24, 1764 (Adm. 1/482); remarks of Thomas Hill in Colvill to Admiralty, July 26, 1764 (Adm. 1/482); log of *Squirrel,* July 10, 1764 (Adm. 51/929); log of *St. John,* July 10, 1764 (Adm. 51/3961); *Newport Mercury,* July 16, 1764.

[90] Colvill to Admiralty, January 12, 1765 (Adm. 1/482); log of *Gaspée,* December 8, 10, 12, 1764 (Adm. 51/3856).

[91] Graves to Admiralty, February 20, 1775 (Adm. 1/485); *New York Journal: or General Advertiser,* February 23, 1775; Margaret Wheeler Willard, ed., *Letters on the American Revolution, 1774–1776* (Boston, 1925), pp. 65–66.

[92] Graves to Admiralty, April 11, 1775, Mowat to Graves, May 4, 1775 (in Graves to Admiralty, May 13, 1775), Barkley to Graves, June 5, 1775 (in Graves to Admiralty, June 22, 1775), Montagu to Graves, June 17, 1775 (in Graves to Admiralty, July 17, 1775) (Adm. 1/485); log of *Scarborough,* May 14, 1775 (Adm. 51/867); log of *Fowey,* July 16, 23, 1775 (Adm. 51/375). Despite the troubles at Marblehead in February, *Lively* was still pressing there in May (Graves to Admiralty, May 13, 1775 [Adm. 1/485]).

[93] Admiralty to Graves, June 24, September 29, 1775 (Adm. 2/549, 550); Graves to Admiralty, September 12, 1775, and List of . . . Press Warrants, January 27, 1776, in Graves to Admiralty, January 1776 (Adm. 1/486); Shuldham to Arbuthnot, June 5, 1776, in Shuldham to Admiralty, July 24, 1776 (Adm. 1/484).

[94] *Massachusetts House Journals,* 2: 300–1; Freeman, *Washington,* 1: 199; *New-York Gazette; Weekly Post-Boy,* August 12, 1754.

[95] *Massachusetts House Journals,* 33, pt. 2: 434.

[96] Hutchinson, *Press-Gang,* pp. 5–7.

[97] Sparks, ed., *Works of Franklin,* 2: 338, 334. For opposition to impressment on the part of the Genevan democrat, Jean Jouis de Lolme, and by the British radical, John Wilkes, see Robert R. Palmer, *The Age of the Democratic Revolution* (Princeton, 1959), p. 148. *New-York Gazette; Weekly Post-Boy,* December 31, 1770; *Annual Register . . . for 1771* (London, 1772), pp. 67, 68, 70–71; R. W. Postgate, *That Devil Wilkes* (New York, 1929), p. 182; Percy Fitzgerald, *The Life and Times of John Wilkes* (London, 1888), 2: 120.

[98] Paine, *Writings,* ed., Foner, 1: 11. For later attacks on impressment by Paine, see *ibid.,* p. 449, and 2: 476. The complaint in the Declaration of Independence alludes to impressment after the outbreak of fighting: "He has constrained our fellow Citizens taken Captive on the high Seas to bear Arms against their Country, to become the executioners of their friends and Brethren, or to fall themselves by their Hands." Carl L. Becker, *The Declaration of Independence* (New York, 1958), pp. 190, 156, 166. Thomas Jefferson to Dr. Thomas Cooper, September 10, 1814, in Andrew A. Lipscomb and Albert Ellery Bergh, eds., *The Writings of Thomas Jefferson* (Washington, D.C., 1907), 14: 183.

[99] James Fulton Zimmerman's *Impressment of American Seamen* ([New

York, 1925], esp. pp. 11–17) treats the practice as almost nonexistent before the Revolution, giving the pre-Revolutionary phenomenon only the briefest consideration, and concluding, on the basis of speculative evidence, that impressment was rare in the colonies. The author does not understand the Sixth of Anne, and thinks it was repealed in 1769. Clark, "Impressment of Seamen," in *Essays to Andrews*, p. 202; Paine, *Ships and Sailors of Salem*, p. 65; George Athan Billias, *General John Glover and His Marblehead Mariners* (New York, 1960), p. 31; Bridenbaugh, *Cities in Revolt*, pp. 114–17, 308–10; and Bernhard Knollenberg, *Origin of the American Revolution: 1759–1766* (New York, 1961), pp. 12, 179–81, all see impressment as contributing in some way to the revolutionary spirit.

[100] Adams, *Works of Adams*, 2: 226n. Neil Stout ("Manning the Royal Navy," pp. 182–84) suggests that impressment did not become a "great issue" of the American Revolution because American "radicals" did not *make* an issue of it, and especially because of the failure of John Adams' attempt to make a "*cause celebre*" in 1769. Stout's approach sides with the navy and minimizes the *reality* of impressment as a grievance. Its implication is that the seaman had in fact no genuine grievance and that he acted in response to manipulation.

[101] President Reed to President of Congress, October 21, 1779 (*Pennsylvania Archives*, 1st ser., 7:762). Reed renewed his complaint of these "Opressions" in the following year (Reed to Pennsylvania Delegates in Congress [*ibid.*, 1st ser., 8: 643]).

[102] Colvill to Admiralty, August 8, 1765 (Adm. 1/482); Sherburne, *Memoirs*, p. 68.

[103] William M. Willett, *A Narrative of the Military Actions of Colonel Marinus Willett, Taken Chiefly from His Own Manuscript* (New York, 1831), pp. 149–51. On the level of leadership, impressment was not a major cause of the American Revolution. But the extent to which the articulate voice a grievance is rarely an adequate measure of the suffering of the inarticulate. Since it is unrealistic to suppose that the victims of impressment forgot their anger, the question becomes not why was impressment irrelevant to the American Revolution—for it had to be relevant, in this sense—but, rather, why were the articulate not *more* articulate about the seamen's anger? In part, perhaps, because much impressment took place offshore and was invisible to all but the seamen directly involved. But the leaders had always perceived even visible impressment more as an interference with commerce than as a form of slavery. As the Revolution approached, impressment as human slavery interested them even less than Negro slavery did; the gap between Jack Tar and the men who made laws for him continued. The failure of the elite to see impressment more clearly as a political issue means only that they failed, as we have, to listen to the seamen.

104 General Gage to Secretary Conway, November 4, December 21, 1765, in Clarence Edwin Carter, ed., *The Correspondence of General Thomas Gage . . . 1763-1775* (New Haven, 1931), 1: 70–71, 79; *New-York Gazette; Weekly Post-Boy* of November 7, 1765, estimated that there were four to five hundred seamen in the mob; the entries of November 1, 7, 1765, *Montresor Journal,* pp. 336, 339, estimated the total mob at "about 2000," and is the only source describing the participation of a professional group other than seamen, estimating three hundred carpenters. See R. R. Livingston to General Monckton, November 8, 1765 (Chalmers Manuscript vol. 4, New York Public Library), for a note signed "Sons of Neptune." Lieutenant Governor Colden to Secretary Conway, November 5, 9, 1765 (O'Callaghan, ed., *Documents,* 7: 771–74); *New York Mercury,* November 4, 1765. For additional information on the leadership of privateer captains, especially Isaac Sears, see William Gordon, *History of the Rise, Progress, and Establishment of the United States of America* (London, 1788), 1: 185–86. The navy continued to press during the crisis. See log of *Guarland,* April 22, 1766 (Adm. 51/386); April 21, 1766, *Montresor Journal,* p. 361. Impressment also limited the navy's activities against the rioting. "As most of our men are imprest," wrote a captain in answer to a governor's request for men to put down a mob, "there is a great risque of their deserting." Marines were needed as sentries to keep the men from deserting. See Archibald Kennedy to Cadwallader Colden, November 1, 1765, in *The Letters and Papers of Cadwallader Colden* (NYHS *Collections,* vols. 50-56 [New York, 1918–1923], 7: 85–86.

105 For a fuller account of the seamen's opposition to the Stamp Act, see Lemisch, "Jack Tar vs. John Bull" pp. 76–128.

106 *New-York Gazette; Weekly Post-Boy,* May 19, 1763; "Essay on the Trade of the Northern Colonies," *ibid.,* February 9, 1764. Even admirals were worried about the prospects of postwar unemployment (see Colvill to Admiralty, November 9, 1762 [Adm. 1/482]). During the French and Indian War, 18,000 American seamen had served in the Royal Navy (*Annual Register . . . for 1778* [London, 1779], p. 201), and a large additional number had been privateersmen. Fifteen to twenty thousand had sailed in 224 privateers out of New York alone, 5,670 of them in 1759 (Fish, *New York Privateers,* pp. 4, 54–82; Bridenbaugh, *Cities in Revolt,* p. 62). A New York merchants' petition of April 20, 1764, expressed the fear that seamen thrown out of work by the Sugar Act might drift into foreign merchant fleets (see *Journal of the Votes and Proceedings of the General Assembly of the Colony of New York* [New York, 1764–66], 2: 742–43). On the eve of the Revolution, maritime commerce employed approximately 30,000–35,000 American seamen (Carman, ed., *American Husbandry,* pp. 495–96; John Adams to the President of Congress, June 16, 1780 in

Francis Wharton, ed., *The Revolutionary Diplomatic Correspondence of the United States* [Washington, D.C., 1889], 3: 789). I am presently assembling data which will allow more detailed statements on various demographic matters involving seamen, such as their numbers, comparisons with other occupations, their origins and permanence. For some further quantitative information on seamen in various colonial ports, see—in addition to the sources cited immediately above—Evarts B. Greene and Richard B. Morris, *A Guide to the Principal Sources for Early American History (1600–1800) in the City of New York*, 2d ed., rev. (New York, 1953), p. 265; E. B. O'Callaghan, ed., *The Documentary History of the State of New York* (Albany, 1849), 1: 493; Governor Clinton's Report on the Province of New York, May 23, 1749, Report of Governor Tryon on the Province of New York, June 11, 1774, in O'Callaghan, ed., *Documents*, 6:511, 8: 446; Main, *Social Structure*, pp. 38–39; Benjamin W. Labaree, *Patriots and Partisans* (Cambridge, Mass., 1962) p. 5; John R. Bartlett, ed., *Records of the Colony of Rhode Island and Providence Plantations . . .* (Providence, 1856–65), 6: 379; also see below.

[107] See, for example, James and Drinker to William Starkey, October 30, 1765 (James and Drinker Letterbook); *New-York Gazette; Weekly Post-Boy*, December 19, 1765.

[108] See, for example *New-York Gazette; Weekly Post-Boy*, November 28, December 5, 1765. For a fuller account of this dispute, see Jesse Lemisch, "New York's Petitions and Resolves of December, 1765: Liberals vs. Radicals," NYHS *Quarterly*, 49 (1965): 313–26.

[109] Edmund S. and Helen M. Morgan, *The Stamp Act Crisis* (Chapel Hill, 1953), p. 162. For a fuller account of the nullification of the Stamp Act, see *ibid.*, pp. 159–79. The seamen's strategy may have been more effective in bringing about repeal than was the strategy of the leaders. Commenting on Parliament's secret debates, Lawrence Henry Gipson, in "The Great Debate in the Committee of the Whole House of Commons on the Stamp Act, 1766, as Reported by Nathaniel Ryder" (*Pennsylvania Magazine of History and Biography*, 86 [1962]: 10–41), notes that merchant pressure was only the "ostensible" cause of repeal and that many members were influenced by the violent resistance in America. I am indebted to E. S. Morgan for calling Ryder's notes to my attention.

[110] See John Swift to Commissioners of Customs, October 13, 1769, Customs Commissioners to Collector and Comptroller at Philadelphia, October 23, 1769, John Hatton, A State of the Case, November 8, 1770, John Hatton to John Swift, November 9, 1770, Customs Commissioners at Boston to Collector and Comptroller at Philadelphia, January 1771, John Swift to Customs Commissioners, February 11, 1772, John Swift to Customs Commissioners, November 15, 1770, Collector and Comptroller at Phila-

delphia to Customs Commissioners, December 20, 1770 (Philadelphia Custom House Papers, 10: 1205, 1209, 1286, 1288; vols. 11 and 12; 10: 1291–92; and vol. 11, Historical Society of Pennsylvania). Swift made the customary contention that the seamen rioted because their captains told them to. For a qualification of this contention, see Arthur L. Jensen, *The Maritime Commerce of Colonial Philadelphia* (Madison, 1963), p. 152. For a mob which attacked a collector of customs and others at the time of the Stamp Act and which may have been led by a seaman, see Morgan and Morgan, *Stamp Act Crisis,* pp. 191–94; log of *Cygnet,* August 29, 30, 1765 (Adm. 51/223); Captain Leslie to Admiral Colvill, August, 30, 31, 1765 (Adm. 1/482).

[111] Dickerson, *Navigation Acts,* pp. 218–19. For seamen's right to import, see Morris, *Government and Labor,* pp. 238–39.

[112] On the participation of seamen in the Boston Massacre, see the testimony of Robert Goddard, October 25, 1770, Ebenezer Bridgham, November 27, 1770, James Bailey, November 28, December 4, 1770, and James Thompson, November 30, 1770 in Wroth and Zobel, eds., *Legal Papers of Adams,* 3: 57–58, 103–6, 114–15, 115n.–20n., 188, 189n. 268–69; also Frederick Kidder, *History of the Boston Massacre, March 5, 1770* (Albany, 1870), p. 288. For Adams' description, see Wroth and Zobel, eds., *Legal Papers of Adams,* 3: 266. For Attucks, see testimony of James Bailey, November 28, 1770, and Patrick Keeton, November 30, 1770, *ibid.,* pp. 114–15, 115n.–20n., 191–92, 262, 268–69; Kidder, *Boston Massacre,* 29n.–30n., 287; Hutchinson, *History of Massachusetts Bay,* 3: 196; Boston Herald, November 19, 1890 [*sic*]; John Hope Franklin, *From Slavery to Freedom* (New York, 1956), p. 127.

[113] Lieutenant Colonel W. Dalrymple to Hillsborough, March 13, 1770 (C. O. 5/759, pt. 3, Library of Congress photostat); Captain Thomas Rich to Admiralty, March 11, 1770 (Adm. 1/2388); Morris, *Government and Labor,* pp. 190–92.

[114] *The Times* (New-York Historical Society broadsides, 1770–1821); Morris, *Government and Labor,* p. 190n.

[115] *New-York Gazette; Weekly Post-Boy* of February 5, 1770, reports on the gang of seamen which went from dock to dock turning out soldiers. *The Times* (New-York Historical Society broadsides, 1770–1821) described what could only be the same group and adds the threat of vengeance.

[116] *New-York Gazette; Weekly Post-Boy,* January 22, February 5, 1770; Dawson, *Sons of Liberty,* p. 117n.; William J. Davis, "The Old Bridewell," in Henry B. Dawson, *Reminiscences of the Park and Its Vicinity* (New York, 1855), p. 61. Thomas Hutchinson noted the death of the seaman and believed that the Battle of Golden Hill "encouraged" Boston, thus leading to the Boston Massacre (Hutchinson, *History of Massachusetts Bay,* 3: 194).

[117] Wroth and Zobel, eds., *Legal Papers of Adams,* 3: 262; see also John Shy, *Toward Lexington* (Princeton, 1965), p. 309.

[118] Douglass Adair and John A Schutz, eds., *Peter Oliver's Origin and Progress of the American Rebellion: A Tory View* (San Marino, Calif., 1961), pp. 65, 94–95, 48, 158, 39, 162, 165.

[119] Louis de Lomenie, *Beaumarchais and His Times,* trans. Henry S. Edwards (London, 1856), 3: 110, see also Paine, *Writings,* ed. Foner, 1: 33.

[120] Dickerson (*Navigation Acts,* p. 219) offers no explanation of the extent or method of his search. Wallace Brown, *The King's Friends* (Providence, 1965), pp. 263, 287–344. Although Brown states that those listed (pp. 261–63) "make up 100 per cent of the claimants," he has excluded those whose occupations are unknown without noting the exclusion. He has also made some minor errors in his calculations (pp. 261–63, 295, 300, 313). The figures given in the text are my own computations, based on corrected data. I would like to thank Mr. Brown for his assistance in clearing up some of these errors. My own examination of New York materials in Loyalist Transcripts (vols. 1–8 and 41–48) and Lorenzo Sabine's *Biographical Sketches of Loyalists of the American Revolution with an Historical Essay* (Boston, 1864) turned up very few loyalist seamen, some of whom were obviously captains. See, for example, Alpheus Avery and Richard Jenkins, Loyalist Transcripts, 18: 11–15, 43: 495–504. Brown (*The King's Friends,* pp. 307–8) also finds five out of a total of nine New York loyalist "seamen" are masters.

[121] See Morison, *John Paul Jones,* pp. 165–66. "The unpleasant subject of the treatment of American naval prisoners during the war afforded fuel for American Anglophobes for a century or more, and there is no point in stirring it up again." For a plea that the horrors of the prisons not be forgotten, see *New Hampshire Gazette* (Portsmouth), February 9, 1779. The following brief account of the prisons in England and America summarizes my full-length study, "Jack Tar in the Darbies: American Seamen in British Prisons during the Revolution," to be completed shortly.

[122] For the prison ships, the standard work at present is James Lenox Banks, *David Sproat and Naval Prisoners in the War of the Revolution with Mention of William Lenox, of Charlestown* (New York, 1909). This contains many useful documents, but the commentary is a one-sided whitewash written by a descendant of Sproat who was not above ignoring evidence that Sproat elicited favorable accounts of conditions in *Jersey* through threats and bribery. Cf. *ibid.,* pp. 12–14, 81–84 with Danske Dandridge, *American Prisoners of the Revolution* (Charlottesville, 1911), pp. 419–23.

[123] For instance, computations based on a list of prisoners in Mill Prison from May 27, 1777, to January 21, 1782 (from the *Boston Gazette,* June

24, July 1, 8, 1782), indicate that 7.7 percent of 1,013 men entered the King's service. This figure may be slightly distorted by the presence of a small number of non-Americans, but there is almost precise confirmation in Adm. 98/11–14, which lists only 190 out of a total of 2,579 Americans, or 7.4 percent, entered from all English prisons. This figure is slightly inflated. See Adm. 98/13, 108. See also John Howard, *The State of the Prisons in England and Wales,* 3d ed. (Warrington, Eng., 1784), pp. 185, 187, 188, 192, 194. I am indebted to John K. Alexander, a graduate student at the University of Chicago, for these figures and for valuable assistance in connection with my research on the prisons.

[124] Charles Herbert, *A Relic of the Revolution* (Boston, 1847), p. 157. See also entry for August 19, 1778, in Marion S. Coan, "A Revolutionary Prison Diary: The Journal of Dr. Jonathan Haskins," *New England Quarterly,* 17 (1944): 430. Clearly, there is plagiarism here, as there was in many other but by no means in all entries in the two journals. For a contention that Haskins is the plagiarist, see John K. Alexander, "Jonathan Haskins' Mill Prison 'Diary': Can It Be Accepted at Face Value?" *ibid.,* 40 (1967): 561–64.

[125] William Russell, "Journal," December 31, 1781; Paine, *Ships and Sailors of Salem,* p. 155.

[126] Sherburne, *Memoirs,* p. 81. For a prisoners' committee in Forton Prison, see January 27, 1779, Adm. 98/11, 442–44; for a trial in Mill Prison for "the crime of profanely damning of the Honrbl. Continental Congress," see the March 4, 1778, entry in Coan "Revolutionary Prison Diary," p. 305. For self-government in *Jersey,* see Dring, *Recollections,* pp. 84–86.

[127] For example, Dring, *ibid.,* pp. 97–116; Herbert, *Relic of the Revolution,* p. 142; Russell, July 4, 1781, Paine, *Ships and Sailors of Salem,* p. 142. For a celebration of the British defeat at Yorktown, see Benjamin Golden to Benjamin Franklin, December 2, 1781, in Franklin Papers, 23: 94.

[128] Max Farrand, ed., *The Records of the Federal Convention of 1787,* rev. ed. (New Haven, 1937), 2: 204–5.

[129] Duke de la Rochefoucauld Liancourt, *Travels through the United States of North America . . . ,* trans. H. Neuman (London, 1799), 2: 672, quoted in Staughton Lynd and Alfred Young, "After Carl Becker: The Mechanics and New York City Politics, 1774–1801," *Labor History,* 5 (1964): 220.

[130] Bailyn, ed., *Pamphlets,* pp. 581–83, 740, *n.* 10; Bailyn quotes the last phrase from George Rudé, "The London 'Mob' of the Eighteenth Century," *Historical Journal* 2 (1959): 17. Bailyn is here contending that the post–1765 crowd was more highly developed than its English counterpart, which was, according to Rudé, not yet "a fully-fledged political move-

ment." See also Gordon S. Wood "A Note on Mobs in the American Revolution," *William and Mary Quarterly*, 3d ser., 23 (1966): 635–42.

[131] See Gustave Le Bon, *The Crowd* (New York, 1960). For a critique of interpretations of the American Revolution which seem to echo Le Bon, see Lemisch, "American Revolution," *passim*, in Bernstein, ed., *Towards a New Past*. Two useful discussions which place Le Bon and those he has influenced in the context of the history of social psychology (and of history) are George Rudé, *The Crowd in History* (New York, 1964), pp. 3–15, and Roger W. Brown, "Mass Phenomena," in Gardner Lindzey, ed., *Handbook of Social Psychology* (Cambridge, Mass., 1954), 2: 833–73. Both Rudé and Brown describe Le Bon's bias as "aristocratic." Also relevant are some of the studies in Duane P. Schultz, ed., *Panic Behavior* (New York, 1964), especially Alexander Mintz's "Non-Adaptive Group Behavior" (pp. 84–107).

[132] Bailyn (ed., *Pamphlets*, pp. 581–83, citing Max Beloff, *Public Order and Popular Disturbances, 1660–1714* [London, 1938], pp. 33, 153, 155), calls Beloff "the historian of popular disturbances in pre-industrial England," thus bypassing at least one other candidate for the title, George Rudé, whom he describes as "an English historian of eighteenth-century crowd phenomena." Rudé has shown (in *The Crowd in History* and elsewhere) that the crowd was purposeful, disciplined and discriminating, that "in the eighteenth century the typical and ever recurring form of social protest was the riot." Rudé finds in Beloff echoes of Burke and Taine; thus the European foundation for Bailyn's interpretation of the pre-1765 American crowd is somewhat one-sided. Compare Bailyn with R. S. Longley's extremely manipulative "Mob Activities in Revolutionary Massachusetts," *New England Quarterly*, 6 (1933): 108, "Up to 1765, the Massachusetts mob was not political. Even after this date, its political organization was gradual, but it began with the Stamp Act."

[133] For a further discussion, see Lemisch, "American Revolution," *passim*, in Bernstein, ed., *Towards a New Past*. Bailyn (ed., *Pamphlets*, p. 581) is not entirely clear on the situation *after* 1765. He denies that "Revolutionary mobs" in America were in fact "revolutionary" and questions their "meliorist aspirations."

[134] For rough-and-ready Jack, see Watson, *Sailor in English Fiction*, pp. 45, 159–60; Hohman, *Seamen Ashore*, p. 217.

[135] *Pennsylvania Archives*, 8th ser., 4: 2971, 2987, 2995–98, 3009; "Extracts from the Gazette, 1742," Labaree *et al.*, eds., *Papers of Benjamin Franklin*, 2: 363–64. Yet even these men can be shown to have had some ideas; their shouts, which included attacks on "Broad-brims," "Dutch dogs," and "You damned Quakers, . . . Enemies to King GEORGE," are similar to those of the European "Church and King" rioters. See Rudé, *The Crowd*

in History, pp. 135–48; E. J. Hobsbawm, *Primitive Rebels* (New York, 1956), pp. 110, 118, 120–23.

[136] E. P. Thompson, *The Making of the English Working Class* (New York, 1964), p. 60.

[137] Deposition of Thomas Austin, December 10, 1769, in Hutchinson to Hillsborough, December 20, 1769 (C. O. 5/759, pt. 2, Library of Congress transcript); *Pennsylvania Packet* (Philadelphia), January 16, 1779; *Colonial Records of Pennsylvania, 1683–1790* (Harrisburg, 1852–53), 11: 664–65; J. Thomas Scharf and Thompson Westcott, *History of Philadelphia, 1609–1884* (Philadelphia, 1884), 1: 403. For some crimes of seamen against masters, see *The King* v. *John Forster,* Indictment for Petty Larceny, filed October 23, 1772, New York Supreme Court, Pleadings K–495; deposition of Captain Elder and examination of John Forster, sworn October 20, 1772, *ibid.,* Pleadings K–457; *New-York Gazette; Weekly Post-Boy,* February 2, 1764.

[138] See above, p. 48.

[139] Thompson, *Making of the English Working Class,* pp. 55, 59, 78; Hobsbawm, *Primitive Rebels,* pp. 2, 7, 10.

The Abolitionists as a Dissenting Minority

Merton L. Dillon

Superficially, the abolitionists were America's most successful radicals: the Emancipation Proclamation and the Thirteenth Amendment, after all, freed the slaves. But Dillon, in "The Failure of the American Abolitionists" (*Journal of Southern History* [May, 1959]), argued that the abolitionists won "only a circumstantial victory" in the Civil War. "Measured against its professed aims and methods"—a moral regeneration of America—the movement "must be ranked not as a triumph but as one of the major failures of our history." Here Dillon returns to this theme, exploring the way in which men who in the late eighteenth century had been essentially "in harmony with the dominant spirit of their time" by the mid-nineteenth centry had become "consciously estranged" from their society.

Dillon approaches his subject with the advantage of having studied the evolution of abolitionism in its earlier and less well known figures. He is the author of *Elijah P. Lovejoy, Abolitionist Editor* (Urbana, 1961) and *Benjamin Lundy and the Struggle for Negro Freedom* (Urbana, 1966). His current research examines the critical response to the War with Mexico in the mid-West. Formerly at Northern Illinois University, Dillon is now a member of the Department of History at Ohio State University.

If the rhetoric of the American Revolution had been taken seriously by its creators, "slavery," so vigorously denounced when only figuratively inflicted by British officials on white colonials, also had to be resisted when it was imposed by white Americans on blacks. Many late-eighteenth-century Americans could not ignore the logic of this, and thus the first wave of vigorous opposition to American Negro slavery formed a coherent part of the revolutionary movement of the age.[1]

So in harmony were early abolitionists with the dominant spirit of their time that they could have sensed little tension between themselves and the society in which they worked. Authority seemed in sympathy with their goals; American Revolutionary leaders, who spoke grandly of the inalienable rights of man, sometimes explicitly condemned slavery as an outworn remnant of barbarism, inconsistent with natural law and the spirit of Christianity.[2] Therefore, paradoxical though it may seem, early abolitionists had little occasion to consider themselves, ideologically or strategically, as revolutionaries. On the contrary, they advocated a program that was entirely consistent with the ideals of their society, as voiced by men in power, and their efforts encountered little articulated opposition.

Later all this would change. Eventually abolitionists would become what they had not been in the eighteenth century: an element in American society that was consciously estranged from its prevailing values. At last aware that they faced formidable opposition, they would launch a crusade to destroy the foundation of southern power and to renovate the spirit of the entire nation. They adjusted their tactics and style to meet new situations; but they never altered their program in a fundamental way. The goals abolitionists sought in the 1780's—freedom for the slave and recognition of his rights as a human being—also were sought by Benjamin Lundy in the 1820's, and in later years by such otherwise varied reformers as William Lloyd Garrison, Theodore Dwight Weld, Thaddeus Stevens, and Wendell Phillips.

Crucial change in ideals and purpose occurred less in the abolitionists than in the American people as a whole, and especially in public leadership. Eventually it became clear that the program abolitionists advocated would not be tolerated, that power was ranged against them. When this happened, and when they realized that it had happened, abolitionists adopted the mode of thought and the style of discourse that customarily is assumed by men who recognize themselves as displaced persons from an old order but advance agents of the new. They became revolutionaries. They assumed this role, however, only after other American leaders had abandoned an ideology they once shared with abolitionists.

Resisting the forces to which others yielded, abolitionists retained earlier ideals and insisted upon applying them to various institutions and social relationships. It is not clear, however, that—despite all their decades of effort before, during, and after the Civil War—they ever succeeded in transmitting their principles to more than a small part of their contemporaries. Indeed, when slavery finally was abolished —an accomplishment often credited to abolitionists—the event followed more upon the actions of southern leaders and the accidents of war than from the moral regeneration of the nation. From this point of view the abolitionists' record was one of persistent failure, and their heirs, who have felt impelled to struggle in the same irrepressible conflict, have of necessity inherited their predecessors' revolutionary role.

I

Before slavery became an important issue of sectional dispute its opponents could be found almost everywhere in America, in the South as well as in the North.[3] It is obvious that the men who spoke and acted in the antislavery cause before 1800 were not motivated by sectional or class antipathies or by political ambition. They were moved, rather, by the humanitarian concern that marked the age. And even ownership of slaves conferred no immunity from liberal ideology. Many southern slaveholders were troubled by the existence of slavery, and for exactly the same reasons as men in the North. However, inasmuch as slaveowners could never be disinterested parties, even the most philanthropic of slaveowners encountered immense difficulty when faced with the prospect of translating their philosophic objection to slavery into action against it. The inhibiting shadow of their self-interest almost always fell between their awareness of the evil of slavery and the act of emancipation. But, in spite of this, sympathy for at least part of the abolitionist program was voiced by slaveholders of vast prestige and power. Such men as George Washington, Patrick Henry, and Thomas Jefferson left burning indictments of slavery, although they attempted little in the public sphere to remedy the evil they condemned.[4]

Non-slaveholders, understandably, found it easier to do such things. Especially in northern states, where the economic interests of slaveholders were less widespread and important, the ideals of religion and the Enlightenment could be expressed in successful emancipation efforts. This did not run counter to the dominant spirit of the time but, instead, expressed it. Men of practical influence and position sometimes aided antislavery efforts, and many more who did not do so appeared to be friendly to such efforts. Although emancipation in the North was not achieved without conflict, would-be emancipators nonetheless could feel they were in harmony with history and could enjoy the security that came from knowing they had friends or ideological allies in high places.[5]

Occasions for apprehension were few. Not many persons recognized in the creation of the Constitution the potential for the control of the nation by a political party that was dominated by slaveholding interests. Few men saw in the new national government a machine that might frustrate antislavery efforts. They did not realize that a westward-moving population would find on the frontier not only enlarged dimensions for liberty but also new opportunities to exploit weaker members of society.[6]

The nineteenth century would disclose such dangers, but, for the present, early antislavery workers enjoyed the confidence that success brings. Having freed the slaves in the North, they anticipated that their example eventually would be followed in the rest of the states. They could help encourage this, they believed, by disseminating antislavery ideas far and wide, and this was their primary task. Meanwhile they had a related work to do close to home. With the abolition of slavery in the North, humanitarians did not count their duty to the Negro finished; there was the further obligation to befriend and elevate the freedman. In an age when sentiments about progress and the goodness and perfectibility of man circulated freely, this task must have seemed a simple matter at first. The newly freed slave might be expected to find that economic opportunities were open to him in a land where much work of all kinds needed to be done. Having secured a sound economic position, he would live decently among other citizens, educate his children, and be accorded a respected position in the community alongside other free, humble men.[7]

None of this happened. Instead, abolitionists soon found oppression by the community replaced enslavement by the master. No longer slaves, but in the eyes of society not yet free to enjoy the rights and benefits of other citizens, Negroes almost universally occupied a very lowly status.[8] Philanthropists had underestimated the force of prejudice and custom, which restrained the freedman's progress. Nor had they foreseen the limitation of an American leadership that would continue to voice slogans of freedom, equality, and opportunity while taking no effective steps to end slavery or to aid the freedman. They had not yet sufficiently taken into account the grasping and pragmatic quality of Americans who, perhaps unthinkingly, sacrificed principle for present material advantage.

Not until after 1800 did many abolitionists for the first time sense that their program of racial justice aimed at a goal shared in no way by the majority. The growth of slavery as a southern economic institution and its defense by various southern spokesmen dampened the abolitionists' expectations of easy triumphs. They began to understand that the dominant forces of their age were working against them. It became evident that a drawn-out, irrepressible conflict was under way, but this fact hardly persuaded them that victory might not eventually be theirs. Having accepted the principles of the Enlightenment and of liberal religion, they still imagined that rational men could be educated to accept moral duty. Thus with undiminished ardor they continued their efforts to abolish slavery while they made a special point of attempting to improve the lot of the freedman. Their purpose in philanthropy among Negroes was twofold: (1) to aid the downtrodden and (2) to persuade skeptics that the progress of free Negroes proved that emancipation need not lead to chaos and the destruction of social order.

In the two most conspicuous centers of early antislavery activity, Philadelphia and New York, philanthropists devoted as much effort to aiding and protecting free Negroes as to attempting to free more slaves. Their program, solely humanitarian and educative in intent, could not yet be thought of as either anti-southern or political. Their work, however, bore such implications, for abolitionists had committed themselves to a course from which the majority of Americans had diverged. They conducted their campaigns in a society that clearly did not wish to be persuaded of the Negro's improvability. Conflict was inevitable.

The clash was delayed, however, because abolitionists for a time concentrated their energies on relatively uncontested activities and in areas where the likelihood of opposition was minimal. In their philanthropic efforts, for instance, early antislavery groups placed special emphasis on establishing schools for northern freedmen. Such schools would aid Negroes in an immediate, practical way, it was thought, by providing them with skills that were essential for living as free citizens. Schools also would accomplish something more subtle and perhaps even more important, abolitionists hoped—the lessening of racial prejudice.[9]

Advocates of abolition had soon discovered more stubborn opposition to their program than was fitting for Christians who were imbued with natural-right theories. Racial prejudice, it seemed, persisted and was all but universal; no other force seemed quite so powerful an obstacle to the antislavery program. In slaveholding areas prejudice was simply a face that self-interest assumed, but it also flourished among persons to whom slavery brought no evident advantage. If racial prejudice could be dispelled, every other obstacle to emancipation could more easily be overcome. Thus the companion aim of abolitionist projects for educating free Negroes was to demonstrate the acceptable intellectual and moral capacity of Negroes. The abolitionists hoped to mold them to fit their ideal of middle-class white behavior patterns and thereby remove a compelling objection to emancipation.[10] This part of their program was less racially chauvinistic than might appear, for most Negroes—then and long afterward—were eager to adopt the ways of the white majority. They did not willingly exclude themselves beyond the social threshold. Only later did the continued rejection force many Negroes into cultural separatism and thereby inaugurate that long and finally irreversible process of alienation that shattered beyond repair the abolitionist vision of a racially integrated American society.[11]

The educative efforts of the early antislavery societies did not succeed in the way their leaders had anticipated, but neither the Negroes nor the abolitionists were responsible for the failure. Abolitionist schools provided ample evidence of the Negro's intellectual capacity. Negro children learned to read and to compute about as well as white children; their handwriting specimens frequently were marvels of elegance; girls in sewing classes sewed fine seams.[12] Although many white persons knew of these skills and accomplishments, they seldom allowed this knowledge to interfere with their prejudices. Although the Negro's successes in education confirmed the optimism of philanthropists, they in no way altered the majority's racial views. None of this helped to persuade slaveholders that they were holding their intellectual equals in bondage.

Indeed, as the years passed, belief in an inherent inferiority of Negroes—repeated often, and by prestigious men—became a principal bulwark of slavery. In passages that create extreme discomfiture today, because of their source in a mind otherwise so enlightened, Jefferson in his *Notes on the State of Virginia* portrayed the Negro and his potential in most unflattering terms. And there is no reason to suppose that his opinions were not generally shared at that time, and long afterward. Southerners rehearsed the inferiority argument until it became gospel, and most northerners accepted it in much the same way.[13]

The early abolitionists contradicted Jefferson's view of racial inferiority and presented evidence of Negro accomplishments to support their opinions.[14] They used every occasion to expand upon their views of the Negro's rights in natural law and religion. But the number of persons they persuaded was small. Appeals to reason and to moral principle waged unequal battle with self-interest and pride. Slavery might be an embarrassment to some southerners, but it had become so useful and familiar to most of them that antislavery arguments could be turned aside and embarrassment could be borne with equanimity. For most northerners, slavery was an evil for which they could not be held accountable, and against which wisdom decreed they ought not interfere. Few Americans, it seemed, could purge themselves of racial bias.

II

As slavery spread across the South after 1800 it became the basis —together with land—of social, economic, and political power; and cotton, accompanying the yeoman farmer westward, democratized slaveholding. Slavery thus became even more firmly entrenched and more widely supported in America than before, and the moment in which it might have been eradicated with minimal trauma and travail receded into the past. As slavery became inextricably tied to economic advance and political power, a man who worked against it was cast, in spite of his intentions, as a foe of national development, even as a revolutionary. The abolitionists' view of the mission of America as the realization of humane ideals and the majority's view of its purpose as the achievement of power and material success came into irrepressible conflict. Abolitionists required at least three decades to accept the full implications of this truth.

In the decade immediately following 1800 the manumission societies in Pennsylvania and New York continued their activity of educating Negroes, condemning slavery, and defending the freedman's legal rights, while a few solitary philanthropists spent their energies trying in other ways to remove the slag of prejudice that overlay the North.[15] These early abolitionists had outlawed slavery in the North and they supported its exclusion from the Northwest Territory; they also had helped enact laws against the importation of slaves. These were not mean accomplishments, but although such measures set the stage for massive sectional conflict, they did nothing in themselves to end slavery in the South or to halt its southwestward advance. Nor did they do anything to improve the lot of freed Negroes in the North.

Abolitionists nonetheless persisted in their agitation throughout the 1820's; even though they had abandoned hope of early victory, and were conscious of living in a society that had rejected much of what they stood for, they still felt obliged to act in accord with their principles and as if victory were possible. If the prospects for support among northerners seemed dim, southern support of the abolitionist program, or any part of it, nearly disappeared. Only in parts of the upper South did antislavery activity continue.[16] Southern slaveholders who still recognized the evil inherent in slavery were increasingly inclined to look to the beneficence of time and to the deity to remedy an evil they considered beyond man's capacity to deal with. A bad situation would only be made worse, they insisted, by large-scale human intervention.[17] Under such circumstances many humanitarians, in the North as well as the South, wearied of the constant, apparently hopeless conflict with prejudice and self-interest. Free blacks could never be absorbed peacefully into American society, they decided, because whites would never accept them. Surrendering to pessimism, they concluded that the most that could be done for the Negro would be to free him from slavery and send him away from a society that degraded, defamed, and exploited him. They became colonizationists.[18]

The expedient offered by the American Colonization Society, wise though it may have been in view of the monumental racial prejudice that flourished in America, could never have succeeded. Even had there been a general commitment to its vast program, the tasks in freeing and transporting the entire Negro population to Africa were quite beyond the resources of the nation. Colonization, moreover, faced opposition from abolitionists, whose moral principles it disregarded. Colonizationists accepted prejudice as inevitable, and catered to it, and thereby probably stimulated it. The removal of prejudice, on the other hand, had always been fundamental to abolitionist doctrine; therefore abolitionists rejected all schemes to encourage or compel Negroes to leave the country. They launched an intense, prolonged battle against the American Colonization Society.

The widespread interest that had been aroused by the colonization society's program was evidence of a growing popular awareness that slavery and racism were problems. The means commonly favored to deal with these problems, however, could only dishearten abolitionists, for they regarded colonization as an evasion of moral duty. The fact that so many political and social leaders advocated such a solution to a moral problem helped convince abolitionists that they were the sole defenders of ideals that had been betrayed. They felt themselves more and more estranged from the dominant forces within their society.

In some respects, it is true, democratic and humane principles seemed triumphant in the 1820's and 1830's, but such progress excluded Negroes. Racial prejudice in no way declined during these decades and the slave system continued to expand and solidify, as abolitionists seemed powerless to influence events. Their sense of alienation and frustration, however, did not paralyze their ability to act. At a time when their prospects for success seemed more remote than ever, a new dynamism in several Protestant churches gave abolitionists renewed purpose and opportunity. The wave of religious revivalism that swept America in the late 1820's brought a new spirit to the already venerable antislavery movement.[19] (Some important abolitionists—Lundy, for instance—remained almost unaffected by the revivalism. Such men maintained their agitation on the already well-established lines, continuing to point out slavery's inconsistencies with the Declaration of Independence, with Scripture, and with economic utility.)

Youthful abolitionists now became agents of an abolitionism that was linked with evangelical fervor, and it was these men who assumed direction of the antislavery movement after 1830. For the new leadership that emerged in the wake of the revivals, abolitionism itself became a kind of religion, or at the very least a necessary part of religion. These young men, most of them born after 1800, felt a new urgency to accomplish God's will in order to renovate the earth and prepare it for judgment.[20] They retained the key points of their predecessors' program to end slavery and grant the freedman full rights in America, but their intensity of commitment, now tied with religious obligation, often seemed greater than that of their elders. Furthermore, their fervor led them to demand more of the American people than most of their predecessors had felt was necessary. With keen realization that the American Revolution had been in part betrayed, they asked Americans to undergo painful confrontations with themselves and with the realities of their society. They asked them to confess that the ideals to which they gave assent on the Sabbath and on patriotic holidays had been compromised—if not debased into cant. They demanded fundamental readjustments in American life. Preaching such a message and program, abolitionists should not have been surprised that they encountered angry opposition.

Negro equality was the abolitionist goal that was most often condemned. If racial prejudice in the 1830's was no greater than it had always been, the evidence of its existence surely became more flagrant.

The appearance of large numbers of free Negroes in northern cities during the 1820's had antagonized many whites and set them against a general emancipation. Few men in positions of power now used their authority to help quell such prejudice. On the contrary, many mayors, governors, and legislators freely acceded to the popular will. Anti-Negro laws were passed in most of the northern states and influential public men often did little to restrain mob action—a frequent manifestation of prejudice in the 1830's—whether it was directed against Negroes or abolitionists.

Such policies and actions should have been expected. Leadership of the states and of the nation had by the 1830's passed to men who had been born too late to share (except at secondhand) in the ideals the Revolution had fostered. Although the new politicians repeated its rhetoric, most of them knew little of its spirit, which in a sense was hardly remarkable. If such Revolutionary leaders as Thomas Jefferson had been forced by circumstances to compromise principles for the sake of solidarity, at the cost of preserving slavery, how could the leaders of Andrew Jackson's day—captives of a slaveholding, Negro-hating democracy—have done more? Indeed, even the new democratic theory seemed to denote acquiescence in public opinion, even if this included racial antipathy.

The dominant political fact of the 1830's was the organization of the new Jacksonian party, which was strongly influenced by pro-southern, pro-slavery interests. In large areas of the North the rise of the Jacksonian Democrats had brought to office men who had strong political ties with the South,[21] and some powerful northeastern economic interests—shipping, textiles, the cotton trade—flourished because of their southern connections. The situation was much the same in the new western states. Although Ohio, Indiana, and Illinois had received an influx of abolitionist refugees from the South, they also had received large accessions of other southern emigrants who may have disliked slavery, but who often disliked Negroes as well.[22] Political parties, Whig and Democratic alike, necessarily represented such views and interests. Neither party dared sacrifice its support by taking antislavery stands.

Thus the abolitionists of the 1830's had to face several disheartening truths: not only did slaveholders refuse to free their slaves voluntarily or to allow the abolitionist argument to enter the South, but northerners generally held anti-Negro views and supported southern anti-abolitionist positions. Slaveholding power dominated the nation.

When abolitionists recognized these facts, the antislavery movement entered a new phase. An abolitionist had once been simply a humanitarian whose program was accepted, at least in theory, by the leaders of American society; his ideals were in harmony with those of the nation at large. Now he advocated goals that conflicted with the interests of most of the important people and with the attitudes of hundreds of thousands of ordinary citizens. No longer could abolitionists regard themselves as the vanguard of a whole society that was moving toward the consummation of noble ideals, as had seemed to be the case in 1780. Now they conceived of themselves as a "saved" remnant, burdened with the responsibility of renovating and rescuing a lost nation.[23] The abolitionist had been converted into a revolutionary and began to think of himself as such.

Abolitionists who had come under the sway of the imperatives of revivalistic religion felt a holy obligation to conduct their crusade against whatever opposition might appear. As far as they could tell, there was no one else to undertake the task in an America in which property rights held priority over human values—where, despite proclamations of equality, caste, class, and racist views flourished. Unlike their predecessors in a more optimistic age, after 1830 abolitionists could not anticipate that the slow working of progress would in time remove great evils. On the contrary, time seemed to be moving the nation toward ends that denied the ideals upon which it had been founded. In such a setting a man who joined the abolitionist crusade was likely to do so in a spirit of resignation, consciously facing the prospect of tragedy and sacrifice, but undertaking a holy obligation that could not be shirked. "I am the one," an abolitionist may be imagined as saying, "And there is no way not/To be me[.]"[24]

III

Initiation into the crusade was likely to begin with an intense, interior drama. "Great moral reforms are all born of soul-travail," wrote the western abolitionist Theodore Dwight Weld, who would have known. "The starting point and power of every great reform must be the reformer's self. He must first set himself apart its sacred devotee, baptised into its spirit, consecrated to its service, feeling its profound necessity, its constraining motives, impelling causes, and all reasons why." The reformer must never count the cost nor calculate the pain of resisting the dominant spirit of his age, Weld asserted. He must gird himself to undertake "desperate struggles to wrench out false principles embedded in public sentiment till petrified into . . . the fossils of ages." [25]

The abolitionist leadership, thus consecrated and ready for ordeal, launched the new phase of its crusade as a battle of the spirit—material power was too formidably ranged against the movement to be challenged directly. Scores of abolitionist agents toured the North, scattering their message across the land. Their call for individual repentance for the sins of slavery and prejudice—the attitude that gave life to slavery, and deadened minds to prospects of its abolition—persuaded only a few and antagonized many. Abolitionists now were asking for a good deal more than adherence to a specific and limited program that aimed at bettering the condition of Negroes; they called for a new vision among Americans, for a change of heart. They sought a renovation of individuals, and through them of society itself. The abolition of slavery, of course, would be a natural consequence of such renovation, but only one of the consequences.

"This anti-slavery discussion is of inestimable value," said Ichabod Codding, a founder of the abolitionist Liberty Party, "in teaching the people a sense of personal responsibility, and in the development of individuality, and giving people a true knowledge of human rights, and the value of men and himself. If not one slave should be liberated, it is worth all that it has cost in trial and sacrifice, to the coming generation." [26] Far-reaching changes in American life might be anticipated as the revolution moved forward. "African slavery was simply one form of the domination of capital over the poor," said the Indiana abolitionist George W. Julian. The antislavery crusade "was not waged for the Negro," he said, "but for humanity . . . for the Rights of Man." [27]

The abolitionists' most urgent or notorious demand was for the immediate ending of slavery. But immediate emancipation alone would not have satisfied them, for the destruction of the institution, as they well knew, would not necessarily destroy the idea that had provided its chief support. Therefore abolitionists in the 1830's and afterward worked as diligently as had earlier reformers to convince their countrymen that the Negro must be recognized as equal in rights to any other man. This transformation of attitude could be accomplished, they believed, through religious reawakening.

If abolitionist efforts to demonstrate the truth of their assumption about racial equality appeared somewhat less intense than those of earlier workers, it was only because the demonstration no longer seemed either essential or effectual. The key point in their program was their call for a change of heart—the shedding of pride—and this must come through faith rather than reason. Americans had already observed demonstrations of the Negro's capacity, and been blind to its import; abolitionists for the most part now were content to rely on the evidence of things *not* seen. But this fact made their program in no way more acceptable.

Had abolitionists sought only the ending of slavery as a matter of economic and political policy, resistance outside the South to their crusade would not have been as strong and determined as it was. They asked for much more, demanding alterations in ideals and practices so fundamental as to entail revolutionary upheaval. They sought a reordering of American values and a restructuring of American society, as well as the abolition of a fundamental American institution. The abolitionists' call for the acceptance of Negroes—and all other men—as equals seemed outrageous enough, but just as disturbing was their demand that individuals resolve to act responsibly and with due regard for the rights of all men. Their call for the acceptance of individual responsibility for the direction of society rather than continued acquiescence in social drift was rejected by most persons who heard them. A moral revival of such intensity was intolerable.

The meaning and character of the abolitionists' message were not lost on their audiences. Had men and women in the 1830's not recognized the revolutionary nature of the antislavery crusade, the anti-abolitionist riots of that decade probably would not have occurred. Abolitionists labored "under a sort of religious hallucination," said an unfriendly St. Louis judge in 1836. "They seem to consider themselves as special agents . . . in fact, of Divine Providence. They seem to have their eyes fixed on some mystic vision—some Zion . . . within whose holy walls they would impound us all, or condemn us to perish on the outside." [28]

It was to be expected, of course, that—on grounds of self-interest alone—slaveholders and those who were allied with them would have resisted every call for emancipation. As sectional controversies deepened, however (and by no means were all of these directly concerned with slavery), northerners might have demanded an end to slavery simply as an anti-southern measure if their own racial prejudice had not precluded their doing this. And it was prejudice, together with the attitudes that gave it birth, that abolitionists had always sought to eradicate. They had always insisted that the Negro was a man who had the same capacities as other men. If he sometimes appeared to be less capable, this, they insisted, was only another consequence of the blighting effects of slavery. Unwillingness to accept the implications of this message was a motivating force in every mob that was formed against the abolitionists and every critique of their activities.

The agitation continued, and eventually, as northerners realized that the abolitionists' revolution would not soon be achieved, the most overt forms of opposition to them decreased. But this did not signify acceptance of their program. Until the abolitionist message had been yoked to the instruments of power, it remained little more than self-expression. Abolitionist speeches—eloquent, moving, and highly persuasive—no doubt had a cumulative effect in leading persons who heard or read them to a hatred of slavery (and slaveholders), but it cannot be demonstrated that they had a corresponding influence in promoting that cleansing of spirit that abolitionists believed would destroy prejudice and lead to national renewal. Abolitionist orators and journalists issued magnificent declarations of moral commitment, and devastating indictments of slavery, but they spoke only for themselves; they were never spokesmen for their society. Under such tutelage, Americans learned every important detail about the conditions of southern slavery. They were acquainted through firsthand observation with the oppression of Negroes in the North. Only a few, however, cared enough to become involved—or even to risk that painful self-examination from which action might issue, or measure the gap between reality and what they imagined themselves and their society to be.

Nonetheless, hostility toward the South increased throughout the areas in which the abolitionists worked. So great did anti-southern feeling become that political parties were formed in the North on anti-southern as well as antislavery principles. Tensions between the sections, which had been felt at least since the Revolution, intensified as the population pushed westward. In the late 1840's these tensions reached new heights.

Southerners had reacted to abolitionist criticism in violent, despotic fashion, and had invoked states' rights and nullification and gag rules as a means of protecting themselves or thwarting the potential menace of antislavery programs. Southern views on banks, tariffs, and internal improvements, on the other hand, appeared to determine national policy. And the annexation of Texas and the Mexican War seemed only to confirm southern dominance.[29] By 1850, therefore, much of the politically conscious northern population had become anti-southern. Because most persons who felt this way understood that slavery was the basis for the South's economy, society, and political power, they inclined to be antislavery. This does not mean, however, that they necessarily sympathized with the plight of the Negro; to be antislavery in this limited political sense did not imply granting Negroes (even within the North) equal political, social, or economic rights. It might entail nothing more positive than a determination to bar slavery from the territories.

The abolitionist message had reached a very large audience, but the message had been accepted only in part; indeed, its essence was ignored by most who heard it. In short, it was quite possible to be an enthusiastic Free Soiler and at the same time display no sympathy whatever for ending slavery (except, perhaps, as a punitive measure against the South) or for extending "privileges" to Negroes. For some northerners "antislavery" was nothing more than a synonym for "anti-southern." [30]

Thus when the Republican Party in 1860 drafted the platform upon which it would elect its first president, it called for the confinement of slavery, not for its abolition. Although the platform incorporated a portion of the Declaration of Independence, it was altogether silent on the issue of Negro equality. This equivocal antislavery position did not please abolitionists, but it satisfied others whose moral sense had been disturbed by slavery and those who resented the "aggressive" gestures of the South. The platform must also have satisfied the large group whose dislike for Negroes was fully as keen as its disapproval of slavery as an immoral southern institution. In effect, the Republican Party leaders offered assurance that the West would be reserved as a white man's country. The Negro would be confined to the South and remain a southern problem—an albatross about the necks of those who deserved him.

If the point requires illustration, one need only recall the remarks the Republican presidential candidate had made during the Lincoln-Douglas debates. The position of Negroes, Lincoln said on those occasions, might continue to be sharply circumscribed by the prevailing racial prejudice. Lincoln was humane, and doubtlessly possessed great capacity for moral growth, but neither in 1858 nor 1860 did he accept the abolitionist position—any more than Jefferson had accepted it before him.[31] No practical politician with an extensive constituency could afford to do differently. Few abolitionists were elected to office; they were still in 1860 what they had become by 1830: a revolutionary minority that advocated a fundamental change in ideas, attitudes, conduct, and institutions. After several decades of agitation they had failed to persuade many northerners of the wisdom or prudence of their message.

This does not mean, however, that their impact in the North had been slight. On the contrary, abolitionists had convinced a wide public that slavery was an immoral institution and that men who held slaves were wicked. They had disturbed the conscience of the nation. They had failed only in not being able to move that conscience to act, because racial prejudice had been too strong. There is no evidence to show that in 1861—as the Civil War began—a considerable number of persons, despite their undoubted knowledge of the facts of slavery in the South and the mistreatment of Negroes everywhere, were determined that such practices should end.

The abolitionists had succeeded only in helping make the North anti-southern. In consequence, southern publicists and politicians were pushed into increasingly militant stands, and finally to secession. Thus the South had allowed itself to be maneuvered into the situation that finally brought an end to slavery. Abolitionists had played a determining role in all this, but events had never occurred in the manner they had sought and never accomplished the ends for which they had worked and prayed. It would be difficult to challenge the statement made during the first year of the Civil War by Charles Godfrey Leland, editor of the Unionist *Continental Monthly*: "This is not now a question of the right to hold slaves, or the wrong of so doing. . . . So far as nine-tenths of the North ever cared, or do now care, slaves might have [interminably] hoed away down in Dixie" had the South not seceded.[32]

After the war, a writer in the *Atlantic Monthly* saw the matter similarly. "The moral significance of the struggle which has just closed is thus found in the fact that the good cause was best served by its bitterest enemies. . . . The immense achievement of emancipating four millions of slaves, and placing them on an equality of civil and political rights with their former masters, is due primarily to such men as Calhoun and McDuffie, Davis and Toombs. . . . The prejudice in the United States against the colored race was strong enough to overcome everything but their [Calhoun *et al.*] championship of it.[33] Western abolitionists also understood the dynamics of the historical situation. They had "forced the slaveholder himself to became a powerful ally, by driving him into extreme measures of defense or aggression," explained George W. Julian. Jonathan Blanchard, an Illinois abolitionist, agreed: The end of slavery was "precipitated as much by the madness of the planters as by the efforts of reform." [34]

IV

The destruction of slavery during the Civil War depended primarily upon military events and the Union army,[35] although the abolitionists had made Americans aware that slavery was a moral issue and thus a matter of prime concern in the war. That the ultimate cause of the Civil War was slavery, Confederate leaders recognized from the very beginning. Although southerners did not conceal the fact that in seceding they were bent upon retaining slavery as the basis for their institutions, northern leaders were not generally determined to destroy it. This fact, of course, horrified abolitionists, who dismissed as wholly inadequate the early war aim of restoring the Union to what it had been. "For one, I don't care a rag for 'the Union as it was.' I want and fight for *the Union better* than it was," wrote Albion Tourgée, an Ohio soldier. "Before this is accomplished we must have a fundamental thorough and complete revolution and renovation. This I expect and hope." [36]

Tourgée's was an abolitionist position; and most northerners came to such a view, if at all, only reluctantly and out of military necessity as the war raged on. "We are not the advocates of immediate and universal emancipation," said a typical essay in *The Biblical Repertory and Princeton Review*. "Nevertheless we believe the war may render emancipation indispensable. . . . If forced to choose between the preservation of slavery and the preservation of the Union, the heart of the nation will not hesitate a moment." [37] Such antislavery sentiment, tentative though it was, had been the creation of abolitionists, who exploited every opportunity during the war to force Lincoln and the Congress into antislavery positions.[38] Yet so uncertain was northern public commitment to abolition that a considerable part of its population fought only to restore the Union, and other northerners reluctantly accepted emancipation as a wartime necessity.[39]

As the war continued (it is difficult not to become "mystical" about this) the crusading atmosphere generated by the wartime experience created a momentary determination to free the slaves and to recognize their rights. The holocaust of war moved the nation through what John Greenleaf Whittier would later describe as a "Red Sea of Revolution." [40] Abolitionists, aided by Negroes, played crucial roles in directing and shaping events during those fateful months. In 1863 Lincoln's Emancipation Proclamation, although limited in its effect and application, nevertheless set forth the ending of slavery as a new war aim, and throughout the North, as Union armies carried destruction into the Confederacy, many of the legal barriers that oppressed northern Negroes in the free states were swept away.

After the collapse of Confederate military resistance in 1865, Reconstruction proceeded rapidly, with the Negro in some sense becoming the key to the process. Abolitionists recognized their great opportunity and resolved that it should not escape them; they insisted on writing safeguards for the Negro's new status into the Constitution. The result was the Thirteenth, Fourteenth, and Fifteenth Amendments, even now the foundation for the Negro's claim to civil and political rights.[41] "You will agree with me, I am sure," a Boston abolitionist-politician told his constituents in a Fourth of July oration in 1866, "that government is not intended for the preservation of property, or the perpetuation of power, or the purposes of conquest, or the establishment of social distinctions—for these and these only. It has a higher duty." George B. Loring, in the Reconstruction crisis, construed this duty as the establishment of Negro rights. "Whatever means are required to secure to the American citizen everywhere, the privileges of the church, the school house, the ballot box and the jury box, should become a part of the machinery of reconstruction. If for this it were necessary to send Grant back to his blazing lines, I would do it. If for this it were necessary to send Sherman back to Atlanta, I would do it." [42]

Abolitionist views such as those expressed by Loring in 1866 coincided with political exigency and—for a fleeting moment—with northern conviction. But the moment soon passed. It had become clear, long before President Rutherford B. Hayes withdrew the last federal troops from the South in 1877, that no deep and long-lasting commitment obtained in the North to secure the gains of the abolitionist crusade. Although abolitionists protested and resisted every concession that was made to racist views, just as earlier they had protested slavery and prejudice, again their efforts were largely in vain. The end of the story is well known.

v

In 1874 some Chicago abolitionists, led by Zebina Eastman, invited their fellow crusaders all over the country to attend a reunion. Besides renewing old friendships, Eastman explained, the antislavery veterans would use the occasion to review their achievements and thereby attempt to find special meaning in their antislavery past. As might have been expected, the assembled abolitionists indulged in a good deal of sentimental reminiscing and self-congratulation, but two themes ran through the speeches and through the letters that were sent by those who could not attend: wonderment at the manner in which slavery had been ended and awareness that abolitionists had not achieved the essence of their reform.

Moral suasion had not succeeded before the Civil War, the speakers agreed—"The perplexing Gordian knot has been cut by the sword." Slavery had been destroyed by revolutionary violence, wrote Whittier, "not, as we hoped, through the peaceful ways of argument, appeal, and constitutional legislation." Northerners had never accepted the abolitionist message, said Francis Gillette; "nothing less terrible than the thunderbolts of war could arouse the country and break the chain of slavery." [43]

Amos Dresser, who as a youth travelling in Kentucky had been whipped because of his abolitionist associations, had a word of counsel for his comrades. The abolitionist aim, he reminded them, had been not solely to end slavery but also to eradicate "the caste and prejudice from which it sprang and on which it fed" and to destroy "all institutions and customs which did not recognize and respect the image of God, and a human brother in every man, of whatever clime, color or condition of humanity. [44]

Even as Dresser spoke, abolitionists, surrounded by evidence of their triumphs, received public honor for having been in the forefront of a great humanitarian crusade. They were popularly credited as having been responsible for ending slavery, but, as Dresser under-

stood, this was a great simplification of history, misleading in its implication that abolition had resulted from moral reform and not from
secession and war. It detracted not at all from the moral grandeur
of the abolitionists to recognize that their victories had been incom-
plete, and in part illusory, and their honors not altogether deserved.

"We will thank God," Dresser said, "that so far as the statute is
concerned slavery is no more, and the odious word 'white' is, or is
about to be, erased from both the constitutions and the statutes of
each State." But he was not convinced, nine years after the Civil War
and in the midst of Reconstruction, that the abolitionist revolution
had yet achieved its aim: "There yet remains a great work to be
done to eradicate the spirit of slavery and the spirit of caste so
deeply rooted in the heart." This, the purpose of the abolitionists
from the beginning, had not yet been accomplished.[45]

It was not clear that the nation was more nearly resolved in 1874
than it had been twenty years earlier to implement the ideals that
abolitionists believed had given meaning to the American Revolution.
Although great strides had been taken in the advancement of human
rights, Negroes for the most part remained outside the American commitment to opportunity and equality. And the drive for power and
gain (to the exclusion of much else) marked the new age even more
triumphantly than the past age. Abolitionists, who had sought to realize the principles upon which they believed the nation had been
founded, remained a prophetic element, as before. The irrepressible
conflict still raged in America.

[1] Bernard Bailyn, *The Ideological Origins of the American Revolution*
(Cambridge, Mass., 1967), pp. 232–46; J. Franklin Jameson, *The American
Revolution Considered as a Social Movement* (Princeton, 1926), pp. 21–26.
For a contemporary view of the ideological conflict between the Revolu-
tion and slavery, see comments in the *American Museum*, 1 (March,
1787): 239.

[2] See George Livermore, *An Historical Research Respecting the Opinions
of the Founders of the Republic on Negroes . . .* (Boston, 1863).

[3] The standard works on the early antislavery movement are still Mary
S. Locke, *Anti-Slavery in America from the Introduction of African Slaves
to the Prohibition of the Slave Trade (1619–1808)* (Boston, 1901), and
Alice D. Adams, *The Neglected Period of Anti-Slavery in America, 1808–
1831* (Boston, 1908).

[4] Slavery and Revolutionary ideology is a major theme in Robert Mc-Colley, *Slavery and Jeffersonian Virginia* (Urbana, Ill., 1964).

[5] See Arthur Zilversmit, *The First Emancipation, The Abolition of Slavery in the North* (Chicago, 1967), esp. pp. 85–229.

[6] For the belief that the Constitutional Convention of 1787 might be prevailed upon to abolish slavery, see New York Manumission Society Minutes, New York Historical Society, N.Y., vol. 1, fol. 72. For the frontier and the treatment of Negroes, see John Hope Franklin, *From Slavery to Freedom, A History of American Negroes* (New York, 1947), pp. 166–67.

[7] The record of early attempts to accomplish these aims may be found in the minutes of the American Convention for Promoting the Abolition of Slavery, the first national organization that was formed to coordinate anti-slavery philanthropy: A.C.P.A.S. *Minutes* (1794–1837), 26 vols. (Philadelphia, Baltimore, and Washington, D.C., 1794–1837).

[8] *Ibid.*, 1794 (Philadelphia, 1794), p. 15. The most comprehensive treatment of the condition of northern free Negroes is Leon F. Litwack's *North of Slavery: The Negro in the Free States, 1790–1860* (Chicago, 1961).

[9] Almost every meeting of the A.C.P.A.S. concerned itself with Negro education. For representative reports, see the 1797 *Minutes* (Philadelphia, 1797), pp. 29–31, and the 1818 *Minutes* (Philadelphia, 1818), p. 13.

[10] See New York Manumission Society Minutes, vol. 1, fols. 83, 87, and *To the Abolition and Manumission Societies in the United States* (August 8, 1817), a printed circular in the collection of the New York Historical Society.

[11] Some evidence of the process can be found in August Meier and Elliott M. Rudwick, *From Plantation to Ghetto: An Interpretative History of American Negroes* (New York, 1966), pp. 70–74, 80, 84.

[12] A typical account of such accomplishments is in the New York Manumission Society Minutes, vol. 8, fol. 2.

[13] See Thomas Jefferson, *Notes on the State of Virginia*, ed. William Peden (Chapel Hill, N.C., 1955), pp. 138–41. For the phenomenon of American racial prejudice, see William S. Jenkins, *Pro-Slavery Thought in the Old South* (Chapel Hill, 1935), and William Stanton, *The Leopard's Spots: Scientific Attitudes toward Race in America, 1815–1859* (Chicago, 1959).

[14] Critiques of inferiorist racist views (not all of them by abolitionists) can be found in Gilbert Imlay, *A Topographical Description of the Western Territory of North America* (London, 1792), pp. 185, 191; George Buchanan, *An Oration upon the Moral and Political Evil of Slavery* (Philadelphia, 1793), pp. 7, 10, 17; Thomas Branagan, *A Preliminary Essay on the Oppression of the Exiled Sons of Africa* . . . (Philadelphia, 1804), pp.

100, 101; and Thomas Hedges Genin, *Selections from the Writings of the Late Thomas Hedges Genin* (New York, 1869), pp. 102, 109–11.

[15] Zilversmit, *The First Emancipation*, pp. 201–26. One of the most active early "free lance" abolitionists was John Kenrick of Newton, Massachusetts. For an account of Kenrick's career see Lydia Maria Child, *An Appeal in Favor of That Class of Americans Called Africans* (Boston, 1833), p. 230; and *The Liberator* (Boston), April 6, 20, and June 8, 1833.

[16] See Gordon E. Finnie, "The Antislavery Movement in the South, 1787–1836: Its Rise and Decline and Its Contribution to Abolitionism in the West" (Ph.D. diss., Duke University, 1962), *passim.*

[17] For an explicit statement by a prestigious southerner of this commonly held opinion, see Fitzhugh Lee, *General Lee* (New York, 1894), p. 64.

[18] For a comprehensive treatment of these efforts, see Philip J. Staudenraus, *The African Colonization Movement, 1816–1865* (New York, 1961).

[19] The classic study of the relationship between revivalism and abolition is Gilbert H. Barnes' *The Antislavery Impulse, 1830–1844* (New York, 1933); see also Anne C. Loveland, "Evangelicalism and 'Immediate Emancipation' in American Antislavery Thought," *Journal of Southern History,* 32 (May, 1966): 172–88, and Merton L. Dillon, *Benjamin Lundy and the Struggle for Negro Freedom* (Urbana, Ill., 1966), pp. 148–56.

[20] See David Brion Davis, "The Emergence of Immediatism in British and American Antislavery Thought," *Mississippi Valley Historical Review,* 49 (September, 1962): 209–30; Ira V. Brown, "Watchers for the Second Coming: The Millenarian Tradition in America," *ibid.,* 39 (December, 1952): 451; and Whitney R. Cross, *The Burned-over District: The Social and Intellectual History of Enthusiastic Religion in Western New York, 1800–1850* (Ithaca, N.Y., 1950), pp. 165, 224.

[21] See Dwight L. Dumond, *Antislavery: The Crusade for Freedom in America* (Ann Arbor, Mich., 1961), pp. 63–75, and Richard H. Brown, "The Missouri Crisis, Slavery, and the Politics of Jacksonianism," *South Atlantic Quarterly,* 55 (Winter, 1966): 55–72.

[22] This is a central theme of Eugene H. Berwanger's *The Frontier against Slavery: Western Anti-Negro Prejudice and the Slavery Extension Controversy* (Urbana, 1967). For an excellent treatment of the subject in a single state, Indiana, see Emma Lou Thornbrough, *The Negro in Indiana: A Study of a Minority* (Indianapolis, 1957).

[23] Antislavery writers had long expressed fears of divine retribution for the nation's sins; for a relatively late example of this, see the *St. Louis Observer,* April 16, 1835.

[24] The quotation is from James Dickey, "Snakebite," *Poems, 1957–1967* (Middletown, Conn., 1967), p. 263.

[25] "Lessons from the Life of Wendell Phillips," in *Memorial Services*

upon the Seventy-fourth Birthday of Wendell Phillips, Held at the Residence of William Sumner Crosby . . . November 29, 1885 (Boston, 1886), pp. 24–26.

[26] *Chicago Daily Tribune,* June 10, 11, 1874.

[27] *Ibid.,* June 11, 1874.

[28] *Missouri Republican* (St. Louis), May 26, 1836. The anti-abolitionist riots at Alton, Illinois, which produced the only murder of an abolitionist, are analyzed in Merton L. Dillon, *Elijah P. Lovejoy, Abolitionist Editor* (Urbana, 1961), pp. 111–70.

[29] A close study of the effect of the Texas issue on the growth of abolitionism in a northern state is Kinley J. Brauer's *Cotton versus Conscience: Massachusetts Whig Politics and Southwestern Expansion, 1843–1848* (Lexington, Ky., 1967).

[30] Berwanger, *Frontier against Slavery,* pp. 30–59 and *passim.*

[31] A reasonable explanation of Lincoln's ambiguous and sometimes conflicting racial views can be found in Richard N. Current, *The Lincoln Nobody Knows* (New York, 1958), pp. 214–36.

[32] "Our War and Our Want," *Continental Monthly,* 1 (February, 1862): 114.

[33] C. H. Coleman, "Moral Significance of the Republican Triumph," *Atlantic Monthly,* 23 (January, 1869): 128.

[34] *Chicago Daily Tribune,* June 10, 11, 1874.

[35] See Dwight L. Dumond, *America's Shame and Redemption* (Marquette, Mich., 1965), pp. 47–48, 90–93.

[36] In Otto H. Olsen, *Carpetbagger's Crusade: The Life of Albion Winegar Tourgée* (Baltimore, 1965), pp. 24–25.

[37] *Biblical Repertory and Princeton Review,* 34 (July, 1862): 521. See also Caleb S. Henry, "Letters to Professor S. F. B. Morse," *Continental Monthly,* 4 (November, 1863): 528.

[38] Their efforts are treated in full in James M. McPherson, *The Struggle for Equality: Abolitionists and the Negro in the Civil War and Reconstruction* (Princeton, 1964).

[39] Evidence for this view can be found in James G. Randall and David Donald, *The Civil War and Reconstruction* (Boston, 1961), pp. 371–98; see also C. Vann Woodward, "Seeds of Failure in Radical Race Policy," in Harold M. Hyman, ed., *New Frontiers of the American Reconstruction* (Urbana, 1966), pp. 125–47, and V. Jacque Voegeli, *Free but Not Equal: The Midwest and the Negro during the Civil War* (Chicago, 1967), *passim,* especially chs. 5 and 6.

[40] In the *Chicago Daily Tribune,* June 11, 1874.

[41] See Kenneth M. Stampp, *The Era of Reconstruction, 1865–1877* (New York, 1965), pp. 214–15.

[42] *Safe and Honorable Reconstruction* (South Danvers, Mass., 1866), pp. 7, 21.

[43] *Chicago Daily Tribune*, June 10, 1874.

[44] *Ibid.*, June 11, 1874.

[45] See Merton L. Dillon, "The Failure of the American Abolitionists" (*Journal of Southern History*, 25 [May, 1959]: 159–77), for speculations on the limits of the abolitionist accomplishment.

The Peculiar Dissent of the Nineteenth-Century South

Carl N. Degler

Dissent within a dissenting region poses special problems. Starting from the premise that the "South's position as a minority within the nation" influenced the shape of dissent within the region, Carl Degler explores the failure of three groups of Southern dissenters from about 1830 to 1880: the anti-slavery advocates, the Unionists, and the native Republicans. This essay sums up his thinking midway through a book on the same subject.

Degler's interpretive work, *Out of Our Past: The Forces That Shaped Modern America* (New York, 1959), has guided innumerable college students to new insights into American history. Specialists are familiar with his challenging articles on slavery and the origins of racial prejudice, the "Locofocos," feminism, and political parties and the growth of the cities. He is the editor of the two-volume *Pivotal Interpretations in American History* (New York, 1966), and his most recent book is *Affluence and Anxiety: The United States since 1945* (Chicago, 1968). In addition to his book on southern dissenters, Degler is now at work on an interpretation of women and the family in America. For many years a teacher at Vassar College, Degler recently joined the Department of History at Stanford University.

Throughout most of the nineteenth century the South was at odds with the rest of the nation, first in its defense of slavery, then in its dissatisfaction with, and secession from the Union, and, still later, in its rejection of the Radical Republican solution to the question of the Negro. If dissent is defined as opposition to the views of the majority, the South was surely a region of dissenters. Indeed, in their secession from the Union the eleven states that came to make up the Confederacy took the most extreme course open to dissenters; they withdrew from the consensus entirely.

Some might contend that true dissent is more than simply a deviation from the majority, it must also be an attempt to alter the status quo, that is, to further social change. Even by such a definition, the South seems to fit the meaning of dissent, for secession clearly was an attempt to change the nature of the Union and to provide a new vision of society in the form of the Confederacy. Certainly to the Buchanan and Lincoln administrations secession represented a new and undesirable path for the Republic, both saw their defenses of the Union as truly conservative measures against those who would alter established practices and attitudes.

I do not, however, want to press too far this conception of the South as a radically dissenting region. Secession, it is true, was a departure from past practices, but it was a radical means for securing a conservative end. Like the revolution of 1776, it was a means for preserving the going society, at least in the South, and not a device for repudiating the regional status quo. It is important to my broad purpose, however, to emphasize at the outset that the typical southerner in the nineteenth century dissented from the opinion of the majority of Americans.

In some ways the South's dissent, even in the ante bellum years, exhibits similarities to the dissent from the "right" in our own time. Although the content of the pro-slavery, secessionist argument of the Old South has little in common with the argument of the radical right of the 1950's and 1960's, the purpose and nature of these two kinds of dissent have much in common. They were—and are—efforts to resist changes taking place in society and politics. Both doubted the value of the national consensus, not because that consensus lacked vision or was slow to make improvements—as is the customary criticism of dissenters—but simply because of its acceptance of the *desirability* of change. The nineteenth-century South, like the radical right today, reminds us that dissent is not always a radical movement, it can also be a means for preserving the present, which is only another way of saying that dissent can be conservative.

These general observations on the South as a region in disagreement with the rest of the nation have more than passing importance in examining those men and women who dissented within the South itself. It is the thesis of this essay that the South's position as a minority within the nation was one of the principal influences in determining the "shape" of dissent within the region.

It has long been recognized, of course, that the great reform movements that surged across the North in the 1830's and 1840's had few or no counterparts in the South. The women's rights movement, the peace movement, the communitarians, the labor movement, the temperance crusade, and, of course, the antislavery agitation were almost entirely absent from the South. In those years, in fact, southern publicists and leaders proudly proclaimed the freedom of their region from strident criticisms of the status quo. The absence of the reform movements that were agitating the North, however, is not the main point of my observation that southern dissent was molded by the minority position of the South within the nation; the point is, rather, that those within the South, who deviated from traditional southern patterns, constituted a peculiarly southern kind of dissent. Despite their deviation from the regional consensus, they also reflected their region's divergence from American cultural patterns in general; and, as dissenters within the South, they nevertheless were southerners in some very fundamental ways. To put the matter another way, the very character of southern dissent was, paradoxically, yet another example of the divergence of the South from the rest of the nation.

Before we can attempt to establish this point we must examine the nature of the men and women who, although living in the South, differed from it. Despite the acknowledged conservatism of the region and the tendency of historians to treat the South as a monolith and an object of, rather than an actor in, reform, the South has not always spoken with a single voice. Throughout the nineteenth century there were southerners who disagreed with their region's dominant social and political stances—a disagreement that surely qualifies them as dissenters. Three significant groups of nineteenth-century dissenters stand out: antislavery advocates; Unionists, or opponents of secession; and, after the Civil War, native Republicans. It is these three groups that I shall examine in an effort to discern the nature and meaning of southern dissent.[1]

I

Let us look first at the character of southern antislavery thought and action. Despite the well-known opposition of the slave South to any agitation of the slavery question, the fact is that prior to 1830—when antislavery ideas began to be silenced in the South—there were more antislavery societies in the South than in any other part of the country. Furthermore, even in the 1830's southern objections to slavery were still being heard. Perhaps the most significant instance of these objections was the celebrated debate in the Virginia legislature in 1831–32, which came hard on the heels of the greatest slave rebellion of the entire ante bellum period, that of Nat Turner. As many as sixty members out of perhaps 135 members of that legislature put themselves on record as opposing slavery. Later, other public efforts at ending slavery were made in the upper South. In 1834, for example, there was an abortive attempt in Tennessee to have the legislature of that state take steps to abolish slavery, and in 1849 several thousand Kentuckians voted for delegates to a constitutional convention who were pledged to end slavery in Kentucky (none of the antislavery delegates, however, was elected).

In addition to these public efforts, which suggest that thousands of southerners, at least in the upper South, opposed slavery, a number of individual and sometimes prominent southerners strongly spoke out against slavery in the years after 1830. It is the antislavery arguments of these southerners that permit us to examine more closely the ideological assumptions and nature of southern dissenting thought.

The arguments southerners leveled against slavery were many. Following Jefferson, who also had opposed slavery, some indicted slavery for its denial of natural rights. Indeed, in early 1832, during the first days of the debates in the Virginia legislature, one of the delegates made this Jeffersonian argument:

> The right to the enjoyment of liberty, is one of those perfect, inherent and inalienable rights, which pertain to the whole human race, and of which they [the slaves] can never be divested, except by an act of gross injustice. . . . Liberty is too dear to the heart of man, ever to be given up for any earthly consideration.[2]

It is worth noting, in passing, that such expressions of concern for natural rights did not necessarily envision an acceptance of the Negro as a civic equal.

Hinton Rowan Helper, who was an avowed believer in the inferiority of the Negro, as well as a Jeffersonian, later expressed himself in much the same way. "No system of logic," he wrote in his celebrated antislavery tract, *The Impending Crisis of the South* in 1857, "could be more antagonistic to the spirit of true democracy" than the argument that the racial inferiority of the Negro justified slavery.

> "It is probable that the world does not contain two persons who are exactly alike in all respects; yet all men are endowed by their Creator with certain *inalienable* rights, among which are life, liberty, and the pursuit of happiness."

Emancipation, he said, would restore to Negroes "their natural rights."[3]

Other antislavery delegates adverted to the contradiction between slavery and religion. "This, sir," a delegate pointed out, "is a christian [*sic*] community," and slavery was morally offensive to it. Virginians "read in their Bibles 'do unto all men as you would have them do unto you'— and this golden rule and slavery are hard to reconcile." [4]

But the most common argument advanced by the opponents of slavery during the Virginia debates in 1831–32 was that slavery constituted a threat to white society. Indeed, one of the reasons for the debate was the terror Nat Turner's uprising of the previous year had brought to the minds of all thinking men. The sixty whites who had been murdered by Turner's band were mute but powerful symbols of a great warning. Would it not be desirable, many legislators asked, to rid the state of that threat once and for all?

Outside the halls of the Virginia legislature as well as within, the most insistent argument was that slavery impoverished the land, retarded the economy, and harmed the non-slaveholder. In fact, this argument was one of the principal arguments of antislavery men in the South throughout the ante bellum years. Daniel Reeves Goodloe of North Carolina, for example, in 1844 published a pamphlet, *Inquiry into the Causes Which Have Retarded the Accumulation of Wealth and the Increase of Population in the Southern States*, which, as the title suggests, principally followed this argument. Like his fellow North Carolinian Helper, who much later published a more famous version of the argument, Goodloe meticulously contrasted the history and the production of the southern states with that of comparable northern states to show that slavery was the cause of southern economic backwardness. Cassius Marcellus Clay of Kentucky, perhaps the best-known antislavery southerner of his time, also employed the argument of the retarding effects of slavery as his principal weapon against the "peculiar institution." Both as a member of the legislature in the 1840's and as the editor of the *True American* in Lexington, Clay advocated abolition as the first, indispensable step for the South to take in developing industry and in raising the income of its people to a level commensurate with that of the North. [5]

In 1847 Henry Ruffner of Virginia carried the same argument forward by ascribing the South's higher rate of white illiteracy and inadequacy of education to the evil effects of slavery. Moreover, he argued, commerce would come to Virginia only if slavery were removed. "Even the common mechanical trades do not flourish in a slave State," [6] he pointed out—as Helper was to repeat ten years later in his *Impending Crisis*. And, like Helper, Ruffner also observed that the raw materials for all the manufactured imports of the South were to be found in the South itself; all that was required to produce them was energy, ingenuity, and free labor. Like so many other antislavery men of the South, Ruffner was an economic liberal. He did not deny that slavery was profitable to the slaveholder; he simply held that it was less profitable than a free labor system would be. Like Goodloe, Ruffner blamed the lack of population growth in the South on slavery; people were compelled to emigrate simply because slavery restricted their labor opportunities. To those who asserted that immigration from Europe was the principal source of northern population growth, Ruffner replied that slavery was the reason immigrants did not come to the South.[7]

Important as the economic or social argument against slavery bulks in the writings of such antislavery southerners as Goodloe, Helper, Ruffner, and others, it was not the only argument. Mary Minor Blackford of Fredericksburg, Virginia, for example, did not publish her diary, but in it she wrote another kind of southern argument against slavery. A deeply religious woman, she found slavery cruel and a limitation on the slaves' opportunity for access to Christianity. Vehemently, if privately, she deprecated the inhumanity she witnessed almost daily in the slave pens of her city, one of which was situated near her home.[8]

A few other antislavery writers in the South also expressed a moral objection to slavery, some publicly. Although Goodloe's primary concern was the political and economic evils of slavery, he objected to the underlying racist defense of slavery that someone like Helper accepted. Speaking of the Negroes under slavery, Goodloe wrote in 1849:

> They are not savages, in any proper sense of the word, though they are for the most part illiterate and degraded in a moral point of view. They have no idea of living by hunting or fishing; they are acquainted with agriculture and the mechanic arts. There is a spirit of mental and moral improvement among them; many have, under every disadvantage, accumulated money sufficient to buy themselves at a high price. These are not the characteristics of savages; and it cannot be pretended that they are wanting in incentives to labor.[9]

Perhaps, from the standpoint of the Negro, the most striking attack on slavery by a white southerner was that of Eli Caruthers, an obscure North Carolina preacher. Caruthers went far beyond any other southern antislavery man, arguing that the racist defense of slavery was both morally and historically wrong. Citing writers on ethnology, he pointed out that such people as the South Sea islanders and Hottentots were quite inferior to African Negroes. If this is so, he asked, how can one logically justify the enslavement of Negroes as the most degraded of men? But, more important, where is the authority for enslavement? he asked. If such tyranny were practised on

> any other portion of mankind we should be horror struck at the recital. Why is the black race thus doomed rather than the *olive*, the *copper* colored or any other? Why should those with nappy hair or any other distinguishing peculiarity be confined to a cruel and hopeless bondage rather than those who differ from them?

And even if they are degraded today, he asked, when did white men get the right to enslave them?

> For long generations they appear to have been the supperior [*sic*] race & to be the admiration of the literary and scientific community, the mutilated and long buried monuments of their greatness have been brought to light on the Nile, the Tigris & the Euphrates. . . . Should we not honor them as a race for what they have done & for what God has done for them & by them. And it surely does not become *us* to treat them thus with contempt & rigor, without a cause, for our ancestors were once very little if any better than the caffres or Hottentots of the present day. In the time of Cesar [*sic*], not long before the Christian era, their priests, the Druids, offered human sacrifices & the people could have sunk very little lower in superstition & wretchedness. Other Roman writers of that age tell us that the Angles or Britons & the Germans, from both of whom, *we*, the Anglosaxons [*sic*], the traducers & oppressors of the Africans, have descended, were exceedingly ignorant, superstitious & degraded.[10]

Despite the intrinsic interest of Caruthers' amazingly modern plea, it was virtually unique and unpublicized. Indeed, Caruthers' book, probably written in 1861, was never published, although the author-preacher was known among his neighbors for his antislavery views. The cogency of his argument, which stands almost alone among antislavery works, stems from a concern for the Negro and the immorality of the white man's hubris, contrasting sharply with the much more common economic arguments against slavery.

The significant fact is that the southern antislavery movement showed very little concern for the Negro. Not all antislavery southerners, to be sure, were as obsessed with Negro-phobia as someone as well-known as Helper was, but their arguments against the peculiar institution were essentially in behalf of the southern white man. This attitude is clearly reflected in the program of the American Colonization Society, the most publicized movement against slavery in the South. It enlisted as members prominent southerners such as Andrew Jackson and John Marshall, and as late as 1849 it boasted of having Henry Clay as its president. The society's solution to the problem of slavery, however, was the removal of the Negro from the South, despite the fact that most slaves and free Negroes had no more acquaintance with Africa than most white men. Although Cassius M. Clay recognized the impracticality of such a solution, he still did not envision equality of rights or treatment for the Negro; certainly he did not see the Negro in the same light as Caruthers.

This insensitivity of the great majority of southern antislavery men toward the Negro is revealing. There were among them no William Lloyd Garrisons, no Theodore Welds, no Charles Sumners arguing for the full equality of the Negro. Such northern abolitionists were dissenters not only on slavery but on the racism of the national culture as well. They strove for a new and full place for the Negro in American life, one that few southerners could countenance. Why was this so? The principal reason was that southern dissent on slavery, like southern culture as a whole, lacked the idealism and the self-criticism that the less isolated and less insulated North displayed at times. This is not the place to inquire into the causes for the difference in cultural outlook between the sections, but that the difference existed is clear. One sign of this difference was the almost total absence of concern for the Negro among southern antislavery advocates. To believe in full equality for the Negro in the 1850's required a great effort of imagination, if not a leap of faith, in the potentiality of the degraded slave. All around them, day in and day out, southerners saw overwhelming evidence of the Negro's alleged social incompetence and dependence. The qualities of imagination or faith necessary to transcend these experiences were denied to southerners by their culture. In the South, as David M. Potter has written, "the culture of the folk survived . . . long after it succumbed to the on-slaught of urban-industrial culture elsewhere." [11] Such a culture, resting on close family ties and direct, personal contact, tends to be narrowly realistic and practical, eschewing the theoretical and the idealistic; observation and experience, not imagination or faith, are the bases of judgment. Hence most southerners, whether they owned slaves or not (and most did not), accepted slavery as both realistic and practical. Those few southerners who came to oppose slavery did so for equally realistic and practical reasons: because it harmed the economy or endangered white society, not because it hurt the Negro.

Belief in the perfectibility of man, which acted like yeast in the thought of some northerners, simply was absent south of Mason's and Dixon's line. Where, one may ask, were the Transcendentalists of the South? How—indeed—could a thoughtful southerner believe in the perfectibility of human institutions when he recognized the compromises he had to make in arguing for liberty for his region while justifying slavery? For many years the principal defense of slavery had been that it was a necessary evil, and from such reasoning a belief in the perfectibility of man cannot issue. As Donald Mathews has shown, southern practicality and narrowly conceived realism smothered the Methodist commitment to antislavery at the end of the eighteenth century and prevented its revival in the 1830's.[12] The particular and narrow realism of southerners also can be seen in their literal interpretation of the Constitution, which led them to states' rights, and in their literal reading of the Bible, which resulted in religious fundamentalism.

In such a climate of opinion there was no chance for the develop-ment of a full-blown belief in the egalitarian potentiality of the Negro. Southern antislavery men, although they may have detested the in-stitution, did not envision the Negro any differently than other south-erners. It is not accidental that those few southerners who saw a vision of a new role for the Negro in American society, such as James Birney or Angelina and Sarah Grimké, left the South; or, like Eli Caruthers, lived in obscurity.

The limits of the antislavery argument in the south not only re-flect the nature of southerners in general but offer additional evidence of the South's difference from the rest of the nation.

II

Virtually all the antislavery southerners we know of were also opponents of secession. Helper, for example, wrote: "No man can be a
true patriot without becoming an abolitionist. . . . Our motto is the
abolition of slavery and the perpetuation of the American Union." [13]
Undoubtedly this correspondence between antislavery and defense-
of-the-Union attitudes stemmed from the recognition that slavery
underlay the drive to secession. But the reverse clearly is not true,
for most southern Unionists were not hostile to slavery. Although the
number of southern antislavery advocates may have been relatively
few, southern Unionists during the 1850's, and throughout the war,
constituted a sizable proportion of the population. In the election of
1860, for example, something like forty per cent of southern voters
cast their ballots for John Bell, who clearly was the Unionist candidate
in the South in that contest.

Actually, Unionism was a protean concept in the South of 1860.
For some people it meant resistance to secession, but only so long as
the Union refrained from the use of force in sustaining itself. For
example, Charles Phillips, a professor at the University of North
Carolina, wrote to a fellow Unionist who had left the South that he
considered himself a Unionist and was denounced as such by secessionists. "Still," he pointed out, "I know not a man who is a *Unionist
per se.*" If the Republican Party, Phillips said, will not repudiate its
stand on slavery, "we will jump over the fence that now surrounds
us & our northern neighbors." [14] But others were much stronger in
their Unionism, men like Governor Sam Houston of Texas, who refused to call a secession convention and who was forced from office
because he would not allow his state to secede. Andrew Johnson of
Tennessee, unlike many of his southern colleagues in the Senate, remained at his post in Washington and represented his state although
his own people repudiated him (along with the government of the
United States) when Lincoln moved to crush secession by force. In
eastern Tennessee, the region Johnson came from, thousands of lesser
figures and farmers rallied to the Union cause, ultimately contributing
some 49,000 soldiers to the Union Army—the strongest proof possible of commitment to the nation. Many other small farmers, mainly
non-slaveholders in western North Carolina, also remained loyal to
the Union, defying the Confederate authorities or fleeing across

Kentucky to Indiana for the duration of the war. Indeed, throughout the Confederacy, wherever slavery was weakly rooted the cause of the Union found adherents and the Confederacy discovered opponents.

Not all Unionists, however, were small farmers or hill-dwellers. Some of the most outspoken were large planters, like James L. Alcorn of Mississippi, who as chief levee commissioner was the most highly paid official in the state, and James Madison Wells of Louisiana, who in 1860 owned three plantations and ninety-six slaves, and Kenneth Rayner of North Carolina, who owned a hundred slaves. Rayner, Wells, and Alcorn, like thousands of other well-to-do Unionists in the ante bellum South, were former Whigs. All through the sectional turmoil of the 1850's the Whigs of the South sought to counter the drift toward secession although they rarely opposed slavery. It was the Whigs who prevented secession in 1850 and 1851, by their vigorous support of the Compromise of 1850. Then, in 1860, another Whig, John Bell of Tennessee, tried to head off secession as the presidential candidate of the Constitutional Union party, but without success.

The plight of the Unionist in the South after the war broke out was clearly a difficult one. If he openly sided with what his neighbors spoke of as the "coercive power" of the Washington government, he would, at best, be ostracized, or imprisoned. Some wealthy Unionists deliberately, went even further. Wells, for example, spoke out against the Confederacy—and carried on his own guerrilla warfare against the southern forces, burning their supplies and hiding from reprisal.[15] Most Unionists, however, were not so courageous. Many of them, when faced with the dilemma, joined the Confederate Army, as did Alcorn and Zebulon Vance of North Carolina. Others, like W. W. Holden of North Carolina, maintained a cautious but defeatist outlook on the Confederacy's struggle and acted as centers of Unionist sentiment. Some retreated entirely from public life, biding their time, as Alcorn did after he left the army. Still others gave various forms of material support to the Union.

Thanks to the research of Frank Klingberg among the records of the Southern Claims Commission, we have some measure of well-to-do southerners' support for the Union.[16] Generally this espousal of the Union cause took the form of voluntarily supplying goods and services to the Union forces when they invaded southern states. Almost 1,500 southerners made claims to the commission for $5,000 or more for aid they had rendered the northern military forces. Twenty thousand more made claims for less than $5,000. Although the largest claims ($10,000 or more) came from every Confederate state, such claims, significantly, were clustered in the rich plantation areas along the Mississippi River in Louisiana, Arkansas, and Mississippi and along the Georgia and South Carolina seacoasts, the locale of many Whig planters before the war. These well-to-do claimants, and the anonymous and humble southerners who joined the Union armies, were the hard core of southern Unionism. These men gave the strongest earnests of their convictions: their property, their safety, and sometimes their lives.

The most striking fact that emerges from any examination of the Unionists, as a group or as individuals, before or after the war, is their conservatism. During the secession winter of 1860/61 the Unionists of the South sought to preserve the status quo; it was the secessionists who were the radicals—as in fact they were called by people in both the North and the South. Within the South, however, Unionists were the dissenters; and if the measure of a dissenter is the cost he pays, materially and psychically, for his deviation, then the southern Unionists certainly deserve the title. Yet they were dissenters of a special kind. They were created and shaped by the fact that the South was a minority within the nation.

The southern Unionists were espousing a cause that was a majority cause in the nation; they stood for the national outlook, against which their section was in rebellion. But instead of providing strength, this fact inhibited their success. Unionism was on the defensive in the South in 1860 because it sought to prevent change, that is, the disruption of the Union. Given this conservative goal of Unionism, it is not surprising that the tactics and the leadership of the Unionist forces in the South lacked the audacity that energizes those who resent and therefore seek to change the status quo.

Southern Unionists were much like the American Tories during the American Revolution; they represented the established order, which was under attack. Both Tories and southern Unionists found it difficult to counter the thrusts of their vigorous and usually younger opponents of the status quo. Like the Tories, southern Unionists were weakened militarily by their physical separation from the larger group to which they remained loyal, as well as by self-doubt and by conflicts in personal loyalties. The psychological burdens, however, were much heavier in the South, where the culture was more homogeneous than that which had shaped the Tories. Moreover, it also was a culture that by virtue of its minority position within the nation made dissent personally difficult as well as socially dangerous.

A few stalwart Unionists such as Andrew Johnson, Hinton Helper, and Daniel Goodloe, it is true, could boldly reject the South during the war by leaving the region, repudiating the Confederacy. But even such men, when Reconstruction came, found that they were emotionally tied to the South. Johnson, Helper, and Goodloe rejected the Radical Republican program in the South partly because of the race issue, but also because the policy was imposed by the North. In both instances the continuing influence of their southern heritage was measured. Again there is an analogy with the Tories, many of whom, after they migrated to England during the Revolution, found themselves out of place—more American in thought and sentiment than they had heretofore been aware.

The remark of August Hurt of Georgia, who had risked his safety and liquidated his property in behalf of the Union, typifies the situation of southern Unionists after the end of hostilities: "My sympathies personally were with my friends who were exposed to danger and their homes to desolation, but politically my sympathies were with the country in the efforts to establish peace and restore good government." [17] The fact of the matter is that few southern Unionists, even those who worked for the Union cause during the war, could bring themselves to denounce the South after Appomattox. Their support of the Union had seldom been a mystical defense of nationalism, but the belief that secession would harm the South. As a Unionist from Mississippi told the conquerors, "If you want me to say, or expect me to say, that I hate the South because they were at war with the Union, I cannot say it." [18]

Again it is evident that dissent in the South was of a different order from that which obtained in the rest of the country. It was clearly conservative, not only in the sense of preserving the status quo but also in standing up for the values of stability, order, and continuity— the values of conservatives everywhere. Nowhere is the essentially conservative character of southern Unionism better illustrated than in the response to Reconstruction. Except for a few rare specimens such as William Brownlow, the Republican governor of Tennessee, the great majority of Unionists in the South worked for a restoration of the Union as it had been before the war. Even a staunch southern Unionist like Andrew Johnson, who had risked all in behalf of the Union, took this position as President, refusing to acknowledge that the war had transformed the Union. In a sense, his humiliating struggle with Congress over Reconstruction policy was a conflict between traditional southern Unionism and the new nationalism that had been born of the war. As conservatives, many southern Unionists, caught in the crisis of secession, war, and Reconstruction, found themselves ever on the defensive. First they had to counter the radical secessionists. After the war they had to confront their erstwhile allies, the Radical Republicans, who had formed a new conception of the Union, one that envisioned not only a slaveless South but a South firmly subordinated to the national authority.

It would be misleading, however, to leave the impression that all southern Unionists found the Radical Republicans undesirable; after the war many of them moved quite easily into the newly founded Republican Party. But it is not quite accurate to speak of southern Republicans as dissenters during Reconstruction. Those years constituted such an unusual (if not unique) period in the history of the region that it is almost impossible to draw valid conclusions about the nature of southern dissent on the basis of the events. It was, after all, a period in which the North dominated the region by force and thereby offered an impetus to dissent that is unique in southern history. Moreover, such interference by the North makes it difficult to know the motives that animated the dissent.

Many southerners became Republicans because they thought the party was "the wave of the future," so to speak, and not because they were dissenters from southern tradition. When the Republican Party failed to catch on as a white man's party in the South, these men soon returned to conformity with their fellow southerners. It is, instead, in the period after Reconstruction, when northern force and influence had been withdrawn, that we can again obtain a clear and unambiguous look at southern dissenters.

III

When Reconstruction ended in 1877, the South was solidly Democratic. In all the southern states Negroes continued to vote, constituting the mainstay of the Republican Party there. Only in North Carolina and Tennessee were there white Republicans worth mentioning. Although this is not the place to examine the causes for the failure of the experiment to build a Republican Party in the South, that failure is germane to another group of southern dissenters that arose in the years after Reconstruction. One of the consequences of the triumph of the "Bourbons" (conservative Democrats) in the southern states was that avenues for new approaches and new ideas were limited. To southerners who wanted to change the South by relieving its poverty, educating its children, and stimulating its industry, the Democratic Party appeared hidebound, stodgy, and conservative in policy, and exclusive and ingrown in leadership. (Indeed, it was because of these characteristics that dissatisfied southerners called the Democratic leaders Bourbons, after the royal house of France, which, upon its restoration after Napoleon's overthrow, was said to have forgotten nothing and learned nothing.)

In the late 1870's anti-Bourbon movements within the Democratic Party erupted in Mississippi, Georgia, North Carolina, and Virginia. Independent candidates ran in both local and Congressional races with some success, but, to defeat the ruling Democrats on a large scale, these anti-Bourbon movements had to win the support of the large, though dwindling, Republican vote. If conditions were right, such a coalition could lick the Bourbons. In no other state, however, did the independents win the kind of success they achieved in Virginia. Other states, it is true, had more obvious advantages than Virginia, such as the large number of Negro voters in Mississippi or the substantial white Republican vote in North Carolina, but Virginia had a leader who could take the inchoate anti-Bourbonism and join it to the Negro vote to shape a program and a party organization. The dissident movement of William Mahone in Virginia during the late 1870's and 1880's therefore engages our attention as a third category of southern dissent.

Superficially, William Mahone was ill suited to the role of leader against great odds; in his dress and his appearance he was the dissenter, not the leader.[19] Only five feet tall and weighing less than one hundred pounds, he looked more like a high-strung gnome than a political chieftain. His voice (like William Lloyd Garrison's) was thin and high-pitched and his oratory was flat and pedestrian. His appearance reflected the carelessness of the stereotypic reformer and included a white, broad-brimmed farmer's hat (which became his hallmark), and a scraggly beard covered his entire chest. Besides these outward eccentricities, Mahone was an outsider in a state where being of the inner circle was the customary first step to political success. Born of poor parents in the black belt of southside Virginia, he owed his education at Virginia Military Institute and his later success in business to his own drive and talent.

During the Civil War Mahone distinguished himself as the audacious leader of the Confederate troops who turned back the Union attack at Petersburg in the dramatic battle of the Crater. At Appomattox, Mahone's division (as he was fond of recalling) was the largest and best equipped in the Army of Northern Virginia, betokening the high morale of his men and his own careful husbanding of the dwindling materiel of the moribund Confederacy. After the war Mahone returned to his prewar activities of railroad construction and promotion. Although an active Democrat, his interest in the party was overshadowed by his efforts to consolidate the railroads of the state and to built up the port of Norfolk, for Mahone was first of all an advocate of a new industrial South.

The issue that shook Mahone out of the traditional political paths of a native white Virginian was the matter of the state debt. In the years immediately after the close of Reconstruction almost all southern states found themselves with large public debts, incurred principally for postwar rehabilitation and railroad construction. Some of the debts were dishonestly or illegally incurred, and all were far in excess of the impoverished states' capacity to pay. Nevertheless, the financially orthodox Bourbon Democrats insisted upon payment in full, even if it meant the neglect of social services and schools, or the imposition of high taxes upon farm land. The more independent-minded Democrats advocated some kind of compromise, which meant, in fact, semi-repudiation, by scaling down the obligations (in Virginia these independents came to be called Readjusters).[20] By 1877 the movement had come to a head in Virginia, with Mahone as its most prominent leader. In 1879 the Readjusters, who still were nominally Democrats, captured the legislature, which thereupon elected Mahone to the United States Senate. In 1881 they obtained their greatest triumph, by electing a governor and a legislature.

Like all the independent movements in the South, the Readjusters began as offshoots of the Democratic Party. In order to win, however, the Readjusters had to enlist Negro support—that is, Republican votes. This was neither easy nor safe, for all Republicans, Negro and white, were suspicious of the motives of erstwhile Democrats; on the other hand, any party that looked to Negro support sullied itself in the eyes of white southerners who might otherwise be attracted to its cause.

Mahone's contribution to the resolution of the dilemmas of the southern dissenter, whether political independent or Republican, was unique. No other southern leader at that time so clearly recognized that economic and social progress in the South required the elevation of the Negro. The Bourbons, for example, wanted a new industrial South, but they gave the Negroes no place in it, except the traditional one of agricultural worker. At a later period, Populists (like Tom Watson and Marion Butler) would accept Negroes as fellow political workers, but they ignored the need for the economic development of the region. Mahone and his Readjusters, then, were dissenters on two grounds: they attempted to overturn both the racial practices of the region and its traditional commitment to agriculture.

In office under Mahone, the Readjusters carried out their promises to scale down the debt, build schools for whites and blacks, and abolish the poll tax (and the whipping post as punishment for felonies). Moreover, in Richmond and elsewhere Negroes received jobs in government offices, that had never been open to them before, as well as a college and a new lunatic asylum. Mahone proudly proclaimed a new era in Virginia for the Negro. In 1882, in a public letter to a group of citizens in Boston, he wrote:

> Virginia has closed the long strife, which Mr. Jefferson foresaw and dreaded as he would dread "the firebell in the night" over the status of the colored man. . . . We are equally gratified with what we are doing for the colored man and what he is doing for himself. He vindicates himself and justifies us in our determined effort for his moral and intellectual advancement. . . . Our purpose is to make the colored man feel his identification with us, and to stimulate in him the feeling of contentment by wise and generous care and consideration that there may be prevented the calamity to the South of a heavy emigration of the colored people.[21]

Education was a concrete measure of the Readjusters' and Mahone's interest in countering the South's traditional attitude toward the Negro. Although neither Mahone nor the Readjusters objected to

segregated education, they sought to reverse the severely discrimina-
tory allocation of funds for Negro schools. In 1886, in response to an
inquiry from Mahone, the state superintendent of instruction reported
that when he took office. in 1882 he found the average white attendance at each school to be 78 pupils while the average Negro attendance was 147. By 1885, he said, "we reduced the discrimination some
and left 73 white to each school and 119 black. I used every effort in
my power to do away with this Godless discrimination—but as you
see with but small success." Bourbons on the local school boards, the
superintendent said, prevented larger gains.[22]

Mahone's efforts to build a biracial political party in Virginia were
successful for four years. In 1883, by raising the cry of Negro domination (in some of the black belt towns, Negroes were on the police
force and sat on governing bodies), the Democrats were able to defeat the Readjusters. Rather than abandon his cause, however, Mahone moved into the Republican Party, to continue his dissent from
the traditional views of his state and the South. Once he had cast his
lot with the Republicans, he never deserted his new party. (In 1884,
after a Democratic victory in the nation as well as in the state, one
of Mahone's followers suggested it might be wise to return to the
Democratic ranks and forget about the Negro. In this way, the friend
suggested, Mahone's reelection to the United States Senate would be
assured. Mahone's response was an unequivocal no and a disclaimer
of any personal political ambition.) [23]

For Mahone, the two chief requirements for a new South—acceptance of the civic equality of the Negro and industrial development—were two sides of the same shield. In 1889, while running for
governor, he told an audience of voters that the cry of "Negro Rule"
was "a mere scare-crow to excite prejudice and fear, in the hope of
diverting the white working man from casting his ballot for the
candidate he honestly prefers." The fact of the matter, he correctly
pointed out, was that the Negro had never sought to rule in Virginia.
Although Negroes constituted a majority in twenty-two legislative
districts, he observed, seventeen of these districts were represented
by white men. "No self-thinking, manly man can be afraid of negro
domination in our affairs," Mahone insisted, "or that his participation
in the selection of the agents of government can in any wise en-
danger our civilization." On the contrary, he asserted that the Negro
was necessary to the welfare of Virginia. "The colored man is here

to stay. He is an essential factor in and to our labor system. He is in great measure the life-giving power to all our industrial pursuits." Mahone made it clear that his vision of the Negro's future was a large one. The Negros' "labor contributes to the wealth of the State," he said, "and the more we enlarge his capabilities and stimulate his efforts the greater will be his contributions. We want here no condition of serfdom, if we would advance our civilization and promote the peace, happiness and prosperity of all." [24]

Mahone hoped to eradicate prejudice against the Negro, which he knew was strong, by education and prosperity; the school and the factory would do the job in time. Poverty and ignorance "on the part of the white laboring people of the South," he argued, constitute "the seat of the prejudice of that class" against the Negroes. Yet the truth is, he continued, that the poor white man had a stake not only in the Negroes' emancipation from slavery but also in "the elevation of that people—the placement of that labor—upon a higher plane." [25]

In economic affairs in the late 1880's, Mahone turned to the protective tariff as a major device for encouraging industrial development in Virginia. He was convinced that such measures would attract capital into the state to develop its natural resources and put its labor to work. Here, too, Mahone stood out against the opinion of his region, which still saw the protective tariff as harmful to its well-being.

As a Republican in the South in the 1880's, Mahone was certainly a dissenter, but—like the southern antislavery and Unionist dissenters we have already looked at—he was quite different from dissenters in the contemporary North. He objected to the majority views of his neighbors, but his objections were really the views of the majority of the nation. Specifically, national policy in the 1880's supported the protective tariff as a means for stimulating economic growth, as did Mahone. And even on the Negro question Mahone—so different from others in the South—was no more radical than the average northern Republican. He made no argument for integrated schools nor even for equality of treatment in politics.

"Our colored people must now realize," Mahone wrote a friend in 1883, "that to preserve their liberties they must let us lead—they must not over burthen us. Predjudices [sic] are still to be consulted. Time will subdue them—but we must be wise not to fight them— even with reason—nothing vs. [against] them avails." [26] All through his public career he feared going too fast on Negro equality. When asked in 1889 what he thought of the rumor that President-elect Harrison would appoint a Negro to the cabinet, Mahone did not conceal his objection to such a possibility. "The time has not come for that," he snorted. "However correct it may be in American citizenship, it is wrong in policy just now. The colored man is entitled to all the rights that properly pertain to him, and I so heartily believe; but his place is not at the extreme front yet." [27] George Washington Cable during the same years, it is true, was even more forthright and radical on Negro rights, as his essays *The Freedman's Case in Equity* and *The Silent South* make clear, but it is significant that he could not—at any rate, did not—remain in the South. Cable's powerful blows against segregation and Negro subordination aroused too much opposition; and with his permanent removal to the North his voice of protest ceased to be southern.

Aside from Mahone's cautious, southern approach to the race question, another aspect of his thought links him with earlier dissenters in the South. Like Hinton Helper and Cassius M. Clay, Mahone desired to change the traditional position of the Negro not from an abstract concern for the Negro but from a very southern, specific, and practical concern for the white man. This does not minimize Mahone's courageous position in behalf of Negro civic equality in a South that refused to concede it, it merely takes cognizance of his truly southern character. In his own time and since, Mahone has been looked upon as a traitor to his region because he espoused Negro equality and the Republican Party, but his actions and words show that he was well within the southern tradition that scorned the utopian or the idealistic and concentrated upon the practical and down-to-earth.

Earlier, contending that slavery was the source of the South's ills, Helper had become a radical critic of the society in order to improve it. Over and over again in *The Impending Crisis of the South* he expressed his conviction that the South must raise itself to equality with the North. The trouble with the South, he wrote, was that it misused the human and material resources it possessed in abundance.

> Instead of cultivating among ourselves a wise policy of mutual assistance and cooperation with respect to individuals, and of self-reliance with respect to the South at large, instead of giving countenance and encouragement to the industrial enterprises projected in

our midst, and instead of building up, aggrandizing and beautifying our own States, cities, and towns, we have been spending our substance at the North, and are daily augmenting and strengthening the very power which now has us so completely under its thumb.

These words could as easily have been written by the great southern pro-slavery advocate J. D. B. De Bow, for the fact is that Helper—aside from his opposition to slavery—was as fervent a southern nationalist as De Bow. Significantly, at the end of his best-known book Helper expressed his goal in almost religious terms: "The time hastens —the doom of slavery is written—the redemption of the South draws nigh." [28]

Much later, Mahone also sought to advance the South into a new industrialized era, modeled after the productive economy of the North. Like Helper and C. M. Clay before him, Mahone wanted to make the South into a land of prosperity rather than poverty, of industry as well as agriculture, of education rather than illiteracy. His concern for the Negro was dictated by his realistic recognition that Negroes constituted a large proportion of the labor force of the South and therefore would have to be included in the political and social affairs of the region. They could not remain hewers of wood and drawers of water if the economy was to develop.

IV

By now it is clear that all three of these southern dissident movements were linked, and sometimes all three were embodied in a single dissenter. Helper, Goodloe, and Cassius M. Clay, for example, were antislavery and pro-Union, and all three of them became Republicans. Alcorn was a Unionist who for a time became a Radical Republican. Mahone had been a Confederate, but in his espousal of industrial development for Virginia and his espousal of the Republican Party he was an intellectual descendant of Helper and C. M. Clay.

These three dissenting movements are interconnected in another way, in that all of them failed to attract a significant number of southern followers. There were, of course, specific reasons for these failures, but a general reason or cause of failure emerges from this examination. Because the South was a minority while its reformers were advocates of the values of the national majority, southern dissenters labored under a double handicap. They not only attacked the status quo but at the same time aligned themselves with the threatening majority. In a South ever conscious of its minority position in the nation, the dissenter suffered not only from his disagreement with his neighbors but also from an added hostility that derived from his espousal of ideas that were congenial to the North. Certainly the antislavery advocates and the Unionists of the South had to bear these burdens before the war, and under such circumstances it is not surprising that many Unionists, however reluctantly, came to support the Confederacy.

In the postwar South, as in the years before the war, merely to be a Republican was to arouse hostility. In 1878, the wife of a southern Republican in North Carolina pleaded with a northern senator to say a word "in defence of the most oppressed people in the United States, the native southern Republican, who since the war have been regarded as pariahs and, with their families have been in all social relations, when possible, entirely proscribed, when not regarded as barely tolerated intruders whom it was a good deed to insult or injure." [29] Another native southern Republican (when turned out of office in Washington in 1885 after the national Democratic victory of the previous year) complained to a fellow southerner that he now had "no state to claim as a home. . . . [It would be] folly to return to my state, Mississippi, to engage in private business, as at the outset I would have to meet that senseless and hence dangerous opposition borne of bigotted and intolerant political prejudice which extends even into home life in the South." [30] Daniel L. Russell, the only Republican governor of North Carolina since Reconstruction, found life almost intolerable simply because he was a Republican. Indeed, during Russell's term in the governor's mansion in the late 1890's, his wife was reduced almost to a state of melancholia as a consequence of the vilification that was heaped upon him.[31] In 1888, when William Mahone asked General James Longstreet, who had become a Republican soon after the war, to come from his native Georgia to speak in behalf of the Republicans in Virginia, Longstreet, with some feeling, gave voice to the trials of being a Republican in the South. Mrs. Longstreet, the general wrote Mahone, "thinks that the bitter feeling engendered against me during this twenty-odd years is quieting down and she dreads to have me give occasion for reopening all the bad feelings of the past. She is more advanced in life now and I find myself less inclined to bring her to new troubles and less disposed to

encounter them myself." Mahone, accepted the refusal with understanding, writing that "the severe cost to which the Confederate is
subjected when he becomes a Republican is not appreciated by those
of the North." [32]

Despite their dissent, the great majority of these critics of the
South exemplified the narrow realism, the "concreteness," the pessimism, and the lack of utopian vision that has long been the hallmark
of the southerner. Even the dissenters of the South, paradoxically, reinforce the view that throughout the nineteenth century the South was
a separate culture, on the edge rather than in the mainstream of the
American experience.

[1] A fourth group, the Populists, has not been included in this essay,
primarily because of lack of space and the large amount of attention it has
already received in scholarly studies. I intend, however, in a book in progress that is devoted to dissent in the nineteenth-century South, to treat them
too. In some ways, as will be evident in this essay, the Populists parallel the
Unionists, for both groups sought to resist particular kinds of changes in the
South. From another perspective, there is a parallel between Populists and
Republicans insofar as the former sought to include the Negro in the political life of the South.

[2] In Joseph C. Robert, *The Road from Monticello* (Durham, N.C.,
1941), pp. 20–21.

[3] *The Impending Crisis of the South: How to Meet It* (New York,
1860), pp. 184–85.

[4] Robert, *The Road from Monticello*, p. 110.

[5] See the essays republished in Horace Greeley, ed., *The Writings of
Cassius Marcellus Clay* (New York, 1848).

[6] In *Address to the People of West Virginia . . . by a Slaveholder of
West Virginia* (Lexington, Va., 1847, Reprinted by the Green Bookman,
Bridgewater, Va., 1933), p. 23.

[7] *Ibid.*, p. 13.

[8] See Launcelot Minor Blackford, *Mine Eyes Have Seen the Glory: The
Story of a Virginia Lady, Mary Berkeley Minor Blackford, 1802–1896, who
taught her sons to hate slavery and to love the Union* (Cambridge, Mass.,
1954).

[9] "A Carolinian" [Daniel Reeves Goodloe], *The South and the North*
(Washington, D.C., 1849), p. 5.

[10] From a manuscript in The Eli Washington Caruthers Papers, Duke
University Library, Durham, N.C., fols. 13–28. It is to be noted, of course,
that Caruthers' history and ethnology, unlike his logic, were faulty.

[11] "The Enigma of the South," *Yale Review*, 51 (Autumn, 1961): 150.

[12] Donald Mathews, *Slavery and Methodism* (Princeton, 1965).

[13] Helper, *The Impending Crisis*, pp. 116, 186.

[14] Charles Phillips to B. S. Hedrick, February 12, 1861, in The B. S. Hedrick Papers, Duke University Library.

[15] See Walter McGehee Lowrey, "The Political Career of James Madison Wells," *Louisiana Historical Quarterly*, 31 (October, 1948): 1009.

[16] See Frank W. Klingberg, *The Southern Claims Commission* (Berkeley, Calif., 1955).

[17] *Ibid.*, p. 194.

[18] *Ibid.*

[19] The standard biography of Mahone is Nelson Blake's *William Mahone of Virginia, Soldier and Political Insurgent* (Richmond, 1935).

[20] The standard study of the movement is C. C. Pearson's *The Readjuster Movement in Virginia* (New Haven, 1917), but it is out of sympathy with the movement and out of date.

[21] From a clipping dated February 11, 1882, probably from the *Richmond Whig*, in Scrapbook 28, The William Mahone Papers, Duke University Library.

[22] From a manuscript in an envelope marked "Virginia Public Schools," Scrapbook 35, The William Mahone Papers.

[23] See Floyd B. Hurt to William Mahone, November 20, 1884, and Mahone's reply, in Letterbook, December 8, 1884, in The William Mahone Papers.

[24] See *Vital Virginia Issues*. Speech delivered at Abingdon, Va., September 23, 1889, University of North Carolina Library.

[25] William Mahone to James M. Swank, October 23, 1886. Letterbook, The William Mahone Papers, Duke University Library.

[26] William Mahone to John Booker, November 17, 1883, in Letterbook, The William Mahone Papers.

[27] From a clipping dated January 18, 1889, probably from the *New York World*, in Scrapbook 39, The William Mahone Papers.

[28] *The Impending Crisis*, pp. 23–24, 413.

[29] In James A. Padgett, ed., "Reconstruction Letters from North Carolina: Part VI Letters to William E. Chandler," *North Carolina Historical Review*, 19 (January, 1942): 94.

[30] Ralph Ballin to Thomas Settle, July 25, 1885 in Thomas Settle Papers, No. 2, Southern Historical Collection, University of North Carolina Library.

[31] See the letter from Russell, quoted in Robert Durden, *Reconstruction Bonds and Twentieth Century Politics* (Durham, N.C., 1962), p. 12. A few weeks after the bloody Wilmington, N.C., riot of 1898, Russell wrote to Benjamin Duke, the brother of James Buchanan Duke, the tobacco king:

"I would not want to resign as Governor until after I get rid of their [Democratic] Legislature. But the irritations incident to being a Republican and living in the South, are getting to be too rank to be borne, and I would not be surprised if they come to you in your proper person, so as to make you hesitate about building that house in Durham, and to cause you to begin to think about living in the civilized North" (Russell to Benjamin N. Duke, December 2, 1898, in The B. N. Duke Papers, Duke University Library.)

[32] James Longstreet to William Mahone, September 8, 1888. Mahone's answer, dated September 21, 1888, is in Mahone's Letterbook, The William Mahone Papers.

Protestantism and the American Labor Movement: The Christian Spirit in the Gilded Age

Herbert G. Gutman

Traditional labor history has not only focused too much on union organizations and leaders but has dealt with workers primarily as "economic factors." In his attempt to get at the "mind of the worker" during the period of rapid industrialization, Herbert Gutman opens a new field for intellectual history. Relying on editorials and especially on letters in the labor press, as well as on the speeches and writings of labor leaders, Gutman draws on the methods of such English scholars as Edward Thompson, Asa Briggs, and Eric Hobsbawm. He finds that "certain strands of pre—Gilded Age Protestantism" sanctioned trade unionism and radical social reform, creating a "working-class social Christianity" that was different from the better-understood middle-class "social gospel."

This essay draws on Gutman's research for a forthcoming comprehensive history of workers from 1860 to 1900, the themes of which have been set forth in a dozen or more articles in recent years. His book, tentatively titled *The Shock of Industrialization*, deals with social stratification, political power, and the subculture of the worker. Gutman, who received his doctorate from the University of Wisconsin, is Associate Editor of *Labor History*. Before he joined the faculty at the University of Rochester he taught history at the State University of New York at Buffalo.

This essay appeared originally in *American Historical Review*, vol. 62: No. 1 (October, 1966), 74–101, and is reprinted with the permission of the American Historical Association and the author. © 1966 by Herbert Gutman.

Labor historians and others have puzzled over precisely how and why American workers, especially those critical of the new industrial order, reacted to the profound changes in the nation's social and economic structure and in their own particular status between 1850 and 1900, but in seeking explanations they have studied almost exclusively working-class behavior and trade-union organization and have neatly catalogued the interminable wranglings between "business" unionists, "utopian" dreamers, and "socialist" radicals. Although their works have uncovered much of value, the "mind" of the worker—the modes of thought and perception through which he confronted the industrialization process and which helped shape his behavior—has received scant and inadequate attention. American workers, immigrant and native-born alike, brought more than their "labor" to the factory and did not view their changing circumstances in simple "economic" terms. So narrow an emphasis ignores the complexity of their lives and experiences and, in general, distorts human behavior. "Events, facts, data, happenings," J. L. Talmon reminds us, "assume their significance from the way in which they are experienced." [1] These pages examine one of several important but overlooked influences on the disaffected worker's thought: the way certain strands of pre-Gilded Age Protestantism affected him in a time of rapid industrialization and radical social change.

Before 1850 relatively few Americans had direct contact with an industrial *society*, but after that date rapid industrialization altered the social structure, and the process left few untouched. Depending upon circumstance, these social changes meant more or less opportunity for workers, but nearly all felt greater dependence and profoundly different patterns of work discipline. In addition, urbanization and immigration changed the structure and composition of the working class and affected its style of life. In ways that have not yet been adequately explored, class and status relationships took on new meaning, too.[2] And a new ideology that sanctioned industrial laissez faire emerged because, as Ralph Gabriel has perceptively written, "the mores of a simpler agricultural and commercial era did not fit the conditions of an age characterized by the swift accumulation of industrial power."[3] The era found much "truth" in the frequent judgments of the Chicago *Times* that "the inexorable law of God" meant that "the man who lays up not for the morrow perishes on the morrow," that "political economy" was "in reality the autocrat of the age" and occupied "the position once held by the Caesars and the Popes," and that cheapened production counted for so much that men did not inquire "when looking at a piece of lace whether the woman who wove it is a saint or a courtesan."[4]

Legal and political theory, academic economics, amoral "social science," and institutional Protestantism emphasized that in industrial America interference with the entrepreneur's freedom violated "divine" or "scientific" laws, and historians have given much attention to the many ways Gilded Age social thought bolstered the virtues of "Acquisitive Man."[5] Two seemingly contradictory ideas especially sanctioned industrial laissez faire. Related to the decline of traditional religious sanctions and the growing importance of secular institutions and values, the first insisted that no connection existed between economic behavior and moral conduct. Gilded Age business practices, Edward C. Kirkland has argued, cannot be understood without realizing that for most entrepreneurs "economic activity stood apart from the sphere of moral and personal considerations."[6] Much contemporary evidence supports this view.[7] The second concept, identified with traditional Calvinist doctrine, reinforced the business ethic by equating poverty and failure with sin.[8] Evidence gathered primarily from national denominational weekly and monthly periodicals, together with a Gilded Age premillennial evangelism (typified by the popular Dwight Moody) that insisted that "until Christ returned none of the basic problems of the world could be solved," convinces its historians that the Protestant denominations and their leaders mostly "lost their sense of estrangement from society" and "began . . . to bless and defend it in a jargon strangely compounded out of the language of traditional Christian theology, common-sense philosophy, and *laissez-faire* economics." [9] Henry May, Aaron Abell, and Charles Hopkins have shown that a small but quite influential group of Protestant clergymen and lay thinkers broke free from institutional Protestantism's social conservatism and traveled a difficult route in pioneering the social gospel,[10] but in the main Gilded Age Protestantism is viewed as a conformist, "culture-bound" Christianity that warmly embraced the rising industrialist, drained the aspiring rich of conscience, and confused or pacified the poor. The writings of an articulate minority suggest to historians that the wealthy busied themselves memorizing Herbert Spencer's aphorisms and purchasing expensive church pews, that the middle classes chased wealth and cheered Horatio Alger, and that the wage earners, busy laboring, found little time to ponder existential questions and felt separated from institutional Protestantism. Workers wandered from the fold, and the churches lost touch with the laboring classes.

Accurate in describing certain themes characteristic of Gilded Age social and religious thought, this view nevertheless tells little about the relationship between Protestantism and the working class because the many functions of religion, particularly its effects on the lower classes, cannot be learned by analyzing what leading clergymen said and what social philosophy religious journals professed. Unless one first studies the varieties of working-class community life, the social and economic structure that gave them shape, their voluntary associations (including churches, benevolent and fraternal societies, and trade unions), their connections to the larger community, and their particular and shared values, one is likely to be confused about the relationship between the worker, institutional religion, and religious beliefs and sentiments.[11] It is suggested, for example, that a close tie between laissez faire and Gilded Age Protestantism developed partly because the post Civil War "burst of technological and industrial expansion . . . created unbridled cheerfulness, confidence, and complacency among the American people" and because "the observational order coincided in a high degree with the conceptual order and . . . such coincidence defines social stability." [12] Such was probably the case for successful entrepreneurs and many lesser folk who benefited from rapid industrialization and the era's massive material gains, but the same cannot be inferred for those whose traditional skills became obsolete, who felt economic dependence for the first time, who knew recurrent seasonal and cyclical unemployment, and who suffered severe family and social disorganization in moving from farm and town to city and in adapting to industrial and urban priorities and work discipline patterns different from traditional norms. Day-to-day experiences for many such persons ("the observational order") did not entirely coincide with the religious and secular ideas and values ("the conceptual order") they carried with them from the immediate past. Some withdrew from the tensions stirred by such conflict, and others changed their beliefs. Many found in Gilded Age Protestantism reason to cheer material progress or comfort in premillennial evangelism. But some, especially trade unionists and labor reformers and radicals, discovered that preindustrial ideology heightened rather than obliterated the moral dilemmas of a new social order and that the Protestantism of an earlier America offered a religious sanction for *their* discontent with industrial laissez faire and "Acquisitive Man." A preindustrial social order had nurtured particular religious beliefs that did not disappear with the coming of industrialism and did not easily or quickly conform to the Protestantism of a Henry Ward Beecher or a Dwight Moody and the secular optimism of an Andrew Carnegie or a Horatio Alger. The material conditions of life changed radically for these workers after 1850, but not the world of their mind and spirit. They saw the nation transformed, but were not themselves abruptly alienated from the past. Older traditions and modes of thought (religious and secular in origin) did not succumb easily to the imperatives of a disorganized industrial society, but, depending upon particular circumstances, often clung tenaciously and even deepened tensions generally characteristic of an early industrializing society.

The recent perspective emphasized by British historians of early industrial England helps clarify the particular relationship between Protestantism and Gilded Age labor reform. "In order to understand how people respond to industrial change," Asa Briggs has written, "it is necessary to examine fully what kind of people they were at the beginning of the process, to take account of continuities and traditions as well as new ways of thinking and feeling." [13] Edward P. Thompson has gathered and organized a mass of data in *The Making of the English Working Class* to argue persuasively that the English working class was not "the spontaneous generation of the factory-system" and that the early social history of industrial England was more than "an external force—the 'industrial revolution'—working upon some nondescript undifferentiated raw material of humanity." [14] Applied to the United States, this general point is quite simple although its particular American characteristics demand a level of conceptualization and a method of research not yet typical of "labor history." Protestantism in its many and even contradictory forms, but particularly the Christian perfectionism of pre-Civil War evangelical and reform movements, lingered on among many discontented *post bellum* workers.[15] It was no different in the United States than in Great Britain, where labor and religious historians have documented the close relationship between Protestant Nonconformity, especially Methodism, and labor reform.[16] None of this should surprise students of social movements. "The bulk of industrial workers in all countries," Eric Hobsbawm notes, "began . . . as first-generation immigrants from preindustrial society . . . and, like all first-generation immigrants, they looked backwards as much as forwards." The new industrial world "had no pattern of life suited to the new age," and so men and women often "drew on the only spiritual resources at their disposal, preindustrial custom and religion." [17]

An additional point stressed in Thompson's recent work offers insight into the Gilded Age labor reformer. "Behind every form of popular direct action," Thompson notes, "some legitimising notion of right is to be found." [18] Thus Boston labor leader and editor Frank K. Foster insisted in 1888: "The dry names and dates furnish but a small part of the history of the labor movement. To understand its real meaning one must comprehend the spirit animating it." [19] Leaders and followers of social movements that challenge an established order or question the direction of a rapidly changing society (such as the United States after the Civil War) are usually "animated" by a "spirit" that sanctions and legitimizes the particular alternative they espouse. It is not enough for them merely to criticize and to offer alternatives. This is the case whether they advocate trade unions in a society hostile to collective activity or urge even more thorough and fundamental social reorganization. They must *feel* that what they propose is justified by values that transcend the particular social order they criticize. For this reason, they often crudely reinterpret the historical past. They either project "new" values or, as is more frequently the case, reinterpret vague and broadly shared national values to sanction their behavior. Then, they can argue that their critique of the dominant order and its ideology is "consistent with very basic values." [20] Such was the case with the generation of trade unionists, labor reformers, and labor radicals who felt the transition from a preindustrial to an industrial society and who bore the social, economic, and psychological brunt of the American industrializing process after 1860.

Two broadly shared preindustrial national traditions especially offered the discontented nineteenth-century American worker a transcendent and sanctioning "notion of right." The first—the republican political tradition— is beyond the scope of these pages. The second was traditional American Protestantism. Frank Foster could explain in 1887: "John on Patmos, Jack Cade at the head of the populace, . . . Krapotine indicting Russian imperialism, the rising wrath of American Democracy—these are all of kinship." Commenting on the American labor movement, Foster went on:

> The "cross of the new crusade" is the cross of an old crusade, old as the passions of the human heart. An idea may take different forms of expression and its ethical purport may be the same, and in whatever direction men may strive for this ambiguous thing we call social reform, if they mean anything at all, they but echo—be they Jew or Gentile, Greek or Christian, Deist or Atheist, Knight of Labor or Socialist—that carol of welcome which was sung to greet the coming of the Carpenter's Son in the centuries long gone by, "peace on earth, good will to men."

"Looking afar off, over the broad ocean of time and space," the Boston editor concluded, " we have faith, like St. Simon at death's door, [we] may exclaim, 'The future is ours.'" [21] Similarly, the *Union Pacific Employees Magazine* comforted fearful trade unionists by reminding them that after the Crucifixion "the rabble rejoiced." "Time," this journal insisted in explaining the difficulties encountered by trade union advocates, "corrects errors. . . . The minority continue to urge their views until they become the majority or the fallacy of them be proven. Advance is made only thus. Time must be had to prepare the way for every step." [22] In another connection, the American Railway Union's *Railway Times* called "sublime idiocy . . . the idea that workingmen of the present, or of any other century, were the first to call attention to the rapacity of the rich." Instead, "the arraignment of the rich by God Himself and His Son, the Redeemer, set the pace for all coming generations of men who would be free from the crushing domination of wealth." Labor's complaints had "the unequivocal indorsement of the Holy Writ." [23] Here, then, was a religious faith that justified labor organization and agitation, encouraged workers to challenge industrial power, and compelled criticism of "natural" economic laws, the crude optimism of social Darwinism, and even the conformist Christianity of most respectable clergymen.

Protestantism affected the American working class in many ways, and a brief article cannot encompass its varied manifestations, but it is possible to indicate some of them.

A subordinate but distinct theme drew from pessimistic premillennialism the apocalyptic tradition that prophesied doom and imminent catastrophe before "redemption." In a period of rapid, unpredictable social and economic change, change itself meant decay and destruction to some. For them, the Christian prophetic tradition did not buoy up the spirit and command reform, but stimulated withdrawal. A Massachusetts ship joiner predicted destructive world-wide war as the result of "the sin of the people, 'covetousness.' " [24] A regular *Coast Seaman's Journal* columnist more than once made the same point.[25] Readers of the Denver *Labor Enquirer* learned from several sermons by Mrs. P. C. Munger of "The World's Final Crisis." She urged violence to speed the end of an evil social order and praised dynamite as a "blessing" from God:

> Socially, the ruling world is a dead leper. In the name of God and man bury it deep in the earth it has corrupted. . . . Dynamite in its line is the last scientific fruit of the Holy Ghost. . . . It is in every way worthy of the giver—God. . . . I thank, I praise, I bless God for dynamite. It is the blast of Gabriel's trumpet. . . . It does the deeds of God. . . . Its fruits are peace, love, joy, goodness, gentleness, meekness, and truth displayed in decent life and government. Is not this boon of heaven worth a blow; worth a blast on the trumpet of doom? . . . Dynamite is a weapon to win; a weapon to conquer; a weapon to kill. It is your only one. God Himself allows you no other; use it or tamely submit and sign your death warrant.[26]

Such violent and apparent psychotic anguish, however, was not typical of even the most extreme premillenarian visionaries. More characteristic was the complaint of an Indiana coal miner's wife who believed that "according to history" a "visitation" took place every two thousand years and quietly complained, "I have heard my mother talk about her girlhood days and how good and religious people were." The world had changed for the worse. "It is no wonder," she feared, "that God sends His voice in thunder through the air as wicked as this world stands to-day. . . . We are living in a land where shadows are continually falling in our pathway." [27] The extraordinary psychological strains of early industrialism thus found expression in the rejection of the secular order and the acceptance of a Protestantism of doom, despair, and destruction.[28]

More widespread than these premillennial prophecies was a postmillennial Christian justification of trade unionism and even more radical social reform. Conservative trade unionists and radical anarchists and socialists (except for the zealous followers of Daniel De Leon) often appealed to Christianity for its sanction. A pre-Civil War utopian and afterward a Knight of Labor and builder of cooperatives, John Orvis claimed "the labor question" was "here in the Providence of Almighty God" and meant "the deliverance, exaltation, and ennobling of labor and the laboring classes to the first rank." [29] Conservative craft unionist and president of the Amalgamated Association of Iron, Steel, and Tin Workers, John Jarrett told a gathering of clergymen that "the climax of the mission of the Savior, beyond a question, . . . is that He came here so that the gospel would be preached to the poor." [30] After being sentenced to death in the aftermath of the Haymarket affair, German immigrant anarchist August Spies linked his beliefs to Thomas Münzer. "He," Spies said of Münzer, "interpreted the Gospel, saying that it did not merely promise blessings in heaven, but that it also commanded equality and brotherhood among men on earth." Spies insisted that "the spirit of the Reformation was the 'eternal spirit of the chainless mind,' and nothing could stay its progress." [31] This sentiment—radical criticism and labor discontent sanctioned by an appeal to Christian tradition—did not diminish by the end of the nineteenth century and remained as common in the 1890's as in the 1860's. No apparent connection existed between a particular brand of labor reform and Christianity; all shared in it.

Prophetic Protestantism offered labor leaders and their followers a transhistoric framework to challenge the new industrialism and a

common set of moral imperatives to measure their rage against and
to order their dissatisfactions. The intensity of religious commitment
varied among individuals: it depended upon particular life experiences, and its sources drew from the many strands that made up the
web of Protestant tradition. But the influence of the Christian perfectionism and postmillennialism identified with Charles G. Finney
and other pre-Civil War and preindustrial evangelical revivalists
seems predominant.[32] Even this tradition, which emphasized God's redemptive love and benevolence and insisted that "progress, in all its
forms, was divinely directed toward the perfection of the world,"
took many forms.[33] A few examples suffice. In the 1860's, William
Sylvis, that decade's most prominent trade unionist, pitted the God
of Christian perfectionism against Malthusian doctrine and asked: "Is
it not reasonable, is it not Christian, to suppose that the all-wise Being who placed us here, and whose attributes are benevolence and
love, could find other means of controlling population than by war,
famine, pestilence, and crime in all its forms?"[34] More than thirty
years later, George E. Ward hailed the coming of the American Railway Union by arguing that "God is infinite and eternal justice," so
that "he who strives to promote and establish justice upon earth is a
co-worker with God." It followed that union men were "the rapidly-
evolving God-men—the *genus homo* vivified by the eternal truths and
energizing principles of the gospel of Christ."[35] Another perfectionist
strain, more "emotional," told of man's "sin," but was nevertheless
distinctly postmillennial. Celebrating Thanksgiving, a midwestern
worker assured the Chicago *Knights of Labor*:

> God has given the earth to the children of men; that a few have
> stolen it all and disinherited the masses, is no fault of God's, but
> the wickedness of man. . . . We could not know the wickedness
> of man, could we not see the goodness of God. . . . It is perfectly
> safe to pray for His kingdom to come, and in that prayer you
> anathematize the present system as bitterly as words could do it.[36]

"Pumpkin Smasher," a Newcomb, Tennessee, coal miner, typified extreme labor evangelism:

> Labor has made this country into a bed of roses so that a few may
> lie therein, and bask in the beautiful God-given sunshine, while the
> laborer or the creator of all this splendor is roaming in rags all

tattered and torn. . . . Cheer up, my brothers, the longest night
comes to an end. It may end by an honest use of the ballot box,
but as that can never be until the great and glorious millennium
with all its attendant beauties set in, brothers we need not look
for deliverance through the medium of the ballot box. But it will
come just the same. It may come like it did to the Israelitish serfs
from down yonder in Egypt, or it may come like it did in France
in those long days of rebellion. Or, my brothers, it may come as it
did to the colored slaves of the South by sword and fire. Let us be
ready to eat the Paschal lamb at any moment the trumpet sounds.[37]

Even the more "conservative" *American Federationist* found room for
labor evangelism. A contributor to the American Federation of Labor's official journal asked for nothing less than "a living Christ moving, living, breathing and dominant in the hearts of a people, not a
dead Christianity, dreaming of a dead Christ, but live Christians as
live Christs, scattering the table of the money changers in the tem-
ples, . . . going down in the poverty-stricken alleys of the robbed
industrial slaves, and raising up its victims." This Christianity he
called *"the real article!"* [38]

Not surprisingly, the labor evangels found the most essential characteristics of the rapidly developing new industrial social order un-
Christian and violative of God's will. As early as the 1860's "Uncle
Sam" told readers of *Fincher's Trades Review* that "the present system of labor . . . is a system begotten by the *evil one, hell-born*," and
that it "warred against the heaven-born creation, the system instituted
by *God* for the good of man." [39] And the Boston *Daily Evening Voice*
justified a living wage and condemned the maldistribution of wealth
by appealing to God: "It is because He has made of one blood all
men—because all are brethren—that the differences instituted by men
—the chief of which is the money difference— are so morally disastrous as they are. . . . The elevation of a false god dethrones the real
one." [40]

Self-protection and trade unionism especially enjoyed the blessings of God. A Louisville cigar maker argued: "The toilers are coming out of darkness into light and . . . have dared to organize, to
come in closer touch with our Lord's will and the teachings of Jesus
Christ." He prophesied: "The time is not far distant when the wage
earners shall stand on the rock of independence and sing, 'Nearer, My

God, to Thee.' We need not fire and sword, but [to] organize, union-
ize." [41] During the bitter bituminous coal strike of 1897 the *United
Mine Workers' Journal* editorialized: "Blessed are the union men.
They are the salt of the earth which keeps uncontaminated the pure
principles of brotherhood in the breast of their fellow toilers, and
which, if allowed to die, would make us doubt the fatherhood of
God." [42] Biblical "history" served well J. A. Crawford, Illinois district
president of the United Mine Workers, as he preached the divinity of
unions:

> The first labor organization mentioned in history, either profane or
> divine, was the one founded just outside of the historic Garden of
> Eden, by God Himself; the charter members being Adam and Eve.
> . . . Noah's campaign among the Antediluvians favorably reminds
> us of the organizing campaigns of the United Mine Workers. . . .
> The third attempt at organizing labor was made by the authority
> of Jehovah, instituted and carried to a successful termination by
> "The Walking Delegates," Moses and Aaron, for the purpose of re-
> deeming Israel from Egyptian task-masters. . . . The next labor
> movement of importance recorded in sacred history begins with the
> beginning of the ministry of the "Nazarene," opposed to all forms
> of oppression of the poor and antagonistic to the operation of "Wall
> street" in the house of His Father, the sanctuary of worship. . . .
> Choose you this day whom you shall serve. If plutocracy be God,
> serve it; if God be God, serve Him.[43]

A *Railway Times* writer summed it up by insisting that "so-called 'labor agitators,' who are such, *not* for the love of money, but for the
love of humanity, are true followers of Christ and are striving to establish upon earth the kingdom of God, for which disciples are taught
to pray." [44] Labor organizers had only to push ahead. "Brother
Knights," a fellow unionist advised, "allow me to say that Moses, while
fleeing from bondage and endeavoring to deliver his people from the
hands of the Egyptian destroyer, received the imperative command
from God, to 'go forward.' The same injunction still comes to us, 'go
forward.' " [45]

The historic and divine person of Jesus Christ loomed large in the
rhetoric and imagery of labor leaders. He served as a model to emulate, a symbol to inspire. An Illinois coal miner later elected to the
state assembly admiringly described trade unionist Richard Trevel-

lick: "While not a preacher of Jesus and Him crucified, yet he was one of His most exemplary followers. . . . My wife thought Dick Trevellick the second Jesus Christ." [46] Much was made of the argument that "the Saviour Himself" had associated "with common fishermen and carpenters." [47] A West Coast seaman reminded his brothers that "Peter and James and John, . . . three sailors, were the chosen of our Saviour." [48] The *Railway Times* called Jesus "an agitator such as the world has never seen before nor since, . . . despised and finally murdered to appease the wrath of the ruling class of His time." [49] William Mahon, the international president of the motorman's union, lectured the Businessman's Bible Class of the Detroit First Congregational Church that Christ was "crucified for disturbing the national order of things . . . [by] the conservative goody good people, whose plans Jesus spoilt." The businessmen learned that the speaker belonged to "the organizations . . . fighting for the very principles laid down by Jesus Christ." [50] The *Coast Seaman's Journal* explained Christ's death:

> Christ taught that all men had souls and were therefore equal in the finality of things. For that He was put to death. But it was not for preaching the doctrine of a common equality before God that the Saviour suffered. The Powers have never objected to changing the conditions and relations of the future: it is the conditions and relations of today they object to altering. Christ was crucified because the doctrine of common equality hereafter, which He preached, led inevitably to the doctrine of common equality now. This is the essence of Christ's teaching.[51]

Christ in an industrializing America would suffer as a labor leader or even a "tramp" suffered. "Had Christ lived in Connecticut, he would have been imprisoned for asking for a cup of water," the Washington *Craftsman* believed.[52]

If Gilded Age businessmen make sense only when it is realized that for them "economic activity stood apart from moral considerations," the opposite is true for most Gilded Age labor leaders. Protestantism helped many of them restore what Oscar Handlin calls "the sense of human solidarity infused with religious values." [53] Prominent Gilded Age trade unionists, labor reformers, and even radicals—with the notable exception of Samuel Gompers and De Leon—shared a common faith in a just God, effused perfectionist doctrine, and warned of divine retribution against continuing injustice.[54] They often condemned the insensitivity of institutional Protestantism to the suffering brought about by rapid industrialization, but their speeches and writings also made frequent allusion to essential religious "truths" that gave meaning to their lives and that sanctioned organized opposition to the new industrialism.[55] Trade unionists and reformers from Catholic backgrounds, such as Joseph P. McDonnell, who had studied for the priesthood, and Terence V. Powderly, frequently quoted the Sermon on the Mount.[56] Important trade unionists and labor radicals reared as Protestants did the same. Sylvis found no contradiction between his sympathies for the First International and his belief that the worker's "task" was "to found the universal family—to build up the City of God" through trade unions which Sylvis called an "association of souls" formed by "the sons of God." America's distinctiveness rested, for Sylvis, on "God's ordained equality of man . . . recognized in the laws and institutions of *our* country." [57] Early trained for the Baptist ministry, Knights of Labor founder Uriah Stephens called excessive hours of work "an artificial and man-made condition, not God's arrangement and order," and insisted the Knights build upon "the immutable basis of the Fatherhood of God and the logical principle of the Brotherhood of Man." Labor organizations had come "as messiahs have ever come, when the world was ready for them." The Knights brought workers together in local assemblies:

> The tabernacle—the dwelling-place of God—is among men. No longer shall men pine for justice, or perish for lack of judgment. "'And He will dwell with them, and they shall be His people." "God and Humanity." How inseparably connected! God, the Universal Father; Man, the Universal Brother! [58]

Trevellick found in God reason to ennoble human labor and asked: "Is He less because His mechanical hand formed the mountains? . . . No fellow toilers; He is not less because He worked; neither are you." [59] Eugene V. Debs bristled with Christian indignation at human suffering and cannot be understood outside that framework. From his prison cell after the Pullman debacle, Debs publicly celebrated Labor Day by declaring that it "would stand first in Labor's Millennium, that prophesied era when Christ shall begin in reign on the earth to continue a thousand years." [60] He compared his jailing with Daniel's treatment by the Persians.[61] Released from Woodstock jail, Debs told an admiring Chicago throng, in an oration punctuated with religious images and analogies:

> Liberty is not a word of modern coinage. Liberty and slavery are primal words, like good and evil, right and wrong; they are opposites and coexistant. There has been no liberty in the world since the gift, like sunshine and rain, came down from heaven, for the maintenance of which man has not been required to fight. . . . Is it worth [while?] to reiterate that all men are created free and that slavery and bondage are in contravention of the Creator's decree and have their origin in man's depravity?

Courts, such as the Supreme Court, had been "antagonizing the decrees of heaven since the day when Lucifer was cast into the bottomless pit." "God Himself had taught His lightning, thunderbolts, winds, waves, and earthquakes to strike," and men, too, would strike, "with bullets or ballots," until they walked "the earth free men." "Angels" had "transplanted sympathy," one of the "perennial flowers of the Celestial City" and the mainspring of human compassion for Debs, "in Eden for the happiness of Adam and Eve," and then "the winds had scattered the seed throughout the earth." Without sympathy, Debs concluded, there could be "no humanity, no elevating, refining, ennobling influences." [62]

The most eloquent Gilded Age labor reformer, George E. McNeill, was an abolitionist turned staunch American Federation of Labor trade unionist and Christian socialist. He was also an essential link between preindustrial American reform and the Gilded Age labor movement. McNeill rarely spoke or wrote without imparting a deep Christian fervor.[63] In 1876 he complained in the socialist *Labor Standard*: "It is the old, old story. . . . Have the Pharaoh's descendants nothing to learn from Pharaoh's fate?" [64] At a meeting eleven years later to condemn the hanging of Albert Parsons, McNeill announced: "I believe in the passive force of non-resistance as 'Him of old.' . . . I come here tonight as a Christian." [65] In 1890 he once again tied labor reform to Christian ethics:

> The Pilgrim leaven still works, true to the fundamental principles of the great Leader of men. . . . The influence of the teachings of the Carpenter's Son still tends to counteract the influence of Mammon. In this movement of the laborers toward equity, we will find

a new revelation of the Old Gospel, when the Golden Rule of Christ shall measure the relations of men in all their duties toward their fellows. . . . Though the Mammon-worshippers may cry, "Crucify Him! Crucify Him!", the promise of the prophet and the poet shall be fulfilled . . . by the free acceptance of the Gospel that all men are of one blood. Then the new Pentecost will come, when every man shall have according to his needs.[66]

Three years later, McNeill found "the religious life" of the labor movement nothing less than "a protest against the mammonizing interpretation of religious truth." He wanted "the kingdom of Heaven (of equity and righteousness) to come on earth," but, more importantly, argued that "religious truth," adapted to the realities of industrial society, had meaning for his America. "A new interpretation of the old truth, 'That the chief end of man is to glorify God and to enjoy him forever,' reads that the glorification of God is the reinstatement of man in the likeness of God; that to enjoy God forever all things must be directed toward the securing for all the largest measure of happiness." [67] McNeill never changed. In 1902, sixty-five years old, he reaffirmed his continued faith in the supremacy of "moral power," but nevertheless warned: "Submission is good, but the order of God may light the torch of Revolution." [68]

Evangelical Protestantism that emphasized the possibility of perfect holiness in this world found expression among trade unionists of less importance than McNeill and other national leaders. Negro activists in the early United Mine Workers of America (1890–1900) reveal such an influence.[69] A preacher and coal miner, William Riley won election in 1892 as secretary-treasurer of the Tennessee district and importuned fellow Negroes to join the union:

> Continue to battle on for the right, seek wisdom and be wise, act honest men and by so doing both white and colored men will love to respect you, and God Himself will bless you. . . . Yes, my people, wake up and ask yourselves these questions: How long am I to live in ignorance? How long am I to be a pullback to my race? How long am I to be a stumbling block for the cause of labor, justice, and humanity? Say as the prodigal did: I will arise and join the labor unions and rally for its [sic] rights, defend its cause and be known among my own craftsmen as a man among men.[70]

The tensions between an active, just God and the day-to-day realities of a Negro coal miner's life strained William E. Clark, a Rendville, Ohio, miner. He reported:

> My mind has wandered from world to world. My first wonder was, I wonder if the other worlds were inhabited? Did they have the same kind of law and government that we have? And my next wonder was, was this world of ours the hell we read about in the good book? If it is not, how can a man stand the punishment twice, and then live through eternity? They burn men alive, skin them, lynch them, shoot them, and torture them." [71]

The most important early UMW Negro leader, Richard L. Davis, elected to the National Executive Board in 1896 and 1897, penned many letters that suggested the influence of evangelical imperatives. He found in the union a secular church that promised redemption from an evil social order. He gave to his work the zeal and devotion expected of a dedicated missionary. Miners who threatened to quit the UMW heard from him the words of Paul in the New Testament: "Except those abide in the ship, ye cannot be saved." Preachers designated the ship as "a church," but Davis called the UMW "the ship" and insisted: "I now exhort you that except ye abide in the ship ye cannot be saved." A common religious rhetoric helped Davis war against factionalism. He denied the charge of fellow Negroes who called the UMW "a white man's organization" and told them: "You yourselves are men and . . . have the same interest at stake as your white brother, because . . . I believe in the principle of the fatherhood of God and the brotherhood of all mankind no matter what the color of his [sic] skin may be." Davis' evangelical fervor was not otherworldly. "I know," he addressed these same Negroes, "that in former days you used to sing 'Give me Jesus, give me Jesus, you may have all the world, just give me Jesus.' But the day has now come that we want a little money along with our Jesus, so we want to change that old song and ask for a little of the world as well." Urging compact labor organization, Davis argued that "we are taught by teachings of the Holy Writ that in unity there is strength." The acquittal of a Pennsylvania sheriff involved in the shooting of several Polish anthracite miners in 1898 caused Davis to lament: "It is as we expected. . . . The miner has no rights that the coal barons are bound to respect. Surely, oh Heaven, this condition of things will not last forever." [72]

Just as Christianity motivated so many labor leaders who organized the reaction against the radical transition from preindustrial to industrial America, so, too, did it serve to condemn particular aspects of that new society and its ideology. A few examples illustrate. The *United Mine Workers' Journal* felt that legal convict-leasing of coal miners proved "the laws of Tennessee . . . in conflict with Christianity, civilization and government." [73] Exploitative child factory labor caused the Chicago *Knights of Labor* to explode: "When Jesus said, 'Suffer little children to come unto me,' He did not have a shirt or cloak factory, nor a planing mill, that He wanted to put them into at forty cents per day. He wanted to bless them and show them the light." [74] The San Francisco Manufacturers' and Employers' Association defense of "free contract" led Andrew Furuseth, secretary of the Sailors' Union of the Pacific, to exclaim indignantly: "If the present system be right, then Christianity is a lie; if the present system be right, then Robert Ingersoll is not a censer-boy in the Temple of Mammon, but the prophet of a new dispensation." [75] Critics of Labor Day learned that "Labor Day is one of the signs of the millennium." [76]

Those who saw in Christianity justification for industrial laissez faire especially felt the sting of labor critics. The *Locomotive Firemen's Magazine* declared the "theory" that "God assigns anyone a station in life . . . preposterous, repulsive, and degrading to God and man." [77] Men who argued that "labor, like flour or cotton cloth, should always be bought in the cheapest market" did so because "an All-wise God, for some inscrutable purpose, has created them" so that workers could see "to what viciousness the antagonism to labor has arrived" and then "beat back to its native hell the theory that . . . laborers . . . are merchandise to be bought and sold as any other commodity—as cattle, mules, swine.[78] Clergymen who upheld the competitive system learned: "The church which allows the competitive system of each for himself, without a never-silent protest, is not a living Christian church; for 'each for himself' is a gospel of lies. That never was God's decree." [79] And the argument that poverty enjoyed God's blessings met the retort: "Do you think it is anything short of insulting to God to pretend to believe He makes of ninety-nine paving material for the one to walk into Heaven over?" [80] Paul's directive to Titus to "obey magistrates" was rejected. If followed "by the patriots of '76," explained the *Locomotive Firemen's Magazine*, "a new nation would not have been born." [81]

Christian example and religious exaltation proved especially important in times of severe discontent and defeat and in challenging dominant Gilded Age "myths." Two examples suffice. After the Pullman strike and boycott and Debs' imprisonment, a Portland, Oregon, railroad worker drew inferences and analogies only from sacred history:

> Were Moses now living, and the Almighty should send him to a General Manager's office to protest against corporation robberies, he would be forthwith arrested and thrown into jail, and if Moses should appeal to the Supreme Court, the infamous proceedings would be sustained and declared constitutional; and therefore, the way I look at it, the corporation slaves of the United States are in a worse condition than were the slaves of Pharaoh. But in the case of Pharaoh, God put a curse upon him. The corporation Pharaohs are not to have their way always. There may be a Red Sea just ahead—but beyond it is the promised land.
>
> Egypt had only one Pharaoh at a time on the throne. Here we have probably a hundred of the abnormal monsters, all engaged in enslaving working people. . . . The Egyptian Pharaoh did not send Moses to prison. . . . He could have done it. He had absolute power. He was a despot with a big D. . . . Here a labor leader is condemned and thrown into prison by a decree of one small contemptible Pharaoh at the suggestion of a General Manager Pharaoh . . . and there is no appeal except to the Buzzards Bay Pharaoh [Grover Cleveland's Summer White House was on Buzzard Bay], which would be like appealing from a pig-stealing coyote to a grizzly bear.[82]

The second example concerns Andrew Carnegie and his belief in the "Gospel of Wealth," the notion of "stewardship." At the time of its enunciation, the *Locomotive Firemen's Magazine* scorned the "Gospel of Wealth" as "flapdoodle" and "slush." Of Carnegie, it said: "While asserting that the ' "Gospel of Wealth" but echoes Christ's words,' [he] endeavors to wriggle out of the tight place in which Christ's words place him." It required "patience" to read about "the 'right modes of using immense fortunes' known to be the product of cool,

Christless robbery." [83] The Homestead conflict in 1892 caused the same journal to call Carnegie and Henry Clay Frick "brazen pirates [who] prate . . . of the 'spirit of Christ' [and] who plunder labor that they may build churches, endow universities and found libraries." [84] In 1894 the conservative *National Labor Tribune* joined in mocking Carnegie's professions:

> Oh, Almighty Andrew Philanthropist Library Carnegie, who are in America when not in Europe spending the money of your slaves and serfs, thou are a good father to the people of Pittsburgh, Homestead and Beaver Falls. . . . Oh, most adorable Carnegie, we love thee, because thou are the almighty iron and steel king of the world; thou who so much resembles the pharisee. . . . We thank thee and thy combines for the hungry men, women and children of the land. We thank thee and thy combines for the low price of iron and steel and the low price paid in iron and steel works. . . . Oh master, we thank thee for all the free gifts you have given the public at the expense of your slaves. . . . Oh, master, we need no protection, we need no liberty so long as we are under thy care. So we commend ourselves to thy mercy and forevermore sing thy praise. Amen! [85]

Such language could not be misunderstood.

Although the evidence emphasized in these pages indicates the existence of a working-class social Christianity and suggests that Protestantism had a particular meaning for discontented Gilded Age labor leaders, social radicals, and even ordinary workers, it is hazardous to infer too much from it alone about the working class. Too little is yet known about nineteenth-century American Protestant workers. Evidence on church affiliation, for example, is contradictory. While many contemporaries like D. O. Kellogg, general secretary of the Charity Organization of Philadelphia, frequently worried over the "widespread skepticism and alienation from Christianity prevalent among the workingmen" and complained that institutional Protestantism often was "out of the poor man's reach." Inadequate but significant statistics for church affiliation among the general population, not just workers, show an increase from sixteen per cent in 1850 to thirty-six per cent in 1900.[86] Until more is known about particular groups of workers and their relations to institutional and noninstitutional religious sentiment and belief, however, it remains impossible to recon-

cile such seemingly contradictory evidence. Scattered but still inconclusive evidence hints at an apparent close connection between
youthful religious conversion and subsequent labor militancy among
certain workers.[87] The considerable but as yet largely neglected variations in the experience and outlook of factory workers and skilled
craftsmen and of self-educated artisans and casual day laborers, as
well as the different social environments of small, semi-rural factory
and mining villages, industrial cities, and large urban centers, suggest
other important analytic problems in exploring the relationship between Protestantism and the "working class."[88] And there are additional complexities. It is risky to assume too close a relationship between religious sentiment and rhetoric and everyday behavior, and it
is equally perilous to view church attendance and affiliation as proof
of religious belief, or not attending church as presumptive evidence
of the opposite. An example of the confusion that might result was
the response of an unidentified worker when asked in 1898: "Why
are so many intelligent workingmen non–church goers?" "Jesus
Christ," he replied, " is with us outside the church, and we shall
prevail with God." [89]

Despite these many difficulties, a perspective over more than one
or two generations suggests tentative connections between the religious mode of expression of many Gilded Age trade unionists and
labor radicals and the behavior of larger numbers of disaffected
Gilded Age Protestant workers. Except for those unions that drew
support primarily from workers living in small towns and semi-rural
or other isolated areas, the language of labor leaders and social radicals and the tone of their press after 1900 displayed a marked decline
in religious emphasis when compared to the labor speeches, editorials, and letters penned between 1860 and 1900. In part this difference
suggests the growing secularization of the national culture, but it also
makes possible a particular view of Gilded Age workers, seeing them
as a transitional generation that bridged two distinct social structures
and was the first to encounter fully the profound strains accompanying the shift to an urban and industrial social order. Not separated
emotionally or historically from a different past, they lived through
an era of extreme social change and social disorder, but carried with
them meaningful and deeply felt traditions and values rooted in the
immediate and even more distant past. This process was not unique
to the United States, but occurred at different times in other rapidly

changing societies and greatly explains the behavior of the "first generation" to have contact with a radically different economic and social structure.[90] Although it is an exaggeration to argue that the violent and often disorganized protest characteristic of so much Gilded Age labor agitation resulted only from the tension between the outlook the worker brought to the Gilded Age and that era's rapidly changing economic and social structure, it is not too much to suggest that the thought and the behavior of Gilded Age workers were peculiar to that generation.

Vital in both pre-Civil War reform movements and evangelical crusades, perfectionist Christianity carried over into the Gilded Age and offered the uprooted but discontented Protestant worker ties with the certainties of his past and reasons for his disaffection with the present by denying for him the premises of Gilded Age America and the not yet "conventional wisdom" of that day. In 1874 the secretary of the Miners' Protective and Progressive Association of Western Pennsylvania, George Archbold, called the trade union a "God-given right" and warned fellow unionists of employer opposition: "The Philistines are upon you, and the fair Delilah would rob you of your locks and shear you of your power." [91] Twenty-three years later, and not in entirely dissimilar language, West Coast labor organizer and sailor Andrew Furuseth celebrated the twelfth anniversary of the Sailors' Union of the Pacific:

> Congress may rob us of our rights as men, and may make us bondsmen. The Judiciary may say "Well done" and uphold them. Yet we have our manhood from nature's God, and being true to our best interests we shall yet as free men turn our faces to the sun. . . . We must organize ourselves and align ourselves with the forces which in our country are making for that brotherhood for which Jesus died. So we must as individuals forget home, self and life, if need be, to reconquer our liberty, to preserve the sacredness of our bodies, which by Paul were called "the temples of the living God." [92]

Such an emphasis was common to men who disagreed on other matters, such as trade union strategy and the long-range purposes of labor organization and reform. That it is found among "business" unionists, Knights of Labor, and socialist and anarchist radicals and was as prevalent in the 1890's as in the 1860's suggests that it characterized no particular segment of organized labor, but was common to a generation of disaffected workers. Even the German Marxist immigrant Adolph Douai revealed its influence. Although he worried that "enthusiasm without reason engenders fanaticism and thus baffles the noblest purposes," Douai nevertheless pleaded in 1887: "Our age needs religious enthusiasm for the sake of common brotherhood, because infidelity is rampant and hypocrisy prevails in all churches—an infidelity of a peculiar kind, being a disbelief in the destiny of men to be brothers and sisters, in their common quality and rights." Douai depicted the Gilded Age labor movement as *the* religion of common brotherhood." [93]

Preindustrial Christian perfectionism offered Gilded Age labor reformers absolute values in a time of rapid social change and allowed the labor reformer or radical to identify with "timeless truths" that legitimized his attack on the absolutes of Gilded Age social thought —the determinism of Spencerian dogma, the sanctity of property rights and freedom of contract, and the rigidity of political laissez faire.[94] "Conditions" had changed, but the "issues" remained as of old, wrote the *Printer's Labor Tribune*, immediate forerunner to the important Pittsburgh *National Labor Tribune*, in arguing that "the war between capital and labor" was being "fought all the time, and [was] . . . identical with civilization itself." Privilege and monopoly were not new. "When Adam commenced business as a farmer, he enjoyed a monopoly, and the same might be said of Noah, but this could not continue," wrote the *Tribune* in 1873. Industrialism merely altered the terms of a historic conflict. "The age of steam, electricity and progress generally shows up a new phase of this old war. We have to fight against the old enemy of the masses, only under a new shape." [95] Coal miner and union organizer W. H. Haskins could declare: "Brothers, the principles of organized labor are as old as the old gray rocks and sand of Mt. Sinai." [96] And Knights of Labor leader Charles Litchman could promise:

> If you ask me to say how this system is to be changed, when the emancipation of the toiling millions on earth is to come, I can only say, "I know not *when* it will come, but I know it will come," because in the sight of God and God's angels the wrongs of the toiling millions on earth are a curse and a crime, and that as God is mercy and God is love, in His own good time the toiler will be free.[97]

Although the labor press frequently complained that institutional Protestantism had "come down to the level of merchandise, and our modern Levites worship the golden calf and offer their wares, like fakirs, to the highest bidder," [98] the *United Mine Workers' Journal* for good reason printed on its first page a sermon by Baptist minister J. Thalmus Morgan. Morgan warned from his Ohio mining-village pulpit:

> God's law of right and wrong are ever the same and cannot be changed until God and man's moral nature shall be changed. Opinions may change, but truth never. Truth is truth to the end of all reckoning. What was right in the time of Moses, Mordecai and Ehud will be right forever. . . . God shall judge the poor of the people; He shall save the children of the needy, and shall break into pieces the oppressor. Yes, He will do the poor justice, for He will delight in doing them good. . . . And [He] shall break into pieces oppression. He is strong to smite the foes of His people. Oppressors have been great breakers, but their time of retribution shall come, and they shall be broken themselves. [99]

The transcendent values that organized labor found in such post-millennial Christian exhortation helped steel it in a transitional era of deep crisis. "The mandate, 'Thou shalt glorify me in thy works,' is Labor's first article of faith," concluded the *Coast Seaman's Journal*. [100]

Although trade unionists and labor radicals were not the only critics of Gilded Age industrial America, the social Christianity they espoused was different from the more widely known and well-studied social gospel put forth by middle- and upper-class religious critics of that society. Both groups reacted against the early disintegrating consequences of rapid industrialization and drew from the same broad religious tradition. But parallel developments are not necessarily synonymous even though they occur at the same time and share a common mode of expression. The available evidence suggests few formal connections between the two "movements," and for several reasons. Before the 1890's, the two groups, so different in their social composition and in the way industrial and social change affected them, rarely addressed each other and usually spoke to different audiences. Despite many diversities (its "radical" and "conservative" fringes), the essential attributes of the early social gospel movement are characterized by Henry May in a way that makes it possible to distinguish it from its working-class counterpart:

> The Social Gospel of the American nineteenth century . . . did not grow out of actual suffering but rather out of moral and intellectual dissatisfaction with the suffering of others. It originated not with the "disinherited" but rather with the educated and pious middle class. It grew through argument, not through agitation; it pleaded for conversion, not revolt or withdrawal.[101]

Critical of business behavior and the individualist ethic of their time and anxious to infuse all social classes with a meaningful Christian ethic, few early advocates of the social gospel identified closely with organized labor and its particular forms of collective organization and protest. Few shared Henry George's belief that "the revolt everywhere" against the "hard conditions of modern society is really the religious spirit." [102] They sought first to mediate between the competing classes and frequently failed to understand the "'immediacy" of labor discontent. Only a small number, May finds, arranged "a successful working relation between their ultimate confidence in the new social spirit and the drab realities of day-to-day struggle." [103] Even the young Richard T. Ely and Washington Gladden, both so typical of the mainstream social gospel movement and both profoundly at odds with the materialism of their times, found it difficult at the start to associate themselves with working-class organizations and their methods and objectives.[104] Of the early social gospel movement, Charles H. Hopkins concludes that its "inclusive panacea" was "Christianity itself." Quoting Gladden, he adds: " 'the power of Christian love' was declared to be strong enough 'to smooth and sweeten all relations of capitalists and labor.' " Society would change mainly "through the converted individual whose changed character would produce a social transformation." [105] Such thought and argument stimulated numerous middle- and upper-class reformers in late-nineteenth-century America, but what May calls its "facile optimism" and its "fatal tendency to underestimate difficulties and to neglect mechanism" cut it off from working-class critics of industrial society.[106]

Protestantism in Gilded Age America permeated the social structure and the value system of the nation more deeply and in different ways than has heretofore been emphasized by that era's historians. The careers and writings of Henry Ward Beecher, Dwight Moody,

Mary Baker Eddy, Washington Gladden, and the trade unionists and labor radicals described in these pages illustrate the complexity of the relationship between religious belief and organization and the component parts of a particular social structure. Although what has been written here must not be interpreted as a single explanation for the little-studied subject of nineteenth-century working-class thought and behavior, it should be clear that the social gospel early found expression among these who professed to speak for the discontented lower classes and that the behavior of these critics of industrial capitalism cannot be understood without first exploring the religious (and secular) dimensions of their thought. For some workers and their leaders, including some of the most prominent Gilded Age trade unionists and radicals, a particular strand of Protestantism offered what Hobsbawm calls "a passion and morality in which the most ignorant can compete on equal terms" and what Liston Pope describes as a religion "intimately related to the everyday struggles and vicissitudes of an insecure life" and "useful for interpretation and succor." [107]

In 1893 one American pondered existential questions:

> While man is nothing more than a human, he has feeling. . . . While I am not a preacher nor one among the best of men, I am one who believes in Christ and His teachings and endeavor each day to live the life of a Christian. . . . My way is not everybody's way, and it would be wrong to even suppose it should be. . . . Now, what is my motive? . . . My reasoning is after this manner: Can man within himself accomplish as much while self exists as when he considers, Am I the only being that lives? and finds in answer, no. But I am one among millions, a pitiful drop in the bucket he thinks at once. . . . Am I right? Man wants everything but that which is best for him and his brother.[108]

These were not the words of Henry Ward Beecher, Russell Conwell, Mary Baker Eddy, Dwight Moody, William Lawrence, Lyman Atwater, John D. Rockefeller, Andrew Carnegie, or even Washington Gladden; they were penned by an unidentified but troubled Belleville, Ohio, coal miner.

[1] J. K. Talmon, "The Age of Revolution," *Encounter*, 21 (September, 1963): 14; see also Richard Hofstadter, *The Paranoid Style in American Politics and Other Essays* (New York, 1965), pp. ix–x. Urging the study of

popular ideology in order to understand more fully political thought and behavior, Hofstadter writes: "The political contest itself is deeply affected by the way in which it is perceived." "This does not mean," he hastens to warn, "that the material interests of politics can be psychologized away or reduced to episodes in intellectual history." A similar admonition is essential in studying labor thought.

2 Evidence on differing contemporary estimates of the status of industrialists and workers in large cities and small industrial towns is found in H. G. Gutman, "The Worker's Search for Power: Labor in the Gilded Age," in *The Gilded Age: A Reappraisal*, ed. H. Wayne Morgan (New York, 1963), pp. 38–68.

3 *The Course of American Democratic Thought* (New York, 1956), p. 154.

4 August 24, 1874, and August 26, 1876.

5 An able summary of the defense of laissez faire in the Gilded Age is found in Sidney Fine, *Laissez Faire and the General-Welfare State: A Study of Conflict in American Thought, 1865–1901* (Ann Arbor, Mich., 1956), pp. 3–166. On the process of legitimizing newly achieved power, see Max Weber, *Essays in Sociology*, tr. and ed. H. W. Gerth and C. W. Mills (New York, 1946), p. 271.

6 "Divide and Rule," *Mississippi Valley Historical Review*, 43 (June, 1956): 3–17.

7 Economist Arthur Perry explicitly said that "the grounds of economy and morals are independent and incommensurable," while the president of the American Exchange Bank found the "laws" of economics separate from but "as sacred and obligatory as . . . those of the Decalogue." Chicago, Burlington, and Quincy Railroad President C. E. Perkins advised an associate: "If I were able, I would found a school of political economy in order to harden men's hearts." Another time Perkins explained: "The question of political economy is not, What is noble? What is good? What is generous? What are the teachings of the Gospel?—but What, if anything, is it expedient to do about [the] production, distribution and consumption of property or wealth?" Like many other men of new wealth and power, this railroad leader worried about those who denounced "the economic law of Adam Smith . . . as too cruel and heartless for a Christian People." Quoted in Fine, *Laissez Faire*, pp. 54, 56, 103; Kirkland, "Divide and Rule"; and Thomas Cochran, *Railroad Leaders, 1845–1890: The Business Mind in Action* (Cambridge, Mass., 1953), pp. 436–37.

8 This view is identified most frequently with Henry Ward Beecher and Russell Conwell. "The general truth will stand," Beecher argued, "that no man in this land suffers from poverty unless it be more than his fault—unless it be his *sin*." (Quoted in Henry F. May, *Protestant Churches and In-*

dustrial America [New York, 1949], p. 69). Conwell made the same point another way: "The number of poor to be sympathized with is very small. . . . To sympathize with a man whom God has punished for his sins, thus to help him when God will still continue a just punishment, is to do wrong, no doubt about it." (Quoted in Marquis Childs and Douglas Cater, *Ethics in a Business Society* [New York, 1954], p. 137.) A variant of this theme urged passivity upon complaining workers, as when the Methodist *Christian Advocate* lectured readers: "John the Baptist set a good example . . . when he advised the Roman soldiers, 'Be content with your wages.'" (Quoted in William G. McLoughlin, Jr., *Modern Revivalism: Charles Grandison Finney to Billy Graham* [New York, 1959], pp. 267–68.)

⁹ Sidney E. Mead, "American Protestantism since the Civil War," *Journal of Religion*, 36 (January, 1956): 1–15; see also Winthrop Hudson, *American Protestantism* (Chicago, 1961), pp. 136–40. Hudson also relates these developments to the new theology, "the doctrine of Incarnation, interpreted as divine immanence, which sanctified the 'natural' man and invested the culture itself with intrinsic redemptive tendencies." The new theology therefore surrendered "any independent basis of judgment." Excellent analysis of the post-Civil War evangelism typified by Dwight Moody is found in McLoughlin, *Modern Revivalism*, pp. 166–281, and Bernard A. Weisberger, *They Gathered at the River: The Story of the Great Revivalists and Their Impact upon Religion in America* (Boston, 1958), pp. 160–219.

¹⁰ May, *Protestant Churches, passim*, but esp. pp. 91–111, 163–203; A. I. Abell, *The Urban Impact on American Protestantism, 1865–1900* (Cambridge, Mass., 1943), *passim*; and C. H. Hopkins, *The Rise of the Social Gospel in American Protestantism, 1865–1915* (New Haven, Conn., 1940), *passim*.

¹¹ See the penetrating and original study of the role of voluntary associations and community institutions among Irish immigrant workers and their children in Newburyport, Massachusetts, between 1850 and 1880 in Stephan Thernstrom, *Poverty and Progress: Social Mobility in a Nineteenth Century City* (Cambridge, Mass., 1964), pp. 166–91.

¹² Hudson, *American Protestantism*; Mead, "American Protestantism."

¹³ In his review of Edward P. Thompson, *The Making of the English Working Class*, in *Labor History*, 6 (Winter, 1965): 84.

¹⁴ *The Making of the English Working Class* (London, 1963), p. 194 and *passim*.

¹⁵ See esp. Timothy L. Smith, *Revivalism and Social Reform in Mid-Nineteenth-Century America* (New York, 1957), *passim*. Smith does not carry his important findings on the relationship between pre-Civil War evangelism, Christian perfectionism, and social reform beyond the Civil War. Clifton E. Olmstead argued that perfectionism "increased steadily in

American evangelical Protestantism throughout and beyond the Civil War." It "flourished primarily in urban areas," Olmstead maintained, "where the social problems and the individual frustrations presented a peculiar challenge to those who believed that Christianity could 'work' to the betterment of mankind" (*History of Religion in the United States* [Englewood Cliffs, N.J., 1960], p. 352). But Olmstead offered no concrete evidence to support this valuable insight. Although he makes little of the strain of labor Protestantism emphasized in these pages, W. G. McLoughlin offers a suggestive framework for understanding the effects of pietistic perfectionism on American social movements in his essay "Pietism and the American Character," *American Quarterly*, 17 (Summer, 1965): 163–86.

¹⁶ Thompson, *Making of the English Working Class*, pp. 350–400; Eric Hobsbawm, *Labouring Men: Studies in the History of Labour* (London, 1964), pp. 23–33; Robert F. Wearmouth, *Methodism and the Working-Class Movements of England, 1800–1850* (London, 1937), *passim*.

¹⁷ *Social Bandits and Primitive Rebels: Studies in Archaic Forms of Social Movement in the 19th and 20th Centuries* (Glencoe, Ill., 1959), pp. 108, 130.

¹⁸ *Making of the English Working Class*, p. 68.

¹⁹ *Labor Leader* (Boston), September 15, 1888.

²⁰ Alvin and Helen Gouldner, *Modern Sociology* (New York, 1963), pp. 634–36.

²¹ *Labor Leader*, August 27, 1888.

²² *Union Pacific Employees' Magazine*, n.d., reprinted in *Journal of the Knights of Labor* (Philadelphia), July 16, 1891. The Crucifixion was but one example this journal cited; it also pointed to the mobbing of William Lloyd Garrison, the hanging of John Brown, and the jailing of Voltaire.

²³ *Railway Times* (Chicago), June 15, 1896.

²⁴ *Labor Standard* (Boston), February 22, 1879.

²⁵ *Coast Seaman's Journal* (San Francisco), November 28, 1888, January 30, 1889.

²⁶ *Labor Enquirer* (Denver), April–May, 1883.

²⁷ *United Mine Workers' Journal* (Columbus, O.), March 8, 1900.

²⁸ Hobsbawm, *Labouring Men*, p. 376.

²⁹ *American Workman* (Boston), June–July, 1869.

³⁰ *Labor: Its Rights and Wrongs* (Washington, D.C., 1886), pp. 252–61.

³¹ *The Accused, the Accusers. The Famous Speeches of the Eight Chicago Anarchists in Court . . . on October 7th, 8th and 9th, 1886* (Chicago, 1886), pp. 5–6.

³² McLoughlin, *Modern Revivalism*, pp. 65–165; Smith, *Revivalism*, *passim*; Olmstead, *History of Religion*, pp. 347–62. See also the subtle but

significant distinctions between the prophetic and the apocalyptic impulses stressed by Martin Buber in his essay "Prophecy, Apocalyptic, and Historical Hour" (1954), reprinted in *idem., Pointing the Way: Collected Essays* (New York, 1957), pp. 192–207. Although authoritative conclusions cannot yet be drawn, it appears that the prophetic rather than the apocalyptic tradition characterized the dominant religious sentiment of dissident Gilded Age workers.

[33] McLoughlin, *Modern Revivalism*, p. 167. There is little direct reference to Finney in post–Civil War labor thought. An exception is found in the *Iron Molder's Journal* (Cincinnati), of October, 1876, which reported the following story about Finney: "He was passing an iron foundry when the works were in full blast and heard a workman swearing terribly. 'Young man,' said the revivalist, addressing the swearer, 'how hot do you suppose hell is?' The workman recognized the questioner, and placed his arms akimbo, and looking him squarely in the face, said, 'Well, Mr. Finney, I suppose it's so hot there that if somebody brought you a spoonful of melted iron, you'd swear't was ice cream.' Mr. Finney had nothing more to say."

[34] James Sylvis, *Life, Speeches, Labors and Essays of William H. Sylvis* (Philadelphia, 1872), pp. 152–65.

[35] *Railway Times*, January 15, 1894.

[36] *Knights of Labor* (Chicago), November 20, 1886.

[37] *United Mine Workers' Journal*, March 29, 1894.

[38] Louis Nash, "Is This a Christian Civilization?" *American Federationist*, 1 (January, 1895): 252.

[39] *Fincher's Trades Review* (Philadelphia), February 2, 1864.

[40] September 2, 1865.

[41] *Cigar-Makers' Official Journal*, 19 (January, 1894): 3.

[42] September 30, 1897.

[43] *Ibid.*, June 15, 1893.

[44] *Railway Times*, January 15, 1894.

[45] *Journal of United Labor* (Philadelphia), September, 1882.

[46] O. T. Hicks, *Life of Richard Trevellick* (Joliet, Ill., 1898), pp. 198–200.

[47] *Craftsman* (Washington, D.C.), May 30, 1885.

[48] *Coast Seaman's Journal*, February 25, 1891. See also the editorials in the *National Labor Tribune* (Pittsburgh), February 3, March 7, 1877, in which trade union organizers and labor reformers are called the "Apostles of Labor" and urged to go among the workers and talk with them as did the early Christians. The Apostles, the *Tribune* reminded readers, "were teachers who traveled without pay, and for no other reason than to spread the new gospel." "Looking back," it noted, "we may wonder how a few

simple-minded men, without education, with nothing but plain, simple honesty, could make such mighty changes."

49 *Railway Times*, February 1, 1897.

50 *The Motorman and Conductor*, 5 (January, 1899): 1–3. See also *Labor Standard* (New York), January 6, 1877. The socialist *Standard* condemned the New York *Herald* for praising Christ's life among the poor and for finding in it "a theory of the conduct of life and of society." The *Standard* believed that "if any man were to follow Christ's example by going amongst the brokers and doing as he did, he would soon find himself an inmate of a Lunatic asylum or a Jail." "Who in these days," asked the *Standard*, "does unto others as he wishes to be done by?"

51 February 22, 1897.

52 December 19, 1885; see also W. J. M., "Christmas Greeting," *Coast Seaman's Journal*, December 21, 1887. The identification of Christ with "tramps" occurred earlier, too, especially during the antitramp hysteria of the middle and late 1870's. Defending "tramps," the *Weekly Worker* reminded readers: "About the only consolation left the truly unfortunate tramp is the thought that Christ was a tramping vagabond" (*Weekly Worker* [Syracuse, N.Y.], August 15, 1875). The *National Labor Tribune* and other labor journals echoed this point in the 1870's. "Christianity," the *Tribune* insisted, "was ushered into existence by tramps. . . . Great movements come from the bottom layer of society, who [*sic*] possess the truest instincts and noblest instincts. Our tramps are but the beginning of a worn-out system" (December 23, 1876).

53 *The Americans* (Boston, 1963), p. 308.

54 An unusual example of Gompers' making a direct appeal to religion occurred in an April, 1891, Pittsburgh speech after the Morewood, Pennsylvania, murder of several East European coke workers. Gompers said: "I say to the capitalists, don't turn your backs on organized labor; don't widen the chasm. . . . Even the Bible lesson of our early childhood will change and we may be compelled to say, 'Whither thou goest I cannot go. . . . Thy people were not my people; thy God is not my God' " (*United Mine Workers' Journal*, April 23, 1891). But see, more typically, Gompers' 1898 attack on "the church and the ministry as the apologists and defenders of the wrong committed against the interests of the people, simply because the perpetrators are possessors of wealth . . . whose real God is the almighty dollar" (quoted in Hopkins, *Rise of the Social Gospel*, p. 85), and other examples of his critical attitude toward organized religion in Bernard Mandel, *Samuel Gompers: A Biography* (Yellow Springs, O., 1963), pp. 9–12.

55 A good summary of the criticism by labor reformers and radicals of institutional Protestantism and "clerical *laissez-faire*" is found in May, *Protestant Churches*, pp. 216–23.

[56] See, e.g., Powderly's speeches in the *Journal of United Labor*, July 17, 1890, December 28, 1892, and McDonnell's editorials in the Paterson *Labor Standard*, December 24, 1881, May 15, 1886, and in *Bakers' Journal*, December 1, 1888.

[57] Sylvis, *Life of William H. Sylvis*, pp. 96–117, 443–46.

[58] Terence V. Powderly, *Thirty Years of Labor* (Columbus, O., 1886), pp. 160–72, 176–77.

[59] *National Labor Tribune*, March 18, 1882.

[60] *Writings and Speeches of Eugene V. Debs*, ed. Arthur M. Schlesinger, Jr., (New York, 1948), pp. 4–6.

[61] *Labor Leader*, October 12, 1895.

[62] *Union* (Indianapolis), January 17, 1896.

[63] Arthur Mann, *Yankee Reformers in the Urban Age* (Cambridge, Mass., 1954), pp. 178–84, contains perceptive comments on the career and importance of McNeill, but most labor historians have minimized his importance.

[64] *Labor Standard*, November–December, 1876.

[65] *Labor Enquirer*, November 27, 1887.

[66] *Labor Leader*, February–March, 1890.

[67] George E. McNeill, *The Philosophy of the Labor Movement* (Chicago, 1893), unpaged pamphlet.

[68] *American Federationist*, 9 (September, 1902): 479–80.

[69] Further details on the role of Negroes in the early United Mine Workers of America are found in Herbert G. Gutman, "The Negro and the United Mine Workers. The Career and Letters of Richard L. Davis and Something of Their Meaning: 1890–1900," in *The Negro and the American Labor Movement*, ed: Julius Jacobson (New York, 1968).

[70] Riley to the editor, *United Mine Workers' Journal*, September 8, 1892.

[71] Clark to the editor, *ibid.*, August 9, 1894.

[72] Davis to the editor, *ibid.*, August 15, 1895; April 18, 1892; February 11, 1897; March 3, 10, 1898.

[73] *Ibid.*, December 8, 1892.

[74] *Knights of Labor*, September 25, 1886.

[75] *Coast Seaman's Journal*, June 29, 1892.

[76] *Railway Times*, June 1, 1895.

[77] 11 (April 1887), 207–208.

[78] *Ibid.*, 10 (September, 1886): 519–20. See also "Hermit of the Hills" to the editor, *National Labor Tribune* (January 1, 1876), who wrote: "No happiness can come to men or nations—no Kingdom of Heaven can descend upon earth—as long as this false system of antagonism—of working each against the other—continues."

[79] *Journal of United Labor*, September 13, 1888.

[80] *Ibid.*, September 20, 1888.

[81] 18 (September, 1894): 877–79.

[82] *Railway Times*, August 15, 1895.

[83] *Locomotive Firemen's Magazine*, 14 (February, 1890): 104–6.

[84] *Ibid.*, 16 (August, 1892), reprinted in *Writings and Speeches of Eugene V. Debs*, ed. Schlesinger, pp. 378–82.

[85] Reprinted in *Coming Age*, February 10, 1894. Such satiric use of traditional religious forms recurred in these years. See, for example, "A Miner's Prayer," *United Mine Workers' Journal* (May 16, 1895): "Oh! Almighty and allwise and powerful coal barons who art living in great and glorious palaces, when thou art not in secret meeting working for our interest and welfare, we hail thy blessed name as the great philanthropist of our commercial world to-day. We bow before thee in humble submission. . . . We are Americans of the modern type, not like Jefferson, Hancock and Washington. . . . We are your fools, liars, suckers; spit in our faces and rub it in. We have no business to want an education for our children or ourselves. We ain't got any sense. We don't want any; it don't take any sense to load coal for thee. . . . Did Dred Scott ever serve his master better? . . . Amen."

[86] D. O. Kellogg, "Some Causes of Pauperism and Their Cure," *Penn Monthly*, 11 (April, 1878): 275–76, 281–82; Olmstead, *History of Religion*, p. 447.

[87] Of the British experience, Hobsbawm writes: "The sect and the labour movement were—especially among the cadres and leaders of the movement —connected . . . by the process of conversion: that is to say, by the sudden, emotionally overpowering realizing of sin and the finding of grace. . . . Conversion indicated, reflected, or perhaps stimulated the kind of unselfish activity which labour militancy inevitably implied. . . . Conversion of some kind is, of course, a commonplace in labour movement" (*Social Bandits and Primitive Rebels*, p. 140). Too little is known about this phenomenon among American trade unionists and social reformers, but Gabriel perceptively points out that Henry George's beginning awareness of the "social problem" in New York in 1869 came to him as a "conversion after the pattern of evangelical Protestantism." George himself wrote: "Once, in daylight, and in a city street, there came to me a thought, a vision, a call—give it what name you please. But every nerve quivered. And there and then I made a vow" (*Course of American Democratic Thought*, pp. 208–11). There is also the case of Samuel Fielden, one of the anarchists convicted in the aftermath of the Haymarket bombing. As a Lancashire youth and factory worker, Fielden was converted to Primitive Methodism and became an active lay preacher. Years later, he wrote: "I felt that that religion . . . which I thought was calculated to better the world was something that was worth while for me to use my energies in propagating, and I did it. I could not help it. . . . So

intense and earnest was I at that time that I was at one and the same time the Sunday School superintendent of a little Sunday school, a class teacher, a local preacher, and what was called an exhorter." Fielden came to the United States in 1868. Some years later he came into contact with secular radical ideology. His description of his "conversion" to socialism suggests a close parallel to evangelical conversion and the process Hobsbawm describes. Fielden explains his growing discontent with industrial America and goes on: "My ideas did not become settled as to what was the remedy, but when they did, I carried the same energy and the same determination to bring about that remedy that I had applied to ideas which I had possessed years before. There is always a period in every individual's life when some sympathetic chord is touched by some other person. There is the open sesame that carries conviction. The ground may have all been prepared. The evidence may have all been accumulated but it has not formed in any shape; in fact, the child has not been born. The new idea has not impressed itself thoroughly when that sympathetic chord is touched, and the person is thoroughly convinced of the idea. It was so in my investigation of political economy. . . . A person said to me Socialism meant equal opportunities— and that was the touch. From that time on I became a Socialist. . . . I knew that I had found the right thing; and I had found the medicine that was calculated to cure the ills of society" (*The Accused, the Accusers*, pp. 36–39).

[88] Asa Briggs, *The Making of Modern England, 1784–1867* (New York, 1965), p. 287.

[89] H. Francis Perry, "The Workingman's Alienation from the Church," *American Journal of Sociology*, 4 (March, 1899): 626.

[90] Hobsbawm, *Social Bandits and Primitive Rebels*, pp. 1–12, 126–49, but especially p. 3, when he writes of this generation: "They do not as yet grow with or into modern society: they are broken into it. . . . Their problem is how to adapt themselves to its life and struggles." See also Max Weber's compelling observation that "whenever modern capitalism has begun its work of increasing the productivity of human labor by increasing its intensity, it has encountered the immensely stubborn resistance of . . . pre-capitalistic labor," and the extensive comments on it in Thompson, *Making of the English Working Class*, pp. 356 ff. Perceptive argument for a "generational" analysis by social historians is found in Marc Bloch, *The Historian's Craft* (New York, 1964), pp. 185–87: "Men who are born into the same social environment about the same time necessarily come under analogous influences, particularly in their formative years. Experience proves that, by comparison with either considerably older or considerably younger groups, their behavior reveals certain distinctive characteristics which are ordinarily very clear. This is true even of their bitterest disagreements. To

be excited by the same dispute even on opposing sides is still to be alike. This common stamp, deriving from a common age, is what makes a generation."

[91] *National Labor Tribune,* January 31, 1874.

[92] *Coast Seaman's Journal,* March 17, 1897.

[93] *Workmen's Advocate* (New Haven, Conn.), May 14, 1887.

[94] Vittorio Lanterari, *The Religion of the Oppressed: A Study of Modern Messianic Cults* (New York, 1965), p. x. "Although each history has its own teleology," Lanterari writes, "the important fact is that the drive which motivates man's practical choices and causes him to struggle and suffer for a better fortune is common to all and rises out of a faith that is absolute. Thus, even while man is aware of the relativity of human values and goals, nonetheless he behaves 'as if' the goal were a final one (*eschaton*) and 'as if' the values he defends were absolute values." In this connection, an editorial in *Railway Times* (November 1, 1895) is of great interest. The official journal of the American Railway Union worried why, although "truth" is "one of the attributes of deity, . . . the disciples of error, the devotees of lies, professing to be champions of truth, have betrayed it and placed it on a thousand scaffolds, from Calvary to Woodstock." The *Times* explained: "There is an intimate relation between truth and freedom. Christ said, 'Ye shall know the truth, and the truth shall make you free.' It is this declaration that solves the problem. If men are free, they will have found the truth, but they will be free only while they cling to it, maintain it, defend it, hold it aloft, swear by it, and fight for it on every battle field where its enemies appear; and if need be die for it." But this labor newspaper worried that in the United States "error has erected its golden god and commands the nation to fall down and worship it."

[95] *Printer's Labor Tribune* (Pittsburgh), November 27, 1873. See also the editorial in the Providence *Sun,* April 14, 1875, a Rhode Island labor weekly, which insisted: "From the Old Testament times the Almighty has had a controversy with those who have robbed the laborer of his wages."

[96] *United Mine Workers' Journal,* January 17, 1895.

[97] *Journal of United Labor* (Philadelphia), August 27, 1888.

[98] *Coast Seaman's Journal,* October 18, 1893. Earlier examples of this critical attitude toward the clergy's dominant social conservatism are found in reviews of Washington Gladden's *Working People and Their Employers* (Boston, 1876) in the *Workingman's Advocate* (Chicago), August 26, 1876, and the *National Labor Tribune,* September 16, 1876. The *Tribune* was especially hard on Gladden: "He is a shallow thinker and writer. Had his book never been written nothing would have been lost. Preachers, as a class, are not able to deal with the Labor problem, and Mr. Gladden is no exception."

[99] June 28, 1894. What Morgan's sermon typified cannot be known because the ideas and social outlook of local clergymen, particularly those in industrial towns and cities and those with predominantly working-class congregations, have not yet been studied, and it is not helpful to infer their thoughts and behavior from national religious periodicals. Scattered but inconclusive evidence suggests that an unexplored dimension of the clerical social gospel may be uncovered by studying the clergy in such communities. A few examples suffice. After discontented and unpaid Erie Railroad shopworkers and repair mechanics stopped trains and took control of the repair shops in March, 1874, eighteen hundred state militiamen went to Susquehanna Depot, Pennsylvania, to restore order. But a local minister preached a severe Sunday sermon against the railroad company. (H. G. Gutman, "Trouble on the Railroads in 1873–1874," *Labor History*, 2 [Spring, 1961]: 228). In 1880 a socialist newspaper editor, Irish immigrant Joseph P. McDonnell, served time in a Passaic County, New Jersey jail for libeling a brickyard owner by publishing a letter that exposed conditions in a Paterson brickyard. Two Paterson clergymen, one a Baptist and the other a Methodist, publicly supported McDonnell and sided with the workers. (*Idem*, "Industrial Invasion of the Village Green," *Trans-action*, 3 [May–June, 1966]: 19–24.) After the fierce violence in 1892 between strikers and Pinkerton police that resulted in more than thirty deaths, a Homestead, Pennsylvania, Methodist preacher said of Henry Clay Frick at the funeral services for three dead strikers: "This town is bathed in tears today, and it is all brought about by one man, who is less respected by the laboring people than any other employer in the world. There is no more sensibility in that man than in a toad." (Leon Woolf, *Lockout. The Story of the Homestead Strike of 1892: A Study of Violence, Unionism, and the Carnegie Steel Empire* [New York, 1965], p. 133). At the time of the 1894 Pullman strike and boycott, William Carwardine, pastor of the First Methodist Church of Pullman, bitterly attacked George Pullman and called his model town "a hollow mockery, a sham, an institution girdled with red tape, and as a solution to the labor problem most unsatisfactory." Carwardine supported the strikers and was joined by Morris L. Wickman, pastor of the Pullman Swedish Methodist Church, who sharply criticized the firm before the United States Strike Commission. (Almont Lindsey, *The Pullman Strike* [Chicago, 1942], pp. 73, 103; May, *Protestant Churches*, pp. 109–11). Although he frequently criticized the social orthodoxy of most institutional Protestant churches and was himself without religious sentiment, Gompers nevertheless interestingly wrote in 1898 that not all clergymen deserved his condemnation: "The men who preach from their pulpits and breathe with every word their sympathy with the great struggling masses of humanity; . . . these ministers you will find always interesting, and not only interesting,

but the churches filled with workers who go to hear them." (Perry, "Workingman's Alienation from the Church," p. 623).

100 August 29, 1894.

101 May, *Protestant Churches*, p. 235.

102 *Labor: Its Rights and Wrongs*, pp. 261–68. George linked all contemporary protest movements, even the most radical, and compared them to early Christian history: "Who are these men, the Socialists, the Anarchists, the Nihilists, and what is it they seek? . . . Is it not for a state of greater equality, for a state of more perfect peace, for a condition where no one will want and no one will suffer for the material needs of existence? That is the ideal those men have before them, blind and wrong their methods though they be. And what is that ideal? Is it not the kingdom of God on earth? What was the reason that a doctrine preached by a humble Jewish carpenter, who was crucified between two thieves, propagated by slaves and fugitives meeting in caverns, overran the world and overthrew the might of legions and the tortures of the amphitheatre and dungeon? Was it for theological distinction that Rome, the tolerant Rome, that welcomed all Gods to her Pantheon, persecuted the adherents of this new Galilean superstition? No. . . . It was because they sought the kingdom of God on earth. It was because they hoped to bring it about there and then. . . . That doctrine of the fatherhood of a common Creator and the brotherhood of men struck at the roots of tyranny; struck at the privileges of those who who were living in luxury on the toil and the blood and the sweat of the worker."

103 May, *Protestant Churches*, 231–65.

104 In 1886 Ely, for example defended trade unions and attacked employer abuses in his significant *The Labor Movement in America*, but nevertheless urged discontented workers to "cast aside envy" and told them: "While the Bible is a good armory from which you may draw weapons of attack, it at the same time points out the right course for you to take. . . . It discourages no good effort; but even James followed his awful condemnation of the oppressor with these wise words, 'Be ye also patient' " ([New York, 1886], pp. v–xiii). Gladden early attacked the industrial abuses of his time, but still found labor unions "often unwise and unprofitable" and argued that "as a general thing" unions "result in more loss than gain to the laboring classes" (quoted in John L. Shover, "Washington Gladden and the Labor Question," *Ohio Historical Quarterly*, 68 [October, 1959]: 335–52).

105 *Rise of the Social Gospel*, pp. 70, 89, 325.

106 May, *Protestant Churches*, p. 233.

107 Hobsbawm, *Social Bandits and Primitive Rebels*, p. 132, and Pope, *Millhands and Preachers* (New Haven, Conn., 1942), p. 86.

108 *United Mine Workers' Journal*, June 29, 1893.

The Radicalism of the Dispossessed: William Haywood and the IWW

Melvyn Dubofsky

"Distorted by the romanticism of novelists and the antipathy of most scholars," Melvyn Dubofsky writes, "the history of the Industrial Workers of the World remains unreal, misunderstood, and relatively meaningless." The fate of "Big Bill" Haywood, the IWW's famous leader, is even worse: patronizing scholars have relegated him to the ranks of merely "colorful" labor leaders. Dubofsky here attempts to reinterpret the IWW through Haywood, offering a "progress report" on a forthcoming full-scale history of the organization.

Dubofsky's work on his previous publications laid the basis for his latest project. His articles on Western labor, in *Labor History*, analyzed the working-class radicalism that spawned the IWW. *When Workers Organize: New York City in the Progressive Era* (Amherst, 1968) explored the relationship between the labor movement and the urban community in the East in the heyday of the IWW. To compensate for the government's destruction of IWW records in the World War I raids, he has used new material in the National Archives and in various collections in the West. Dubofsky, who holds a doctorate from the University of Rochester, taught history at Northern Illinois University before he joined the Department of History at the University of Massachusetts.

I thought, and still think, that he was one of the most remarkable men that ever lived. . . . He became one of the great leaders of our time. It was something inborn in his personality that made him such a great leader. He had a personal and physical magnetism that nobody could resist.

He was an outstanding human being. No matter what he engaged in, he would have made a success of it.

—Mary Gallagher, in an Oral History Interview, Bancroft Library, University of California, Berkeley, pp. 13–14

He is the embodiment of the Sorel philosophy, roughened by the American industrial and civic climate, a bundle of primitive instincts, a master of direct statement. He is useless on committee; he is a torch amongst a crowd of uncritical and credulous workmen. I saw him at Copenhagen, amidst the leaders of the working-class movements drawn from the whole world, and there he was dumb and unnoticed; I saw him addressing a crowd in England, and there his crude appeals moved his listeners to wild applause. He made them see things, and their hearts bounded to be up and doing.

—J. Ramsay MacDonald, *Syndicalism: A Critical Examination*, pp. 36–37

Clio's fickleness never ceases to amaze. The man who made so strong an impression upon Mary Gallagher and Ramsay MacDonald, and the labor organization he personified, aroused dreadful anxieties among most "respectable" middle-class Americans early in the twentieth century. But few people today know anything about the man and the movement which once frightened a less affluent America.

That man—William D. Haywood—and his organization, the Industrial Workers of the World, represented America's early twentieth-century generation of dispossessed workers. Little remembered today and less understood, the IWW and Haywood tell us much about the nature of radicalism in America, the limits of dissent in a purportedly free society, and the prospects, if any, for radical transformations in American society. For the IWW, like the Negro militants and the "New Left" of the 1960's, despised the "power structure" and confronted established authority with nonviolent direct action. "Wobblies" also preached power and promised revolution, beliefs which sometimes involved their organization in riots and violence. Moreover, Wobblies, like today's young radicals, practiced an anti-organizational, semi-utopian, almost anarchistic radicalism. To understand where the new radicalism is today, and where it is headed tomorrow, we might well look back to see where it was only yesterday.

But it is difficult to come to grips with the IWW's place in American history. Posing a threat to the American establishment just before and during the First World War, after Versailles the IWW survived only on the fringes of society. Some of its leaders had been lynched or imprisoned; others had died or joined livelier causes; and the organization itself vanished into what Dan Wakefield has called "haunted halls." In 1923 federal agents added insult to injury when they incinerated the IWW files they had used to persecute and prosecute Wobblies, thereby denying scholars of a later generation an opportunity to perform a decent autopsy.

With the IWW no longer a threat to constituted authority after 1919, and its papers destroyed, novelists and folklorists seized upon the travails of prewar Wobblies to weave a legendary web around their very real exploits. John Dos Passos, earlier than most other novelists, utilized the Wobbly myth in *The 42nd Parallel,* in which the hero, Mac, deserted the girl he loved to join the IWW class war in Nevada. Thirty years later, James Jones also introduced the IWW into fiction; in *From Here to Eternity* an army old-timer lectures a young recruit: "You don't remember the Wobblies. You were too young. Or else not born yet. There has never been anything like them before or since. They called themselves materialist-economists but what they really were was religion. They were workstiffs and bindlebums like you and me, but they were welded together by a vision we don't possess." The religion and the vision gave Wallace Stegner material for his novel, *The Preacher and the Slave*, and Barrie Stavis material for his play, *The Man Who Would Not Die*, both of which were based upon the life of the Swedish-born IWW organizer, bard, and martyr Joe Hill, who melodramatically declaimed before facing a Utah firing squad, "Don't mourn for me. Organize." [1]

Folklorists and folksingers also discovered a usable past in their version of the IWW legend. For Wobblies had sung as they organized, their bards composing lyrics on picket lines and in prison cells. The IWW put its songs together in the *Little Red Song Book*, where a later generation of folksingers could rediscover them to sharpen discontent among protesting civil rights marchers—not oppressed workers as the Wobblies had intended.

Scholars who have investigated the IWW, however, have not been as kind as literary folk. Where novelists discovered an admirable Wobbly tradition, scholars, with one or two exceptions, have been either patronizing or hostile. Either devotees of the American Federation of Labor's official line or products of post–World War II prosperity, euphoria, and Cold War conservatism, these scholars have deprecated the IWW as an association of gun-slinging frontiersmen more famous for its singing than for its accomplishments and for its oratory rather than its organizing—an organization which offered "merely an over-simplified, anti-poltical Marxism" and therefore "quietly withered on the radical vine without leaving many tangible fruits." [2]

Left-wing scholars have also been critical of the Wobblies. Notwithstanding the IWW's commitment to working-class solidarity and industrial unionism, the Marxist historian Philip Foner and the Communist Party chairman William Z. Foster (himself a Wobbly *ca.* 1909–12) derogate it as infantile disorder inflicted upon the more mature, realistic Marxian left. They indict the IWW for failing to participate adequately in politics and for dividing the American labor movement, thereby weakening radical influences within the house of labor. Foner in particular, measuring the IWW against his version of

Marxism-Leninism, naturally finds the Wobblies wanting. Even Ray Ginger, a non-communist scholar, castigates the IWW for splitting the labor movement. Only William D. Haywood escaped the full wrath of the IWW's left-wing critics. He seemed more committed politically than the organization he led, and he later followed the road to Moscow, becoming a Communist Party member in 1919 and an exile to Russia in 1921—unlike most Wobblies, who after 1920 chose to ridicule Soviet communism as industrial autocracy under a new name.[3]

I

Distorted by the romanticism of novelists and the antipathy of most scholars, the history of the IWW remains unreal, misunderstood, and relatively meaningless. Almost the same can be said of William D. Haywood, its most famous personality. If little is known about the IWW as a labor organization, less is known about Haywood as a person. If the IWW story is encrusted in legend, Haywood's life is pure myth.

Haywood contributed to this myth. Allowing Communist Party hacks to ghost-write his 1927 autobiography, Haywood, by then a gravely ill man, produced a book telling of the exploits of a Western frontiersman. Homesteader, gun-slinger, advocate of the homemade justice of the Colt .45, organizer of a cowboys' union, Haywood leaps from the pages to duel with sheriffs and deputies at pistol point. The picture in *Bill Haywood's Book* is that of a rugged frontiersman who ended his life believing in Karl Marx and communist revolution, not in the rugged individualism of Horatio Alger.[4]

But the real William Haywood differed as drastically from the "Big Bill" of autobiographical recollection as the historical IWW differed from the Wobblies of novelists, playrights, and poets. The real man and the real organization matured in an America in which the primitive frontier was giving way to an urban and industrial environment. The workers Haywood knew and the IWW organized lived in cities and worked for corporations. The agricultural workers they spoke for toiled in "factories in the field," not on small farms. Wage workers, not frontiersmen, followed the call of Haywood and the IWW.

Haywood's America counted its dispossessed by the millions: workers whose skills had been rendered obsolete by technological innovation; Negroes emancipated by law but denied the social and economic freedom to make emancipation meaningful; European immigrants drawn to the land of promise only to dwell in urban slums and to work in dark mills; sons of farmers forced off the land and searching for work wherever it could be had.

The America of Haywood's youth and early manhood also fit the historical context out of which Oscar Lewis sees the "culture of poverty" emerging. It featured, in the four decades after 1877: (1) a cash economy, wage labor, and production for profit; (2) a persistently high rate of unemployment and underemployment for unskilled labor; (3) low wages; and (4) a paucity of social, political, and economic organization, whether on a voluntary basis or by government imposition, for the low-income population. Its values, imposed by the dominant class, stressed the accumulation of wealth and property and the possibility of upward mobility through thrift, and attributed low economic status to personal inadequacy.[5]

Haywood's life, as much as we know of it, was that of an individual who experienced "family disruption, violence, brutality, cheapness of life, lack of love, and lack of education." [6] Born in the American West, to be sure, he was neither rugged frontiersman, frustrated homesteader, nor gun-slinger. Rather, he led what—based upon his own testimony, twice offered under oath—must have been a typical Western working-class life.[7]

His life, at least as much of it as can be reconstructed accurately because of the paucity of Haywood's papers and the inaccuracies with which friends and scholars have surrounded it, developed in five distinct phases which flowed smoothly one into the other. He was born in Salt Lake City in 1869. Beginning with few advantages of family, education, or wealth, Haywood had to earn his own way at an early age. By age 15, he had become a hardrock miner; for the next twelve years he worked in Western mining camps, seldom remaining in one place long enough to establish roots. From these early work experiences in an industry unusual for its labor solidarity and violence he probably derived his beliefs about the worker's place in American society and the irrepressibility of conflict between capital and labor. During the next decade (1896–1905), after settling down in one community, Haywood served first as a local union official and then as an officer in his international union. Service in the cause of trade unionism taught him the limitations as well as the advantages of the American labor movement. Aware of its inadequacies, he became a crusader for industrial unionism and socialism.

The third phase of his life saw his role as labor leader diminish as his activities as a Socialist Party politician rose. But seven years of Socialist Party struggles (1906–13) left Haywood disillusioned with the ability of American Marxists to make a revolution in his native land. Recalled from the party's National Executive Committee in 1913, he began a new phase in his career: national leader of the apolitical, syndicalist, and revolutionary ɪww. At last finding full satisfaction in his work, Haywood again became a diligent and efficient union administrator, as well as a fire-eating, spell-binding advocate of revolution. But his success ended in federal repression of the ɪww, which brought Haywood's life to its final phase: political exile in the Soviet Union, unable to promote radicalism in the land of his birth or to build the new society in the land of his exile. Such, in brief, is a summary of the various phases through which Haywood's life passed.

Little is known about Haywood's family antecedents. Salt Lake City, his first home, with its well-planned streets, carefully tended gardens, and superior public services, may have been a terrestrial paradise for its Mormon founders; it was anything but that for Haywood. His father died when Haywood was only three, and the boy had little home or school life. Moving with his mother back and forth between Salt Lake City and his stepfather's home in the mining camp of Ophir, where he suffered the childhood accident that cost him an eye, young Haywood soon began to earn his own way. As an adolescent in Salt Lake City he spent his days scrambling for the various jobs open to an uneducated, working-class youth. By fifteen he was a strapping young man with broad shoulders, stout legs and bulging muscles, ready to go down into Nevada's mines with his stepfather, who introduced him to work in the hardrock mining industry.[8]

Haywood's life is hardest to reconstruct during the years 1888 to 1894, when he drifted around the widely scattered mining camps of Utah, Colorado, Nevada, and Idaho. His autobiography said that he had cowboyed and homesteaded during this period (a claim given credence by scholars who were attracted to the portrait of Haywood as a frustrated frontiersman), yet in sworn testimony about his life Haywood never mentioned either a homestead or life as a cowboy. Nor can his associates offer evidence to substantiate such assertions. We do know that about this time Haywood married and began to raise a family. His wife, "Nevada Jane" Minor—as described in her husband's autobiography—was the classic frontier woman, waging a losing struggle against the forces of nature, drudgery, and loneliness when the man of the family was absent from home for long stretches. Few photographs exist of "Nevada Jane," but one that was taken after she had been invalided and separated from her husband shows a slender woman with penetrating eyes, a homely, unexpressive face, and clear signs of having lived a hard life.[9] Possibly wanting sons, like most workingmen, Haywood had only daughters, but his two girls, Vern Florence and Henrietta Ruth, though clearly their father's daughters, and even more handsome, were never close to their father.

On the skimpy evidence available, one can only conclude that Haywood had a family but was not a family man. His wife, invalided as a result of childbirth and attracted to the mysteries of Christian Science, grew more frail and less attractive as the years passed— hardly the sort of woman to keep a virile husband at home. By 1900, when he had become a national union official, Haywood's marriage was failing. By the time he had become a national celebrity, after his arrest for murder in the notorious Steunenberg assassination case of 1906, it was a fiasco. Indeed, Pinkerton detectives seized their prime suspect in a Denver brothel, almost within walking distance of the family home where his wife lay ill in bed.[10]

In the ensuing trial the advice of the defense counsel, Clarence Darrow, brought a family reconciliation, and "Nevada Jane" and the two girls played a prominent role in court. It was hard for a jury to believe that a defendant with a frail wife and two attractive children, all of whom professed their man's absolute innocence, could be a cold-blooded mass murderer as the prosecution charged. The purpose of the courtroom charade accomplished, Haywood was acquitted and the family separated, this time permanently.[11] Haywood would make his career and establish his fame as a radical labor leader unencumbered by wife or children.

Whatever Haywood did between 1888 and 1895, in 1896 he worked in the mines of Silver City, Idaho, where he met Ed Boyce and the Western Federation of Miners and began a new phase of his life. The WFM had grown directly out of the corporatization of the Western mining frontier and the efforts of large corporations, backed by state and federal power, to "discipline" the previously powerful and independent Western workers. Founded in 1893, the WFM barely survived infancy; the 1893 depression and incompetent leadership made the union's first three years perilous. Prosperity returned in 1896, however, and an effective leader, Ed Boyce, assumed the WFM's presidency. That same year Boyce came to Silver City to organize a WFM local in which Bill Haywood became a charter member, finally finding a career for himself and a purpose in life.[12]

Haywood rose rapidly within the union's ranks. As secretary of the Silver City local he organized a determined campaign to win the union shop in local mines. So successful was he that only two Silver City miners remained outside the union. He cautiously led his fellow unionists along the accepted route of American trade unionism, concentrating upon job security, higher wages, shorter hours, and union-sponsored protection and benefits against illness, injury, and death.[13] His successful administration of local union affairs enhanced Haywood's reputation as an effective "business unionist" within the high echelons of the Western Federation. Elected secretary-treasurer of the WFM at its 1900 convention (a position he would hold for almost eight years), he looked forward to repeating his local triumphs on a national scale.[14]

When Haywood assumed national union office in 1900 the WFM had already left the labor movement's mainstream. Confronted by the united power of capital and the state during an industrial conflict at Leadville, Colorado, in 1896–97, the WFM, as a recent American Federation of Labor affiliate, had vainly pleaded with President Samuel Gompers and the AFL's 1896 convention for assistance. Boyce's experience at this convention so convinced him of the failure of traditional trade union tactics that, in a bitter exchange with Gompers, Boyce even denied that he was a trade unionist as Gompers defined the term.[15]

By 1896 Gompers and the AFL were moving to make their peace with the American system. Although the AFL had once preached the inevitability of class conflict and the need to abolish the "wage-slave" system, it now proclaimed the beauties of class harmony and the possibilities inherent in a beneficent capitalism. By 1900 Gompers faithfully served the needs of the AFL's rank and file—men who possessed valuable and scarce skills, belonged to powerful craft unions, were treated better than the mass of workers, and quarreled over their share of what capitalism produced rather than with the system itself.[16]

Vehemently disagreeing with Gompers' approach to trade unionism, Boyce led the WFM in establishing the Western Labor Union, a dual, schismatic labor federation. Formed in 1898 largely by Boyce with Western Federation funds, it claimed that the AFL emphasized the needs of labor's skilled elite whereas the WLU stressed a policy "broad enough in principle and sufficiently humane in character to embrace every class of toil, from the farmer to the skilled mechanic, in one great brotherhood." Where the AFL stressed the absolute autonomy of the national craft union, the Westerners favored the industrial union, free transfer from union to union, and union solidarity. Where the AFL sought to close America's gates to newcomers, the Westerners welcomed them.[17] Where the AFL preferred such traditional trade union tactics as strikes, boycotts, and collective bargaining, the WLU insisted that industrial technology and corporate concentration had made the traditional tactics obsolete, leaving the working class but one recourse: to vote socialist.[18]

This was the labor environment in which Haywood matured as a union official, keeping the WFM's books and for a time editing its official journal, the *Miners' Magazine.* Haywood's editorials in the *Magazine* reflected a growing disenchantment with "business unionism" and an increasing distaste for many aspects of American society. From his early pieces extolling the value of union labels and promoting cooperation with AFL affiliates, he moved on—in awkward metaphors— to compose passionate pleas for union ownership of mines, to celebrate the eventual triumph of socialism, and to issue vitriolic comments on Gompers and the AFL. As secretary-treasurer he managed the international's affairs as efficiently as he had once handled those of his Silver City local.[19]

Under the combined leadership of Boyce and Haywood the WFM thrived; radicalism proved no impediment. The WFM chartered more new locals and recruited more new members from 1900 to 1903 than at any other time in its history. Between 1900 and 1902 it added 55 locals and ten thousand members; and during 1903 it increased its total membership by a third, raising it to between thirty-five thousand and forty thousand. In 1902, when Boyce retired from the union's presidency, he left behind him an organization which seemed secure.[20]

Up to this point in his life Haywood had proved himself an able union official, one who had traveled ideologically from the pure and simple policies employed at Silver City to the industrial unionism and political socialism of the Western Federation, the Western Labor Union, and the American Labor Union.[21] As early as February, 1902, however, he had a premonition that his career as an ordinary union official would soon end. In an editorial he wrote for the *Miners' Magazine*, and which seemed to refer directly to its author's ambitions, Haywood commented: The agitator "is the advance agent of social improvement and fully realizes that reforms are not achieved by conservative methods." [22]

II

Within a year of this remark events in Colorado transformed Haywood from a rhetorical radical into a revolutionary activist. Until 1903 he had maintained that social change would come to the working class through organization, education, and legislation. He even derided the need for class conflict, informing Colorado officials and businessmen: "We [the WFM] are not opposed to employers . . . it is our purpose and aim to work harmoniously and jointly with the employers as best we can under this system, and we intend to change the system if we get sufficiently organized and well enough educated to do so." [23]

One year later Haywood would drastically reverse himself, for class warfare in Colorado in 1903 and 1904 taught him the limitations inherent in seeking to cooperate with private employers and public officials. Before engaging in industrial conflict the WFM had offered to negotiate with Colorado employers, but the businessmen preferred to smash the union—an "un-American," seditious, even criminal organization. And a pliant governor who had no scruples about authorizing illegal searches and seizures, unwarranted arrests, and suspension of due process, taught Haywood and the WFM just how "impartial" government was.[24]

The militia that was sent to the Cripple Creek and Telluride strike districts by the Colorado governor, James H. Peabody, made its purpose clear. "To hell with the Constitution," an officer proclaimed; "we aren't going by the Constitution." In Colorado the state was indistinguishable from private capitalism. The governor provided the troops and the mine owners paid for them; the governor employed and paid Pinkerton detectives, and the mine owners supervised their work in the field.[25]

The Western Federation went into the Colorado labor conflict a dynamic and growing organization; it came out a crushed and declining one. Haywood went into the conflict as a full-time union official, part-time agitator, and equivocal revolutionary; he came out a part-time union official, a full-time agitator, and a committed revolutionary.

The Colorado experience made Haywood and the wfm cynical about the value of education and legislative reforms, and they now began to emphasize direct labor action. Colorado had convinced them that America's disinherited had to discover new weapons to win social change. Traditional trade unions, political action, even radical politics had been found wanting. Haywood later told the United States Commission on Industrial Relations: "It was during the period of those strikes that the Western Federation of Miners realized the necessity of labor getting together into one big union. . . . There seemed to be no hope for such a thing as that [solidarity] among any of the existing labor organizations." [26] To find new weapons Haywood and the wfm, together with other discontented American radicals, created the Industrial Workers of the World.

Chairman of the iww's founding convention, the keynoter, and afterward the eulogizer of its accomplishments, Haywood epitomized the spirit of the convention of June, 1905. He spoke to delegates who represented the Socialist Trades and Labor Alliance, splinter labor unions, "paper" labor unions, a few real unions (his own, of course), and to delegates who represented only themselves (Debs, Mother Jones, Lucy Parsons, and Algie Simons, for example) as an experienced, successful union official. Also, he stood above the nasty and petty sectarian socialist squabbles many delegates had brought with them to Chicago as he stressed the convention's essential purpose. From the opening moment, when Haywood called to order "the Continental Congress of the Working Class," he spoke of the need to emancipate America's working-class masses from capitalism through the power of an organization that could destroy the existing system and the prevailing relationships of production. Haywood advised the assembled delegates to create a new labor organization as the voice of the unskilled, the unorganized, the powerless. "What I want to see from this organization," he said, " is an uplifting of the fellow that is down in the gutter . . . realizing that the society can be no better than its most miserable." [27] Following Haywood's sentiment, the iww opened its doors to all workers, skilled and unskilled, native and immigrant, child and adult, male and female, black, white, and even yellow. It provided for low uniform initiation fees, still lower dues, and free universal transfer of union cards.

In order to train the powerless in the uses of power the ɪww vested ultimate organizational authority in the rank and file, establishing—on paper—the most democratic decision-making procedures in the history of American trade unionism. All actions taken by ɪww national officials were made subject to appeal to the general convention, whose decisions, in turn, might be put to a general-membership referendum. In practice, the ɪww's anti-organizational, implicitly anarchic spirit hindered the effective functioning of its general headquarters and allowed ɪww affiliates even more local autonomy and freedom than the organization's constitution offered them in theory. Even the locals usually practiced a form of rotation of officials that was so effective it would have shocked Andrew Jackson himself.[28]

The delegates at the ɪww's founding convention must have found Haywood impressive. Well over six feet tall, broad shouldered, with ample girth and a pock-marked but handsome face set off by a patch over his right eye, Haywood's features bore witness to the battles he had waged and the suffering he had endured. His appearance proclaimed his strength. Neither stamping, pounding, bellowing, nor bullying, he used simple, direct, working-class expressions. Listening to "Big Bill" speak, an observer commented, and "stripping Haywood of all the attributes which usually enable labor leaders to lead, we end by finding in him two qualities, rare ones: genuine power and genuine simplicity." [29]

Haywood, however, had less endearing qualities by American Victorian standards. He was as much "at home" in the saloon and brothel as on the speaker's platform or in the union office. Whoring and drinking, however, added to the image of his virility and apparently did not lessen his appeal to workingmen, although this may have diminished his ability to serve the labor movement. At any rate, Haywood never had a chance to put his strength or his imagination to work for the ɪww; he would be isolated in an Idaho prison for the next two years.

On the afternoon of December 30, 1905, ex-Idaho Governor Frank Steunenberg was assassinated. Two days later, on January 1, 1906, local police apprehended the presumed assassin, Harry Orchard, who after several weeks of subtle interrogation by famed Pinkerton agent

James McParland (the man who had brought Pennsylvania's notorious Molly Maguires to "justice" thirty years earlier) confessed to the governor's murder and to countless other crimes, all of which he alleged he performed at the behest of the Haywood-dominated "inner circle of the WFM." [30] McParland's men then kidnapped Haywood, George Pettibone (a former WFM member, close friend of Haywood and Moyer, and then a small businessman in Denver), and WFM President Charles Moyer on February 17, 1906. Unable to communicate with friends, family, or attorney, the three abductees were sped to Idaho on a special train, where a month later they would be indicted on murder charges. They remained in jail, without bond, for more than a year while McParland unsuccessfully searched for evidence to corroborate Orchard's confession. [31]

Meanwhile, Wobblies and members of the Western Miners organization fought among and between themselves; indeed, an open factional battle erupted at the 1906 IWW convention about whether the IWW should be an uncompromising revolutionary organization, or whether it should concentrate upon unionism and the achievement of improved working conditions. The majority at this second Wobbly convention, calling themselves revolutionists, purged their opponents, even abolishing the office of president. During the convention struggle the Western Federation's delegates divided, bringing the Wobblies' civil war into their own union. The western miners disagreed about whether to endorse the new "revolutionary" IWW, or whether to create a non-revolutionary industrial union federation, until the 1907 WFM Convention voted to withdraw from the IWW. [32]

The struggle raged even within the prison walls. Moyer, after the WFM's 1904 defeat in Colorado, had begun to rethink his support of radical socialism, dual unionism, and constant industrial conflict. His arrest and confinement hastened the reassessment. In the future, he decided, he would lead his union toward the AFL—that is, toward less radicalism and more cooperation with employers. Many WFM members who had never taken to radical unionism or to socialism or who had fought the IWW "revolutionists" at the 1906 convention could be counted upon to support Moyer. No discernible shift toward the right could be detected in Haywood, however; if anything, arrest and imprisonment impelled him toward more radical views. Haywood claimed in his autobiography that reading radical literature while in prison had reinforced his own intuitive judgments. More likely, however, Haywood's personality was more rebellious than Moyer's, and perhaps he had a desire for martyrdom—what a Freudian might call a death wish. Further research into Haywood's early life would doubtless turn up many more examples of his rebellious nature inasmuch as several documents suggest Haywood's strong assertiveness well before the founding of the iww and his formal break with Moyer (who apparently was a contented family man).[33]

Thus divided, Moyer and Haywood could do nothing to bind the iww's wounds nor, for that matter, to temper the conflict within the miners' union. Moyer threw in his lot with the dominant wfm faction, which by 1907 was on the road to a reconciliation with the afl. Haywood, however, found himself alone. Although critical of the men who had dominated the 1906 iww convention, he could not endorse their opponents. Still a member of the Socialist Party and a believer in political action, Haywood was leery of an iww dominated by Daniel De Leon's Socialist Labor Party and Vincent St. John's apolitical direct actionists.[34]

III

In May, 1907, Haywood was finally brought to trial, and was acquitted (partly because Orchard's confession was uncorroborated and partly because Orchard's testimony during cross-examination was contradictory). But he left prison a union leader without an organization, an agitator without an immediate cause. The Western Federation, which by then had withdrawn from the iww and restored Moyer to the presidency, wanted no part of the radical Haywood, and early in 1908 it unceremoniously dropped him. Contrary to the version of Charles Madison, Patrick Renshaw, and Carl Hein, Haywood's attitude toward the feeble iww was similarly cool. A Denver iww official complained: "So much does Haywood think of the I.W.W. that he has never been near our headquarters or our meetings, here in Denver, since his acquittal." [35]

The Idaho incident, however, had opened a new phase in Haywood's life. Converted into a national celebrity by his trial, he proved exceedingly useful to the Socialist Party, and he was accommodating. Even while he had been in prison he had run for the governorship of Colorado on the Socialist Party ticket in 1906. Rejecting the lucrative lecturing and writing offers that awaited him on his release, he chose instead to speak for the party. In 1908 he took a prominent part in Debs's "Red Special" campaign for the presidency.

Even among Socialists, who elected him to the party's National Executive Committee in 1909, Haywood proved a dissenter. His experiences had convinced him that no capitalist law was worth a laborer's respect, no capitalist's property was worth a worker's life; and he increasingly counseled law-breaking, sabotage, and direct non-political action. On one occasion Haywood defiantly informed an audience of Socialists: "I despise the law, and I am not a law-abiding citizen." To American Socialists who, unlike Debs, feared imprisonment, Haywood said: "Those of us who are in jail—those of us who have been in jail—all of us who are willing to go to jail—care not what you say or do! We despise your hypocrisy. . . . We are the Revolution!" Yet he represented a party that by and large respected the law and opposed the destruction of property. In 1913 his continued advocacy of sabotage would lead to his recall from the party's National Executive Committee.[36]

Sent to Europe in 1910 as an American delegate to that year's Copenhagen Congress of the Second International, Haywood spent most of his time with trade union activists and his European contacts influenced him to end the phase of his life that had been dominated by Socialist Party politics and oratory. Like William Z. Foster, who visited the continent at the same time and whom Haywood met in Paris (the two American radicals, however, were never close friends), Haywood became intrigued with the militancy of European labor, its appeal to the less skilled workers, and its effective use of direct-action tactics. It was in Europe that Haywood decided to resume his connection with the IWW. Interviewed in a French syndicalist paper, Haywood declared his belief in industrial unionism as represented by the IWW. Returning to America, he appeared on the rostrum at New York City's Yorkville Casino in December, 1910, as an accredited IWW speaker. The enthusiastic audience welcomed the lost son back to the fold.[37]

The IWW and Haywood now thought alike and acted alike. In 1908 the IWW had suffered a second purge that expelled Daniel De Leon, the self-proclaimed high priest of revolutionary socialism, and those who shared his belief in the primacy of political over economic action. Vincent St. John, a former WFM official who had allied himself with the IWW "revolutionists" in 1906 and later had left the Western Federation, now took firm control of the IWW. Under his leadership the organization divorced itself from all political parties and concentrated upon direct economic action that would deliver "the goods" to America's underpaid and overworked but unorganized laborers. Like Haywood, St. John stressed direct action and militant tactics in his leadership of the IWW, disdaining to hide his abomination of the law and private property.[38] Finally finding an organization that was suited to his personality and in need of his unique talents, Haywood entered upon the most significant phase of his life.

IV

Haywood, St. John, and the IWW created a derivative but distinctly American radicalism. IWW beliefs must be understood in terms of those to whom the organization appealed and those whom it tried to organize. After 1908 the IWW concentrated upon workers who had been neglected by the mainstream American labor movement. To "timber beasts," hobo harvesters, itinerant construction hands, the exploited East and South European immigrants, racially excluded Negroes, Mexican, and Asian Americans the IWW promised a new day. As Haywood told an inquisitive reporter: "Here were millions and millions of people working desperately and barely able to exist. All I needed was to stir those millions into a sense of their wrongs."[39]

Rexford G. Tugwell aptly described the kind of worker to whom the IWW carried its radical gospel. Writing about the Pacific Northwest logger, Tugwell noted:

> "His eyes are dull and reddened; his joints are stiff with the rheumatism almost universal in the wettest climate in the world; his teeth are rotting; he is wracked with strange diseases and tortured by unrealized dreams that haunt his soul. . . . The blanket-stiff is a man without a home. . . . The void of his atrophied affections is filled with a resentful despair and bitterness against the society that self-righteously cast him out." [40]

Wobbly recruits were Marx's *Lumpenproletariat*, individuals who felt marginal, helpless, dependent, inferior. Impotent and alienated, they harbored deep-seated grievances against the institutions of the ruling class: police, government, and church.[41] Although IWW leaders did not come from the ranks of these disinherited, they shared their alienation.

The disinherited joined the ɪww by the thousands because it offered, in the words of Carleton Parker, "a ready-made dream of a new world where there is a new touch with sweetness and light and where for a while they can escape the torture of forever being indecently kicked about." To migratory workers the ɪww promised "the only social break in the harsh search for work that they have ever had: its headquarters the only competitor of the saloon in which they are welcome." [42]

More important, the ɪww also promised its followers a way out of their "culture of poverty." It endowed them with class consciousness, organization, solidarity, hope for the future; that is, with a sense of identification with larger social groups that might destroy the psychological and social core of their marginality, dependence, and impotence. It tried to give them what revolutionaries the world over usually see as an absolute necessity: a sense of self-respect, importance, and power—a feeling that the disinherited were humanity's last best hope.

ɪww ideology visualized the downtrodden emerging from the abyss. They would seize industry for themselves; mere crumbs from their masters' tables were not enough. "We are many," proclaimed the ɪww's newspapers. "We are resourceful; we are animated by the most glorious vision of the ages; we cannot be conquered, and *we shall conquer the world for the working class.*" Simply put in the ɪww's favorite revolutionary hymn, the *Internationale*: "We have been *naught*—We shall be All!" [43]

But Wobblies did not expect their revolution to make itself. It was inevitable, but they would help the course of history. "Our organization is not content with merely making the prophecy," insisted *Solidarity*, "but acts upon industrial and social conditions with a view to shaping them in accord with the general tendency." [44] To help history, the Wobblies followed the pattern of all modern revolutionaries: they proposed a program, developed a doctrine concerning the transfer of power, and elaborated a system of organization. Unlike most other modern revolutionaries, however, with the exception of the anarcho-syndicalists whom they resembled, Wobblies rejected purely political tactics and organizations. The Wobblies believed they could best make history by obtaining power. Who held power ruled society!

The IWW proposed to transfer power from the capitalists, who held it and used it for antisocial purposes, to the proletariat, who would exercise power for the benefit of humanity. Jack London in *The Iron Heel*, a novel referred to often and lovingly by Wobblies, expressed better than any IWW editorial or pamphlet the organization's feelings about power. London's hero, Ernest Everhardt—a fictional Haywood—affirmed that "Power . . . is what we of the working class preach. We know and well we know by bitter experience, that no appeal for the right, for justice, for humanity, can ever touch you. . . . So we have preached power." And he concluded, as coldly as London's capitalist, "Power will be the arbiter, as it has always been the arbiter. . . . We of the labor hosts have conned that word over till our minds are all a-tingle with it. Power. It is a kingly word." [45]

The doctrine had Darwinian overtones. In its widely circulated organizing pamphlet for lumber workers the IWW emphasized: "It is the law of nature that the strong rule and the weak are enslaved." George Speed, a veteran West Coast trade unionist and charter member of the IWW, expressed the IWW concept tersely: "Power is the thing that determines everything today. . . it stands to reason that the fellow that has got the big club swings it over the balance. That is life as it exists today." Thus workers had to develop their own sources of power; nobody could do it for them—neither Socialists, political action, nor legislation. "That is my contention," argued Speed. "They have to learn to do it themselves, and they are going to suffer until they do learn." [46]

IWW antipathy toward political action reflected the status of its members. Migratory workers moved too often to establish legal voting residences. Millions of unnaturalized immigrants lacked the franchise. So did Negroes, and women, and children, to whom the IWW opened its doors. As Haywood informed the Commission on Industrial Relations: "The wage earner or producing classes are in the minority; second . . . they are not educated to the game of politics . . . their life is altogether industrial." [47] Even immigrants and the native born who had the right to vote nourished a deep suspicion of government. The state, symbolized by the policeman's club and the magistrate's edict, hardly treated the poor kindly. Wobblies realized that the power of the state was used against them. Who knew better than an IWW, who had been imprisoned for exercising his right of free speech or clubbed by a cop while peacefully picketing for higher wages? Wobblies never believed that stuffing pieces of paper, even socialist ones, into a ballot box would transform this repressive state into a humane one.

If the workers could not use political power to alter the rules of the game, what remained? Wobblies thought they had the answer. "Political power," said one, "is a reflex of economic power, and those who control economic power control the political power of the state." Another concluded: "Without economic power working-class political action is like a house without a foundation or a dream without substance." [48]

iww leaders therefore taught their followers how to achieve economic power. "Get it through industrial organization." "Organize the workers to control the use of their labor power." "The secret of power is organization." "The only force that can break . . . tyrannical rule . . . is one big union of all the workers." [49]

Through organization the iww could exert direct action, its essential means of bringing the new society into existence. By direct action it meant "any economic step taken by the workers. . . . It includes sabotage . . . passive resistance . . . and covers the ordinary strike, the intermittent strike, the silent strike, and the death blow to capitalism in the form of the social general strike." "Shall I tell you what direct action really means?" another iww manifesto asked. "The worker on the job shall tell the boss when and where he shall work, how long, and for what wages and under what conditions." Direct action, according to Haywood, would eventually reach the point where workers were strong enough to say: "' Here, Mr. Stockholder, we won't work for you any longer. You have drawn dividends out of our hides long enough; we propose that you shall go to work now, and under the same opportunities that we have had.' " [50]

Wobblies, in their emphasis on direct action, liked to compare themselves to ante bellum abolitionists, who had also defied the laws that sanctioned human bondage and who had publicly burned the American Constitution. "We are the modern abolitionists fighting against wage slavery," proclaimed general organizer James Thompson.[51] Wobblies were willing to unsheath the Lord's terrible swift sword.

Although the iww employed the vocabulary of violence, more often than not it utilized passive resistance and was itself the victim of violence that was instigated by law-enforcement officials, condoned by the law-abiding. The IWW, in fact, sought through organized activities to channel the frustrations and antisocial rage of the dispossessed into constructive courses. Even Haywood, whose career with the Western Federation had been associated with labor violence, told a reporter during the 1912 Lawrence textile strike: "I should never think of conducting a strike in the old way. . . . I, for one, have turned my back on violence. It wins nothing. When we strike now, we strike with our hands in our pockets. We have a new kind of violence—the havoc we raise with money by laying down our tools. Pure strength lies in the overwhelming power of numbers." [52]

Wobblies also looked to nonviolent tactics in order to expose the brutality of their enemy and to win sympathy for their suffering. Passive resistance, editorialized *Solidarity*, "has a tremendous moral effect; it puts the enemy on record; it exposes the police and city authorities as a bunch of law breakers; it drives the masters to the last ditch of resistance. 'Passive resistance' by the workers results in laying bare the inner workings and purposes of the capitalist mind. It also reveals the self-control, the fortitude, the courage, the inherent sense of order, of the workers' mind. As such, 'passive resistance' is of immense educational value." [53]

But IWW passive resistance should not be confused with pacifism. Nonviolence was only a means, never an end, and if passive resistance led only to beatings and deaths, the IWW threatened to respond in kind. Arturo Giovanitti, a sometime poet, sometime Wobbly, put the IWW's position bluntly: "The generally accepted notion seems to be that to kill is a great crime, but to be killed is the greatest." And Haywood cited Abraham Lincoln's alleged advice to citizens who suffered from hunger as a result of wartime food speculation: "Take your pickaxes and crowbars and go to the granaries and warehouses and help yourselves." That, said Haywood, "is a good I.W.W. doctrine." [54]

In keeping with its commitment to nonviolence (at least when lacking the power to employ violence), the IWW even saw its revolution coming peaceably. It would come, according to Haywood, when "labor was organized and self-disciplined [so] it could stop every wheel in the United States . . . and sweep off your capitalists and State legislatures and politicians into the sea." The only violence involved, he added, would occur after labor had drained the capitalists' pocketbooks. [55]

The nonviolent overthrow of capitalism would result from a general strike. Neither Haywood nor any other Wobby, however, ever precisely defined the general strike, but Haywood explained it as the stoppage of all work and the destruction of the capitalists through a peaceful paralysis of industry. Ben Williams insisted that it was no strike at all—simply "a 'general lockout of the employing class' leaving the workers in possession of the machinery of distribution and production." Whatever the exact definition of the general strike, Haywood wrote, whenever its day came "control of industry will pass from the capitalists to the masses and capitalists will vanish from the face of the earth." [56] This utopian day would come peaceably if workers had their way, and violently if capitalists attempted to postpone it with "roar of shell and whine of machine-guns."

In Haywood's dream of his utopia, "there will be a new society sometime in which there will be no battle between capitalist and wage earner, but . . . every man will have free access to land and its resources. In that day . . . the machinery can be made the slave of the people instead of a part of the people being made the slave of machinery." Another Wobbly's utopia would have no room for poverty, jails, police, the army and marines, Christians, churches, heaven and hell. Its cities would be clean and beautiful, with wide streets, parks, flowers, and fine homes and its workers "no longer stoop shouldered and consumptive looking." Prudery would disappear, along with heaven and hell, and naked children would frisk on the grass and bask in the sunshine. With economic freedom in this utopia and an abundance of food, shelter, clothing, and leisure, and education for everyone, "all hearts and minds [would be] turned towards solving the mysteries of the Universe." [57]

Wobblies never quite explained how this paradise would be governed; they agreed, however, that the state—as most Americans knew it—would be nonexistent. "There will be no such thing as the State or States," Haywood said. "The industries will take the place of what are now existing States." "Whenever the workers are organized in the industry, whenever they have a sufficient organization in the industry," added St. John, "they will have all the government they need right there." [58]

Somehow, each industrial union would possess and manage its own industry. Union members would elect superintendents, foremen, secretaries, and managers. The separate industrial unions would then meet jointly to plan for the welfare of society as a whole. This system, "in which each worker will have a share in the ownership and a voice in the control of industry, and in which each shall receive the full product of his labor," was variously called "the Cooperative Commonwealth," "the Workers' Commonwealth," "the Industrial Commonwealth," "Industrial Democracy," and "Industrial Communism." Unsure of its proposed system, the iww could not label it definitively.

Like European syndicalists, the Wobblies aimed to abolish capitalism by nonpolitical means; and, like them, they also emphasized direct action. In the iww's new society, as in that projected by European syndicalism, the political state would not exist; workers would administer industry directly through their industrial unions. The iww even took over the French syndicalist concept of the militant minority. "Our task," said an iww paper, "is to develop the conscious, intelligent minority to the point where they will be capable of carrying out the imperfectly expressed desires of the toiling millions." As a perceptive Socialist theorist noted, notwithstanding superficial variations caused by different economic and political conditions in different countries, "this living spirit of revolutionary purpose unifies French and British syndicalism and American Industrial Unionism (the iww)." [59]

Industrial unionism, Haywood once stated, was socialism "with its working clothes on." After 1913, however, when Haywood was recalled from the Socialist Party's highest council, iww industrial unionists and American Socialists had little in common. When Socialists talked of capturing control of the government through the ballot box and of transforming the capitalist state into the "Cooperative Commonwealth," the iww responded: "A wise tailor does not put stitches into rotten cloth." [60]

Wobblies might obey the law, use the voting booth, and temporize on their revolutionism, but they could never—despite the intellectuals among them—entirely forego anti-intellectualism. To Socialists who prided themselves on their intellectual abilities, Haywood said: "Socialism is so plain, so clear, so simple that when a person becomes intellectual he doesn't understand socialism." iww ideology always remained that of the poor, not of the educated; it was intended to motivate the disinherited, not to satisfy the learned. As an iww member noted, reviewing John Graham Brooks' *American Syndicalism*: "It is not the Sorels . . . the Wallings, LaMontes and such figures who count for the most—it is the obscure Bill Jones on the firing line, with stink in his clothes, rebellion in his brain, hope in his heart, determination in his eye and direct action in his gnarled fist." [61]

v

In the last analysis, the Wobblies and Haywood must be remembered more for what they did than for what they thought, more for what they fought for than what they learned. In 1914, the year he became the ıww's top official, Haywood succinctly explained the organization's role. "It has developed among the lowest strata of wage slaves in America a sense of their importance and capabilities such as never before existed. Assuming control and responsibility of their own affairs, the unorganized and unfortunate have been brought together, and have conducted some of the most unique strikes, fights for free speech and battles for constitutional rights." [62] And that is just what the organization did both before and after Haywood took command of the ıww. From 1909 to 1917 it led workers who were neglected by other labor organizations in struggles that raised their self-esteem and improved their conditions of life.

By fighting for free speech in Spokane, Fresno, Missoula, Sioux City, and Minot (among other cities), the ıww proved to long-brutalized migratories that authority could be defeated through direct action and passive resistance. Taking to the streets in defense of their civil liberties, Wobblies courted arrest, and those arrested were quickly replaced on soap boxes by other free-speech speakers. Wobblies flooded the jails, paralyzed the courtrooms, and strained the purses of the cities they confronted. Most civic authorities, unable to cope with such passive resistance on a mass scale, succumbed to ıww demands; but some authorities, like San Diego's, dealt with the ıww "menace" by methods later made infamous in Mussolini's Italy and Hitler's Germany. The ıww also achieved reforms in private employment agencies that had traditionally exploited migratories, and improved working conditions in farming and forestry.

In industrial centers such as McKees Rocks (steel, in 1909), Lawrence (textiles, in 1912), Paterson (textiles, in 1913), and Akron (rubber, in 1913), the ıww showed mass-production workers the possibilities of industrial unionism. It also tempered ethnic divisions by organizing without regard to distinctions of national origin. Most important, the ıww taught previously unorganized mass-production workers how to wage their own struggles for improvement. IWW members learned industrial warfare and union tactics in the manner Marxist theorists and even John Dewey prescribed—by doing! If Wobbly strikers wanted higher wages, shorter hours, and better conditions, their organizers let them fight for them. If workers wanted agreements with their employers, IWW leaders let their followers negotiate them. The IWW organized, agitated, advised; but it was the workers themselves who led and decided. When authorities queried IWW strikers about their leaders, the men and women could respond in a single voice: "We are all leaders."

After the Wobblies' surprising strike victory at Lawrence in 1912, the revolution seemed near at hand. Commentators forgot about the rising tide of socialism and began to worry about the more dangerous threat of revolutionary industrial unionism. Such intellectuals as Max Eastman and the young John Reed saw in the IWW the agency that would accomplish the Nietzschean transvaluation of the values of existing society. And they saw William Haywood as the archetypal Nietzschean superman, as Jack London's Ernest Everhardt come to life. Haywood became the darling of New York's Greenwich Village rebels, enjoying the role of star proletarian performer in Mabel Dodge Luhan's Fifth Avenue salon.[63]

But the IWW's revolutionary threat disappeared as quickly as it had come; victory in Lawrence was followed by defeat in Paterson, Akron, and other Eastern cities. Economic adversity aggravated organizational ills. When the American economy declined in 1913 and 1914, IWW membership, never more than thirty thousand before 1916, fell to about fifteen thousand in 1915. By December, 1914, Haywood reported a bankrupt treasury and the IWW seemed on the verge of extinction. No longer did leading journals warn about the dangers of industrial unionism.[64]

From 1909 to 1915, although the IWW had demonstrated to a segment of the American proletariat the virtues of organization, solidarity, and direct action, it could not keep them organized or united. It contended against forces that were simply too powerful to defeat. Employers, supported by local, state, and federal authorities, could vitiate IWW organizing efforts either through outright repression, or with the aid of progressive reforms, could offer workers immediate palliatives.

Throughout its history the IWW faced paradoxes the organization never resolved. If it offered only perpetual industrial warfare, how could it maintain its membership, let alone increase it? But if it won better contracts, and union recognition, and improved life for its members, what was to keep them from forswearing revolutionary goals and from following the established AFL pattern? If it declared a truce in the class war, how could it bring about the ultimate revolution? In the end, IWW leaders, including Haywood, subordinated reform opportunities to revolutionary necessities; the rank and file, when it could, took the reforms and neglected the revolution.

In adversity and decline, however, the IWW learned important lessons. In the summer of 1914 it began to concentrate upon the hardcore disinherited—the migrant workers who harvested the nation's wheat, picked its hops, cut its lumber, built its railroads, and mined its copper. To these men the IWW offered a purpose in life and a sense of identity and value; to the IWW they, in turn, gave allegiance and strength.

Migratories joined the IWW in increasing numbers as the organization demonstrated that it could improve their conditions of work. When Haywood took over the general headquarters in November, 1914, the IWW was almost broke. A year later, after its Agricultural Workers' Organization had begun an organizing campaign in the wheat belt, the IWW had a surplus in its treasury and thousands of new members on its roster, and it paid organizers to carry its word to lumber and construction workers and hardrock miners. The message Wobbly organizers carried in 1915 and 1916 emphasized organization, not revolution, and immediate gains, not utopian ideology. The new message was heard. Membership rose between 1915 and early 1917 to between sixty thousand and one hundred thousand. By 1916 the Wobblies could charter new industrial unions for lumber workers, hardrock miners, and construction hands.[65]

As its membership and treasury increased, the IWW's tone seemed to alter. The 1916 convention was the first convention that fully asserted the authority of general headquarters; separate industrial unions were to be subject to closer supervision by Haywood's new, centralized Chicago office. Those who disagreed with the new emphasis or disliked Haywood's predominant influence left the IWW or were relegated to obscurity within the organization. After 1916 Elizabeth Gurley Flynn, Joseph Ettor, Arturo Giovanitti, and Carlo Tresca (among others)—leaders who had once shared the headlines and national publicity with Haywood—were pushed into the background.

They were replaced by a new breed of Wobblies, those who propagandized less and organized more. Over this new ıww, which flourished as never before, presided William D. Haywood.[66]

Sitting behind his large roll-type desk at the new ıww headquarters on Chicago's West Madison Street, Haywood never seemed happier than early in 1917. Ralph Chaplin, then the editor of *Solidarity,* later remembered that Haywood, his boss and close friend, appeared more self-assured, more firm of voice, and more youthful as he worked among busy clerks and secretaries. Haywood seemed " a revolutionary tycoon whose dream was coming true." His enthusiasm infected everyone at ıww headquarters, which, in its effort "to build the new society within the shell of the old," became one of the liveliest places in Chicago.[67] But Haywood's happiness and enthusiasm would prove shortlived; so, too, would the ıww's success and growth. The factors that had brought the ıww prosperity presaged its death, and Haywood's exile.

The European conflict contributed greatly to ıww resurgence under Haywood, as war orders poured into the American market. Rising production brought rising profits and increasing labor scarcity. In a tight labor market the ıww could not only organize successfully, it could also win material improvements for its members inasmuch as employers were loath to sacrifice wartime profits to anti-union principles. But when America intervened in April, 1917, employers discovered how they could have profits without the ıww.

The ıww had long preached antimilitarism and antipatriotism as basic principles, and the war did not make any changes in this, but the ıww now concentrated upon organization, direct action, and on-the-job activities. It was too busy organizing harvest hands, lumber workers, and miners to lead antiwar campaigns. It was too busy fighting for higher wages and shorter hours to waste its time in an anti-conscription drive. The ıww did nothing directly to interfere with the American war effort, but it did organize and strike in industries that were vital to that effort.[68]

In the spring of 1917 ıww strikes threatened the lumber industry, copper mining, and the wheat harvest. Stories were spread which received credence in the Justice and War Departments, that ıww strikes were German-inspired and German-financed.[69] Western employers pleaded with state and national authorities to suppress the ıww in the interest of national security; they also took direct action of their own, organizing Citizens' Alliances and Vigilante Leagues, some of these with the sanction of the Justice Department. These vigilantes hunted out every worker who threatened war profits.

Everywhere the iww found itself beset by enemies. Local and state officials joined private businessmen in persecuting Wobblies. If their action proved ineffective, officials demanded federal intervention, and before long federal troops patrolled West Coast docks, Northwest woods and farmlands, and the mining towns of Arizona and Montana. Simultaneously, the Justice Department and Military Intelligence infiltrated agents into the iww. Between Pinkertons, Thiel detectives, and federal agents, spies had the iww under constant surveillance. Even the Labor Department, less anxious and more realistic about Western labor conflicts than the War and Justice Departments, did its part to curb the iww. Labor Department agents, however, also tried to use the war crisis to improve working conditions, as well as to induce iww laborers to join AFL affiliates. With Gompers' hearty approval and direct cooperation, the Labor Department attacked the iww menace, promoting the AFL cause.[70]

When these efforts failed to end the iww's threat to Western industries, the federal government—pressured by private business, state governors, United States attorneys, and influential congressmen—took the final step. With presidential approval, the Justice Department proscribed the iww. In a nationwide series of raids on September 5, 1917, the department's agents invaded every important iww headquarters, seizing everything they could lay their hands on (including rubber bands, paper clips, and Ralph Chaplin's love letters).[71] Sorting through tons of confiscated material, the Justice Department assembled the evidence to indict iww leaders for sedition, espionage, and interference with the war effort.

By the end of 1917 almost every important iww official, including Haywood, was in prison. In the interests of national security, industrial harmony, and business profits, the government put the iww under lock and key. Due process followed, but what happened in the courtrooms in which Wobbly leaders were tried, convicted, and sentenced was only a legal charade. Whether in Chicago, Wichita, or Sacramento, the trial evidence was always the same, as were the results. In every case the iww—as an organization, not its individual leaders or members—was placed on trial. In every case the iww was judged not for what it had done but for what it said and wrote, although most of the "seditious" writings and speeches antedated America's overseas involvement and, to a great extent, 1914.[72]

Some subordinates in the Justice Department realized that the government did not have a valid case against the iww. They suggested that, in the interest of justice, trials be postponed until wartime hysteria subsided, but the Justice Department would not listen to such an argument. To its top officials, many drawn from Wall Street law offices, and often associates of leading businessmen, the iww represented a real menace, both to America's war effort and to business profits. The trials went on and Wobbly leaders were sent to Leavenworth.[73]

Thus ended the iww's threat to the prevailing order. New and inexperienced Wobbly leaders took to fighting among themselves, becoming easy prey to the Pinkertons and military intelligence agents who continued to infiltrate the organization. And thus ended Haywood's role in the history of American radicalism. In 1917 he had led a dynamic organization that posed a growing threat to the established order. In 1918, after smashing the iww, the United States government in effect said to Haywood and his fellow Wobblies what Leon Trotsky had said to Martov and the Russian Mensheviks after the Bolsheviks' November revolution: "You are miserable isolated individuals. You are bankrupt. You have played out your role. Go where you belong, to the dustheap of history." [74]

VI

Most convicted Wobblies, accepting their punishment and what they thought of as martyrdom, went to Leavenworth, but Haywood refused to surrender. Plagued by a history of ulcers and diabetes, and perhaps by cirrhosis of the liver, and fearful of another prison term, he jumped bail and turned up in the Soviet Union in 1921. Neither his close friends nor inveterate critics knew why he declined martyrdom and chose political exile. Whatever the reason, that decision betrayed Haywood's bail backers, brought them financial loss (and in one case suicide), and turned most of his former iww comrades against him.[75]

Escape to Russia, however, did not save Haywood from history's dustheap. Not really a Bolshevik, he did not fit into Lenin's or Trotsky's schemes for a new and better world. Expecting to find the

Wobblies' utopian workers' state—or nonpolitical anarcho-syndicalist society—he found instead a system busily constructing its own political and industrial bureaucracy. The IWW's anti-organizational approach proved as unacceptable to Russia's new rulers as it had to America's. For a time Haywood directed a labor project in the Kuznets district, but by 1923 his dream of building a Wobbly utopia in Russia had soured.

Tired, sick, the strength draining from his huge body, Haywood retired to a room in Moscow's Lux Hotel. He later married a Russian national, but almost nothing of substance can be discovered about this marriage. Haywood usually kept to his Moscow hotel at the time Alexander Trachtenberg, an American Communist leader, made his pilgrimages to Moscow in the 1920's. Later, Trachtenberg remembered Haywood as a desperately lonely man, alien to Moscow's new society, who found solace only in the bottle and in the companionship of old Wobblies who somehow drifted into his hotel room. They would join their former chief in drink and song, going through the *Little Red Song Book* from cover to cover interminably, until they collapsed in a drunken stupor.[76]

Such was Haywood's Moscow exile; he played no part in the construction of Soviet society. Ailing and frequently hospitalized, he tried to keep abreast of labor developments at home, and he found time to complete his unsatisfactory and distorted autobiography. On May 28, 1928, he died unmourned in a Moscow hospital. Russian officials placed part of his ashes alongside those of John Reed beneath a plaque in the Kremlin wall, and the remaining ashes were shipped to Waldheim Cemetery in Chicago for burial beside the graves of the Haymarket Riot martyrs.[77]

To President Theodore Roosevelt, Haywood was an undesirable citizen; to Frank P. Walsh, reform Democrat and chairman of Woodrow Wilson's Commission on Industrial Relations, he was the "rugged intellectual, with his facility of phrasing, his marvelous memory and his singularly clear and apt method of illustration." To conservatives, Haywood was the voice of anarchy; to friends and admirers, he was the epitome of sweet, simple reason. To such labor foes as Samuel Gompers, he was an inept propagandizer and a smasher of trade unions; to his supporters, he was an effective administrator and a talented organizer. To Mary Gallagher, who directed the campaign to free Tom Mooney, he was a great leader in every way; to Ramsay MacDonald, he was a rough-hewn agitator, splendid with crowds but ineffectual as an administrator.

Scholars have done little to interpret Haywood's character other than allude to his rebellious spirit and frontier heritage. The essays of Charles Madison and Carl Hein tell us nothing that cannot be found in Haywood's autobiography; and in Patrick Renshaw's recent history of the IWW his treatment of Haywood is notable for the number of errors he makes in only three pages. Haywood's grossly inaccurate autobiography is a masterpiece of precise history compared to Renshaw's summary.[78] Perusing the comments of Haywood's contemporaries and the analyses of scholars gives us no understanding of his personality. Unfortunately there is little evidence to support any of the differing versions of Haywood's life.

The only comment one can make with certainty is that Haywood, like most Wobblies, was neither an original thinker nor a theoretician. Haywood, in short, was not plagued by the "hobgoblin of little minds": consistency; his life is a tale of inconsistency.

During his early years with the WFM he displayed outstanding ability as an administrator and organizer. Willing to work long hours and to drive himself furiously, Haywood mastered the intricacies of trade unionism. From 1914 to 1917, in a later and vastly different environment, he also proved to be an industrious union official. During those years, when the IWW experienced its most rapid growth, Haywood gave the Wobblies their first taste of effective administration under a rationalized central office. Between these tours of duty as a union official he devoted himself to agitation and to freewheeling revolutionary oratory in which he impressed many observers with his anti-disciplinarian, anti-organizational, anarchistic personality.

The inconsistencies abound. In a life that was shadowed by violence, few radicals ever expressed the doctrine of passive resistance so forcefully or played so prominent a part in nonviolent labor demonstrations. A denigrator of effete intellectuals, Haywood nevertheless had intellectual pretensions of his own. He harangued strikers in the working-class vernacular, but he also read widely (and deeply), and wrote with considerable skill. It is impossible to pinpoint the time when he began to read serious fiction and nonfiction, but during his incarceration in 1917–18 he wrote movingly to Frank Walsh about the latest Mark Twain he had read. As a writer—he was temporary editor of the *Miners' Magazine,* a contributing editor to the *International Socialist Review,* and a regular commentator in the IWW press—Haywood developed from an immature and awkward stylist into a master of the caustic comment and the philippic phrase, if not an author of graceful and closely reasoned economic and social treatises. In his writings and speeches on economics, politics, sex, and religion he wielded one pen in the modern camp of harsh realism and the other in maudlin Victorian romanticism. Haywood appealed to immigrant workers in the East and to migrant workers in the West, as well as to such bohemian intellectuals as John Reed and Max Eastman.

In the last analysis, Haywood fits no pattern. Unlike the typical labor leader, who begins his career as a radical, finds success, and becomes more conservative, Haywood began his union career as a conservative, discovered success, and became a radical. A man of many talents—administrator, organizer, agitator, speaker, writer— he developed none of these to its utmost, which was perhaps his gravest failing. A labor leader who was at home both with wage workers and intellectuals (an unusual combination in the United States), he led a labor organization that was out of touch with most workers and he frustrated many intellectuals by his refusal to accept martyrdom in 1921. In Russia, he neither served American radicalism nor built the new utopia.

Haywood's life and the history of the Wobblies support an ambivalent conclusion about the results of dissent in America. Dissenting at the outset, Wobblies maintained that poor immigrants and dispossessed native Americans could be organized, given a sense of purpose, and taught to confront authority nonviolently. As they proceeded to do just this, American society accommodated the Wobbly-induced radicalism within the existing system. Rexford Tugwell, commenting upon the IWW's ability to organize casual workers, remarked in 1920: "No world re-generating philosophy comes out of them and they are not going to inherit the earth. When we are a bit more orderly they will disappear."

Tugwell was right. During World War I the federal government influenced Western employers to be more "orderly"; lumbermen established company unionism and the eight-hour day, and owners of copper mines improved working conditions and created grievance machinery. Many Wobblies watched American society vitiate their radicalism by accommodating to it, and ended up by joining that society. Ralph Chaplin is the best example of this process: he became a member of the Congregational church, an ardent patriot, and an even more ardent anti-Communist.

Wobblies who did not opt for reform capitalism lost the faith for other reasons. The ıww's anti-organizational credo, its utter abomination of existing institutions, and its refusal (or, perhaps, inability) to conceptualize an alternative of its own to the structural arrangements of American society (so much like the dilemma of the contemporary New Left) resulted in internal anarchy and recurrent secessions, divisions, and organizational collapses. Thus some Wobblies—Elizabeth Gurley Flynn, James P. Cannon, William Z. Foster are good examples —eventually located the disciplined organization they craved in the Communist Party. Others kept the original faith, never losing their belief in a utopian society bereft of a coercive state. When their dissent moved from speech to action, from criticism to resistance, they felt the heavy hand of a repressive state. If America was capable of domesticating its radicals by offering them reforms, it could also smash them with a vengeance.

Never able to forget his 1915 utopian dream, yet unable to adjust to Communist discipline, Haywood's ashes were divided between the land of his miserable exile and America, among an earlier generation of martyred dissenters.

[1] See John Dos Passos, *The 42nd Parallel* (vol. 1 of *U.S.A.*) (New York, 1930), pp. 89–93, 100–9. Dos Passos also wrote biographical sketches of Haywood (whose name he misspelled Heywood), *ibid.*, pp. 94–97, and of Joe Hill and Wesley Everest, in *1919* (vol. 2 of *U.S.A.*) (New York, 1932), pp. 421–23, 456–61; James Jones, *From Here to Eternity* (New York, 1951), pp. 513, 640–42, 644, 647–48; Wallace Stegner, *The Preacher and the Slave* (Boston, 1950); Barrie Stavis, *The Man Who Would Not Die* (New York, 1954), pp. 3–114. For earlier fictional accounts, see Winston Churchill (the American novelist), *The Dwelling Place of Light* (New York, 1917), and Zane Grey, *The Desert of Wheat* (New York, 1919); cf. Dan Wakefield, "The Haunted Hall: I.W.W. at 50," *Dissent*, 3 (1956): 414–19.

[2] Philip Taft, *Organized Labor in American History* (New York, 1964), pp. 289–98; and esp. Robert L. Tyler, "The I.W.W. and the West," *American Quarterly*, 12 (Summer, 1960): 175–87; *idem*, "The Rise and Fall of an American Radicalism," *Historian*, 19 (November, 1956): 48–65; *idem*, "Rebels of the Woods and Fields," *Oregon Historical Quarterly*, 55 (March,

1954): 1–44. For a more sympathetic recent account, see Patrick Renshaw, *The Wobblies* (New York, 1967), a book as notable for its factual errors as for its equitable portrayal of the ɪww. For a judicious if dry and tediously institutional study by a scholarly contemporary of the Wobblies, see Paul F. Brissenden, *The I.W.W.: A Study of American Syndicalism* (New York, 1919).

³ Philip S. Foner, *History of Labor in the United States*; vol. 4: *The Industrial Workers of the World, 1905–1917* (New York, 1964) (also see my review of Foner's volume in *Industrial and Labor Relations Review*, 21 [October, 1967]: 129–30); William Z. Foster, *From Bryan to Stalin* (New York, 1937), pp. 48–58; Ray Ginger, *The Bending Cross* (New Brunswick, N.J., 1949), pp. 256–57.

⁴ *Bill Haywood's Book: The Autobiography of William D. Haywood* (New York, 1929). Ralph Chaplin and Richard Brazier, old and trustworthy friends of Haywood, maintained that his autobiography was ghostwritten by Communist Party members (Chaplin, *Wobbly* [Chicago, 1948], pp. 348–49, and my interview with Brazier on May 10, 1965). The autobiography's errors and internal inconsistencies make it all the more unlikely that Haywood wrote it himself.

⁵ Oscar Lewis, *La Vida* (New York, 1965), p. xliii.

⁶ *Ibid.*, p. xlv.

⁷ Much of my evidence concerning Haywood's life is based upon his testimony at two trials and one federal investigation: "Transcript of the State of Idaho v. Haywood"—June 4–July 30, 1907, Idaho State Historical Society, Boise (microfilm); *Final Report and Testimony of the United States Commission on Industrial Relations* (hereafter referred to as *Commission on Industrial Relations*), 12 vols. (Washington, D.C., 1915), 11: 10569–73; *Evidence and Cross-Examination in the Case of U.S.A. v. W. D. Haywood, et al.* (n.p., n.d.).

⁸ *Bill Haywood's Book*, pp. 10–12, 19–20.

⁹ *Ibid.*, pp. 32–55; also see the sources cited in n. 7, and my interviews with Brazier, May 10, 1965, and Fred Thompson, October, 1966.

¹⁰ James McParland to Governor Frank Gooding, February 8, 1906, in "Relating to the Western Federation of Miners, 1906–1907," Pinkerton Reports, Idaho State Historical Society, Boise (microfilm); cf. David Grover, *Debaters and Dynamiters* (Corvallis, Ore., 1964), p. 65.

¹¹ *Bill Haywood's Book*, pp. 206–7; Clarence Darrow, *The Story of My Life* (New York, 1932), pp. 129–40.

¹² Vernon Jensen, *Heritage of Conflict* (Ithaca, N.Y., 1950), ch. 6.

¹³ Minute books of Local 66, Western Federation of Miners, Silver City, Idaho, Bancroft Library, University of California, Berkeley.

¹⁴ *Bill Haywood's Book*, pp. 81–89.

[15] See Melvyn Dubofsky, "The Leadville Strike of 1896–1897: An Appraisal," *Mid-America*, 48 (April, 1966): 99–118.

[16] Bernard Mandel, *Samuel Gompers* (Yellow Springs, O., 1963), chs. 9–14.

[17] Butte (Mont.) *Reveille*, May 14, 1901, p. 1; Butte *People*, November 9, 1901, p. 1; *Miners' Magazine*, 2 (February, 1901): 31–33. The miners, however, demanded exclusion legislation against Asians.

[18] Butte *Reveille*, September 11, 1900, p. 5, September 18, 1900, p. 6, and April 9, 1901, p. 4.

[19] See *Miners' Magazine*, vols. 1 and 2 (1900 and 1901).

[20] *Official Proceedings of the 1902* [WFM] *Convention*, pp. 8–10; *Miners' Magazine*, 3 (July, 1902): 23–33, and 4 (July, 1903): 28.

[21] For the American Labor Union, see Melvyn Dubofsky, "The Origins of Western Working Class Radicalism, 1890–1905," *Labor History*, 7 (Spring, 1966): 150–51.

[22] 3 (February, 1902): 6.

[23] "Stenographic Report of the Advisory Board Appointed by Governor James H. Peabody to Investigate and Report upon Labor Difficulties in the State of Colorado and More Particularly at Colorado City," pp. 80–81, 84, 109, 118, in The James H. Hawley Papers, Idaho State Historical Society. This document, unknown to previous scholars, reveals a great deal of new and significant information about Haywood's state of mind in 1903.

[24] Jensen, *Heritage of Conflict*, ch. 10; Dubofsky, "Origins of Western Radicalism," p. 147; 58th Congress; 3d sess., Senate Document No. 122, *A Report on Labor Disturbances in the State of Colorado, from 1880 to 1904* (Washington, D.C., 1905), pp. 115–282. Ample evidence of the Governor's anti-labor attitudes and actions was found in the official papers of James H. Peabody, Colorado State Archives, Denver. *Miners' Magazine*, vols. 4 and 5 (1903 and 1904), offers the WFM's version of the Colorado struggle.

[25] Jensen, *Heritage of Conflict*, pp. 130–31, and correspondence in The Peabody Papers.

[26] *Commission on Industrial Relations*, 11: 10572–73.

[27] *Proceedings of the First Annual Convention of the Industrial Workers of the World* (New York, 1905), pp. 18, 153–57.

[28] See Brissenden, *The I.W.W.*, pp. 96–103.

[29] André Tridon, "Haywood," *New Review*, 1 (May, 1913): 502–6.

[30] For the assassination and the ensuing investigation and trial, see Grover, *Debaters and Dynamiters*, an anti-Haywood, anti-IWW version; for a similar analysis in a more popular vein, see Stewart H. Holbrook, *The Rocky Mountain Revolution* (New York, 1956); see also James McParland

to Governor Gooding, January 8 and January 25, 1906, in The Pinkerton Reports.

31 McParland to Gooding, February 8, 1906, and succeeding reports in *ibid.*, cf. Grover, *Debaters and Dynamiters*, pp. 65–69.

32 *Proceedings of the Second Convention of the IWW* (Chicago, 1906), *passim.; Miners' Magazine*, 8 (October 11, 1906): p. 7, and (October 18, 1906): 12–13.

33 Charles Moyer to Albert Kirwan, n.d., in *Proceedings of the 1907 Convention*, pp. 579–80; Moyer to Charles Mahoney and A. Kirwan, October 30, 1906, *ibid.*, pp. 580–81; Haywood to Kirwan, October 16, 1906, *ibid.*, pp. 582–83. McParland, in his reports to Governor Gooding, stressed the personality differences between Haywood and Moyer, and Haywood's testimony before Governor Peabody's advisory board also demonstrated his more assertive character.

34 Haywood to St. John, March 17 and 24, 1907, in *Proceedings of the 1907 Convention*, pp. 584–86; Haywood to Fred Heslewood, April 2, 1907, *ibid.*, p. 621.

35 *Industrial Union Bulletin*, December 1, 1907, p. 2; Charles Madison, *American Labor Leaders* (New York, 1950), pp. 270–71; Carl E. Hein, "William D. Haywood and the Syndicalist Faith," in Harvey Goldberg, ed., *American Radicals* (New York, 1957), pp. 179–98; Renshaw, *The Wobblies*, pp. 100–4.

36 Haywood in the *International Socialist Review*, 12 (February, 1912): 467, and 13 (September, 1912): 246–47.

37 *Industrial Worker*, December 15, 1910, pp. 1, 4; *Solidarity*, December 31, 1910, p. 2.

38 *Industrial Union Bulletin*, October 10, 24, November 7, December 12, 1908, and February 20, 27, 1909.

39 Arno Dosch, "What the I.W.W. Is," *World's Work*, 26 (August, 1913): 417.

40 "The Casual of the Woods," *Survey*, 44 (July 3, 1920): 472; cf. Carleton Parker, "The I.W.W.," *Atlantic Monthly*, 120 (November, 1917): 651–62.

41 See Oscar Lewis, *La Vida*, pp. xiv, xlv–xlvi, for lower-class alienation from and hostility to society's dominant institutions.

42 Parker, "The I.W.W.," p. 656; Rex Tugwell to the editor, *Survey*, 44 (August 16, 1920): 641–42.

43 E. F. Doree to "Fellow Workers," *Industrial Worker*, November 7, 1912, p. 4; John Sandgren, "Industrial Communism," *Solidarity*, July 31, 1915, p. 12; *ibid.*, March 22, 1913, p. 2.

44 *Solidarity*, March 14, 1914; *Commission on Industrial Relations*, 5: 4239.

45 *The Iron Heel* (New York, 1957), pp. 96–99.

46 *The Lumber Industry and Its Workers* (Chicago, n. d.), p. 59; *Commission on Industrial Relations*, 5: 4940 and 4946–47.

47 *Ibid.*, 11: 10574.

48 *Ibid.*, 5: 4942; *Solidarity*, July 9, 1910, p. 3.

49 *Solidarity*, July 9, 1910, p. 3; Vincent St. John, "Political Parties Not Endorsed by Us," *Industrial Worker*, August 12, 1909, p. 3; *Commission on Industrial Relations*, 11: 10575; *Lumber Industry and Its Workers*, p. 59.

50 *Lumber Industry and Its Workers*, p. 73; *Industrial Worker*, June 6, 1912, p. 2; *The Silent Defense* (Chicago, n. d.), n. p.; *Commission on Industrial Relations*, 11: 10578.

51 *Commission on Industrial Relations*, 5: 4237.

52 Dosch, "What the I.W.W. Is," p. 54.

53 *Solidarity*, December 24, 1910, p. 2.

54 Arturo Giovanitti "Syndicalism: The Creed of Force," *The Independent*, 76 (October 30, 1913): 210; Commission on Industrial Relations, 11: 10578.

55 *Commission on Industrial Relations*, 11: 10583, 10592; Haywood and Joseph J. Ettor, "What the IWW Intends to Do to the U.S.A.," reprinted from the *New York World* in *Solidarity*, June 27, 1914, p. 3.

56 Haywood, as quoted by Dosch in "What the I.W.W. Is," p. 417; Ben H. Williams, "American Labor in the Jungle: The Saga of One Big Union" (unpublished reminiscences, Wayne State University Labor Archives, Detroit).

57 *Commission on Industrial Relations*, 11: 10574; John Pancner, in *Solidarity*, August 24, 1912, p. 2.

58 *Solidarity*, November 1, 1913, p. 2; *Commission on Industrial Relations*, 2: 1449, 1455, 1459, and 11: 10574, 10588.

59 *Industrial Worker*, January 9, 1913, p. 2; John Sandgren, "The Syndicalist Movement in Norway," *Solidarity*, February 14, 1914, p. 3; Robert R. LaMonte, "Industrial Unionism and Syndicalism," *New Review*, 1 (May, 1913): 527.

60 *Commission on Industrial Relations*, 10: 10583.

61 W. D. Haywood, "Socialism: The Hope of the Working Class," *International Socialist Review*, 12 (February, 1912): 461–71; *Industrial Worker*, May 8, 1913, p. 3.

62 W. D. Haywood, "Appeal for Solidarity," *International Socialist Review*, 14 (March, 1914): 545.

63 Louis Levine, "The Development of Syndicalism in America," *Political Science Quarterly*, 28 (September, 1913): 451–79; Mabel Dodge Luhan, *Movers and Shakers* (New York, 1936), p. 89; Max Eastman, *En-*

joyment of Living (New York, 1948), p. 445; R. L. Tyler, "The I.W.W. and the West," pp. 175–87.

[64] Brissenden, *The I.W.W.*, p. 359; Vincent St. John to Mark Litchman, May 9, 1914, The Litchman Papers, University of Washington Archives, Seattle.

[65] See Philip Taft, "The I.W.W. in the Grain Belt," *Labor History*, 1 (Winter, 1960): 56–57; Tom Connors, "The Industrial Union in Agriculture," in *Twenty-Five Years of Industrial Unionism* (Chicago, 1930), pp. 37–42; E. Workman, *History of "400" A.W.O.* (New York, 1939); Brissenden, *The I.W.W.*, p. 359. In its 1917 indictment of the IWW the federal government estimated its membership at 200,000, a considerable exaggeration.

[66] *Official Proceedings of the 1916 Convention*, pp. 30–37, 47, 61, 74–80, 105–11, 146.

[67] Chaplin, *Wobbly*, pp. 199–200.

[68] William Preston, Jr., *Aliens and Dissenters: Federal Suppression of Radicals, 1903–1933* (Cambridge, Mass., 1963), pp. 88–91.

[69] *Ibid.*, ch. 4.

[70] *Ibid.*, chs. 4–5. The records of the Federal Mediation and Conciliation Service (in the National Archives, Social and Economic Division, Record Group 280) contain the full story of Labor Department–A.F. of L. cooperation.

[71] Preston, *Aliens and Dissenters*, pp. 118–19; Philip Taft, "The Federal Trials of the IWW," *Labor History*, 3 (Winter, 1962): 60–61; Michael Johnson, "The I.W.W. and Wilsonian Democracy," *Science and Society*, 28 (Summer, 1964): 268–74.

[72] Preston, *Aliens and Dissenters*, pp. 120–51; Taft, "Federal Trials," pp. 61–80.

[73] *Ibid.*, n. 72.

[74] Quoted in James Joll, *The Anarchists* (London, 1964), p. 11.

[75] Chaplin, *Wobbly*, pp. 286, 298–99, 302–5; *Bill Haywood's Book*, p. 361; interview with Brazier, May 10, 1965.

[76] Chaplin, *Wobbly*, p. 334; *Bill Haywood's Book*, pp. 363–65; conversations with Alexander Trachtenberg on various occasions in 1965 and 1966.

[77] Copy of a letter from William D. Haywood to David Karsner, February 11, 1928, given to me by Richard Brazier; Attorney General Homer Cummings to Secretary of State, January 25, 1934, Department of Justice, Record Group 60, File 188032, National Archives; R. Walton Morse to Cummings, September 5, 1934, *ibid.*; Harold Shantz to Secretary of State, August 16, 1934, *ibid.*

[78] Renshaw, *The Wobblies*, pp. 71–74; Madison, *Labor Leaders*, pp. 264–94; Hein, "Haywood," pp. 179–98.

The Radical Confrontation with Foreign Policy: War and Revolution, 1914-1920

Milton Cantor

Present-day radicals are mistaken if they think their forerunners always shared their preoccupation with American foreign policy. The pre—World War I generation, Milton Cantor argues, persistently "turned inward," and shifted very reluctantly and disunitedly to confront the war. In the phenomena he highlights, however, some may see the beginnings of a pattern: the failure of radicals to analyze foreign policy or the nature of the war, the cannibalistic splits within the radical camp, the co-opting of some radicals by Wilsonian idealism and the easy alliance of other radicals with the liberal opponents of the war, and, finally, the enthusiasm of radicals for the Communist revolution in Russia.

Cantor wrote this essay after the completion of *Max Eastman* (1968), an intellectual study of one of the central figures of the prewar left. It is part of a larger research project into alienation and the American intellectual.

Specialists are familiar with Cantor's forays into a wide range of subjects in early American history: Joel Barlow, John Randolph, the colonial image of the Negro (in Seymour L. Gross and John E. Hardy, eds., *Images of the Negro in American Literature* [Chicago, 1966]). His articles have appeared in the *William and Mary Quarterly*, the *American Quarterly*, and the *New England Quarterly*. He is Managing Editor of *Labor History*. Cantor received his doctorate at Columbia; he taught at Williams College and is now at the University of Massachusetts.

Until the onset of World War I in Europe, American radicals seemed singularly insulated from and indifferent to events abroad; the *cri de coeur* of the Socialists and the Industrial Workers of the World was against capitalist society.

Typically, the Social Democratic Party, that short-lived organization founded by Eugene Debs, Victor Berger, and Frederic Heath in 1897, declared for "cooperative production and distribution." It demanded a program of immediate reforms: national insurance of working people against accidents, lack of employment and want in old age, a system of public works and improvements for the employment of the unemployed, reduction of the hours of labor, adoption of the initiative and the referendum. Then, in its sole gesture toward external affairs, it asked for the "abolition of war . . . and the introduction of international arbitration instead." The Socialist Party, which grew out of the sdp, took over its predecessor's program virtually intact, stressing similar "immediate demands." Even Daniel De Leon, who condemned these "palliatives" and favored the overthrow of capitalism, focused almost exclusively upon the American scene.

This emphasis on domestic affairs is all the more striking because it occurred at a time when the United States was making a dramatic bid for an overseas empire. The Socialist Party's unity convention of 1901, like its first convention in 1900, disregarded the recent war with

Spain, the Filipino insurrection, and even the larger issue of imperialism. Although imperialism was the "paramount issue" in Bryan's 1900 campaign, those who attended the various state and national Socialist Party gatherings would hardly know it existed. Indeed, Debs rejected it altogether: "What but meaningless phrases are 'imperialism,' 'expansionism,' 'free silver,' 'gold standard,' etc. to the wage worker." Thus the socialist onslaught against American capitalism was narrowly conceived; it had narrow, reformist objectives.[1]

For those who were committed to an authentic radicalism in the early 1900's, American foreign policy and the popular response to it could only be sources of despair. Populists and progressives alike endorsed a big navy and a continuing expansionism, and few Americans resisted the moralistic-pietistic syndrome that played such a pivotal role in our diplomacy. The bohemians, the *poètes maudits*, the alienated in those pre-war years had literary or artistic commitments exclusively; their revolts were largely against the Spoon Rivers and Tilbury Towns. A new generation of writers concerned itself with the Zeniths and Winesburgs, or attacked the social conditions that produced strikes at Lawrence, Massachusetts, and in the coal fields. An older generation of reformers saw that the nation, faced with stern domestic realities, seethed with insurgency, but few radicals challenged the fiercely proprietary spirit with which Americans, with very minor exceptions, viewed the United States' overseas practices. Many persons were being radicalized in those years, but the swelling leftist criticism, when not diverted or aborted by progressivism, or absorbed by liberalism, was turned inward.

I

Middle- and upper-middle-class progressives retained their leadership of those who criticized United States foreign policy. Urban progressives, for example, were prominent among those who welcomed Russia's revolutionary leaders to America before the 1906 revolution, and the social workers were especially active, thereby prefiguring their anti-war role in 1917. Even America's Jewish radicals, presumably tied to the Russian Bund (an organization of Jewish revolutionary workers) by an international web of religious and ideological beliefs, responded less enthusiastically than Jane Addams and Lillian Wald to the anti-Czarist revolutionaries who solicited funds among them.[2] These radicals, furthermore, had scant regard for other overseas developments that, presumably, should have moved them to action. They reacted, as would the left generally for the next three decades, with a kind of selective hostility toward particular events and institutions.

Ironically, it was the middle and upper-middle-class progressives —the social workers and the Brahmin aristocrats—who subjected American foreign policy to its most sustained and intensive critique in the prewar years. There was, for example, the New England Anti-Imperialist League (still the elitist body of opposition to expansionism), which consistently opposed the Philippine annexation and America's involvement in Mexico, Santo Domingo, Nicaragua, and Honduras. The prototype anti-imperialism organization and the only one still in the field after 1903, the league displayed consistent opposition to American overseas investments and to Democratic foreign policy. It was, however, an essentially impotent force as it crusaded against spheres of influence and trusteeships with diminished vitality and a dreadful sense of *déjà vu*. Its leading figures were elegant and faded patricians, graybeards who lacked a principled overview that went beyond devotion to democratic ideals.[3] Their targets were the objects of many spirited earlier forays against expansionism but their criticism was not anchored (unlike that of radicals generally) to the common belief that society itself, being grossly defective, required fundamental and sweeping reconstruction.

If "radical" is so defined, then radical priorities in the early 1900's began with internal affairs, and if it is so defined, we must look for those who sought alternative forms of society. Sharing this loosely formulated objective, radicals of course differed sharply on methods, given their varying legacies. Some were the heirs of nineteenth-century romanticism or Manchester liberalism; some were profoundly influenced by continental radicalism; some were beholden to no one for their historical vision. Consequently, they sometimes adopted methods that were considered egregious by orthodox standards, that took them outside the traditional political framework, but often they expressed militancy within the system as they worked for welfare measures or with liberal and minority groups.

No matter how an authentic radicalism is defined, one factor seems constant: its votaries aim at qualitative institutional change. Given such a criterion, we must necessarily exclude liberal spokesmen and their house organs, such as the *Nation* and *New Republic*.

Such a decision may be *ex parte*, to be sure, since these spokes-men and journals have frequently been outstanding opponents of American foreign policy and since it is sometimes difficult to define the term liberal, for this term connotes a category that is more com-plex and less monolithic than first appears. Witness, for example, the liberal posture vis-à-vis World War I when two distinct groups ap-peared: an old school, which recoiled from the war in horror, and the "progressive democrats" or "war liberals" (as Christopher Lasch has called them), who were equivocal about the overseas conflict and who eventually supported mobilization and America's participation. Because these liberal reformers, as well as church leaders and mem-bers of the old peace organizations, have been studied elsewhere and skillfully analyzed, there is no point in retelling the lamentable story of their devolution to an uncritical Wilsonism, especially since they are not really within the radical fold. This conclusion also seems ap-propriate for those who were raised in the same house but who seemed to betray the citadel from within; namely, Randolph Bourne and the less passionate Harold Stearns. Bourne, after all, was no radi-cal or socialist. An anti-war liberal possessed of a vision of an organic national culture, he generally shared the *New Republic*'s hope for an efficient and humane social order that would transcend "internal class struggle." [4]

Nor need the prewar student movement be considered. Van Wyck Brooks notes its "apostolic role," but campus radicalism was negligible and campus response to the war was divided. One contingent, of which Joseph Freeman was emblematic, opposed the war spirit but enlisted in the R.O.T.C. after Brest-Litovsk; another contingent's radical-ism melted away as soon as the United States joined the hostilities.

The pacifists fell in between the usual categories of liberal and radical. Closer to the former in their non-programmatic and non-ideological attitudes, they nonetheless drew back from advocating military assistance to the Allies and military intervention abroad. There were some socialists among them, although the party's execu-tive secretary, Morris Hillquit, was among those who explicitly re-jected such a marriage. But Jessie Hughan, for instance, was both socialist and pacifist. She urged a firm anti-war stand after Sarajevo, pressed a general strike upon socialists, argued against preparedness, and in 1915 helped organize the No-Conscription League. [5]

Dismayed by what seemed obvious war preparations after 1914, pacifists began to organize and their societies mushroomed across the country. Two of their most influential leaders, David Starr Jordan of Stanford and Jane Addams of Hull House, believed America's duty was to remain out of the conflict and to mediate it. The Woman's Peace Party (WPP) founded (1915) and chaired by Jane Addams, proposed "a convention of neutral nations in the interests of an early peace." Its most active anti-preparedness branch, which was dominated by Crystal Eastman in New York City, soon evolved into the American Union against Militarism (AUAM), which, like the WPP, included many social workers. So did the Anti-Preparedness Committee (APC) a heterogeneous agency that was composed of non-resistant Tolstoyans, advocates of defensive war (like Lillian Wald), and a pacifist-socialist combination.[6]

The AUAM, probably the most active pacifist organization in the field, was most successful in challenging preparedness and in dispelling or quieting fears of a German invasion of the United States. It had three aims before 1917: to guard against militarism; to stop the overseas conflict, or at least block American participation; and to help organize the world for peace.[7]

It is significant that the unequivocally radical opponents of the war shared common ground with pacifist groups, since it suggests their ideological flaccidity. Even the Industrial Workers of the World embraced a vaguely defined pacifism. It condemned militarism "in all its forms and functions" at its first convention in 1905, and this position had not altered a decade later. "We as members of the industrial army," the 1914 convention resolved, "will refuse to fight for any purpose except for the realization of industrial freedom." But the Wobblies were immediately placed on the defensive by government actions and were forced to direct their considerable energies toward survival, thus abdicating their leadership of the radical opposition to Wilsonian policies.[8]

Among the most outstanding anti-war opponents of the chief executive were those who, although formally attached to one or another radical organization, more often than not spoke for themselves alone or "in the name of the masses." Scott Nearing, John Reed, and Max and Crystal Eastman were among the most prominent. They began a campaign that became more powerful over the years, particularly after the United States declared war and the Bolsheviks seized power. These two developments converted them from anti-war publicists to journalists and ideologues who were dedicated to a radical reconstruction of society. Reed's campaigns against American intervention and against conscription again suggest the closeness of pacifist and radical positions before the October revolution. Reed, who warned against the "judicial tyranny, bureaucratic suppression, and industrial barbarism, which followed inevitably the first fine careless rapture of militarism," was joined by the Eastmans—and Randolph Bourne and Amos Pinchot *inter alios*—in a crusade against American participation abroad. With this eventual participation, Scott Nearing declared, "the American plutocracy has won [its greatest victory] over the American democracy since the declaration of war with Spain." [9]

II

The Socialist Party, in the twilight days of peace, had been deprived of a considerable audience by Wilsonian idealism, shaken by the anti-sabotage clause in its constitution, and divided by Haywood's recall from the party's National Executive Committee, with the attendant Wobbly defections. David Shannon, however, quite properly notes that historians have exaggerated the extent of the defections and expulsions of 1912. Although it declined in these ante bellum years, the party hardly suffered a catastrophic erosion of strength, and the outbreak of war halted its decline. Indeed, it lost less than 10,000 members between 1916 and 1918, a period of anti-socialist raids and repression, and it scored some major election successes in 1917. The vote, primarily a protest vote, registered the anti-war animus of many electors. [10]

In New York City's mayoralty campaign, for example, the Socialist Party candidate, Morris Hillquit, took a militant peace stance: "We are for peace. We are unalterably opposed to the killing of our manhood and the draining of our resources in a bewildering pursuit of an incomprehensible 'democracy.' " The Democratic candidate, John Hylan was swept into office, but the Republican incumbent, John Mitchell, who ran on a support-the-war program, defeated Hillquit by only 150 votes. In other cities, too, the war was the main issue in the Socialist campaign. James Maurer, the Socialist president of the Pennsylvania Federation of Labor, told Reading voters "You have on one side a party which has plunged you into war . . . on the other hand you have the Socialist Party which is opposed to war and demands an immediate peace." [11]

Although effective "mass opposition" to the war was a socialist daydream, it would nonetheless appear that the party's position was relevant and popular; but this position was not of sudden inspiration in response to overwhelming public sentiment. Local officials, to be sure, observed that "war protest meetings are the real attraction now," and urged the promotion of this tactic upon national headquarters, but most Socialist Party leaders continued to oppose the war for orthodox reasons: the war was essential for the continuance of capitalism and, conversely, the working classes, which "contribute most of the soldiers and make the greatest material sacrifices," were naturally anti-war. Small wonder, therefore, that party locals condemned Europe's parliamentary socialists "who have seen fit to support the militaristic policies that are arraying the workers of Europe under the various nationalistic banners in defiance of our international program." One local even urged expulsion from public office of any socialist who "officially approves of or votes for any appropriation of public moneys in support of the army or navy of the United States." [12]

The Socialist Party's executive committee endorsed a "national campaign for national and international disarmament and international peace" as early as mid-December, 1914. The "Proposed Manifesto and Program of the Socialist Party of America on Disarmament and World Peace" was published later that month. Advancing the orthodox argument that "the fundamental causes [of war] are economic" and that capitalism "with its vast armaments, secret diplomacies and undemocratic governments" was responsible, the manifesto found that the "supreme duty" of socialists was rededication to the "imperishable principles of international socialism." Publication of the manifesto set off a bitter intra-party debate, with especially vehement criticism focused on the no-indemnities and disarmament clauses. This criticism, suggestive of the deep divisions that plagued party leadership, had been made for many years—certainly long before the Emergency National Convention of April, 1917, when the existence of internal schisms became public knowledge. [13]

The party had been divided into a left and a right wing, with a reformist center, almost from the outset. These divisions reflected differing positions on a number of critically important issues, but war did not produce divisions until European hostilities commenced. Before that there had been factionalism, to be sure, but, because of the party's theoretical looseness, factionalism had not torn the organization apart as the war would do. The doctrinal elasticity that enabled the Socialist Labor Party, the Industrial Workers of the World, the anarchists, and other symbiotic ideologists to work in cooperation with socialists on some occasions ceased to mollify party friction when war became the paramount concern. The reformist group dominated the highest Socialist circles prior to 1914; with the war, the left—a loose amalgam of syndicalistically inclined socialists and embryonic Bolsheviks—came into its own. For a while, of course, reformist elements, and even the right wing (represented by such officials as Victor Lewis Berger), supported party policy although they would have preferred a milder anti-war program.[14]

All party factions, long before the outbreak of the war, had said it was inevitable and had denounced it as the result of imperialist rivalry, but this often repeated litany had not prepared them for the events of 1914. Human decency, scientific enlightenment, fidelity to socialist principles, all were diminished by the conflict. "There are evidently flaws in our human nature which make our idealism a tragic joke," Floyd Dell concluded; while Hillquit, conveying the same sense of shock, admitted: "In common with hosts of others I was dismayed by the sudden collapse of human reason." Hillquit and Max Eastman, in a mindlessly un-socialist conclusion, blamed the war on "blind tribal instincts" and "a native impulse of our constitution," which derived from Nietzsche and Darwin, two figures then *de rigeur* in intellectual circles. Such views suggest the confusions of mood and response in socialist circles.[15]

Significant defections among prominent party members, particularly among socialist intellectuals, further clouded the issue. Their public statements, coming after the St. Louis anti-war resolutions of April 1, 1917, repudiated the official pacifist-inclined policy and produced "strong psychic tensions" among party members, which in turn caused more defections. The resultant turmoil made decisions about specific tactics, such as a general strike, all the more difficult.

Nor were matters clarified when John Spargo, one of the most prominent of those who resigned, declared that apprehensions about German miltarism prompted his action. Many socialists shared these fears, and the *Nation* quite accurately reported that some of the "most pronounced radicals now talk of volunteering against the Germans." Eastman's insistence that "the Kaiser and his military machine must be whipped back into Russia and smashed" held pernicious implications for those who rallied to the cause of international socialism and who found that all the belligerents were merely one or another kind of capitalist power. Eastman's view, however, attracted many supporters, including William J. Ghent, George Herron, Louis Fraina, Robert Rives La Monte, and Floyd Dell.[16]

The insistence on this indispensable condition for universal peace, that Germany be "smashed," produced a foreseeable result: "contradiction within socialist ranks," which, Joseph Freeman recalled, "we could neither understand nor resolve" and which would "drive us frequently to the cynicism of despair." Another reason for uncertainty and disillusionment was abandonment of the vaunted cause of international socialism by many European socalist parties that, instead, embraced nationalist attitudes. "We had been led to believe," Freeman disconsolately stated, "that international socialism was thoroughly bankrupt." Hillquit, Spargo, Isaac Hourwich, and Louis Boudin also commented morosely upon what was an almost unbearable shock for most socialists.[17]

Forced to respond publicly to the "plutocrats'" ridicule in the newspapers, Louis Boudin and Louis Fraina, two leading left-wing socialist theoreticians, forthrightly emphasized proletariat internationalism and insisted that "the workingman has no nation." Most socialists replies, however, were defensive, apologetic, tentative, forgiving. Witness, for example, the tortured and unconvincing conclusion in an editorial defense of French socialists: "If this is really to be the last war on earth . . . the Socialists must be in it. If they do not start now they cannot finish the capitalist system at the end." And Hillquit, attempting to explain the action of Germany's socialists, mildly observed: "They acted on impulse. . . . It was not a decision, not a policy—it was history, and history cannot be scolded or praised; it must be understood." [18]

Left-wing reaction to the war itself scarcely differed from that of the reformers. The left wing's analyses, which appeared in the *New Review*, the *Masses*, and the *International Socialist Review*, variously interpreted the hostilities as a trader's war, a militarist's war, a munitions manufacturer's war, a war between feudalism and capitalism, a war between democracy and autocracy, and so forth. Paradoxically, the left saw the war as presenting a matchless opportunity for advancing the cause of social revolution. Louis Fraina, who denounced the conflict, nonetheless thought it would bring an irreversible trend of collectivism in its wake. "War is a Socialist opportunity," the *Call* proclaimed. "There is no cause for despair," Debs counseled in 1915. "The world is awakening and we are approaching the sunrise," and, pursuing a boldly opportunistic approach, he added: "To end the war prematurely, were that possible, would simply mean another and perhaps even bloodier catastrophe." His plea found sympathetic listeners. "Let the war go on," Eastman said, "for the sake of the German people and of all nations." [19]

Conversely, an important bloc of socialists, led by Hillquit, favored an immediate end to the conflict. They believed that "all governments [are] equally militaristic and reactionary"; they urged the party's peace program (of May 15, 1915) of "no indemnities," "no transfer of territory," "no appropriations" for war purposes; they opposed preparedness and conscription. Eastman, for example, having come around to an anti-war and anti-draft position by 1917, scored the drafting of "free citizens" in order to ship "them over a bloody sea to Europe, to be slaughtered in a war waging [*sic*] between other countries than their own." He praised the majority resolution at the St. Louis meeting, which denounced war, and he condemned the "military minorities in the party convention," an obvious reference to Ghent, Russell, Sinclair, Stokes, Walling, *et al.*[20] This bloc of immediatists invariably rejected the contention that its end-the-war-now position could be equated with pacifism. It denied any similarity between socialists and (in Walling's term) "bourgeois pacifists," and affirmed its opposition to the war. Carefully distinguishing between themselves and pacifists, the immediatists were not, to quote from Debs' classic statement of their case, "opposed to all war." [21]

The immediatists and their opponents, however, were in general agreement—even though privately held—on an Allied victory; this was the viewpoint of Debs, Hillquit, Haywood, and Fraina. The real dilemma, therefore, arose from being against Germany and against the other belligerents as well, a dilemma that was heightened by the 1916 election. Eastman and Reed, for example, supported Wilson. Eastman, following tortured logic, criticized the Socialist Party for nominating Allan Benson, but voted for Benson although he endorsed the chief executive. Eastman's endorsement of Wilson derived from the fact that "he has kept us out of war" and "has not succumbed to the epidemic of militarism." Even the revolutionary *International Socialist Review*, in criticizing Berger's *Milwaukee Leader* for its attack on Wilson, took the same position: "To howl suspicions of militarism against a president who has kept the working class of America out of war during a hair-trigger period is a species of treachery to the working class that does no good." [22]

There was further confusion in the party's theoretical discussion of causation and inevitability. One of the articles of socialist faith, in the words of the party's platform of 1916, was "that the competitive nature of capitalism is the cause of modern war." Another clause insisted upon disarmament as "essential to an assured and permanent peace." "Our opposition to war," Walling concurred, "must be based on our opposition to capitalism." But Walling's conclusion was regarded as disastrous by some pacifically inclined socialists: "War can be abolished neither by armament or [*sic*] disarmament." [23]

The early peace proposals of the Socialist Party were remarkably non-specific; the left wing apparently had little to offer. "It is our task to *prepare* for peace, not to bring peace," Fraina somewhat cryptically affirmed, and he denounced the 1915 party program as "apologetic, incompetent and pro-German." This program, however, would later be virtually identical to that of the Bolsheviks, as both stipulated no indemnities, national self-determination, and no military or arms exportation. One senses that Fraina's splenetic opposition derived primarily from the fact that Hillquit and reform elements had been influential in framing the platform, but, in any event, the party's policy became menacingly specific by 1916. Workers were urged to refuse "to mine the coal, to transport soldiers, to furnish food or other supplies for military purposes, and thus keep out of the hands of the ruling class the control of armed forces." Such proposals inferred a general strike, which the lone Socialist congressman, Meyer London, had already advanced, but there was little talk of this, or of ways of implementing it, and an earlier motion to this effect (should "the United States start to mobilize her troops for war") died in committee "for lack of seconds." The left wing, to be sure, talked of "mass action," but it would not or could not go beyond resistance to recruiting drives "by means of mass meetings, street demonstrations, . . . educational propaganda," and strikes against industrial conscription.[24]

When, in 1915, the administration's preparedness campaign went into high gear, socialists were in the vanguard of opposition. Rallies were held, and pamphlets on the order of *No Conscription, No Involuntary Service, No Slavery!* were run off socialist presses. The Intercollegiate Socialist Society (ICSS) kept up the pressure against preparedness and military training on the campuses. "These are days unequalled in opportunities for the American college student of socialism," wrote one observer of a Columbia University anti-preparedness demonstration, urging similar rallies at other schools.[25]

The majority resolution at the 1917 St. Louis meeting upheld the shaky left-center alliance. It condemned the war in the sharpest terms, encouraged "mass movements in opposition to conscription," and called for "continuous, active, and public opposition to the war through . . . all other means within our power." The most extreme passages approached the worker-has-no-country theme, rejected defensive as well as offensive wars, and strongly urged a general strike. Such rhetoric split the left wing, alienated the right wing, and displeased the center, although it had been written by Hillquit and was subscribed to by Berger. The result was the highly publicized desertion of the pro-war bloc, the discreet bolt of pro-socialist (and pro-war) trade unionists, and the destruction (as Daniel Bell tells us) of the precarious balance of socialist forces. The Communist Party's formation two years later would complete the disruption.[26]

Socialists, though not advocates of an unqualified pacifism, did not necessarily repudiate pacifists, and, as we have seen, they occasionally worked together. The American Union against Militarism included Lillian Wald (as chairman) and John Hayne Holmes and Rabbi Stephen Wise, who were pacifists, but Max Eastman was only one of many socialists who belonged to the organization. Both elements had a bond of common grievances at this time, and the AUAM was one of the vehicles of organized opposition to conscription and to the war itself. After the United States intervened overseas, however, these elements became increasingly isolated, and by mid-April, 1917, they began to consider a cordial organizational entente. They found their model in the workingman's councils of socialist Russia, and their indigenous form, they hoped, would resist both Wilson's and Gomper's pro-war policies.[27]

III

The March revolution in Russia and the Bolshevik peace proposals

provided a program around which pacifists and socialists could solidify, and the declaration of war in April and the Conscription Act
provided the catalyst. Pacifists now "turned from a negative policy of
protest against war to constructive proposals for an early peace." A
series of conferences was held during the spring of 1917, in which
representatives of the Emergency Peace Federation, the Woman's
Peace Party, the Socialist Party, and the American Union against Militarism participated, with the goal of evolving a peace policy upon
which they could unite. An organizing committee was formed, with
Hillquit and Norman Thomas among the Socialists and Louis Lochner
and Rebecca Shelley among the pacifists, and from their deliberations
came the decision to stage a Madison Square Garden meeting on May
30 and 31, 1917, which would be called the First American Conference for Democracy and the Terms of Peace. Dr. Judah L. Magnes,
the Jewish pacifist who served as chairman, denied (in his address)
that the conference was "obstructionist"; he insisted it was interested
only in seeking "a speedy and universal democratic peace." At the
second session, William Hull of Swarthmore warned the President
against European involvement, and Victor Berger, in a speech titled
"The War and High Finance," bitterly attacked Wall Street. James
Maurer opened the third session with an attack upon the AFL for its
pro-administration position, and Eastman and other speakers assailed
Wilson or Gompers or both before the rally ended. Other delegates,
opposing conscription and militarism, urged "international cooperation to maintain peace." It was this two-day conference that spawned
the People's Council of America (PCA), an organization of socialists
and pacifists who ardently opposed the President, his war program,
and the AFL.[28]

The groundwork for the council's operations was completed by
June 1, 1917. Cooperation between socialists and pacifists came easily inasmuch as they belonged to the American Union against Militarism, or the Emergency Peace Federation, or the Woman's Peace
Party, the three major groups that joined forces to help form the PCA.
The merger, of course, was not popular with all of the liberal members of the various groups—certainly not with Jane Addams and
David Starr Jordan, who were justifiably fearful of the obvious
growth of socialist power. Their anxiety was not misfounded since
such socialists as Hillquit and Berger were eager to assume leadership
of the new council. Socialists played a prominent role in its affairs,

and by June 1 the Socialist Party was directing what would become the strongest peace movement in the United States.[29]

The PCA, however, was beset by many difficulties, internal and external. Rabbi Magnes, for example, charged that it was dominated by politically oriented socialists and pacifists, and not, as was desirable, by laborers and farmers. Newspapers, which attacked its socialist coloration and objectives, claimed that the council worked "for a German peace," and they usually identified it with bolshevism. Jane Addams soon "escaped any special identification" with the organization, and Hillquit, overburdened by Socialist Party duties, resigned.[30]

But external factors occasionally worked in the council's favor. In Russia, the Bolsheviks' accession to power gave new life and immediacy to the divided council and its peace efforts, which in November, 1917 began a nationwide anti-war campaign to capture the loyalty of American labor. We need not linger on details but it must be emphasized that the council's moderates retained control—officials such as Louis Lochner—and there were no demands for the government's overthrow nor for the establishment of a republic along Soviet lines. The council merely redoubled its efforts to obtain labor's support for peace terms that were based upon the Bolsheviks' formula.[31]

The council's problems were complicated by its failure to raise funds and by the widening schism between its right- and left-wing socialists, particularly on the issue of the recognition of Bolshevik Russia. William Z. Foster, then a left-wing socialist and union organizer, accused Hillquit of "sabotaging the Party's anti-war aims," a charge that received a sympathetic hearing from some council members, but Foster (and Scott Nearing, a member of the socialist center group,) thereby inadvertently confirmed public fears about the PCA and its Bolshevik tendencies and hence contributed to its unpopularity with the public.[32]

Socialists, meanwhile, remained openly hostile to the war effort, which in 1917 brought about the severe repressive measures of the federal government. Division within Socialist Party ranks on the war and the recognition-of-Russia issues, as Louis Waldman recalled, together with "recriminations and criminal prosecutions growing out of the opposition to the war, constituted . . . the first steps in [its] eventual decline." The European socialists, who became "social patriots" and in the main supported their governments, escaped the fate of Socialists in the United States. Had American Socialists imitated their

overseas brothers, their party might well have adjusted to wartime
exigencies, retained its reform constituency, and survived. In a real
sense, therefore, the party was a wartime casualty because some of its
leaders refused to betray the ideals of the Second International. Nevertheless, this refusal to betray the canons of proletarian internationalism
and to support the war gave the party a surprising degree of popularity down to 1918.[33]

IV

The Russian Revolution (although it would later be an important
factor in widening the fissures within socialist ranks) at its outset
presented the image of a raw but vibrant land, free from the economic and spiritual slavery that beset capitalism. This image exhila-
rated even the "war liberals," who had been disillusioned by the
excesses and repressions of war, by rabid postwar nationalism, and
by a peace that sought "to disintegrate the German nation." These
developments had reduced their ranks, and postwar prosperity would
further deplete them. The Soviet experiment, then, was initially useful as an emotional foil, and later in documenting their critique of
the United States. Hence the revolution signaled an accelerated radicalization for liberals as well, or at the very least a swing to the
optative mood.[34]

Radical enthusiasm for the Russian Revolution assumed monumental proportions; the hopes of all—socialists, syndicalists, anarchists—were shaped by the dream of a new society in Russia. These
first converts continually offered incense at the shrine of bolshevism
and flooded Moscow with fraternal greetings. This conversion was
striking, both in its nearly instantaneous character and its wide representation. Prominent literary figures such as Theodore Dreiser and
journalists such as Lincoln Steffens and Eugene Lyons rushed to a
beseiged Russia and found the future there. Floyd Dell jumped bail
and fled to Russia in the hope that the new nation would need his
talents. Newcomers such as Norman Thomas and Benjamin Gitlow
identified with the emerging socialist state, and older radicals such as
Debs and Reed hailed the revolution from prison cells. Albert Rhys
Williams and Max Eastman found that Russia embodied their personal values of joy, struggle, experimentation—a new day for mankind. Moderate socialists, Morris Hillquit chief among them, saw
Russia "standing in the vanguard of social progress"; right-wing so-

cialists echoed Victor Berger, who on the revolution's first anniversary proclaimed: "Here is a government of the people and for the people in actual fact"; and even such a pro-war socialist as Daniel Hogan announced that all socialists must give "unqualified support to Soviet Russia." [35]

Small wonder that the vast majority of socialists hailed the Revolution. Indeed, the Socialist Party in one of its proclamations urged cooperation with Russia in abolishing imperialism; and in another proclamation the party was joined by socialist-dominated groups to press the Bolshevik peace plans—no annexation, no indemnities—upon the United States. [36]

A long editorial in a Negro socialist journal ended with the exclamation: "Long live the Soviet Union." "If to fight for one's rights," another Negro socialist publication declared, "is to be Bolshevist, then we are Bolshevist." Aside from orthodox socialists, even Arne Peterson, the Socialist Labor Party's national secretary, joined the orthodox membership in supporting the revolution, although he had reservations at the outset. Most Wobblies did not share the doubts of their general executive board, which eventually caught up with its members and urged them "to assist the Soviet Government of Russia in fighting the world's battle against capitalism." Emma Goldman's *Mother Earth* was filled with praise for the Bolsheviks, and her autobiography confessed immediate loyalty to the revolution. In short, with only a few significant exceptions, all radical groups could unite on this issue. [37]

Young radicals and intellectuals had been insisting on experimentation and improvisation for several years, which helped bring this unity about more easily. They had come out of village and small-town America in the pre-war years; they renounced society's values, assaulted the provincialism they had escaped, read *America's Coming of Age* almost as a breviary, and sponsored "little magazines," such as the *Masses*. The last was a heady mixture of humor and rebellion, art and life, the experiential and the impertinent. Its columns and its readers proclaimed the value of anarchism, syndicalism, socialism, free love, birth control, suffrage reform—among other things. Wartime chauvinism partially eroded some of these beliefs, but the phenomenon had been strong and it left its mark on radical America. Russia's treatment of these issues—its insistence on birth control, woman suffrage, liberal divorce laws—immediately made it the radicals' cynosure. These reforms seemed so intelligently humane that feminists, progressives, social workers, and liberals generally would be enormously attracted to the new socialist society. But the response of these groups has been chronicled at length elsewhere, and, as Trotsky said, they would never have been more than "fellow travelers." [38]

At the outset, however, liberal and radical reactions varied only in degree, nor were their responses to other, non-revolutionary issues very far apart. The sad facts of war and the peace settlement shocked both groups. For the liberals, it was a liberating experience; it gave them greater flexibility, accelerated the devolution from Wilsonism, and enabled them to grasp the implications of events in Russia. Socialists, freed from their erstwhile fealty to Wilson's crusade, also were vehement in denouncing the Versailles conference. Speaking at the tenth annual convention of the Intercollegiate Socialist Society, Nearing characterized the League of Nations as a "Holy Alliance" against Russia "under the control of the most reactionary forces in the capitalist world." In 1914 the Socialist Party had officially favored a league of nations, as well as a world court and other international agencies, but by the war's end it had shifted to the belief that the league was formulated by "predatory elder statesmen of European and Asiatic imperialism." With some notable exceptions, such as Horace Kallen and Louis Boudin, most socialists would follow Eastman's path, changing from a belief in "international federation" (which he had urged in 1915) to an attack upon "the imperialistic alliance of the Five Victorious Allies, known to polite literature as the League of Nations." [39]

Liberal-radical reaction to American foreign policy toward Russia more or less converged for a decade. William Hard's attack on the State Department for its support of Admiral Kolchak, published in the *New Republic*, could as easily have appeared in the *Liberator*. M. J. Olgin, a leading Jewish-Russian radical, used the *New Republic* for a highly favorable account of Soviet industrial organization. The two most critical foreign policy issues, intervention and recognition, also evoked similar comment. The Allied intervention in Russia in August, 1918, was a final shock for liberals and drove many of them to make emotional—and frequently literal—pilgrimages to Russia. The radical attitude differed from the liberal only in being more vehement. Max Eastman, who because of American intervention came full circle, now condemned Wilson's "self-righteous emotions" and charged that the "Red Terror," the pretext for the intervention, was wholly fabricated—that the Murmansk and Vladivostok landings revealed "the piratical purpose at the heart of the war for democracy," "Hands off Russia," the theme of his nationwide speaking tour in 1919, would be adopted by Norman Thomas, who was then emerging as a prominent socialist. From a prison cell, Debs also assailed the action, found Wilson responsible for it, and appealed for the withdrawal of all foreign forces from Russia. Recently returned from bearing witness to the ten days that shook the world, John Reed condemned the intervention, for which he was arrested and indicted.[40]

In like manner other radicals, with a frequency almost impossible to document, conducted a tireless campaign against Allied expeditions to Russia. This campaign was waged by all of the radical groups: socialist, socialist labor, the iww, the newly formed Communist and Communist Labor parties, and so on. Acting independently, they and their crusade nonetheless took on a semblance of unity and cooperative action. The American Communist Party, which was established early in September, 1919, made its first campaign "the struggle to arouse the workers against the blockade of Soviet Russia." The Communist Labor Party distributed "hands off Soviet Russia" literature that urged American workers to follow the example set in Western Europe and to refuse to load ships with ammunition and provisions that were destined for the foes of Soviet Russia. The Socialist Party, its membership now sharply reduced by factionalism, exhorted its followers to condemn America's "war upon Russia." Its New York State branch denounced the attempt "to invade Russia by force and overthrow the government of the Russian people"; its St. Louis local unanimously adopted resolutions that called for the immediate withdrawal of foreign troops (as did the National Executive Committee). Norman Thomas pleaded that the Russians be "left alone"; endorsing this plea, the pca, at a Madison Square Garden meeting, also urged that the troops be recalled. "What the Allied governments are afraid of," one of the pca spokesmen observed, "is not the Red Terror, nor the force of Bolshevik bayonets, but the power of the Soviet idea." Delegates to the tenth annual Intercollegiate Socialist Convention approved Scott Nearing's attack upon the invasion of "an ally without even the pretense of a declaration of war." [41]

The issue of recognition produced the same kind of near-unanimity among radicals. The liberals provided the leadership here but, *mutatis mutandis*, their attitude merely underscored the attitude that had been advanced by the entire left wing. For example, the Friends of the Russian Revolution, having changed its name to the Friends of New Russia, sponsored recognition at a December, 1917, mass meeting. A Soviet Recognition League was organized, Alexander Trachtenburg stated, "to conduct meetings, to furnish the press with true reports about the doings of the Soviet Government of Russia, and to urge official recognition of the Soviet Government." John Reed supported this policy: "The Soviet Government of Russia is there to stay; it is based on the almost universal will of the Russian masses." [42]

Socialists were hardly of one mind on all issues that pertained to the Soviet Union. They sharply disagreed on the wisdom of a "separate peace," on the revolution's lessons for the United States, and even on whether Russia was a socialist state; and a considerable bloc was troubled by the persecution of the Social Revolutionaries. There was, however, no deviation on the recognition question. Socialists such as Norman Thomas appealed for immediate recognition and trade—as did the socialist journal that would provide his major opposition within the party in the early 1930's. Until 1933, when recognition was granted, the *New Leader* supported the action on the expedient grounds that it would aid American business and weaken Hitler.[43]

The radicals' flirtation with bolshevik Russia grew into a heady love affair as the twenties wore on, while socialists remained dutifully wedded to the Soviet Union and some individuals made dramatic separations, to be sure. Max Eastman, a guiding star of many postwar radicals, was the first conspicuous defector, with his exposé of the triumvirs (Stalin in particular) and his critical but passionate advocacy of Trotsky's cause. J. B. Hardman, another early supporter of Trotsky, also felt betrayed by events in Russia after Lenin died. Others followed in the pathetic and often agonizing journey down the road toward compromise with capitalism, and eventually, for most, to anti-communism. A new spirit appeared, sharper, more dogmatic, and more specifically partisan. The characteristic radical view was that of John Dos Passos, who, writing in 1928, found that the Russians were "nearer . . . a solution to the strange and horrible world industrial society had produced than we were in America." But fratricidal struggle continued to beset the Socialist Party and the Communist parties, which led a romantic but unavailing underground existence during much of the decade.[44]

These parties, of course, managed a fragile ad hoc unity on the issue of United States foreign policy vis-à-vis the Soviet Union. They managed to maintain this unity through the decade, or at least until the late twenties, when the Communist Party, going into its "third period," resorted to extreme sectarianism. The "social fascism" of the entire non-communist left became a Communist byword; the Socialist Party was designated "the hangman of the Revolution"; and Norman Thomas, once dismissed as merely a "bourgeois reformer," became a "hypocritical apologist for the bloody rapacities of Wall Street." These problems were not confined only to the Communists; the left and right opposition were little more than agitational centers that mutually exchanged bitter reproaches and charges when they did not fling them at the Communist Party.[45]

v

Reproaches and ruptures were the special characteristics of American radicalism even in the pre-Harding years. The tendency to schism and the inability of radical leaders and the movements they shaped to maintain a common ground in foreign policy prefigured developments in the late twenties and thirties. The battles had been too costly, the casualty lists too long, the polemics too lacerating to permit collaboration, despite determined Communist efforts in behalf of a popular front and the fact (unlike the situation today) that radicals shared a common moral and intellectual stance. It was preferable to declare war *à outrance* against fellow radicals rather than against the enemy outside. It was much easier to form alliances with liberals although time and again, as we have remarked, liberals and radicals had almost identical outlooks on the world. Both groups had been repelled by the rabid wartime and postwar nationalism, by their common suspicion of the League of Nations, by what Herbert Croly has called "the spiritual distempers of mankind." Nor can we forget that, unlike today's "nuclear generation," radicals never really soured on America, however much (paradoxically) they endorsed the Soviet Union in mindless admiration and deference. They never displayed a determination to transform American society; rather, they almost instinctively opted for the democratic capitalism so warmly espoused by middle-class liberals.

After Versailles, pacifists, socialists, liberals, and Communists could eschew Wilsonian policies and unite in support of Bolshevik peace terms and of bolshevism itself. In the early mid-twenties, they could endorse all the free-wheeling attacks on American imperialism, whether these were made by the Anti-Imperialist League or by William Z. Foster. It was hardly accidental that a major liberal organization, the American Civil Liberties Union, emerged from the socialist-led American Union against Militarism, or that on such issues as militarism and disarmament there were very few differences among left-of-center opinion. *The Freeman*'s attack upon armament programs was subscribed to by Communists, who, significantly, would not demur when the proposed approach to disarmament was legislative. Indeed, neither of the two major radical parties sustained a doctrinaire anti-parliamentarian stand, which again highlights their basically insular and populist qualities.

In the late twenties and early thirties events in Europe drew liberals and radicals into ever closer cooperation, but the situation was more complex and subtle than has often been suggested. It would be misleading to say there was a monolithic liberal capitulation to radical politics, or that all left-wing organizations advanced the same foreign policy views. Liberalism and radicalism must be understood in terms of conflict, tension, differing tendencies; the Communist Party was a wonder of spineless flexibility, the Socialist Labor Party was not. Nevertheless, the absence of firm ideological positions made liberal-radical collaboration, however informal and ad hoc, a feasible strategy that was reinforced by events abroad.

The example of the Soviet Union shaped the basic Communist position more definitively than it shaped the Socialist position. In fact, however, developments in Russia and Russian-American foreign affairs had a powerful impact upon *all* radicals, affecting them at least as much as events on the domestic scene. Almost two decades after the Spanish-American war and radical preoccupation with the wage earner, their outlook and emphasis had shifted sharply. Consequently, the depression, the New Deal's innovations, and even the CIO's organizational drives may not have been more important to them than Trotsky's fall from grace, the adoption of popular front tactics, the show trials of the mid-thirties, and the Nazi-Soviet pact of 1939.

The rise of Hitlerism was uniquely responsible for American radicalism's shift to internationalism after two decades of concern with internal conditions. This departure, however, was not consonant with the American experience, which possibly accounted for the continuing isolation of radicals from the mainstream of national life. Perhaps their perpetual internal rifts, their occasional search for doctrinal purity, their opposition to World War I, and their approval of bolshevism (which gave offense to Americans) also help explain their dysfunctional and artificial character. So be it. After all, it was their lack of opportunism in wartime that helped destroy them. If the present generation would recall the mistakes of earlier radicals, it should also remember their courage and high idealism.

[1] See Eugene V. Debs', "Outlook for Socialism in the United States," *International Socialist Review,* September, 1900; Theodore Debs', "The Birth of the Socialist Party," *New Leader,* April 28, 1934; also *Proceedings of the Tenth National Convention of the Socialist Labor Party; Social Democracy Red Book,* 1900, pp. 132–33; and Ira Kipnis', *The American Socialist Movement, 1897–1912* (New York, 1952), pp. 152–53.

[2] See Lillian D. Wald, *The House on Henry Street* (New York, 1915), pp. 230–33; Alice Stone Blackwell, *The Little Grandmother of the Russian Revolution: Reminiscences and Letters of Catherine Breshkovsky* (Boston, 1917), pp. 111–25, 332–33; Jane Addams, *Twenty Years at Hull House* (New York, 1926), chap. 17.

[3] *Report of the Eleventh Annual Meeting of the Anti-Imperialist League* (Boston, 1909), pp. 32, 33; *Report of the Seventeenth Annual Meeting of the Anti-Imperialist League* (Boston, 1915), p. 14.

[4] For an abrasive though interesting attempt to define liberals, see Eugene Lyons, "When Liberalism Went Totalitarian," in Irving De Witt Talmadge, ed., *Whose Revolution?* (New York, 1941), pp. 116–18. The "war liberals" rejected Jane Addams' despairing cry, "This [war] will set progress back for a generation" (cited in Charles Hirschfeld, "Nationalist Progressivism and World War I," *Mid-America* 45 [July, 1963]: 141). These "guardians of culture," as Henry May has termed them, included liberal reformers, church leaders, and the older peace organizations; they lent their energies to mobilization. See Randolph Bourne, "War and the Intellectuals," in *Bourne, Untimely Papers* (New York, 1919), pp. 22–26, and Harold Stearns, *Liberalism in America* (New York, 1919), *passim.* Oswald Garrison Villard, for example, sharply attacked militarism in 1915, but greeted the news of war "steadfastly and cheerfully" two years later (Villard, "Shall We Arm for Peace?" *Survey,* 35 [December 11, 1915]: 299).

[5] Joseph Freeman, *An American Testament* (New York, 1936), pp. 125.

"Socialism is not inherently a pacifist creed," Morris Hillquit declared, and "the philosophy of Karl Marx is one of struggle. The founders of the modern Socialist movement appraised every war by the practical test of its probable effects on the condition of the working class and the progress of democracy. They frankly supported the more promising side and did not reject war as war" (Hillquit, *Loose Leaves* [New York, 1934], p. 147). For another rejection of pacifism, see Eastman, "A Separation," *Masses* (May, 1917). For Jessie Hughan, see Hughan, "Preparedness," *Intercollegiate Socialist* (February–March, 1916); see also an untitled ms. on socialists and war, circa 1915, in Jessie W. Hughan Papers, Swarthmore (College) Peace Collection, Swarthmore, Pa., and Hughan, *The Beginnings of War Resistance* (New York, 1937), p. 7.

⁶ Together with other pacifists (Louis Lochner, the secretary of the Chicago Peace Society, Rebecca Shelley, *et al.*), Jane Addams toured the continent and became increasingly active in peace groups after her return; she lectured at leading colleges on "the cruelty and barbarity of war" (Addams, *Peace and Bread in Time of War* [New York, 1922], pp. 2, 4). For the WPP, see Marie Degen, *The History of the Peace Party*, (Baltimore, 1939), pp. 40–41.

⁷ Like the WPP, but more extensively, the AUAM challenged other presidential policies: American imperialism in Latin America, intervention in Mexico, etc. Addams, *Peace and Bread*, p. 57; Lillian Wald, *Windows on Henry Street* (Boston, 1934), pp. 290–99, 310; R. L. Duffus, *Lillian Wald* (New York, 1938), pp. 155–58; Donald Johnson, *The Challenge to American Freedoms* (Louisville, Ky., 1963), pp. 23–25; Wald, "Swinging around the Circle against Militarism," *Survey* 36 (April 22, 1916): 95; Crystal Eastman, "War and Peace," *Survey*, 37 (December 30, 1916): 363–64.

⁸ Paul Brissenden, *The I.W.W.* (New York, 1919), p. 92; see also the October 3, 1914, issue of *Solidarity*.

⁹ Granville Hicks, *John Reed* (New York, 1936), *passim*. Eastman rejected the decision of his former teacher, John Dewey, condemned the *New Republic* for its "highly intellectualized lust for bloody combat" (Eastman, "Revolutionary Progress," *Masses* [April, 1917]). See also Scott Nearing, *The Great Madness* (New York, 1917), p. 5.

¹⁰ Daniel Bell, "The Background and Development of Marxian Socialism in the United States," in Donald D. Egbert and Stow Persons, eds., *Socialism and American Life* (Princeton, 1952), p. 328. Bell's claim that the party, by opposing the war, embraced a "policy bordering on adventurism" and thereby "isolated itself completely from the mainstreams of American political life" is indirectly questioned in David Shannon, *The Socialist Party of America* (New York, 1955), p. 104, and directly challenged in James Weinstein, "Socialism's Hidden Heritage: Scholarship Reinforces Political

Mythology" *Studies on the Left* (Fall, 1963), and, more importantly, in *idem,* "Anti-War Sentiment and the Socialist Party, 1917–1918," *Political Science Quarterly,* 74 (1959): 223–24. Joseph Freeman claimed that in 1916 "the general desire to keep out of the war was so strong in America that every candidate ran on a 'peace' platform" (Freeman, *An American Testament,* p. 38).

[11] Fear of the socialist vote drove the major parties into fusion in Dayton, Toledo, Reading, and elsewhere. The *New York Times,* November 7, 1917. Consonant with the party's St. Louis program, Hillquit called for an international conference to end the war on the principle of no annexation and no indemnities, and he announced his refusal to buy Liberty Bonds. See "Pinchot Sees War Protest in Hillquit Vote," *The Call,* (November 8, 1917). The large vote (21.7 percent of the total) might have been even larger except for "some non-socialists pacifists [who] voted for Hylan as more practical" (*Survey,* [November 10, 1917]).

[12] J. L. Stark to Walter Lanfersiek, Nat. Secy., August 24, 1914, in SPUSA Papers, Duke University Library, Durham, N.C. William E. Walling, *The Socialists and the War* (New York, 1915), p. 38. See also the proposed referendum submitted by the South Huntington, Long Island, local, in *American Socialist* (February 27, 1915), and another from the Branch 15 local, Los Angeles, *ibid.* (April 3, 1915). The expulsion proposal, with slightly revised phrasing, became a plank in the report of the Committee on the Constitution of National Committee (see Minutes of the National Committee Meeting, May 13, 1915, *ibid.* [May 22, 1915]) and was added to the national constitution (sec. 6, art. II, national constitution and platform of the socialist party [Chicago, 1917], p. 2).

[13] The full text of "Proposed Manifesto" is in the *American Socialist* (December 26, 1914).

[14] Algie M. Simons, who led the attack on the proposed manifesto, argued that there was a "ghastly simplicity" about Socialists who talked of "offensive war" when all of the nations involved claimed their response had been "defensive" (Simons, "The Socialist War Policy," *ibid.* [January 9, 1915], and *idem,* "Compromising with Hell, *New York Sunday Call,* January 10, 1915). Hillquit, although approving the "Proposed Manifesto," did not endorse the "no indemnities" clause (Hillquit to Carl Thompson, January 6, 1915, Duke University Library). The editors of *Appeal to Reason* demurred because the manifesto failed to provide for absolute disarmament, and Charles Edward Russell attacked the manifesto because it did not mention even limited disarmament (Russell to Carl Thompson, January 15, 1915, *ibid.*). For a later commentary on the internal divisions, see Eastman's "The New International," *Liberator,* 2 (July, 1919): 30. For the intra-party maneuvering at this time, see Theodore Draper, *The Roots of*

American Communism (New York, 1963), pp. 92–95, and Julius Faulk, "The Origins of the American Communist Movement," *New International* (Fall, 1955), pp. 165–66.

[15] Norman Thomas, *A Socialist's Faith* (New York, 1950), p. 11; Hillquit, *Loose Leaves*, p. 145; Walling, *Socialists and the War*, p. 381. For Eastman's infatuation with Darwinism, see his *Love and Revolution* (New York, 1965), p. 30, and "War Psychology and International Socialism," *Masses' Review* (August, 1916). Elsewhere, he condemned as "utopian" the "attempts to remove from man's nature the bellicose-patriotic" tendencies ("The Only Way to End the War," *Masses* [December, 1915]). Some socialists demurred from the view that human nature impelled men to war, for example, Allan L. Benson in "War and Human Nature," *Appeal to Reason* December 18, 1914); but this fashionable Darwinian view was irresistible for most. For a liberal's expression of the view, see Bourne's comments on the "herd instinct" in Louis Filler, *Randolph Bourne* (Washington, D.C., 1943), pp. 122–24.

[16] Walter Rideout, *The Radical Novel in the United States, 1900-1952* (Cambridge, Mass., 1956), p. 50. The list of those who openly supported the Allied cause is impressive: Jack London, Ernest Poole, Ellis O. Jones, Upton Sinclair, J. G. Phelps Stokes, Charles E. Russell, W. J. Ghent, and William E. Walling (possibly the best socialist theoretician). Their "Practical Program for Socialists" urged party members to "adjust themselves to events" (Minutes, SPUSA, April 7, 1917, in Tamiment Institute Library, New York University). Those in opposition were, in Russell's eyes, "dirty traitors" who "sympathized with Germany." For an attack on the minority's "repellent . . . national military position," see Eastman, "Socialists and War," *Masses* (June, 1914). For support of the minority, see Sinclair, *The Autobiography of Upton Sinclair* (New York, 1962), p. 217, and Spargo, *Americanism and Social Democracy* (New York, 1918), p. 171, and Spargo's article in *The Call* (March 18, 1917). Spargo was joined by Frank Bohn, the syndicalist associate editor of the *International Socialist Review*, by A. M. Simons, and by George Herron, the prominent Christian socialist (see his "What of the Proposed Congress?" *American Socialist* [December 5, 1914]). New York's seven socialist aldermen supported the war, as did Allan Benson two years before he became the socialist's candidate for President. Nathan Fine, *Labor and Farmer Parties* (New York, 1961), p. 303. Louis Fraina, an important left-wing spokesman, insisted that "the neutral nations cannot allow, must not allow Germany to win. Germany must be beaten if it takes the whole world to do it" (*New Review*) [July, 1914]. See also *ibid.*, January, March, June, 1915. Max Eastman, while hardly consistent, frequently focused on German militarism in contrast to superior French culture ("The Uninteresting War," *Masses* [September 1915]). For

contradictory observations, see "Let the War Go On," *ibid.* (October, 1914), and Eastman's "Editorial," *ibid.* (March, 1916); see also Lilian Symes and Travers Clement, *Rebel America* (New York, 1934), p. 303.

[17] Freeman, *American Testament,* pp. 77, 78, 87–88; Hillquit, *Loose Leaves,* p. 145. John Spargo bleakly observed: "The outbreak of war revealed the fact that proletarian internationalism was a frail wand" (Spargo, *Americanism and Social Democracy,* p. 103). Isaac Hourwich and Louis Boudin, both staff members of the *New Review,* condemned the German Social Democrats for voting the special war appropriation (Hourwich, "Socialism and the War, October, 1914; Boudin, "Current Affairs," July, 1915, and March, 1916). But not even on this issue were American socialists unanimous. The New York *Volkszeitung,* the organ of German-American socialists, declared that Jules Guesde and Marcel Sembat only did their duty by entering the French cabinet, and William Robinson, although finding the German socialists "craven cowards," praised Guesde, Sembat, and Emil Vandervelde, the Belgian socialist (Robinson, "The War and Socialism," *New Review* [November, 1914]).

[18] *The Call* (August 22, 28, 1914); see also Walling, *Socialists and the War,* p. 380.

[19] *The Call* (August 13, 28, 1914). Debs, in *American Socialist,* January 9, 1915. Eastman, "Let the War Go On"; see also *American Socialist* (January 9, 1915) for the refusal of John Kennedy, secretary of the Illinois Socialist Party, to consider immediate disarmament. Louis Boudin inquired: "Peace—At What Price" and vaguely suggested "a *lasting* peace upon terms that are just and under conditions that will be conducive to the progress of mankind" ("Current Affairs," *New Review* [May 1, 1915]).

[20] Walling, *Socialists and the War,* p. 6; see also H. C. Peterson and G. Fite, *Opponents of War* (Madison, Wis., 1957), pp. 24, 31, 307; "A Socialist Digest," *New Review* (June 15, 1915); *Appeal to Reason* (May 12, 1917). For the response of Boston socialists, see the *Evening Call,* December 8, 1917. Eastman, "Conscription for What?" *Masses* (July, 1917); *idem,* "Socialists and War," *ibid.* (June, 1917).

[21] See, for example, Robert H. La Monte, "Preparedness," *New Review* (December 15, 1915); Walling, "The Great Illusion," *ibid.* (June 1, 1915); Eastman, "A Separation," *Masses* (May, 1917). "Nor am I opposed to fighting under all circumstances," Debs said, "and any declaration to the contrary would disqualify me as a revolutionist." ("When Shall I Fight?" *Appeal to Reason* [September 11, 1915]).

[22] Eastman, "War and Politics," *Masses* (August, 1916). Writing as late as February, 1917, Eastman stated (in the *Masses*): "I think that Wilson's party is going to be the genuine progressive—the state capitalistic

—reform party." See also his editorial in *International Socialist Review* (August, 1916).

[23] *Appeal to Reason* (March 31, 1917). Joseph Freeman recalled that the orthodox socialist position was contained in the Stuttgart resolution adopted by the Seventh International Socialist Congress in 1907: "Wars between capitalist states were the outcome of their competition in the world market. . . . Wars would cease only when the capitalist system was abolished" (*American Testament*, p. 74). See also *The Call* (December 8, 1917). A. M. Simons, endorsing this viewpoint, rejected disarmament as the *ignis fatuus* of the party; see his article in *American Socialist* (January 9, 1915). See also Walling, "The Great Illusion," and *idem, Socialists and the War* p. 475. In the debate on the inevitability of war, Hillquit affirmed the inevitability of conflict under capitalism (*American Socialist* [September 1, 1914]) (see also Walling, *Socialists and the War*, p. 22). But Louis Boudin perceived "no inevitability about war, such as is supposed to flow from the very existence of the competitive system" (*New Review* [January 1, 1916]). Victor L. Berger, giving priority to nationalism and militarism, concluded that "capitalism is only one cause and a minor one at that" (*Milwaukee Leader*, August 23, 1915).

[24] Louis Fraina, *New Review* (September, 1915). See also "Socialist Party Platform Adopted by Party Referendum Closing September 16, 1916" (Mimeograph, Duke University Library). In late February, 1917, the Emergency Committee of the party—consisting of Victor Berger, John Work, and National Secretary Adolph Germer—adopted a statement to remind public officials that socialists had adopted the slogan "Starve the war and feed America" at the outbreak of hostilities; the party now reiterated this demand by urging that "a complete embargo be placed upon all shipments of whatsoever kind from the United States to any and all belligerent countries" ("Statement Adopted by the Emergency Committee, Socialist Party," in Trial Record of the Trial of the United States of America *v.* Victor L. Berger, *et al.*, 5-vol. typescript, 2: 1042-43, Duke University Library). For an early general strike motion, which had been proposed by National Committeeman Ferguson of Oregon at the October, 1914, meeting of the NEC, see *American Socialist* (September 5, October 3, 1914). For strikes against industrial conscription, see Louis Waldman, *Labor Lawyer* (New York, 1944), p. 67–68.

[25] Peterson and Fite, *Opponents of War*, p. 22. See also the Lusk Committee Reports (New York Legislature, Joint Committee Investigating Seditious Activities) in *Revolutionary Radicalism*, 4 vols. (Albany, 1940), 1: 617, and Paul Kennaday, "In Time of Peace, Stick to It," *Intercollegiate Socialist*, 3 (February–March, 1915): 7–8. See also Jessie Hughan, "Pre-

paredness," and Alexander Trachtenberg, "Military Training and the Student," *ibid.*, 4 (April–May, 1916): 14–16. For an opposite view of the socialists' anti-preparedness activities, see "A Socialist Digest," *New Review* (December 15, 1915), which reports Charles E. Russell's position in favor of preparedness.

[26] Alexander Trachtenberg, ed., *American Labor Yearbook 1917–18* (New York, 1918), p. 374. See also Bell, "Marxian Socialism," in *Socialism and American Life*, p. 311 and Draper, *Roots of American Communism*, pp. 92–94.

[27] Peterson and Fite, *Opponents of War*, p. 22. See also Lawrence Levine, *Defender of the Faith* (New York, 1965), p. 88, for a defense of Bryan by Meyer London, the Socialist congressman from New York; London compared Bryan to Tolstoy. Eastman, Pinchot, Lillian Wald, and Jane Addams, among a group of socialists and pacifists, joined Bryan in Washington on February 28, 1917, in a futile effort to influence the President and Congress. For a careful discussion of Henry Ford's "peace ship" and of the pacifists in general, see Devere Allen, *The Fight for Peace* (New York, 1930), Merle Curti, *Peace or War: The American Struggle* (New York, 1936), and Herley Netter, *Origins of the Foreign Policy of Woodrow Wilson* (Baltimore, 1937). Netter (p. 639) says that pacifists were very active and articulate at this time and dismayed by the rise of preparedness societies, such as the National Security League.

[28] A somewhat vague account is Hillquit's *Loose Leaves*, p. 170. A clearer but biased version is in *Revolutionary Radicalism*, 2: 1020–22. Gompers was invited to the conference but refused to attend, and wrote to Louis Lochner: "I prefer not to ally myself with the conscious or unconscious agents of the Kaiser in America" (Gompers to Lochner, May 10, 1917, Gompers Microfilms, AFL Archives, Washington, D.C.). The convention's preamble proclaimed an organization that would "aid our government in bringing to ourselves and the world a speedy, righteous, and lasting peace"; and the delegates endorsed the Bolshevik peace terms "Report of First American Conference for Democracy and Terms of Peace," May 30, 1917, 1st sess., People's Council File, Tamiment Library). See also *The Call* (June 1, 1917). Magnes' address is reported in the *Appeal to Reason* (June 16, 1917) and Hillquit's in "Report of First American Conference for Democracy and Terms of Peace."

[29] The Emergency Peace Federation withdrew from the coalition with the WPP and the American Union against Militarism, and was disbanded in April, 1917. The WPP became increasingly radical, and at its 1918 annual meeting adopted the formidable name Woman's International League for Peace and Freedom, Section for the United States (Addams, *Peace and Bread*, p. 178). Jane Addams would withdraw from the PCA before its

national convention; she was never comfortable with its increasingly radical program, considering herself only a pacifist. But before she left, she and Jordan were eagerly sought after as PCA speakers. The PCA's opposite number, the Workers' Alliance, was the product of AFL concern that socialists might capture the American labor movement. A number of Eastman's "military minority" among the socialists, led by Spargo and Stokes, favored (as the latter stated) "Gompers' stand on the war issues" (Stokes to Chester Wright, July 12, 1917, J. G. Phelps Stokes Papers, Columbia University Library, New York). Spargo suggested that the alliance's structure be independent of the AFL because otherwise it would not appeal to the pro-war socialists who did not wish to associate directly with the AFL (Spargo to Gompers, July 30, 1917, Gompers Microfilms [no. 2], AFL Archives). For the government's support of the alliance, see Creel to Gompers, July 28, 1917 (Committee on Public Information Papers, Library of Congress; Gompers, *Seventy Years of Life and Labor* [New York, 1925], 2: 381; and *The Call* [June 2, 1917]).

[30] Minutes of Organizing Committee (9th sess.), June 20, 1917, People's Council of America (Swarthmore Peace Collection). For the newspaper responses, see the *New York Times*, June 24, 1917; Frederick L. Paxon, *America at War*, 2 vols. (Boston, 1939), 1:55; *The New York Times*, September 20, 1917; *The Call* (September 2, 5, 1917). Jane Addams described the leadership as divided between "good people," such as Lochner, and "self-seekers" (Addams to Jordan, October 2, 1917, David Starr Jordan Papers, Stanford University Library, Stanford, Calif.). Her decision to resign and Jordan's, was made easier when the chairmanship fell into the hands of Scott Nearing, a revolutionary socialist, who soon clashed with PCA moderates, such as Lochner (who also resigned). Many pacifists opposed military preparedness and United States involvement overseas, and played important roles in various peace organizations, but after America declared war most of them—however agonized their decision—gathered around the flag. See Johnson, *The Challenge to American Freedoms*, pp. 1–25; Paul Kellogg, "The Fighting Issue," *Survey*, 37 (February 17, 1917): 572–77; "War Resolutions Adopted by the Settlements," *ibid.*, 38 (June 16, 1917): 265; Ray Abrams, *Preachers Present Arms: A Study of the War-Time Attitudes and Activities of the Churches and the Clergy in the United States, 1914–1918* (Philadelphia, 1933).

[31] For the PCA's Midwest efforts, see Frank Gates to Gompers, November 5, 1917 (Gompers Microfilms [no. 2], AFL Archives); for the West Coast peace campaign, see Executive Committee report of November 8, 1917, People's Council of America (Swarthmore Peace Collection). See also People's Council *Bulletin*, vol. 1, no. 12 (December 28, 1917 [Tamiment Library]). *The New York Times* reported, no doubt with satisfaction,

the "ebb of pacifism in America" (December 23, 1917). Indeed, the PCA's efforts to obtain labor's support were rejected at this time as the American worker became absorbed in reading about the terrors of the Russian revolution. Two instances of the effectiveness of the Alliance's loyalty program were its pro-war performances at the AFL convention in Buffalo (November, 1917) and among New York City's garment workers (where war contract awards were used to buy off pacifist garment workers, particularly among the Amalgamated Clothing Workers). See Robert Maisel to Gompers, November 15, 1917; Gompers to Maisel, December 3, 13, 1917; Charles Pafiner to Gompers, December 18, 1917 (Gompers Microfilms [no. 4], AFL Archives).

[32] William Z. Foster, *From Bryan to Stalin* (New York, 1937) p. 37; see also Lewis A. Brown, "Bolshevism in America," *Forum* 59, (June, 1918): 703–17; *Congressional Record*, 65th Cong. 2d sess., July 29, 1918 (Senate), pp. 9185–86; *The Call* (June 2, 1917). Foster and Nearing were opposed by the moderates; the now right-wing leader, Hillquit, even wrote to Elihu Root to assure him that the Socialist Party supported United States forces overseas (Hillquit to Root, August 12, 1918, Hillquit Papers, University of Wisconsin).

[33] Waldman, *Labor Lawyer*, p. 46.

[34] The *Nation*, which opposed military expeditions to Russia, urged "sympathy [with] and forbearance of the governments which were once its friends" (editorial of August 24, 1918). See also *New Republic* editorial, September 20, 1918.

[35] Of the almost countless instances of congratulatory resolutions sent by radical-socialist groups to the "New Russia," see the resolution of the Cleveland local of the Socialist Party in its *Socialist News* (November 25, 1917); and the *New York Call*, November 26, 1917 and January 7, 15, 1918. On February 4, 1918, the Socialist Party's National Executive Committee adopted two resolutions in support of the Bolshevik revolution and program (Socialist Party Collection, Duke University Library). Benjamin Gitlow, *I Confess: The Truth about American Communism* (New York, 1940), p. 12; Debs, in *Class Struggle*, 3 (February, 1919): 1–4; *Ohio Socialist* (January 8, 1919); *New York Call*, September 12, 1918; and Debs, "The Soul of the Russian People," *New York Call*, April 21, 1918; *Milwaukee Leader*, November 7, 1918; Floyd Dell, *Love in Greenwich Village* (New York, 1926), p. 118; Eugene Lyons, *Assignment in Utopia* (New York, 1937), pp. 37, 38; Ella Winter and Granville Hicks, eds., *The Letters of Lincoln Steffens*, 2 vols. (New York, 1938), 1: 462–63, 466. On its second anniversary the U.S.S.R., Hillquit exulted, remains "strong and stable, confident and invincible, dreaded and cursed by the oppressors of all lands, acclaimed and cherished by the forward-looking workers of all

nations and races" ("Socialist Russia vs. the Capitalist World," *New York Call*, November 7, 1919). For John Reed, see the *New York Call*, September 16, 1918, and Reed, "The First and Second Revolution," *Revolutionary Age* (November 8, 1918); Eastman, "November Seventh, 1918," *Liberator*, 1 (December, 1918): 22–23; Dreiser, *Dreiser Looks at Russia* (New York, 1928), p. 19. Steffens, in *The Freeman* (November 3, 1920), p. 181; *Autobiography of Lincoln Steffens* (New York, 1931), pp. 759–60; Norman Thomas, "The Thirties in America as a Socialist Recalls Them," in Rita J. Simon, ed., *As We Saw the Thirties* (Urbana, Ill., 1967), pp. 114–15.

³⁶ "Proclamation on Russia" adopted by Conference of State Secretaries and Socialist Party Officials, August 10–12, 1918, in *Special Official Bulletin*, September 17, 1918 (Duke University Library). See also the *New York Call*, August 14, 1918.

³⁷ In the 1920's, William E. B. DuBois, not yet a Communist, said in Red Square: "If what I have seen with my eyes and heard with my ears in Russia is Bolshevism, I am Bolshevik" *Crisis*, 34 (1927): 70; Du Bois, *Dusk of Dawn* (New York, 1940), p. 287; editorial in *Crusader* (May–June, 1918); *Weekly People* (November 24, 1917); Peterson, "The American Who Lenin Says Originated the Soviets," *Weekly People* (December 22, 1918); editorial, "All Hail to the Bolsheviki," *New Solidarity* (January 24, 1920). Wobbly leadership believed the "real great revolution," namely, industrial democracy, still had to be tried; it questioned "the state character of the Soviets," banned Harrison George's pro-Soviet pamphlet *The Red Dawn*, and admonished against any attempt to introduce Russian institutions in this country (John Sandgree, "Fate of Bolshevism," *One Big Union Monthly*, 1 [June, 1919]: 18). But many rank-and-file members remained champions of the Soviet state, and the ɪww General Executive Board, for all its doubts, expelled a Philadelphia local for loading ammunition destined for "White" Russian forces (*Seattle Union Record* [August 14, 1920]). See also *Industrial Solidarity* (August 14, 1920) and *New York Call*, August 19, 1920; Emma Goldman, *Living My Life* (New York, 1934), pp. 644–45.

³⁸ Speaking for all of them, the *Nation* editorialized: "In a world that is sick with diseases that breed from capitalist-imperialism, the vitality of Russia may hold out the best hope for civilization" (117 [November 7, 1923]: 501). "The social worker," according to one scholar, "was ready to see the Soviet Union as a kind of Hull House on a national scale, as the land of public health and mental hygiene" (Lewis Feuer, "American Travelers to the Soviet Union, 1917–1932," *American Quarterly*, 14 [Summer, 1962]: 121). For Lillian Wald's enthusiastic comments on public health achievements in Russia—"far-reaching" and "extraordinary"—see Wald, *Windows on Henry Street*, pp. 255–71, and *idem*, "Public Health in Soviet Russia," *Survey*, 53 (1924): 272–74. John Dewey was envious of Russia's

intellectuals, who "have a task that is total and constructive." Dewey also found that "the essence of the Revolution [was] its release of courage, energy and confidence in life" ("Leningrad Gives the Clue," *New Republic* [November 14, 1928], and "The Great Experiment and the Future," *ibid.* [December 19, 1928]).

³⁹ "The Tenth Annual Convention," *Intercollegiate Socialist* (February–March, 1919), p. 26. Eastman, "Knowledge and Revolution," *Masses* (February, 1915); *idem,* "Revolutionary Progress," *ibid.* (February and April, 1917); *idem,* editorials in *Liberator* (May, 1919). In 1915 Socialists officially endorsed a league of nations as well as a world court and other international agencies; predictably, the pacifists also promoted international federation. Degen, *History of the WPP,* pp. 204, 207–12; Addams, *Peace and Bread,* p. 51. For socialist youths' attitudes toward the League of Nations, see "The Conference Speakers," *Intercollegiate Socialist* (October–November, 1916), and Spargo and Rose Pastor Stokes, "What Are the Terms?," *ibid.* (December–January, 1918–19).

⁴⁰ William Hard, "Anti-Bolsheviks: Mr. Sack," *New Republic,* 19 (July 23, 1919): 385–97; M. J. Olgin, "Soviet Industrial Organization," *ibid.* (July 20, 1921), p. 216. For the *Nation's* arguments in favor of recognition, see its April 6, 1921, editorial (p. 494); "Recognize Russia," *ibid.* (March 30, 1921), p. 468. The Communist-dominated Unemployed Councils also urged "resumption of trade with Russia," on the grounds that it would help both countries. *The Toiler,* December 31, 1921. See also A. Coyle, "Our Future Trade with Russia," *Nation* (April 10, 1920), p. 454, and editorial in *ibid.* (April 24, 1920), p. 535. Typical of liberal responses to military intervention were the following: "How Not to Help Russia," *Nation* (June 1, 1918), p. 639, and "The Rescue of Russia," *New Republic,* 16 (October 12, 1918): 301–4. For the radical reaction, see Eastman, "November Seventh, 1918," and his editorials in *Liberator,* vol. 2 (June, 1919); Reed, "On Intervention in Russia," *ibid.,* 1 (November, 1918): 14–16; Ray Ginger, *The Bending Cross* (New Brunswick, N.J., 1949), pp. 382, 401.

⁴¹ The Communist Party's executive committee distributed a break-the-blockade-of-Russia declaration ("Declaration of the Executive Committee of the Communist Party") in *The Communist* (October 18, 1919). For a similar statement, see *The Toiler* (the organ of the Communist Party) of August 27, 1920. Communist Labor Party statement in the *Ohio Socialist* (November 19, 1919). The St. Louis local of the Socialist Party unanimously adopted a resolution for the "immediate withdrawal of troops." *New York Call,* December 1, 1918; the party's national executive committee, meeting in Chicago, did likewise (*Ohio Socialist* [December 29, 1919]), and locals across the country were getting ready "to hold impres-

sive demonstrations as a protest against intervention of the Allied forces in Soviet Russia" (*New York Call*, July 19, 1919, and August 30, 1919). See also Hillquit in the *Socialist World* (August, 1920). New York's Socialists denounced the attempt "to invade Russia by force and overthrow the government of the Russian people" (*New York Call*, July 1, 1918). The *Call*'s editorial of August 9, 1918, rejected an "uninvited invasion of any country by foreign powers, however small its forces and however unavowedly benevolent its purpose." See Norman Thomas in *The World Tomorrow* (February 19, 1919), and *Justice to Russia: Ten Thousand Demand Justice for Russia*, bulletin of the PCA. For Scott Nearing's attack on intervention, see "The Tenth Annual Convention," *The Intercollegiate Socialist* (February–March 1919), 24.

[42] For a pro-recognition statement of the Unemployed Councils, see *Labor Unity* (July 16, 1930). For the liberal position, see the following: "Russia and Recognition" editorial, *Independent*, 116 (January 30, 1926): 119–20; Jerome Davis, "Should America Quarantine the Russian Soviet Government?" *Annals*, 126 (July, 1926): 120; Louis Fischer, *Why Recognize Russia?* (New York, 1931), pp. 211, 219, 287. The Socialist Party's position became clear by December, 1917, and thereafter it urged recognition. *New York Evening Call*, December 22, 1917. Trachtenberg's statement appeared in *Advance* (June 11, 1918), Reed's in the *Liberator* (July, 1918).

[43] Thomas, *As I See It*, p. 73; *New Leader* editorials: January 19 (1924), p. 12; May 24 (1926), p. 4; January 10 (1931); October 28 (1933), p. 2; and "The Socialist Party" (October 28, 1933), p. 2. Hillquit thought Russia was "a travesty of socialism" (*The New York Times*, November 24, 1930); and Soviet repression evoked socialist hostility (see *New York Call* [March 23, 1922]). The *New Leader*, rejecting Russia's claim that it was a proletarian dictatorship, emphasized its censorship and one-party system (see editorial of May 23, 1925, [p. 6]). There was, however, little disagreement on the issues of intervention and recognition (see, for example, Harry Laidler, "An International Program," *L. I. D. Monthly*, 10 [February, 1932]: 4).

[44] *Advance* 15 (January 25, 1929). See also Draper, *Roots of American Communism*, chs. 12–14.

[45] George Rawick, "From Faith to Dogma," *South Atlantic Quarterly*, 53 (April, 1954): 195.

Socialism and the Progressives: Was Failure Inevitable?

Kenneth McNaught

The failure of American socialism is a hardy perennial subject among scholars. Unlike most American scholars, however, Kenneth Mc-Naught believes that in the World War I era the collapse of socialism and the "triumph of majoritarian progressivism" were not inevitable. He writes from the vantage point of a Canadian, as well as that of a scholar who has studied the American left through their trans-atlantic correspondence with British Fabians. This essay is part of a comparative history that is tentatively titled *The Left in Britain and America since 1880*, which will give special attention to "the reasons for American 'uniqueness.'"

Kenneth McNaught is the author of *A Prophet in Politics* (Toronto, 1959), a biography of J. S. Woodworth, the founder of Canada's Social-Democratic Party, and *Manifest Destiny* (Toronto, 1965), a short history of the United States. He received his Ph.D. from the University of Toronto, where he is now Professor of History. He has written a history of Canada that will soon appear in the Pelican series, and he is a contributing editor of *Saturday Night*, a Canadian journal of public opinion.

This article originally appeared as "American Progressives and the Great Society" in the *Journal of American History*, 53, 3 (December, 1966): 504–20, and is reprinted with the permission of the *Journal of American History*.

In the past few years the study of progressivism has reflected dramatically the consensus trend of American historical interpretation which has been so well described by John Higham.[1] Not only does the Bell toll, it positively celebrates the end of ideology. The cumulative portrait of progressivism worked by historians such as Samuel P. Hays, Samuel Haber, George E. Mowry, Robert H. Wiebe, Russel B. Nye, Gabriel Kolko, and Thomas C. Cochran [2] is of a movement to achieve the rationalization of business through government regulation. Regulation of semimonopolistic competition in areas such as banking, railroading, natural resources development, and food and drug production was promoted and formulated by big business while the Underwood-Simmons Tariff was successfully defended as a necessary function of government-supported export drives. A big navy and imperialism, endorsed by populist-progressivism, were equally espoused by business once it got over its springtime jitters of 1898.[3] Indeed, traditional business-agrarian expansionism simply acquired in the progressive period some new slogans, such as the Open Door, Dollar Diplomacy, and the White Man's Burden. In the consensus view of these years, William Howard Taft and Philander Knox rest comfortably in the progressive palladium.

While the consensus view concedes a certain amount of business disunity in the progressive period, it also portrays clearly enough a skillful neo-mercantilist or corporatist development, a mastery over drift which was achieved not in accordance with Walter Lippmann's original purposes but more in fulfillment of the efficiency fetishes of a Brooks Adams or Frederick W. Taylor. As the crest of the Wilson-Roosevelt historical flood approaches, the prevailing impression is the absence of any practical difference between Wilson's and Roosevelt's policy achievements, although students may still be happily at work on cut-and-dried comparisons of the New Freedom and the New Nationalism. The progressive as conservative emerges as the true type while Harold U. Faulkner exits stage left. A recognizably Jacksonian political process is seen to have absorbed the particularist reform groups such as the social gospelers, settlement workers, farm creditists, antimonopolists, advocates of the vote for women, and proponents of the direct-democracy panacea. Municipal reformers emerge as businessmen who deplored inefficiency, while even the fighting Robert M. La Follette is forced into the old-hat role of a Jacksonian machine politician.

Documentation of the revised version is formidable, but the success of the revision seems seriously to imperil the very balance which it is designed to redress. Not only does the new school downgrade the traditional social-justice motives of progressivism and proclaim efficiency and old-family status-seeking as the essential drives of the progressive period, the new version also exhibits the kind of success snobbery which is the hallmark of most conservative history. Even where it is critical of what happened, revisionism comes down heavily in favor of the thesis that "this is the way it had to be." [4] From John D. Hicks through Richard Hofstadter, Arthur M. Schlesinger, Jr., and Louis Hartz there runs the theme (a kind of counterpart to the uninhibited business Calvinism of Allan Nevins) of the inevitable disappearance of third parties and continual return to Lockean consensus. Efforts to organize political dissent outside the major parties—and to give that dissent some ideological content—are deplored on the ground that Americans are not required to bear the essentially European burden of ideology. Arthur Mann seems to share this collective frown of disapproval when he writes: "Hofstadter has won his point that there can be no going back to the intellectual worlds of the Populists and Progressives. . . . The pragmatic center was unquestionably better, as Schlesinger has reminded us, than any of the ideological solutions proposed during the depression." [5] Thus, the most prominent of the historians who have examined the social-justice drive of progressivism coalesce with those who have celebrated the business initiatives of the progressive period, and the two groups find common ground in the New Deal and the Great Society. The circle of inevitable progressive consensus has been closed, and given an incongruous ideological gloss by Hartz, who proclaims America itself to be an ideology within which the absence of a feudal-aristocratic tradition has decreed that private-property liberalism must be the only criterion of political judgment. Because of its inevitable consensus, according to Hartz, America is unique, and its all-embracing, patriotic liberalism is what explains the failure of the ideological wings of progressivism, and particularly the failure of socialism.

The collapse of American socialism, and thus of all twentieth-century attempts to organize a political basis of ideological dissent outside the major parties, could scarcely be more crucial as a determinant of the nature of the present Great Society. Certainly the continuing political impotence of the left marks America as unique within the western world whether or not the failure is seen as historical or inevitable. It is therefore significant that most recent historians of American socialism more or less concur in the general thesis of the inevitable triumph of majoritarian progressivism.[6] While they give varying weight to identifiable aspects of the socialist failure, such as the factionalism that beset the Socialist Party of America, the vagaries of Eugene Debs' leadership, the opportunities of life in the United States, failure to win over the American Federation of Labor, the absence of class consciousness, the free gift of the ballot, and the unhappy consequences of the SPA's antiwar policy, the basic explanation offered is that socialism was ideological, of foreign origin, and therefore bound to fail. Daniel Bell sums it up thus: "The socialist movement, by its very statement of goal and in its rejection of the capitalist order as a whole, could not relate itself to the specific problems of social action in the here and now, give-and-take political world." [7] Socialism, he argues, could not enter the pragmatic consensus of American society and was therefore certain to fail.

The central proposition of the newly established version is clear: Any American political movement that rejects the Lockean basis (or the possessive individualism) of American society is so alien to that society that it cannot represent a serious political challenge, and the other factors of size, the Constitution, immigration, and the rest simply reinforce the definitive function of the "liberal tradition." Into this interpretation can be fitted nearly everyone who is supposed to have benefited from the emergent *quid pro quo* corporatism of the progressive period: farmers, unionists, small and large businessmen (if they were good), and even consumers. But this total explanation, like others of the genre, distorts the available information and minimizes those facts that appear awkward and angular.

Most of the distortion comes in the realm of opinion-facts, or what some Americans thought about the condition and prospects of their country. But such distortion is then taken as proof of the "objective" facts that are said to underlie the opinion. For example, because numerous spokesmen proclaimed America to be a classless society, it is frequently assumed that America was a classless society. Yet the briefest glance at the statistics of income distribution, at the story of industrial warfare, or at the roles played by the Supreme Court or the Bureau of Corporations suggests that the condition of the majority of Americans was no less debilitated by class domination than was the case in Britain. Again, the fact that most Americans were persuaded that socialism was alien is taken as proof that socialism was alien. Yet many of the facts of socialist growth indicate quite the reverse: that a major myth-making campaign was required to make socialism alien despite the widespread existence of conditions favorable to its survival. It is the success of that mythology that has called forth Hartz' ideological superstructure: America is classless because Americans thought it was classless; they thought this because they had no aristocratic-feudal legacy to combat; because there was no focal point of aristocracy, liberalism and socialism could not coalesce. The two points about this argument that seem weakest may be stated thus: While a case can be made that in Europe the struggle for democracy frequently strengthened the political left, in Britain after the 1880's there was no greater focusing on the need to extend democracy as such than there was in the United States. Indeed there was probably less. And there the growth of socialism resulted from concentration on precisely the same problems of industrial and finance capitalism that were also the objects of muckraking, progressive, and socialist concern in the United States.

Yet the irrelevance of the aristocratic legacy in any comparison of British and American socialism is not total. Curiously, while Hartz has a good deal to say about Alexis de Tocqueville, he develops only one side of De Tocqueville's American theme. In noting that the absence of an aristocratic tradition left little room for the growth of an American counterpart to European conservatism, he minimizes the French aristocrat's fears for liberalism—fears which stemmed from precisely the same source. In other words the aristocratic vacuum, while it weakened conservatism, also weakened the resources of individualism in any resistance to whig-dominated conformism. As a result of Hartz' partial use of the aristocratic vacuum it is quite possible to reverse his statement of the problem and come up with an answer which fits more of the facts and at the same time exorcises the specter of inevitability. Thus one can argue that American liberalism is weak in its defense of dissent against majoritarian democracy precisely because it lacks an aristocratic legacy. American liberalism has been weakened and not strengthened by this lack, and the failure of the socialist phase of liberalism is the measure of the weakness.

Some of the difficulty in this analysis flows from the tendency to use liberalism and democracy as interchangeable terms. Whig-guided democracy was able to capture the bulk of the progressive movement and lead to the extinction of party-based dissent not because American society was essentially liberal but because that society lacked an aristocratic tradition of eccentricity and intellectual discipline. The validity of this is strongly suggested by any comparison with the British experience; the longing of many American socialists for the intellectual and social independence that characterized the Fabian Society expressed their envy of a political-social milieu which could ensure safe passage into the age of democracy without loss of the great liberal strengths inherited from an aristocratic tradition. Yet, while the American failure to sustain an independent social-democratic party was rendered more likely in the absence of an aristocratic tradition, that failure was by no means inevitable; nor was socialism any more alien to or incompatible with American society than were other ideas imported from time to time from overseas. The failure has called forth an inevitability interpretation principally because of the ease with which American "moralism" and "patriotism" were employed by expansionist-whig politicians to subvert challenges to their policies. The successful hoodwinking of socialistic progressivism by business progressivism and the fact that Theodore Roosevelt, Woodrow Wilson, and their colleagues discerned in socialism the principal threat to corporate capitalism does not mean that the outcome was inevitable; it does mean that the resources of dissent in America were more slender than they were in Britain. That Wilson could cut as much political ice as he did with the declaration "I will not cry 'peace' so long as there is sin and wrong in the world" [8] is not so much a tribute to the inner liberalism of America as it is to the fear of American democrats that dissent might be termed un-American.

This central problem was clearly seen by Sidney Webb as early as 1889. Observing that Henry George's recent statements had included many socialist proposals, Webb commented:

> Why then does Mr. George object to the name Socialist? The answer is, I think, that Mr. George is an American citizen, and Socialism in the United States is not in exactly the same phase as Socialism here. The American Socialist is apt to be, though there are many worthy exceptions, either an Individualist or an Anarchist, despising and utterly rejecting the whole Law of Rent, or else a fanatical devotee of Marx, an alien and an aggressive atheist, often not yet freed from the illusions of "physical force" and a cataclysmic economic revolution. . . .
>
> The consequent unpopularity of Socialism in the United States, when presented under that name, is greatly to be regretted, and I will frankly add that I think it would have been nobler and better if Mr. George and others had faced the unpopularity, and, by casting in their lot with the Socialists helped to live it down.[9]

Superficially Webb's statement might be seen as further witness to the validity of Hartz' proposition that socialism was alien to America, and certainly the course followed by many other left-wing Americans of the day might also seem to support the Hartz argument. Florence Kelley, for example, writing to Henry D. Lloyd in 1896 deplored "the practice of expelling everyone who can speak English from the Socialist Labor Party." [10] The triumph of Hartz' Americanism seemed inevitable in the face of a literally alien domination of some aspects of the American socialist movement, and Florence Kelley went on through frustration to the "practical" meliorative reformism of the Progressive era.

Yet to jump from individual decisions to general laws can be dangerous, and one weakness of the Bell-Hartz interpretation is its own conceptual rigidity. Pointing to the alienation of doctrinaire

Marxian socialism from American life, it leaps to the illogical conclusion that all socialism was alien. American socialism, in much of the recent writing, becomes a monolithic concept with a fixed life of its own, a conceptual entity whose life was determined not by cumulative individual decisions but by the ghostly immanence of a host of socio-economic abstractions. Jeffersonian ideals, American dreams, Lockean underpinnings, and Algerism dictated that socialism could be in but not of American society. While the effects of Americanism as ideology cannot be denied, neither its definition at any given time nor its self-motivation may correctly be assumed. As a defense of the status quo its role is clear, but surely it was a puppet's role without Pinocchio connotations. The point that is obscured by the grand new terminology is that Americanism was used and was not a force in itself. Diversion of the reform drive from its leftward course was accomplished by individuals who saw this possible function of an Americanism properly clothed in moral dress. Hundreds of progressive statements illustrate this point. One such, from the bulging Wilson records, may be taken as typical: "One really responsible man in jail, one real originator of the schemes and transactions which are contrary to public interest legally lodged in the penitentiary, would be worth more than one thousand corporations mulcted in fines, if reform is to be genuine and permanent. It is only in this way that we can escape socialism." [11]

The more business-oriented reformers contemplated the swelling leftist criticism of American society the more consciously they formulated their alternatives as an answer to socialism. To assert that American whig-progressives were not required to confront socialism (because it was not a part of Americanism), or that socialism aborted because a liberal-socialist alliance was not required to combat a non-existent aristocratic conservatism, is to minimize or ignore the most obvious facts. The majoritarian progressives spent a good deal of time, in private and in public, confronting the socialist "menace." Wilson and Roosevelt were equally concerned to undermine it, and both men, together with many of their supporters, early discerned the real nature of the confrontation. Roosevelt smeared the muckrakers, for example, not because he thought their writings false but because he feared a socialist result from their revelations. Writing to Taft he observed, "Some of these are socialists; some of them merely lurid sensationalists; but they are all building up a revolutionary feeling which will most probably take the form of a political campaign." [12]

The letters of Lincoln Steffens in 1912 document clearly enough the whig-progressive success as well as the effect of that success upon one undoubted American:

> The most to be hoped for from President Wilson is a few laws that won't do much good; some more prosecutions that won't do much harm; and,—this is best: the splitting of the Democratic party in two. Then, next election . . . the Democratic progressives and the Republican progressives will all be in one party, probably under Wilson, and the conservatives will have a party of their own, under somebody (or over somebody). And then? Well, then the actual conservatism of the Progressives will appear; and nothing much will be done.[13]

Steffens expressed a concern that was shared by hundreds of other left-wing progressives who flocked to join the Socialist Party or other socialist organizations such as the Inter-Collegiate Socialist Society which had been started by Upton Sinclair in 1905. By 1913 the ISS had forty-three chapters. In 1915 it had chapters in sixty colleges and included in its membership Randolph S. Bourne, Paul Blanshard, Clarence S. Darrow, John Dewey, Louis Budenz, Stuart Chase, Freda Kirchwey, Broadus Mitchell, Selig Perlman, Walter Weyl, and Norman Thomas.[14] Not only was socialism not un-American, it was becoming respectable. It was both in and of American society. With a press which included thirteen dailies, three hundred weeklies, and a number of monthlies reaching a total circulation of two million in 1912, and with some of the most influential writers and professors in its ranks, socialism merited the fears of the orthodox. Both the majoritarian progressives and the socialists recognized what the new version is at pains to minimize: America was a class-ridden society, and the arguments that were nourishing British socialism were equally valid in the United States.

Mann has indicated how American progressives of all shades used English thought and experience to indict laissez faire economics and social Darwinism.[15] American reformers found appealing the British aristocratic tradition of noblesse oblige and the role of intellectual leadership. But the decision of thousands of middle-class American socialists not to stay with their socialist party when the weather stiffened remains crucial. That decision, frequently repeated, suggests the significance for American radicalism of the dominance of the democratic over the liberal or aristocratic tradition in the United States. British Fabians laughed at the idea of their being alien, while their American counterparts were frequently unnerved by such an idea. As a result American socialist intellectuals largely abandoned the effort to influence union leaders, to educate public opinion, and to provide a constant rallying point from which to oppose the moralistic superpatriots of preparedness and antibolshevism. They permitted the myth of alienation to grow by default and from fear of the democracy. Much of this is plainly suggested in transatlantic Fabian-progressive correspondence. To read in that correspondence is to confront continuously the great questions of free will and inevitability.

The fairly widespread American interest in British socialism was expressed by Lillian Wald of the New York Henry Street Settlement when she wrote to congratulate Ramsay MacDonald on his 1906 election: "This victory must mean great things for 'our' party and we shall be eager to watch affairs of state across 'the pond.' . . . The problems of London and New York are not very different, so that it seems like an experiment of our own for our own. You see you will be in the generous position of doubtless making some mistakes by which we can profit." [16]

For many American socialist-progressives Graham Wallas expressed what seemed best in British radicalism, particularly the challenging idea of an intellectual elite's social responsibility. Wallas' American lecture tours and his books—especially *Human Nature in Politics* (1908) and *The Great Society* (1914)—appealed strongly to such widely separate people as William James and Wallas' chief American disciple, Walter Lippmann. James summed up the American response best when he wrote to Wallas about the first book: "The concreteness and the humour make it a characteristically English piece of work. I should think it might have a powerful effect, being *real* political philosophy. . . . The power of certain individuals to infect (for better or worse) others by their example is to me almost the all in all of social change." [17]

Yet it was symptomatic, as the 1900's advanced, that socialistic progressives gave increasing emphasis to the "boring from within" aspect of Fabianism and less to the role of an independent political party. While they continued to applaud the work of Fabians, Labour, and the ILP, and even to support socialist organization in America, more and more they felt the attraction of the less rocky road of consensus.

The rationalization implicit in this trend was evident in a letter one American wrote after the American election of 1908: "We are still 'at it' in these United States pushing along some very good Socialism mainly through the old parties and we have emerged from the recent elections with a good deal of cheer to everybody." [18]

The course followed by Lippmann in these years reveals much about the potential strength and ultimate debility of independent socialism in the United States. In political philosophy Lippmann was tutored by Wallas, and in municipal socialism by Steffens. His *Drift and Mastery* was, as he told Wallas when he was writing it, aimed "at popularizing your *Human Nature in Politics*." [19] In 1912 Lippmann was a Fabian socialist and tried his hand briefly at practical politics. When the socialists won the municipal election in Schenectady, Lippmann was drafted as secretary to the young minister who became mayor. He reported his experience succinctly to Wallas:

> It wasn't long before I discovered that to raid saloons and brothels, to keep taxes below the usual rate, and to ignore the educational problems were the guiding principles of their "socialist" administration. . . . On every vital question the socialists ignored their own point of view and fell in with what we have come to know as "good government" or "goo-goo" politics.
>
> I fought as hard as I could within the "organization" without any result. When I saw that the policy and program were settled . . . I resigned and attacked the administration in a socialist paper. This brought down upon me the wrath of the leaders. [20]

While Lippmann remained sympathetic to socialism after this experience, he gave up the practical side of socialist politics. Indeed, almost from the start he showed an inclination away from the politics of independence and toward hopeful boring from within—an instinct that seems to have been latent in most of his middle-class colleagues. As early as the summer of 1912 Lippmann wrote: "We are all elated that Wilson has got so far. . . . If elected we all expect him to outgrow his party in short order. For once he begins to handle the situations he must face, his conglomerate supporters will drop off." [21]

Few British Fabians would have made the same judgment about Henry Campbell-Bannerman, Lloyd George, or Winston Churchill. Instead, like R. C. K. Ensor, they continued speaking to and working for the local Labour Representation Committees and Labour parties and building up their influence with trades union leaders.[22] As Alfred Zimmern noted during an American visit in 1911, "Wilson, if elected, would be very much hampered by his reactionary southern following." While Zimmern met and liked Lippmann, he felt most American intellectuals lacked depth of understanding when compared to English intellectual socialists.[23] Doubtless a casual assessment, Zimmern's comment nevertheless touches an important aspect of the transatlantic comparison. The aristocratic tradition of intellectual discipline in British universities gave a consistent logical toughness to socialist analysis and action in the United Kingdom that was much less frequently evident in the United States. This difference was reflected in American political ambivalence. In a letter reflecting on the 1912 election, Charles Zueblin of Chicago seems to illustrate this point:

> Wilson was the best man in the field, but I had to support Roosevelt because the Progressive party is a generation ahead of the Democratic party. It has a definite, though moderate, Socialistic trend, while the Democrats are still harping on States Rights and competition. Our hope is that Wilson's independence will smash the Democratic party as Roosevelt's did the Republican party, and then we shall get a new alignment.
>
> Meanwhile the Socialist vote is growing. They are getting more and more local offices but are threatened by disruption by Syndicalism. That will also be a good thing. I incline more and more to small parties that one can join conscientiously and where he will feel at home.[24]

With Eugene V. Debs at the peak of his influence in 1912, Zueblin's is a curious comment; his later loyalty to Republicanism suggests the common pattern of individual refusals to sustain party-organized political dissent. Perhaps Wallas' understanding of individual reluctance to brave the wrath of the American democracy made him so very popular among a wide range of left-inclined progressives. When his book *The Great Society* appeared, it seemed almost to endorse the difference between British and American possibilities. As A. N. Holcombe wrote to Wallas, "perhaps I ought not to say it . . . but your books seem to me thoroughly American rather than English, by which I do not mean to disparage either what is English or what is American, but simply to indicate a difference." [25] Judge Learned Hand, whose conservative appreciation of Wallas was not as surprising as might appear at first glance, also noted the difference and, by implication, its significance:

> I remember you told me last January that you agreed with me in thinking we Americans should go rather slowly here till we have developed better machinery for collectivistic enterprises. I wish you would impress it upon Walter Lippmann and the other "New Republicans" who are disposed to condemn a provisional attitude. . . . I am really a little puzzled, to speak frankly, to know how the man who wrote *The Great Society* lived for so many years in intimate collaboration with that small body of men and women (the Fabians) who did so much, it is true, to make present England, but who do not seem to me, to put it mildly, to have ever looked at politics with the spirit of genial toleration or a sense that their message might not after all be the last word on the subject.[26]

Judge Hand's worry about New Republican extremism was, of course, unnecessary. As Felix Frankfurter noted, in soliciting Fabian subscriptions for the new journal, "the New Republic's philosophy will be a faith rather than a dogma." [27] From the outset Mrs. Straight's "kept idealists" of Greenwich Village gave voice to that democratic patriotism which, in the guise of radicalism, spelled the end of middle-class intellectual leadership of American socialism.[28] Herbert Croly, Weyl, and Lippmann all flirted with socialism, but the most consistent *New Republic* themes were those of direct democracy, strong executive leadership, and nonpartisanship. In 1919–1920 the *New Republic* called occasionally and quietly for an independent labor party or a farmer-labor alliance; [29] but when the need of vigorous, independent socialist advocacy was greatest, and when it could have given the necessary extra vitality and coordination to the large but inchoate socialist groupings of 1912–1916, the *New Republic* gave way before the blandishments of Wilson's brief progressivism and the mounting clamor of patriotic preparedness. It was left for the *New Republic*, disillusioned by the pseudo-progressivism which the Crolyites had helped make possible, to lament in 1919 that "a parvenu middle class, with a stake in the game, had appropriated the national inheritance and branded it with its own seal. . . . Americanization, which ought to mean a regeneration of mankind in this hemisphere with an open mind toward the future, became . . . a thing to frighten children with." [30]

Those middle-class intellectuals who abandoned independent socialist political action did so almost with a sigh of relief. The alleged need to work within a major party—a "need" which cloaked the cumulative individual decisions to which historians now give the force of law—could be justified by the foreign domination of the Socialist Party. Although such domination as there was by the end of 1916 was principally the result of withdrawal by native Americans rather than influx of hyphenated Americans, the process was at the time, and continues to be, misrepresented. Lippmann, for example, wrote at the end of 1915, "The Socialists have become purely negative and orthodox."[31] In fact, as Ira Kipnis has observed, the socialists might more justly be condemned for having modified their doctrine too much than for remaining too doctrinaire.[32] As early as December, 1914, the *New Republic*, while it was busy lecturing Wilson for backsliding, described the socialist platform as "progressively watered so that the flaming red of a generation ago becomes a delicate pink."[33] Socialism had become Americanized but was debilitated principally by the unwillingness of most of its intellectuals to face the testing time of patriotic consensus.

For many the process of alienating socialism was justified by the growing importance of international affairs. They transferred their idealism from the difficult domestic arena to the international stage where progressive consensus might more readily be organized behind respectable patriotism. As is seen in the Lippmann-Wallas correspondence, the passage was both strange and definitive. Writing at the end of 1915, when Roosevelt reappeared on the political scene, Lippmann confessed, "It's the most difficult political decision I have ever had to make. Wilson is impossible. He has no sense of organization and no interest in the responsibilities of the socialized state. He has no grasp of international affairs and his pacifism is of precious little help to the peace of the world. . . . Roosevelt alone of men who are possible has any vision of an integrated community."[34] By May of 1916, Lippmann's concern for the responsibilities of a socialized state, let alone about independent political action, waned as the assumption took root that a proper relationship to the European struggle required unsullied Americanism.[35] And in August, 1916, he could write:

> I have come around completely to Wilson chiefly because I think
> he has the imagination and the will to make a radical move in the

organization of peace. . . . Of course the campaign depends above
all on what the former progressives do. If Wilson can get 20 percent
of their votes he will be re-elected. . . . Wilson is by far the best
party leader the Democrats have ever produced.[36]

Perhaps the oddest aspect of the intellectuals' exodus from American socialism was the inability of most of those who took part in it
to foresee the consequences of abandoning the rallying point of independent party organization. Few seemed to realize as deeply as did
Wilson himself the full implications of patriotic consensus. In a democratic nation which lacked the aristocratic tradition it was doubly important, if additionally difficult, to maintain a strong center of dissent.
As a visiting Fabian remarked in February, 1917: "I wish I could see
more signs of the trained young American getting down to the job of
thinking some of these things out. . . . The prospect, if America should
should come in [to the war], is unimaginable." [37]

While Lippmann was absorbed by his work for Colonel Edward
M. House's "Inquiry," and while others of the "New Republic circle,"
like Zechariah Chafee, watched civil liberties go to jail with Eugene
Debs, the ferment in British Labour attracted rueful attention.[38] But
without adequate bridges to the empire of Samuel Gompers, and with
the Socialist Party now in fact alienated, there was no vehicle of radical reconstruction in the United States. A misplaced faith in Wilson
and consensus had left socialists scattered and defenseless before the
successive waves of the Sedition Act and the Red Scare. When not
even a civilized peace emerged from the transfer of ideals to foreign
affairs, disillusionment became fashionable. The young Harold Laski,
viewing the scene of radical desolation while he awaited an invitation to dine again with the Harvard Overseers, put his finger neatly
on the problem: "The worst of it is that the liberals have no real pro-
gramme beyond sporadic protest. . . . There is interest in the teachers'
sufferings one day and it dies before the strike at Lawrence the next,
which, in turn, gives way to riots on May Day. . . . The most hopeful
thing I see here is twofold in aspect—the movement toward a labour
party and the restlessness of the undergraduates." [39] The founding of
the New School of Social Research and the uneasiness of socialist union leaders were what betrayed Laski into his moment of optimism.
The flight of the intellectuals from the party of dissent, from the pace-
making base of the American left, and their new-found luxury of dis-

illusionment, eliminated the possibility of a British type of labor party —and condemned American socialism to the disruption and continuing alienation of the 1920's. At the beginning of 1920 a conservative described the real nature of the most basic American political fact. Hand wrote to Wallas:

> What you said in your last lecture [at the New School] made me sorrowful, for I realized your disappointment. However, as I look back now at it I am not surprised, as you are. I remember on your trip in 1914 you seemed to see here a good deal more that was hopeful than I did. . . . We never had the foundations in this country, in my time, for a genuine spirit of toleration. It is a country where you are expected to conform and if you don't you are looked on with suspicion. We all knew this, or at least knew it at times and in spots long before the war taught us. . . . The conception of America as a place of warm-hearted acceptance and toleration was always a mistaken one, I think, and the change is not so great as it seems. . . . Do not despair of us, by any means. We are not very temperate . . . but we will stop long short of the logical implications of what we have been doing.[40]

The most surprising thing in all this is that the very large group of American intellectuals who admired Wallas and endorsed from afar the developing program and action of the British Labour Party failed themselves to apply the central principles of *The Great Society*. For a brief spell the inventive role of a quasi-aristocratic intellectual elite was played by some American progressives in planning with British liberals for a "peace without victory."[41] But the infinitely more important function of such leadership—the establishment of firm union connections and the support of an independent party of socialist dissent—was foresworn. Yet even the people most closely involved in what had happened fell back upon abstract forces rather than individual decisions as explanation. "There is no pretending that the atmosphere is cheerful here," Lippmann wrote Wallas shortly after Harding's inauguration. "It is not. The hysteria has turned to apathy and disillusionment in the general public, and cynicism in most of my friends. I feel that we shall not have much immediate influence in America for perhaps a decade, but I'm not discouraged because we can use that time well to re-examine our ideas."[42]

By the time that decade had passed, Frankfurter's young men were ready to lend a hand with the "bold experimentation" of the New Deal. And by the time three more decades had passed, presidential speechwriters were able to resurrect Wallas' 1914 title and present the new Great Society swept clean of organized political dissent. The triumph of majoritarian, whig-led progressivism in the new Great Society looks very much like the similar triumph recorded in the most recent historical accounts of the traditional progressive era.

It remains, however, extremely doubtful that such triumphs were inevitable. It is even more doubtful that they resulted from impersonal forces—except inasmuch as such forces were created by many individual decisions. Most dubious of all are the contentions that socialism was by definition alien to American society and that the absence of an aristocratic tradition, by enfeebling American conservatism, made America inevitably liberal. The evidence, both factual and opinionative, suggests very strongly the reverse. Socialism was very relevant, was directly confronted by whig-led democracy, and was defeated largely because nonaristocratic and antiliberal tendencies in the American democratic tradition weakened dissent on the left rather than conformity on the right.

[1] In "Beyond Consensus: The Historian as Moral Critic," *American Historical Review*, 67 (April, 1962): 609–25.

[2] Samuel P. Hays, *Conservation and the Gospel of Efficiency: The Progressive Conservation Movement, 1890–1920* (Cambridge, Mass., 1959); *idem, The Response to Industrialism: 1885–1914* (Chicago, 1957); Robert H. Wiebe, *Businessmen and Reform: A Study of the Progressive Movement* (Cambridge, Mass., 1962); Gabriel Kolko, *The Triumph of Conservatism: A Reinterpretation of American History, 1900–1916* (New York, 1963); George E. Mowry, *The Era of Theodore Roosevelt: 1900–1912* (New York, 1958); Russel B. Nye, *Midwestern Progressive Politics: A Historical Study of Its Origins and Developments, 1870–1958* (East Lansing, Mich., 1959); Samuel Haber, *Efficiency and Uplift: Scientific Management in the Progressive Era, 1890–1920* (Chicago, 1964); Thomas C. Cochran, *The American Business System: A Historical Perspective, 1900–1955* (Cambridge, Mass., 1957).

[3] William E. Leuchtenburg, "Progressivism and Imperialism: The Progressive Movement and American Foreign Policy, 1898–1916," *Mississippi Valley Historical Review*, 39 (December, 1952): 483–504; William Appleman Williams, ed., *The Shaping of American Diplomacy*, 2 vols. (Chicago, 1956).

4 See Richard Hofstadter, *The Age of Reform: From Bryan to F. D. R.* (New York, 1955); Daniel Aaron, *Men of Good Hope: A Story of American Progressives* (New York, 1951); Arthur Mann, "British Social Thought and American Reformers of the Progressive Era," *Mississippi Valley Historical Review*, 42 (March, 1956): 672–92.

5 Arthur Mann, "The Progressive Tradition," in John Higham, ed., *The Reconstruction of American History* (New York, 1962), p. 177.

6 David A. Shannon, *The Socialist Party of America: A History* (New York, 1955); Ray Ginger, *The Bending Cross: A Biography of Eugene Victor Debs* (New Brunswick, N.J., 1949); Ira Kipnis, *The American Socialist Movement: 1897–1912* (New York, 1952); Max Eastman, *Reflections on the Failure of Socialism* (New York, 1955); Howard H. Quint, *The Forging of American Socialism: Origins of the Modern Movement* (Columbia, S.C., 1953); Donald Drew Egbert and Stow Persons, eds., *Socialism and American Life*, 2 vols. (Princeton, N.J., 1952).

7 Daniel Bell, "Socialism: The Dream and the Reality," *Antioch Review*, 12 (March, 1952): 3–17.

8 Woodrow Wilson, "The Bible and Progress" (address at Denver, May 7, 1911), in Ray Stannard Baker and William E. Dodd, eds., *The Public Papers of Woodrow Wilson*, 6 vols. (New York, 1925–27), 2:294.

9 Sidney Webb, "Henry George and Socialism," *Church Reformer* (January, 1899), copy in Passfield Papers, 7:1, 10 (London School of Economics).

10 Florence Kelley to Henry D. Lloyd, June 18, 1896, Henry D. Lloyd Papers (Wisconsin State Historical Society, Madison).

11 Woodrow Wilson, "The Author and Signers of the Declaration of Independence," *North American Review*, 622 (September, 1907): 30.

12 Theodore Roosevelt to William H. Taft, March 15, 1906, in Peter Lyon, *Success Story: The Life and Times of S. S. McClure* (New York, 1963), p. 208.

13 Lincoln Steffens to Allen and Lou Suggett, November 19, 1912, in Ella Winter and Granville Hicks, eds., *The Letters of Lincoln Steffens*, 2 vols. (New York, 1938), 1:313.

14 James Weinstein, "The Socialist Party: Its Roots and Strength, 1912–1919," *Studies on the Left*, 1 (Winter, 1960): 5–27.

15 Mann, "British Social Thought and American Reformers of the Progressive Era;" *idem, Yankee Reformers in the Urban Age* (Cambridge, Mass., 1954); also see Quint, *The Forging of American Socialism.*

16 Wald to MacDonald, February 13, 1906, Ramsay MacDonald Papers (Malcolm MacDonald, London). Curiously, Lillian Wald is listed by Mann as one who was "unaffected, at least directly, by British social thought." See Mann, "British Social Thought and American Reformers, p. 690. A

similar point of view was expressed by H. D. Lloyd, writing to Graham Wallas, July 9, 1902 (Graham Wallas Papers, London School of Economics): "Is it not perfectly plain that the escape we have all been hoping for and working for must come by some philosophy and performance far more radical than any we have yet committed ourselves to?"

[17] James to Wallas, December 9, 1908, Graham Wallas Papers.

[18] Wald to Wallas, November 14, 1908, *ibid.*

[19] Lippmann to Wallas, July 31, 1912, *ibid.*

[20] *Ibid.*

[21] *Ibid.*

[22] R. C. K. Ensor Papers, *passim* (Corpus Christi College, Oxford).

[23] Zimmern was not optimistic. He wrote: "Meeting educated people here makes me appreciate the Oxford grounding; they are so incredibly casual and superficial in the way they attack complex, concrete problems. . . . What I come back to again and again as a determining factor in American psychology is the size of the country. Americans live on too large a scale to live deep. . . . The result is that they seem only to think with the front of their head. What Meredith called 'fundamental brain work' is so absent from most of their books and utterances that nobody even thinks of asking for it. Their speeches consist not of argument, but of anecdote and generalization. . . . What is wanted is a new, more serious and steady habit of mind; otherwise, with this system of government, the good done in one whirlwind campaign will be swept away in the next." Zimmern to Wallas, December 24, 1911, Graham Wallas Papers.

[24] Zueblin to Wallas, November 12, 1912, *ibid.*

[25] Holcombe to Wallas, June 28, 1914, *ibid.*

[26] Hand to Wallas, August 19, 1914, *ibid.* Wallas was perhaps the prototype of mid-Atlantic man. On one occasion, after dinner in a London club, his host was asked, "Who was that Yankee dining with you?" *ibid.*, box for 1914.

[27] Frankfurter to Wallas, September 21, 1914, Graham Wallas Papers.

[28] The liberal E. L. Godkin early saw the way in which progressives were hoodwinked by the consensus patriotism of the day and proclaimed that Roosevelt was establishing "a sort of Tory Democracy, fed on promises of a social heaven on earth" (*Nation*, 79 [August 11, 1904]: 110). The overt appeal for consensus remained throughout these years a major stumbling block for independent party organization. *McClure's Magazine* hammered the theme conscientiously: "The coming 'ism' is not Socialism; the coming 'ism' is Patriotism" (21 [July, 1903]: 336). And, there is "a new righteousness which shall become a new passion—*the Love of Country*. We shall see that new passion develop in the American people until we have obedience to the law, *because it is the law*, and the will of the state will be

sufficient" (S. S. McClure, "The Increase of Lawlessness in the United States," *McClure's Magazine*, 24 [December, 1904]: 171). On the New Republicans, see Charles Forcey, *The Crossroads of Liberalism: Croly, Weyl, Lippmann, and the Progressive Era, 1900–1925* (New York, 1961).

[29] See, for example, vol. 21 (February 18, 1920): 329.

[30] 19 (June 14, 1919): 210–11.

[31] Lippmann to Wallas, December 18, 1915, Graham Wallas Papers.

[32] "Like other movements sworn to change the American economy, it had proven too willing to settle for a few favors and promises from the dreaded enemy" (Kipnis, *The American Socialist Movement*, p. 429).

[33] 1 (December 12, 1914): 11.

[34] Lippmann to Wallas, December 18, 1915, Graham Wallas Papers.

[35] *Ibid.*, May 21, 1916.

[36] *Ibid.*, August 29, 1916. The *New Republic*, agonizing between Roosevelt and Wilson and over the decisive abandonment of socialism, was heavy going. The Fabian journalist, S. K. Ratcliffe, reported to Wallas: "The N.R. group makes New York much more enjoyable than it would otherwise be. But what a solemnity broods over the place! They are the gravest set of youngsters in the world. Walter Lippmann by the side of his colleagues is a knockabout comedian!" (March 5, 1915, *ibid.*). Other Americans who were working for American support of Britain, such as A. Lawrence Lowell of Harvard, Ellery Sedgwick of the *Atlantic Monthly,* or Learned Hand, did not have to agonize. As Hand noted in a letter to Wallas: "I have liked Wilson's attitude throughout and he has the support of everyone except the besotted Germans and the indescribable Bryan" (June 29, 1915, *ibid.*).

[37] Ratcliffe to Wallas, February 1, 1917, *ibid.* Felix Frankfurter, on the other hand, commenting on his Harvard Law School protégés, was more optimistic: "Those boys are a wonderful lot and I can't help but feel that a different purpose moves them. There is a more critical self-examination as to what their part in the country's business is than bothered the minds of the men when I was a student" (Frankfurter to Wallas, July 14, 1915, *ibid.*). But Frankfurter's young men were preparing to deal socialist dissent its second and fatal blow in the 1930's.

[38] "Everywhere there is the most eager interest in our labour situation; the manifestoes are being keenly studied" (Ratcliffe to Wallas, June 15, 1918, *ibid.*).

[39] Laski to Wallas, May 12, 1919, *ibid.*

[40] January 17, 1920, *ibid.*

[41] See Laurence W. Martin, *Peace without Victory: Woodrow Wilson and the British Liberals* (New Haven, Conn., 1958).

[42] March 29, 1921, Graham Wallas Papers.

Feminism as a Radical Ideology

William L. O'Neill

If socialism has been overworked by students of American radicalism, feminism is a neglected field. Indeed, it may surprise some scholars that William L. O'Neill can isolate and analyze a radical feminism, and then draw distinctions between it and the suffragist movement, "social feminism," and "hard-core feminism." Tracing these three strands of thought from the nineteenth century to the present, O'Neill analyzes the failure of feminists to define their problem clearly, and argues that if today's feminists are to succeed, they must "construct an ideology for themselves that will be superior to anything that has been seen in America."

O'Neill is the author of *Divorce in the Progressive Era* (New Haven, 1967), the first study of the public debate over marriage and divorce. Earlier, he edited *Echoes of Revolt: The Masses, 1911-1917* (Chicago, 1966), which includes the opinions of its Greenwich Village radical editors on "the woman question." The present essay is a by-product of a book and collection of documents on feminism that is now in progress. O'Neill, who holds a doctorate from the University of California, Berkeley, taught at the University of Colorado before he joined the Department of History at the University of Wisconsin.

Several years ago, in his cogent and provocative essay on the changing place of women in American life, Carl Degler argued that feminism failed because it was unable to construct a viable ideology.[1] Feminism, however, produced an immense literature, and much of it was ideological in that it attempted to frame the "woman question" in such a way as to force solutions.[2] Instead of writing off this material as inadequate—although it was—I think something is to be gained from tracing the principal lines of thought that feminism developed in order to pinpoint the weaknesses that permitted it to collapse once equal suffrage had been secured.

Because feminism was such a widespread, indistinct, poorly defined phenemenon, feminists never developed a precise vocabulary. Indeed, the vagueness of their language reflected larger confusions of thought and perception that kept them from building a successful ideology. No historian, to my knowledge, has found it necessary to remedy this defect, but, because I intend to show that there were several kinds of feminism, a word about terms is necessary.

The phrase most commonly used by women in the nineteenth and early twentieth centuries to describe their expanding activities was "the woman movement." This movement included not only those things pertaining to women's rights but almost any act or event that enlarged woman's sphere, increased her opportunities, or broadened her outlook. It covered everything from woman suffrage and social reform down to the individual accomplishments of gifted, ambitious women. "Feminism," a more limited word, related specifically to the advancement of women's legal and political rights. The feminist movement, in turn, was broadly divided into two wings, but, because feminists themselves did not recognize this until the very end of the period, i.e. in the 1920's, I have coined the phrases "social feminism" to describe that part of the movement that put social reform ahead of women's rights and "hard-core" or "extreme feminists" to describe those who put women's rights before all else. A "suffragist" was simply one who worked for equal suffrage, irrespective of her views on other questions.[3]

I

During much of its history feminism was considered extremely radical; indeed, suffragists did not triumph until after they had persuaded the public that they constituted a "bourgeois, middle-class, . . . middle-of-the-road movement."[4] Although equal suffrage was an absurdly controversial issue, and there was little basis for the repeated charge that it was revolutionary, for a long time there was good reason to think that the feminist program—of which suffrage was only a part—had revolutionary implications. This was so because, by the Victorian era, women were locked into such a tight domestic system —their role so narrowly defined—that granting them real equality was impossible without overhauling the entire social structure. Full equality required drastic readjustments on two levels. If women were to have an equal chance with men to develop themselves, not only would they need equal educational and vocational opportunities but they would somehow have to be relieved of the domestic obligations that bound most of them to the home. And, because every system encourages the attitudes that are appropriate to it, the whole complex of ideas and assumptions that "justified" women's inferior status would have to be changed.

At the beginning of the nineteenth century the only acceptable roles for women were domestic; there was virtually nothing for them to do except stay at home or hire out as maids, governesses and, before long, teachers. A handful made other places for themselves, but until the middle of the century they were too few to affect the system. The cultural rationale that kept women in the home, however, was more complex and demands further attention. The Victorian woman was part of a network of ideas, prejudices, and religious emotionalism that simultaneously degraded and elevated her. "The cult of true womanhood" (as one historian calls it) emphasized women's piety, purity, submissiveness, and domesticity. Religious work was almost the only form of outside activity permitted women because it did not take them away from their "true sphere." "From her home woman performed her great task of bringing men back to God." [5] Woman, it was believed, was morally and spiritually superior to man because of her highly developed intuition, refined sensibilities, and especially because of those life-giving maternal powers that defied man's comprehension. But woman was physically weaker than man, inferior to him in cognitive ability, and wholly unsuited to the rough world outside the home. This was just as well, however, because women were largely responsible for "The Family," the chief adornment of Christian society and the foundation of civilized life.[6]

Although the concept of women as wan, ethereal, spiritualized creatures bore little relation to reality by mid-century, when women operated machines, worked in the fields, hand-washed clothing, and toiled over kitchen ranges, it was endorsed by science and by religion. A vast and constantly growing body of polemical literature was churned out by physicians, clergymen, and journalists in support of this thesis. Even fashion conspired to the same end; the bustles and hoops and the corsets and trailing skirts in which women were encased throughout much of the century seemed designed to hobble them and prevent all but the most desperate from leaving their homes for long. (The weight of metal, cloth, and bone that women were expected to bear should itself have disproved the notion that they were peculiarly delicate creatures, but of course it did not). Feminine "delicacy" was considered the visible evidence of their superior sensibilities, the "finer clay" of which they were made. Women who were not delicate by nature became so by design. In the end, the fashion was self-defeating for it aroused fears that women would become so ornamental as to be incapable of discharging their essential functions. The Civil War helped wake middle-class women from "their dream of a lady-like uselessness," and in 1861, when Vassar College was founded, its trustees put physical education at the head of their list of objectives.[7]

The Victorian idealization of women was self-defeating in another and more important way. The Victorians attempted to compensate women for their domestic and pedagogic responsibilities by enveloping them in a mystique that asserted their higher status while at the same time guaranteeing their inferiority; hence the endless polemics on the moral purity and spiritual genius of woman that found its highest expression in the home and that had to be safeguarded at all costs from the hopelessly corrupting effects of the man-made society without. But, as William R. Taylor and Christopher Lasch have suggested,

> the cult of women and the home contained contradictions that tended to undermine the very things they were supposed to safeguard. Implicit in the myth was a repudiation not only of heterosexuality but of domesticity itself. It was her purity, contrasted with the coarseness of men, that made woman the head of the home (though not of the family) and the guardian of public morality. But the same purity made intercourse between men and women at last almost literally impossible and drove women to retreat almost exclusively into the society of their own sex, to abandon the very home which it was their appointed mission to preserve.[8]

Thus the "woman movement" had its origins in the sexual segregation that Victorians considered essential for an ideal domestic system. Beginning with church societies and a few women's clubs, associationism grew and grew, until by the end of the century millions of women were caught up in it, and their old isolation was broken.

As we noted earlier, the woman movement was not the same thing as feminism. Women who worked for their church or met in literary societies were, however, indirectly helping themselves by developing aspirations that promoted the larger growth to come. They began to press for more education and to manifest intellectual and literary interests. The acute Englishwoman, Harriet Martineau, noted that "in my progress through the country I met with a greater variety and extent of female pedantry than the experience of a lifetime in Europe would afford. " This pedantry, she hastened to add, "was not to be despised in an oppressed class as it indicates the first struggle of intellect with its restraints; and it is therefore a hopeful symptom." [9]

Even more hopeful, of course, was the next step that these developments made possible: the formulation of a distinct women's rights movement. In the 1830's women were stirred by the currents of reform that were sweeping the country, and those who were moved to action discovered that their status as women told against their ambitions as abolitionists, temperance workers, or whatever. Sarah M. Grimké was inspired to write the first American feminist tract of consequence [10] because some clergymen objected to her antislavery work. Elizabeth Cady Stanton was started on her career as a women's rights leader after she was denied a seat, by reason of her sex, at a World Anti-Slavery Convention in London. Susan B. Anthony became a feminist after she was discriminated against by her male colleagues in the temperance movement.

In 1848 these separate streams of dissent came together at the first Woman's Rights Convention in Seneca Falls, New York. The "Declaration of Sentiments" that was adopted by the meeting indicated another element that infused the early feminist movement: the libertarianism of the age of reform. Modeled in part on the Declaration of Independence, this manifesto declared that "the history of mankind is a history of repeated injuries and usurpations on the part of man toward woman, having in direct object the establishment of an absolute tyranny over her." [11] It was, in fact, a decidedly radical document —not that it called for an end to private property, or anticipated a good society along socialist lines, but in storming against every iniquity from votelessness to the double standard of morals it made demands that could not be satisfied without profound changes in the social order. The most sophisticated feminists appreciated, in some measure at least, that they were not merely asking for their rights as citizens, that what they wanted called for new institutions as well as new ways of thinking. They seem to have been feeling their way toward a new domestic order. Mrs. Stanton, who denounced marriage as "opposed to all God's laws," wanted to begin its reformation by liberalizing divorce.[12] The magazine she and Susan B. Anthony ran after the Civil War, *Revolution*, was full of references to the "marriage question" at a time when no orthodox person was willing to admit that there was a marriage question.

Logic alone had forced extreme feminists to sail these dangerous waters because even then it was clear that if women were fully emancipated by law, their domestic obligations would nevertheless prevent them from competing with men on an equal basis. There are only two (by no means mutually exclusive) ways of dealing with this problem: Either women must be supported by the kind of welfare measures (guaranteed maternity leaves with pay, family allowances, and the like) that the advanced social democracies have devised, or marriage and the family must be more flexibly defined.

Because the first alternative did not exist in the mid-nineteenth century, far-sighted women had to consider how the essential domestic institutions could be revised to free women from the tyranny of home and family; they had some precedents to guide them. For their own reasons the Mormons practiced polygamy, while the Shaker communities went to the opposite extreme by abolishing not only marriage but sexual relations as well. A number of perfectionist groups explored the varieties of free love, such as John Humphrey Noyes, who (at Oneida, New York) combined the equality of the sexes, perfectionism, socialism, and "complex marriage" (the sharing of spouses) in a bizarre but strikingly successful way. In such an atmosphere it was natural for the boldest feminists to flirt with radical approaches to the domestic problem. It is impossible to tell where these speculations would have led Mrs. Stanton and her followers, but the Victoria Woodhull affair suggests a likely possibility.

Victoria Woodhull and her equally vivid sister, Tennessee Celeste Claflin, 'burst upon the New York scene in 1868. Although nominally lady stockbrokers, they were agitators and evangelists by persuasion, and enthusiasts for everything radical, or just plain wild—socialism, spiritualism or women's rights. Their magazine, *Woodhull and Claflin's Weekly*, promoted such causes, as well as the peculiar interests of their mentor, Stephen Pearl Andrews, a self-proclaimed universal philosopher and linguist. The surprising thing about the raffish sisters is that they rapidly became celebrated champions of the cause of women, admired by such shrewd and experienced figures as Elizabeth Cady Stanton and Susan B. Anthony. In 1871, for example, Victoria Woodhull persuaded a congressional subcommittee to hold hearings on woman suffrage, and she testified before it with great effect.

Their *Weekly* was interested in marriage from the beginning. Stephen Pearl Andrews believed in free love in the usual Victorian sense (that is, in extramarital sexual relationships contracted as a matter of principle), and the Claflin sisters had practiced free love long before they understood its theoretical possibilities. Having thrown out a good many hints, Mrs. Woodhull finally called a mass meeting and on the stage of Steinway Hall declared herself a free lover. She seems to have been genuinely astonished at the ferocious reaction to this public confession; newspapers hounded her, cautious feminists snubbed her, and the sisters fell on hard times, financially and emotionally. Victoria struck back by disclosing that Henry Ward Beecher, the most famous preacher of the day and a good friend of woman suffrage, had been having an affair with the wife of Theodore Tilton, Mrs. Woodhull's friend, her biographer, and perhaps her lover. The ensuing scandal destroyed the Claflins and the Tiltons; but Beecher survived it, thanks to his great reputation, considerable courage, and influential friends.[13]

The effect of this debacle on the suffrage movement's fortunes is hard to determine because the cause was already in bad shape when the Claflins took it in hand. Suffragists had been disappointed at the end of the Civil War when they were asked to sacrifice votes for women to secure votes for Negro men. Some of them refused to admit that the freedman's need was greater than theirs and, because of this and other frictions, the suffrage movement had divided into two organizations: the staid, Boston-based American Woman's Suffrage Association and the more aggressive National Woman's Suffrage Association, led by Miss Anthony and Mrs. Stanton. Both groups were tarnished by the Beecher-Tilton affair, but the AWSA suffered less because it had always been anti-Claflin. The NWSA came in for a larger measure of abuse because of its closer association with the sisters, but the unquestionable virtue and integrity of its leaders saved it from total eclipse. It used to be thought that the affair had set back equal suffrage for decades; today, however, the movement's temporary decline seems to have been only one feature of the conservative backlash of the Gilded Age. Suffragists had expected too big a reward for their services during the Civil War as nurses, propagandists and sanitary commission volunteers. The country was grateful to them, but not all that grateful—as the defeat of woman suffrage in the hotly contested Kansas referendum of 1866 demonstrated. In freeing and enfranchising the Negro, America, it seemed, had exhausted its supply of liberalism.

The Woodhull affair had one lasting effect, however: it reaffirmed the general conviction that suffrage politics and radical speculations, particularly those affecting marriage and the family, did not mix. In consequence the movement, although it never disowned the social goals that women's votes were presumably to implement, emphasized the most conservative aspects of the suffrage question. The vote was shown to be compatible with the existing domestic economy, and— at best—with those reforms that would elevate and refine domesticity to the level of perfection for which society yearned. Suffragists thereafter, vigorously resisting the temptation to think seriously about the domestic institutions that ruled their lives, made sexual orthodoxy their ruling principle.

II

In the long run these shocks had two important consequences: feminism rapidly became more conservative and more altruistic. Its conservatism—thanks but little to Victoria Woodhull—stemmed from the tightening up of morals and manners that occurred in the high Victorian era. Bills like the Comstock Act (1873) made it impossible for John Humphrey Noyes and other sexual radicals to use the mails, choking off the lively debate that had flourished earlier. The porous or open quality that had characterized American life in the age of reform gave way to the censorious prudery we associate with Victorianism. It is very likely that the extreme feminists would have had to abandon their tentative explorations, if only because of social purity. Earlier there had been sporadic attempts by organized women to eliminate the double standard of morals by holding men to a higher level of conduct. The radical feminists who toyed with free love approached the same goal from an opposite direction, by proposing a sort of convergence in which men and women would occupy a middle ground between the old extremes of absolute license and complete chastity. After the war, however, all doubts as to which line feminists would follow were relieved by the social purity movement, which enlisted the energies of public-spirited women all over the country in a crusade to abolish prostitution and infidelity.[14] Mrs. Stanton continued to advocate free divorce, to the great embarrassment of her younger followers, but she was very much the exception.

At the same time that feminists abandoned their more advanced positions they took on a great range of activities that often had little to do with women's rights. Extreme feminists, for example, displayed a keen sense of self-interest in the struggle over Negro suffrage after the Civil War. The Stantonites as a rule were more radical and more sensitive to the needs of others than the Boston faction, but when they were forced to choose between the Negroes' interests and their own they unflinchingly went down the line for feminist objectives.

The feminism of later years, however, was much more generous and diffuse. A hardy band of suffragists fought the good fight for the vote while most feminists devoted themselves to charities, philanthropies, and reforms. As social workers, settlement house residents, members of women's clubs, advocates of the reform of child labor and women's working conditions, of municipal government, public health, education and housing, and as temperance workers and conservationists they submerged their interests as women in a sea of worthy enterprises. These social justice activities became the principal justification for feminism, and are what historians most admire about the movement, but feminists paid a high price for their good deeds in two important ways. First, these activities drained off personnel from the women's rights movement and protracted the suffrage struggle. Second, they led to ideological confusions that played a large role in the collapse of feminism once the vote was won.

Social feminism also perpetuated the confusion between class and sex, that false sense of solidarity that characterized the entire woman movement. In a way this was natural, because all women suffered from disabilities that were imposed upon men only discriminatingly. It was not possible to have a "man movement" because most men enjoyed all the rights and opportunities that God and nature presumably intended them to have. Equal rights for women, however, did not mean the same thing to a factory girl that it meant to a college graduate, and feminists invariably refused to admit that differences in station among women were of any importance. In the beginning this hardly mattered, because the early feminists were mainly bourgeois intellectuals who were struggling to improve their own immediate circumstances. As the woman movement matured, however, its sociological evasions and self-deceptions attained critical proportions.

This analytic failure, which was characteristic of a movement that (with the notable exceptions of Elizabeth Cady Stanton and Charlotte Perkins Gilman) produced few intellects of the first rank, was compounded by an insistence that women were united in a selfless sisterhood by their maternal capacities, real or potential. "Women," it was declared over and over again, "stand relatively for the same thing everywhere and their first care is naturally and inevitably for the child." [15] Maternity was not only a unifying force but the enabling principle that made the entrance of women into public life imperative. As another suffragist put it in 1878, "the new truth, electrifying, glorifying American womanhood today, is the discovery that the State is but the larger family, the nation the old homestead, and that in this national home there is a room and a corner and a duty for mother." [16] Not only was the nation a larger home in need of mothering, but, by impinging upon the domestic circle, it made motherhood a public role.

As Jane Addams saw it, "many women today are failing properly to discharge their duties to their own families and household simply because they fail to see that as society grows more complicated it is necessary that woman shall extend her sense of responsibility to many things outside of her own home, if only in order to preserve the home in entirety." [17] Thus the effort to escape domesticity was accompanied by an invocation of the domestic ideal: women's freedom road led in a circle, back to the home from which feminism was supposed to liberate them. Feminism was made respectable by accommodating it to the Victorian ethos that had forced it into being.

Given the plausibility and flexibility of this contention, women were (perhaps inevitably) lured into using it to secure their immediate aims; but in retrospect it does not seem to have been an unqualifiedly successful ploy. The Women's Christian Temperance Union is a case in point. Although one historian recently hailed Frances Willard's "supreme cleverness" in using "this conservative organization to advocate woman suffrage and child labor laws and other progressive legislation always in the name of purity and the home," [18] the history of the wcτu illustrates the weakness of an argument that begins by accepting the opposition's premise. In conceding that better homes were of equal importance to feminists and anti-feminists alike, these women reduced their case from one of principle to a mere quarrel over tactics. All the opposition had to do to redeem itself was prove that its tactics were superior. This apparently is what happened to the wcτu after the death of Frances Willard (which coincided with a significant change in its social composition), when new leaders came to believe that temperance was more crucial to the home than suffrage, child welfare, and other progressive causes. Perhaps this new orientation would have come about in any event, but surely such wctu suffragists as Frances Willard made it much easier by their willingness to utilize the cult of domesticity in pursuit of quite separate and distinctively feminist objectives.

The truth was that while these feminists resented the demands made upon them in their roles as wives and mothers, they were insufficiently alert to the danger presented by even a partial accommodation to the maternal mystique. Gravely underestimating the tremendous force generated by the sentimental veneration of motherhood, they assumed they could manipulate the emotions responsible for the condition of women without challenging the principles on which these feelings rested. Moreover, while denying that under the present circumstances mothers could be held accountable for the failings of their children, they implied that, once emancipated, women could legitimately be indicted for their progenies' shortcomings. In 1901 Susan B. Anthony declared that "before mothers can rightfully be held responsible for the vices and crimes, for the general demoralization of society, they must possess all possible rights and powers to control the conditions and circumstances of their own and their children's lives." [19] Her remark would seem to mean that, once granted political equality, mothers would have to answer for all the ills of society. This was a great weight to lay on female posterity, and such statements contributed to the unhealthy and unrealizable expectations that feminism encouraged.

A further hazard of the feminist emphasis on motherhood was the support it lent the notion that women were not only different from men, but superior to men. Julia Ward Howe, a moderate and greatly admired feminist, persistently implied that emancipation was intended to make women better mothers as well as freer persons.

> Woman is the mother of the race, the guardian of its helpless infancy, its earliest teacher, its most zealous champion. Woman is also the home-maker, upon her devolve the details which bless and beautify family life. In all true civilization she wins man out of his natural savagery to share with her the love of offspring, the enjoyment of true and loyal companionship.[20]

Definitions like this left men with few virtues anyone was bound to admire, and inspired women to think of themselves as a kind of super-race that had been condemned by historical accident and otiose convention to serve its natural inferiors.

Such indeed was the case with women who, encouraged by the new social sciences (especially anthropology, which demonstrated that matriarchies had existed and may once have been common, if not universal), took themselves with a new seriousness that few men could share. Elizabeth Cady Stanton argued that prehistoric women had been superior to men, or at least equal to them, but that Christianity, and especially Protestantism, had driven the feminine element out of religion and had subordinated women to the rule of men. Society thereby had lost the beneficent moral and conservative forces of the female intellect and the mother instinct.[21]

With this line of argument Walter Rauschenbush, no enemy of women's rights, was compelled to take issue. Alarmed by what he regarded as the feminists' moral pretensions, he wrote: "Many men feel that women are morally better than men. Perhaps it is right that men should instinctively feel so. But it is a different matter when women think so too. They are not better. They are only good in different ways than men." [22] Rauschenbush believed in the emancipation of women, but he reminded his readers that the feminine virtues could easily be exaggerated, and that in recent times both Christian Science and theosophy had demonstrated a particular appeal to women even though both stressed authority and unexamined belief.

As Rauschenbush's observation suggests, the attempt to demonstrate women's superior nature led nowhere. In essence it was just one more variation of the Victorian mystique, another way of exploiting the belief that woman's unique power was rooted in the mystery of her life-giving capacities. Taken one way, it led back to a preoccupation with motherhood. Read differently, it supported so complete a rejection of men that women could retain their integrity and spirituality only in spinsterhood. Or—by subscribing to the principles of Ellen Key, who elevated motherhood even above marriage and made the right to have illegitimate children the central aspect of feminism—women could have their cake and eat it too.[23] They could realize their generative and instinctual potential without an unseemly dependence on the contaminating male. Deliberately having an illegitimate child necessitated an act of masculine cooperation, and in a delicious reversal of ancient custom man became an instrument of woman's purpose and his ungoverned passion the means to her full emancipation. This was radicalism with a vengeance, but a radicalism that had curiously little to do with the normal objects of revolutionary ardor.

III

Most organized women, however, were neither radical nor especially feministic. The woman movement as a whole, and most social feminists in particular, were satisfied with the comparatively modest programs of the wctu and the General Federation of Women's Clubs. These programs, despite the fears of conservatives, were no threat to what Mrs. Gilman scornfully called the domestic mythology; in fact, they rested largely on the domestic and maternal mystique that was characteristic of the Victorian era. Not only did organized women continuously invoke "home and mother," for the most part their serious enterprises dealt with such related social matters as pure foods and drugs, child welfare, and working mothers. Whenever suffragists were able to tie in the ballot with a specific problem of special interest to women, they gained adherents. Through most of the nineteenth century suffragists maintained that women were entitled to vote as a matter of right and that they needed the vote to protect themselves and to advance the causes that were important to them. Neither argument was very persuasive in the age of Victoria, and always the suffragists' greatest obstacle was the indifference of their own sex.

As late as 1908 Theodore Roosevelt could comfortably, and quite rightly, say that "when women as a whole take any special interest in the matter they will have suffrage if they desire it." [24] But only a few years later the picture had changed entirely. In 1914 the General Federation of Women's Clubs endorsed woman suffrage in the name of its two million members; in 1917 membership in the nwsa soared to something like two million; and in that same year 500,000 women in New York City alone put their signatures to a suffrage petition. By 1917 it was obvious that women wanted the vote, and by 1920 they had it.

Few feminists seemed to realize that although winning the vote had been a feminist victory, it had not been won for feminist reasons. Suffragists had merely persuaded the organized middle-class women, who had become a potent force for reform in the Progressive era, that they needed the vote in order to secure the healthier and broader domestic life that was their main objective; feminists had not, however, convinced bourgeois women that they were greatly deprived and oppressed and that they had vast unrealized capabilities. From a strictly feminist point of view, the vote had been wrongly obtained. It neither reflected nor inspired a new vision of themselves on the part of most American women. Moreover, the suffrage could not but demoralize feminists who had worked so hard for so long, only to find that success had little effect upon the feminine condition.

The immediate consequence of feminine emancipation, then, was the fading away of the woman movement as it became apparent that the great organizations had less in common than they supposed. Moreover, the organizations themselves were changing in character. The WCTU was obsessed with prohibition (although it did not entirely lose interest in other social problems during the 1920's). The NWSA was transformed into the League of Women Voters; and although the league struggled valiantly to advance the old causes beloved of women reformers, it lacked the drive, funds, and numerical membership of its predecessor. The General Federation suffered least, because it had always been less committed to major reforms than its sister groups, and if its member clubs slackened their efforts, the national leadership continued to support the federation's traditional interests. The best evidence of the movement's decline was the fate of the Women's Joint Congressional Committee, which had been formed in 1920 to lobby for bills in which organized women took a special interest. Although it enjoyed some success (it helped keep Muscle Shoals out of private hands and it preserved a measure of federal support for mothers' pensions and other welfare programs), it lost more battles than it won, especially in the crucial struggle to ratify the Child Labor Amendment.

In the 1920's the split between social feminism and hard-core feminism emerged as a fundamental distinction. During the voteless years a common interest in women's suffrage and a general if vague commitment to women's and children's welfare had saved feminists from having to chose between equal rights and social reform. Then, in the twenties, a sharp cleavage opened between feminists in the League of Women Voters and the Joint Committee—which labored mainly for civic-virtue and welfare measures—and the militant Woman's Party, which singlemindedly pursued a narrow program that was signified by the title of its periodical *Equal Rights*. The most divisive feature of the Woman's Party program was its espousal of an equal rights amendment to the Constitution. Social feminists were alarmed by the Lucretia Mott Amendment (as the Woman's Party called it) because of the possibility that the courts would define equal rights as equal treatment. If this happened, the entire array of protective legislation that had been enacted for the benefit of working women during the Progressive era would be swept away. Inasmuch as the courts had already interpreted the Clayton Act to the disadvantage of working men, had twice declared congressional child labor bills unconstitutional, and had struck down minimum wage laws for women, this was not an unreasonable fear. The Woman's Party insisted that equal rights and equal treatment would not be confused, or, if they were confused, so much the better: protective laws discriminated against working women by denying them the competitive advantages of men, who could work whatever jobs and hours they pleased. In reality the competition issue was relevant mainly to business and professional women who had to function in the job market as individuals. It hardly applied to wage-earning women, who could not bargain individually over wages, hours, or working conditions. Thus, feminists of every kind discovered that women did not constitute a real social class but were subject to the same distinctions that obtained among men.

Throughout the decade, and indeed long afterward, an unseemly struggle was waged over equal rights and protective legislation, but this quarrel was only symptomatic of the deeper confusions into which the entire movement had fallen as a result of the Nineteenth Amendment. It was not merely a question of whether complete equality was more risky than advantageous, nor even where, having won the vote, feminism ought to go, but what being a woman in America really meant. In short, feminists had traveled a long, circuitous, ascending path—to find themselves in 1920 about where they had been in 1830. They had not failed to better their condition along the way, but in avoiding fundamental questions for the sake of immediate advantages they had merely postponed the inevitable confrontation with themselves. Now the day of reckoning was at hand.

In the 1920's, then, it became clear that the anti-suffragists had been right all along in saying that the vote would neither change the lives of women as individuals nor greatly aid the causes in which organized women were most interested. Most women soon lost interest in overthrowing such remaining barriers to full emancipation as the WP urgently, and the LWV rather perfunctorily, called to their attention. The surviving hard-core feminists abandoned the fight for social justice (except for themselves), while the social feminists devoted themselves to such causes as peace, poverty, and prohibition, which had little to do with the status of women.

Under these circumstances it was no longer possible to speak with accuracy of a "woman movement," and the term fell into disuse, although such organizations as the International Woman's Suffrage Alliance and the International Council of Women perpetuated the cosmopolitan and cooperative spirit that had been such a striking and useful feature of the old movement. Hard-core feminism, on the other hand, contracted in size and spirit, so that it came to resemble its own mid-Victorian predecessor.

IV

In the 1920's the movement's focus of interest shifted from organized to unorganized women, from the sober clubwoman and earnest social worker to the flapper. This in turn signaled a rebirth of the old popular sociology that considered women only as individual members of an undifferentiated mass. Although the greatest achievement of the woman movement had been to expand the definition of woman, the movement had only modified, not rejected, the biological imperatives of the Victorian ethos; and when the movement began to subside it left the contradiction between woman's sexual identity and her unique persona to be resolved, if possible, in a wholly new context. This new environment was created partly by feminism's successes, partly by its failures, and to a large extent by things over which it had no control. The movement admired daring and independence, to a degree, but it associated these qualities with large and generous purposes. The "new woman" of the twenties was indeed bold and venturesome—but in pursuit of what the older generation considered trivial if not ignoble objectives. The woman movement wanted to eliminate the double standard in morals by making men practice the sexual ethics they preached. The flapper also endorsed a single standard of morality, but she wanted sexual ethics to conform to reality rather than the reverse. Most of all, of course, young women in the postwar era were molded by the characteristic novelties of the period: the ebbing of reform, the demoralizing aftermath of the "war to end war," the emergence of mass society and mass culture, the new technology, and the higher standard of living that permitted the merchandising of pleasure on an immense scale.

The change in feminine sexual behavior was not only the most sensational aspect of these changes but a striking evidence of the shift in women's lives from organization to individuality. Woman suffrage had been a public question that enlisted collective energies; sexuality was a private concern that women had, perforce, to cope with as individuals. Our own atmosphere is so sexually charged and we hear so much about the "sexual revolution" that it is easy to forget the significant changes that took place more than a generation ago. Not only was sex discussed publicly and with a previously forbidden candor in the twenties, there is good reason to think that people, especially women, experienced sex in a different manner. At the end of the decade a gynecologist remarked that in 1885 his typical patient was "the woman 'who would rather die than be examined.' In the early nineties the patient instantly covered the least bare spot with the sheet, but in 1920 full exposure is taken for granted by the young." [25] In another of those remarkable studies that preceded the Kinsey reports a psychiatrist discovered that the sexual experiences of one hundred women correlated with their year of birth. In his admittedly small and arbitrary example, of fifty women who had been born before 1890 only seventeen had engaged in either pre- or extramarital intercourse, compared with thirty of the fifty women who were born after 1890. It seemed to him that the sexual behavior of men and women was converging. [26]

These few bits of evidence lend substance to the feeling of most contemporary observers that important changes in the sexual patterns of the young were taking place during the 1920's. But the new sexuality was accompanied by new attitudes of even greater importance. A juvenile court referee wrote that the younger generation did not admire its parents. The old maxim that age and experience command respect no longer carried weight. Girls and young women were much more aggressive in finding husbands than their mothers were. They expected to work after they were married, mostly for the added income, but they were vague about what they would work at and reluctant to train for particular occupations. A girl "intends to marry at a more specific date if she can bring it about, have a definite number of children at desirable intervals, and earn a definite sum toward the upkeep when she needs to." Most disturbing of all, the younger generation had rejected the idealism of the previous generation. "So for lack of other vision they believe in themselves." [27]

Over and over again the same refrain was heard. Even when girls expressed more or less traditional sentiments, they did so for sensible reasons, which were very different from the principled stands of their mothers. Thus a study of 252 middle-class girls disclosed that although they thought chastity good and promiscuity undesirable, they generally advanced practical rather than moral arguments for this position. Only one girl in three said that in every case she would disapprove of a friend's affair. [28]

A thoughtful ex-suffragist writer for the League of Women Voters (which was distressed by its difficulties in recruiting young members) pointed out that "the feministic movement isn't at all smart among the juniors. But it is interesting to observe that such rights as the old feministic movement has already won for the females of the species, the young accept as a matter of course. Especially when these rights mean personal and individual privileges." [29] Her informants used the First World War, much as a later generation would use The Bomb, to deflate what they regarded as the moral pretensions of their elders and expose the uselessness of their advice.

At least one young woman struck closer to home when she bluntly observed that the previous generation always put off its own ambitions until after some job of reform had been done. "They were all going to return to their personal knitting after they had tidied up the world. Well look at the world! See how they tidied it up! Do you wonder that our generation says it will do its personal knitting first?" Indeed, this girl expressed a high degree of moral fervor in proclaiming her amoral credo:

> But we're not out to benefit society, to remold existence, to make industry safe for anyone except ourselves, to give any small peoples except ourselves their rights. We're not out for submerged tenths, we're not going to suffer over how the other half lives. We're out for Mary's job and Luella's art, and Barbara's independence and the rest of our individual careers and desires. [30]

In one sense this outburst suggests that there was a feminist equivalent of Dada: an insistence that the private vision takes precedence over the social will, that art exists for its own sake and woman for her own sake, a repudiation of the grand causes and glorious rhetoric that had moved the older generation. It was also a logical conclusion to the feminist hardline.

We have seen how dismaying this attitude was to the social feminists who had viewed women's rights as only one aspect of the good society that women could bring into being if given the chance, but it was almost as disconcerting to those who saw feminism as an end in itself. A collective impulse is not the same thing as a social movement, and to the privatized young women of the twenties, luxuriating in their emancipation, the demand of the Woman's Party that they rise up and strike another blow for freedom seemed ludicrous and anachronistic. They had all the freedom they could use; the problem was what to do with it. Having rejected both the woman movement's thesis that the purpose of emancipation was service and the feminists' call to compete fiercely with men at every occupational level, what else remained?

v

What remained, as events would soon demonstrate, was the "feminine mystique." The feminine mystique, as Betty Friedan recently defined it in her lively polemic, is not much different from the nineteenth century's cult of domesticity. It too glorifies the role of woman as wife and mother, finds domestic impulses at the heart of woman's nature, and warns against the dangers of feminine competitiveness. It updates the old familial ideology, however, in several ways. Feminine emancipation brought with it a better-educated womanhood, with higher cultural and aesthetic expectations. Because the home could no longer be defended with religious sentimentalities, moral authorities joined with the mass media to depict the home (in the words of an advertising man) as "the expression of her creativeness. We help her think of the modern home as the artist's studio, the scientist's laboratory." [31] Women were encouraged to regard childrearing and home economics as complicated, lofty enterprises that demanded a skillful mixture of exact science and aesthetic inspiration. This development, already well under way in the Progressive era, required almost no effort to convince bewildered young women in the post-suffrage area that the home—cleansed of its imperfections by modern science, capitalism, and enlightened thought—was a fit object for their attention and a worthy challenge to their sharpened talents.

The task of pouring old wine into new bottles was made easier by psychoanalysis, which offered a popular solution to the problem of reconciling sexual freedom with the necessary limitations of domestic life. The woman movement had drawn a line between eroticism and sex. It accepted, with qualifications, the role of women as fundamentally determined by sex, but it vigorously rejected any suggestion that sexuality was a human right. As it turned out, however, motherhood and sensuality were largely compatible with one another. Premarital intercourse could be and was justified as preparation for that perfect physical union that modern science insisted was a necessary ingredient of married bliss. Freud seemed not only to rationalize a sexuality that society would in any case have to live with, he did this in the context of a remarkably conventional view of feminine nature. Freud, after all, was a Victorian, and his American popularizers translated his concept of women as inherently passive, dependent, and childlike creatures as meaning that women were most in harmony with their true natures when they functioned as sexually fulfilled housewives.[32]

Thus the popular science of the twentieth century recapitulated the popular science of the nineteenth century in discovering that the laws of nature decreed woman's sphere to be the home. The revolution in morals was, then, no revolution at all. Without for a moment denying the importance of that measure of erotic libertarianism that was gained in the 1920's, and admitting that the emancipation of women really broadened their opportunities (although most of the broadening took place before 1920), woman in the twentieth century looks surprisingly like woman in the nineteenth century.[33]

With the emergence of the feminine mystique we can see more clearly the ideological failure that kept feminists from preventing the collapse of their movement. This failure consisted largely of an inability to determine where their interests lay. Because they could not clearly define their problem, they could not devise a successful strategy for solving it. The most perceptive of the first-generation feminists understood that overcoming the prohibitions that confined them to the home made it necessary for them to challenge the polarized definitions of male and female nature upon which the prohibitions rested. This meant, in practice, denying that there were any important differences between the sexes, apart from the inescapable fact that only women bear children. So direct a challenge, of course, provoked extreme responses, which frightened all but the bravest women, but led the more far-sighted among them to consider what would happen if the formal barriers were removed. Obviously, women would still be at a disadvantage because of their maternal obligations, and in the first half of the nineteenth century there was only one way this handicap could be minimized: marriage and the family would have to be reorganized. Because the Woodhull affair had vividly demonstrated the risks inherent in this line of thought, feminists withdrew to a more defensible position, which enabled them (so they believed) to exploit the successes of the woman movement. The movement, and especially its social feminist divisions, employed a sort of moral judo against the masculine establishment by relating its goals to the Victorian steretoype. Woman, the argument ran, needed to be free in order to fulfill her larger destiny as mother of the nation.

This strategy, however, was fatal to the feminists' long-range objectives. Although social feminism promoted many desirable reforms, few of them did much for women's rights, and when social feminism secured a notable feminist objective (such as equal suffrage), it did so in ways that undermined the movement's larger program. Moreover, this alliance with the woman movement led to such confusions and evasions among feminists that it prevented them from formulating an ideology that was adequate to the complex circumstances in which they found themselves. From the outset, feminists had defined their position negatively; they were against a host of specific disabilities—unequal laws, closed professions, votelessness—and their concentration on these barriers made them vulnerable to the opportunism that characterizes political movements, which puts action ahead of theory. Their need for allies, as well as their intellectual failures, made it even harder for them to resist the blandishments of the woman movement. It is a historiographical cliché that in America such opportunism is normal, even desirable, but pragmatism (as political expediency is always called) has the defects of its virtues. If ideological formlessness promotes flexibility, moderation, and useful alliances, it also blurs the vision and encourages what can be a fatal confusion between ends and means.

After women's suffrage was won, feminists discovered that it cost more than anyone a generation earlier could have foreseen. Social feminism was discredited when the vote failed materially to assist organized women in getting what they wanted. Hard-core feminism suffered for lack of an issue that could rouse women as equal suffrage had—and also because, in calling upon women to consider their own interests first, it went against the whole tradition of selfless altruism that had become firmly associated with organized womanhood. Valuable and ennobling as this tradition was, it prevented women from addressing their problems as women, from coming to terms with their disadvantaged status, and from organizing effectively to deal with it. The decline of the woman movement after 1920 further discredited organization along sex lines as an approach to public questions. Thus the post-suffrage era was characterized by the view that women were so different from men that real integration was out of the question, by the failure of organization as a distinctively feminine tactic, and by a general refusal to recognize that women constituted a disadvantaged group that was entitled to pursue its interests in the way that minority groups have historically done in America.

Since 1930 American women have lost ground in relation to their peers in other industrial societies and in relation to their position in the twenties. Not only Russia and Scandinavia but most western countries have a higher percentage of women who are physicians than does the United States. There are more women in Parliament than in Congress. The number of women pharmacists and dentists is negligible here but noteworthy in Sweden and France. The percentage of A.B. and Ph.D. degrees awarded to women in America has declined since 1920. Today the percentage of women who work is larger than ever before, but their occupational segregation is as great as it was in 1900, and the dollar gap between the incomes of working men and women has been rising steadily since World War II. Measured by almost any index, the position of American women, almost half a century after their formal emancipation, is neither enviable nor admirable. Countless articles and books, most notably Betty Friedan's, have in recent years documented these points and made us aware that feminism has failed and that the conditions it struggled against remain.[34]

If my analysis is correct, modern women will have to do two things to secure equality of opportunity and treatment. They must organize in a serious, deliberate, and self-interested fashion, which would seem obvious were it not for the fact that women's right to function as a pressure group is generally denied. Most Americans will admit that individual Negroes and workers may improve their circumstances without affecting the overall position of Negroes and workers in the slightest, but this principle is rarely applied to women, who are expected to deal with their problems by going to college, taking a job, undergoing psychotherapy, or by finding another personal solution.

The reason for this analytical myopia seems to be related to the same anxieties that kept Victorian society from penetrating to the heart of the woman question. The woman movement allayed the nineteenth century's worst fears by showing that formal emancipation and a high degree of organization were largely compatible with the existing social order. Unfortunately this development, tactically sound though it was, disregarded what was most fundamental and important about feminism as a response to modern conditions. It now appears that the unrest of women is directly related to those fundamental institutions, monogamy and the conjugal family, that the Victorian world was so determined to preserve. In theory women today are free to do as they please; in practice, their heavy obligations as wives and mothers prevent them from exercising the rights they nominally enjoy.

This brings me to the second task that confronts a new feminist movement, should one emerge from the present unrest. Before women can organize effectively they must clearly understand what it is they mean to effect. They must construct an ideology that will be superior to anything that has been seen in America; but those who now are engaged in the field of women's rights seem to me insufficiently aware of this need. Such organizations as the President's Commission on the Status of Women and its counterparts on the state level, the National Woman's Party (which still is working to secure equality of women by constitutional amendment), and Mrs. Friedan's National Organization for Women operate too much as their predecessors did. They see the problem in negative terms and they appear to take it for granted that the basic questions have been answered—that we know who women are, what they can do, and what they need.

More than anything else, women must understand the Victorian roots of their situation. The social feminist route (marvelous as it was from a humanitarian point of view) led to a dead end. The radical feminist solution was aborted before it had a real chance to work, but it may well be the key to a genuine feminist renaissance. Radical feminism was suppressed because it threatened to revolutionize the domestic structure, as it still does. I think, however, that the whole of the American experience shows that nothing less profound will give women the freedom in fact that we concede them only in theory.

It may be that little can be done along these lines, that woman's dilemma is one of those facts of life that simply have to be endured. But if a social revolution is wanted, and a drastic change in the position of American women would amount to just that (however unrelated it may seem to the economic problems that are the usual objects of radical concern), it must be preceded by deep and serious thought which up to this point has been conspicuously absent. To put it another way, feminism must have its Marx before it can expect a Lenin.

[1] See Carl N. Degler, "Revolution without Ideology: The Changing Place of Women in America," in *The Woman in America* (Boston, 1965), pp. 193–210. The best guide to the history of women's rights is Eleanor Flexner, *Century of Struggle* (Cambridge, Mass., 1959). A good analysis of the movement's thought in its salad days is Aileen S. Kraditor's *The Ideas of the Woman Suffrage Movement* (New York, 1965).

[2] See, for example, Professor Degler's evaluation of the movement's best ideologue, "Charlotte Perkins Gilman on the Theory and Practice of Feminism," *American Quarterly*, 8 (Spring, 1956): 21–39.

[3] "Suffragette" was the English equivalent of "suffragist." The former term was used in America mainly as a derisive term by critics of woman suffrage.

[4] "A Bourgeois Movement," *The Woman Citizen*, July 7, 1917, p. 99.

[5] Barbara Welter, "The Cult of True Womanhood: 1820–1860," *American Quarterly*, 18 (Summer, 1966): 162.

[6] For a more complete description of this idea, see my *Divorce in the Progressive Era* (New Haven, 1967), pp. 58–61.

[7] Amy Louise Reed, "Female Delicacy in the Sixties," *Century*, 68 (October, 1915): 258–70.

[8] "Two 'Kindred Spirits': Sorority and Family in New England, 1839–1846," *New England Quarterly*, 36 (March, 1963): 35.

[9] In *Society in America*, 3 vols. (London, 1837), 3: 107.

[10] *The Equality of the Sexes and the Condition of Women* (Boston, 1838).

[11] *History of Woman Suffrage*, 1: 70. This immense documentary history of the suffrage movement from 1848 to 1920 ran to six fat volumes and

was published between 1881 and 1922. The first three volumes (1881, 1882, 1887) were edited by Elizabeth Cady Stanton, Susan B. Anthony, and Matilda Joslyn Gage. Volume 4 (1902) was edited by Susan B. Anthony and Ida Husted Harper, and volumes 5 and 6 (1922, 1922) by Miss Harper.

[12] A letter to Lucy Stone, November 24, 1856, in *History of Woman Suffrage*, 1: 860.

[13] For a compact description of these events, see Robert E. Riegel, *American Feminists* (Lawrence, Kan., 1963), pp. 144–50. A recent biography of Victoria Woodhull is Johanna Johnston's *Mrs. Satan: The Incredible Saga of Victoria C. Woodhull* (New York, 1967). The best single source on these events is the *Weekly* itself, a fascinating publication that deserves more attention than most historians have given it.

[14] For this important but little-studied reform, see David Jay Pivar's "The New Abolitionism: The Quest for Social Purity, 1876–1900," (Ph.D. diss., University of Pennsylvania, 1965).

[15] Mrs. Ellis Meredith at the 1904 NWSA convention, in *History of Woman Suffrage*, 5: 101.

[16] Elizabeth Boynton Harbert, *ibid.*, 3: 78–79.

[17] "Woman's Conscience and Social Amelioration," in Charles Stelzle, ed., *Social Applications of Religion* (Cincinnati, 1908), p. 41.

[18] Andrew Sinclair, *The Better Half* (New York, 1965), p. 223.

[19] In *History of Woman Suffrage*, 5: 5–6.

[20] Florence Howe Hall, ed., *Julia Ward Howe and the Woman Suffrage Movement* (Boston, 1913), p. 158.

[21] See her paper, "The Matriarchate, or Mother-Age," in Rachel Foster Avery, ed., *Transactions of the National Council of Women of the United States* (Philadelphia, 1891), pp. 218–27.

[22] "Moral Aspects of the Woman Movement," Biblical World, 42 (October, 1913): 197.

[23] See esp. Key's *Love and Marriage* (New York, 1911).

[24] In a letter to Lyman Abbott, dated November 10, 1908, published in "An Anti-Suffrage Meeting in New York," *Remonstrance*, (January, 1909), p. 3.

[25] Robert Latou Dickinson and Lura Beam, *A Thousand Marriages* (Baltimore, 1931), pp. 12–13.

[26] See Gilbert V. Hamilton, *A Research in Marriage* (New York, 1929). Although Hamilton's sample was a small one, his findings "parallel those of Kinsey for the same grouping of subjects 20 years later" (in Aron Krich, ed., *The Sexual Revolution* [New York, 1965], p. xii).

[27] Eleanor R. Wembridge, "The Girl Tribe—An Anthropological Study," *Survey* (May 1, 1928), p. 198.

[28] See Phyllis Blanchard and Carlyn Manasses, *New Girls for Old* (New York, 1937), chap. 5. (This book was completed in 1930 but was not published until 1937.)

[29] Anne O'Hagan, "The Serious-minded Young—If Any," *Woman's Journal* 13 (April, 1928): 7.

[30] *Ibid.,* p. 39.

[31] In Betty Friedan, *The Feminine Mystique* (New York, W. W. Norton, 1963), p. 217.

[32] For an exceptionally astute critique of Freud's views on women, see Ronald V. Sampson, *The Psychology of Power* (New York, 1966).

[33] Physically (or outwardly), of course, modern women look very different from their Victorian predecessors, thanks especially to the revolution in women's dress that was completed in the twenties. The early feminists placed great emphasis on dress reform, but they gave this up after the "Bloomer fiasco," even though such men as Gerrit Smith thought it was the most desperately needed reform of all. Certainly few other changes that were desired by women have benefited so many people for so long a time. Ironically—as was so often the case—women were liberated from the crippling burdens of their dress by accident rather than by intent; fashion, not reason, called the turn.

[34] For the declining position of women, see also Degler's essay cited in n. 1. Mabel Newcomer, *A Century of Higher Education for American Women* (New York, 1959), also is illuminating. For the position of women workers, Mary Keyserling's "Facing the Facts about Women's Lives Today" (*New Approaches to Counseling Girls in the 1960's* [Washington, D.C., 1966], pp. 2–10), is compelling. Sex discrimination is accurately demonstrated in Edward Gross, "*Plus ça change* . . . The Sexual Structure of Occupations over Time," a paper Gross delivered to the 1967 meeting of the American Sociological Association in San Francisco, Calif.

*Black Power and the American
Radical Tradition*

Martin Duberman

To understand the dilemmas and likely directions of the contemporary Black Power movement, Martin Duberman compares it to the "personnel, programs and fates" of two earlier radical movements he is familiar with: the abolitionists and the anarchists.

Duberman's scholarship on the abolitionists is well known. He is the author of biographies of Charles Francis Adams (Boston, 1961), the anti-slavery leader (but no abolitionist), and James Russell Lowell (Boston, 1966), the abolitionist poet—and of the much-discussed essay "The Abolitionists and Psychology." He edited *The Anti-Slavery Vanguard: New Essays on the Abolitionists* (Princeton, N.J., 1965), which summed up the current generation's sympathetic scholarship on that much-maligned group. His commitment to the cause of equality also was expressed in the eloquent documentary play *In White America* (New York, 1963), which enjoyed success off-Broadway and on tour, and is being made into a movie.

His interest in the history of American anarchism is not as well known but is expressed in "Anarchism Left and Right" (*Partisan Review* [Fall, 1966]) and in a play on the life of Emma Goldman, which he has "temporarily put aside." Currently, he is writing a history of Black Mountain College, which pioneered in experiments in education and the arts. He is a member of the Department of History at Princeton University.

"Black Power and the American Radical Tradition" also appeared in *Partisan Review*, 35, 1 (Winter, 1968): 34–68. © 1968 by Martin Duberman.

The slogan "Black Power" has caused widespread confusion and alarm. This is partly due to a problem inherent in language: words necessarily reduce complex attitudes or phenomena to symbols which, in their abbreviation, allow for a variety of interpretations. Stuart Chase has reported that in the thirties, when the word "fascism" was on every tongue, he asked one hundred persons from various walks of life what the word meant and got one hundred widely differing definitions. And in 1953, when *The Capitol Times* of Madison, Wisconsin, asked two hundred people "What is a Communist?" not only was there no agreement, but five out of every eight admitted they couldn't define the term at all. So it is with "Black Power." Its definition depends on whom you ask, when you ask, where you ask, and, not least, who does the asking.

Yet the phrase's ambiguity derives not only from the usual confusions of language but from a failure of clarity (or is it frankness?) on the part of its advocates and a failure of attention (or is is generosity?) from their critics. The leaders of the Student Nonviolent Coordinating Committee (SNCC) and the Congress of Racial Equality (CORE) who invented the slogan, including Stokely Carmichael and Floyd McKissick, have given Black Power different definitions on different occasions, in part because their own understanding of the term continues to develop, but in part, too, because their explanations have been tailored to their audiences.[1]

The confusion has been compounded by the press, which has

frequently distorted the words of sNCC and CORE representatives, harping on every connotation of violence and racism, minimizing the central call for ethnic unity.

For all these reasons it is still not clear whether Black Power is to be taken as a short-term tactical device or a long-range goal—that is, a postponement or a rejection of integration; whether it has been adapted as a lever for intimidating whites or organizing blacks, for instilling race hate or race pride; whether it necessitates, permits, or encourages violence; whether it is a symptom of Negro despair or of Negro determination, a reaction to the lack of improvement in the daily lives of Negro-Americans or a sign that improved conditions are creating additional expectations and demands. Whether Black Power, furthermore, becomes a constructive psychological and political tactic or a destructive summons to separatism, violence, and reverse racism will depend at least as much on developments outside the control of its advocates (like the war in Vietnam) as on their conscious decisions. For all these reasons it is too early for final evaluations; only time, and perhaps not even that, will provide them. At most, certain limited, and tentative observations are possible.

I

If Black Power means only that Negroes should organize politically and economically in order to heighten self-regard and to exert maximum pressure, then the new philosophy would be difficult to fault, for it would be based on the truism that minorities must argue from positions of strength rather than weakness, that the majority is far more likely to make concessions to power than to justice. To insist that Negro-Americans seek their goals as individuals and solely by appeals to conscience and "love," when white Americans have always relied on group association and organized power to achieve theirs, would be yet one more form of discrimination. Moreover, when whites decry sNCC's declaration that it is tired of turning the other cheek, that henceforth it will actively resist white brutality, they might do well to remember that they have always considered self-defense acceptable behavior for themselves; our textbooks, for example, view the refusal of the revolutionaries of 1776 to "sit supinely by" as the very essence of manhood.

Although Black Power makes good sense when defined to mean further organization and cooperation within the Negro community, the results which are likely to follow in terms of political leverage can easily be exaggerated. The impact is likely to be greatest at the county level in the Deep South and in the urban ghettos of the North. In this regard, the Black Panther Party of Lowndes County, Alabama, is the prototype.

There are roughly twelve thousand Negroes in Lowndes County and three thousand whites, but until 1964 not a single Negro was registered to vote, while white registration had reached 118 percent of those eligible. Negro life in Lowndes County, as Andrew Kopkind has graphically recounted, was—and is—wretched.[2] The median family income for whites is $4,400, for Negroes $935; Negro farmhands earn three dollars to six dollars a day; half of the Negro women who work are maids in Montgomery (which requires a forty- to sixty-mile daily round trip) at four dollars a day; few Negroes have farms, since ninety percent of the land is owned by about eighty-five white families; the one large industrial plant in the area, the new Dan River Mills textile factory, will employ Negroes only in menial capacities; most Lowndes Negroes are functional illiterates, living in squalor and hopelessness.

The Black Panther Party set out to change all this. The only path to change in Lowndes, and in much of the Deep South, is to "take over the courthouse," the seat of local power. For generations the courthouse in Lowndes has been controlled by the Democratic Party; indeed there is no Republican Party in the county. Obviously it made little sense for SNCC organizers to hope to influence the local Democrats; no white moderates existed and no discussion of integration was tolerated. To have expected blacks to "bore from within," as Carmichael has said, would have been "like asking the Jews to reform the Nazi party."

Instead, Carmichael and his associates established the separate Black Panther Party. After months of work SNCC organizers (with almost no assistance from federal agents) registered enough Negroes to hope for a numerical majority in the county. But in the election of November, 1966, the Black Panther Party was defeated, for a variety of reasons—which include Negro apathy or fear and white intimidation.[3] Despite this defeat, the possibility of a better life for Lowndes County Negroes does at last exist, and, should the Black Panther Party come into power at some future point, that possibility could become a reality.

Nonetheless, even on the local level and even in the Deep South,

Lowndes County is not representative. In Alabama, for example, only eleven of the state's sixty-seven counties have black majorities. Where these majorities do not exist, the only effect independent black political parties are likely to have is to consolidate the whites in opposition. Moreover, and more significantly, many of the basic ills from which Negro-Americans suffer—inadequate housing, inferior education, limited job opportunities—are national phenomena and require national resources to overcome. Whether these resources will be allocated in sufficient amounts will depend, in turn, on whether a national coalition can be formed to exert pressure on the federal government. Such a coalition—of civil rights activists, church groups, campus radicals, New Class technocrats, unskilled, un-unionized laborers, and certain elements in organized labor, like the United Auto Workers or the United Federation of Teachers—would, of course, necessitate Negro-white unity, a unity that Black Power at least temporarily rejects.[4]

The answer that Black Power advocates give to the "coalition argument" is of several pieces. The only kind of progressive coalition which can exist in this country, they say, is the mild, liberal variety which produced the civil rights legislation of recent years. And that kind of legislation has proven itself grossly inadequate. Its chief result has been to lull white liberals into believing that the major battles have been won, whereas in fact there has been almost no change, or change for the worse, in the daily lives of most blacks.[5]

The evidence for this last assertion is persuasive. Despite the Supreme Court decision of 1954, almost eighty-five percent of school-age Negroes in the South still sit in segregated classrooms. Unemployment among Negroes has actually gone up in the past ten years. Title VI of the 1964 Civil Rights Act, with its promising provision for the withdrawal of federal funds in cases of discrimination, has been used in limited fashion in regard to the schools but not at all in regard to other forms of unequal treatment, such as segregated hospital facilities. Under the 1965 Voting Rights Act, only about forty federal registrars have been sent into the South, though many areas have less than the fifty percent registration figure which would legally warrant intervention. In short, the legislation produced by the liberal coalition of the early sixties has turned out to be little more than federally approved tokenism, a continuation of paper promises and ancient inequities.

If a *radical* coalition could be formed in this country—that is, one willing to scrutinize in depth the failings of our system, to suggest structural, not piecemeal, reforms, to see them executed with sustained rather than occasional vigor—then Black Power advocates might feel less need to separate themselves and to concentrate on local, marginal successes. But no responsible observer believes that in the foreseeable future a radical coalition on the left can become the effective political majority in the United States; we will be fortunate if a radical coalition on the right does not. And so, to SNCC and CORE, talk of further cooperation with white liberals is only an invitation to further futility. It is better, they feel, to concentrate on encouraging Negroes everywhere to self-respect and self-help, and in certain local areas, where their numbers warrant it, to try to win actual political power.

As an adaptation to present realities, Black Power thus has a persuasive logic. But there is such a thing as being too present-minded; by concentrating on immediate prospects, the new doctrine may be jeopardizing larger possibilities for the future, those which could result from a national coalition with white allies. Though SNCC and CORE insist that they are not trying to cut whites out of the movement, that they merely want to redirect white energies into organizing whites so that at some future point a truly meaningful coalition of Negroes and whites can take place, there are grounds for doubting whether they really are interested in a future reconciliation, or, if they are, whether some of the overtones of their present stance will allow for it. For example, SNCC's so-called position paper on Black Power attacks white radicals as well as white liberals, speaks vaguely of differing white and black "psyches," and seems to find all contact with all whites contaminating or intimidating ("Whites are the ones who must try to raise themselves to our humanistic level").[6]

SNCC's bitterness at the hypocrisy and evasion of the white majority is understandable, yet the refusal to discriminate between degrees of inequity, the penchant instead for wholesale condemnation of all whites, is as unjust as it is self-defeating. The indictments and innuendos of SNCC's "position paper" give some credence to the view that the line between Black Power and black racism is a fine one, easily erased, that, as always, means and ends tend to get confused, that a tactic of racial solidarity can turn into a goal of racial purity.

The philosophy of Black Power is thus a blend of varied, in part contending, elements, and it cannot be predicted with any certainty which will assume dominance. But a comparison between the Black

Power movement and the personnel, programs, and fates of earlier radical movements in this country can make some contribution toward understanding its dilemmas and its likely directions.

Any argument based on historical analogy can, of course, become oversimplified and irresponsible. Historical events do not repeat themselves with anything like regularity, for every event is to a large degree embedded in its own special context. An additional danger in reasoning from historical analogy is that in the process we will limit rather than expand our options: by arguing that certain consequences seem always to follow from certain actions and that therefore only a set number of alternatives ever exist, we can prevent ourselves from seeing new possibilities or from utilizing old ones in creative ways. We must be careful, when attempting to predict the future from the past, that in the process we do not straitjacket the present. Bearing these cautions and limitations in mind, we can still gain some insight from a historical perspective. For if there are large variances through time between roughly analogous events, there are also some similarities, and it is these which make comparative study possible and profitable. In regard to Black Power, I think we gain particular insight by comparing it with the two earlier radical movements of abolitionism and anarchism.

II

The Abolitionists represented the left wing of the antislavery movement (a position comparable to the one SNCC and CORE occupy today in the civil rights movement) because they called for an *immediate* end to slavery everywhere in the United States. Most northerners who disapproved of slavery were not willing to go as far or as fast as the Abolitionists, preferring instead a more ameliorative approach. The tactic which increasingly won the approval of the northern majority was the doctrine of "nonextension": no further expansion of slavery would be allowed, but the institution would be left alone where it already existed. The principle of nonextension first came into prominence in the late 1840's, when fear developed in the North that territory acquired from our war with Mexico would be made into new slave states. Later the doctrine formed the basis of the Republican Party, which in 1860 elected Lincoln to the presidency. The Abolitionists, in other words, with their demand for immediate (and uncompensated) emancipation, never became the major channel of northern antislavery sentiment. They always remained a small sect, vilified by slavery's defenders and distrusted even by allies within the antislavery movement.

The parallels between the Abolitionists and the current defenders of Black Power seem to me numerous and striking. It is worth noting, first of all, that neither group started off with so-called extremist positions (the appropriateness of that word being, in any case, dubious).[7] The SNCC of 1968 is not the SNCC formed in 1960; both its personnel and its programs have shifted markedly. SNCC originally grew out of the sit-ins spontaneously begun in Greensboro, North Carolina, by four freshmen at the all-Negro North Carolina Agricultural and Technical College. The sit-in technique spread rapidly through the South, and within a few months the Student Nonviolent Coordinating Committee (SNCC) was formally inaugurated to channel and encourage further activities. At its inception, SNCC's staff was interracial, religious in orientation, committed to the "American Dream," chiefly concerned with winning the right to share more equitably in that dream and optimistic about the possibility of being allowed to do so. SNCC placed its hopes on an appeal to the national conscience, which it expected to arouse by the examples of nonviolence and redemptive love and by the dramatic devices of sit-ins, freedom rides, and protest marches.[8]

The abolitionist movement, at the time of its inception, was similarly benign and sanguine. It, too placed emphasis on "moral suasion," believing that the first order of business was to bring the inequity of slavery to the country's attention, to arouse the average American's conscience. Once this was done, the Abolitionists felt, discussion could, and would, begin on the particular ways and means best calculated to bring about rapid, orderly emancipation. Some of those Abolitionists who later became intransigent defenders of "immediatism"—including William Lloyd Garrison—were willing, early in their careers, to consider plans for preliminary apprenticeship. They were willing, in other words, to settle for gradual emancipation *immediately begun* instead of demanding that freedom itself be instantly achieved.

But this early flexibility received little encouragement. The appeal to conscience and the willingness to engage in debate over means alike brought meager results. In the North the Abolitionists encountered massive apathy, in the South massive resistance. Thus thwarted (and

influenced as well by the discouraging British experiment with grad-
ualism in the West Indies), the Abolitionists abandoned their earlier
willingness to consider a variety of plans for prior education and
training, and shifted to the position that emancipation had to take
place at once and without compensation to the slaveholder. They also
began (especially in New England) to advocate such doctrines as
"dis-union" and "no-government," positions which directly parallel
Black Power's recent advocacy of "separation," and "de-centralization,"
and which then as now produced discord and division within the
movement, anger and denunciation without.

But the parallel of paramount importance which I wish to draw
between the two movements is their similar passage from "moderation" to "extremism." In both cases there *was* a passage, a shift in attitude and program, and it is essential that this be recognized, for it
demonstrates the developmental nature of these—of all—movements
for social change. Or, to reduce the point to individuals (and to
clichés): "Revolutionaries are not born but made." Garrison did not
start his career with the doctrine of immediatism; as a young man, he
even had kind words for the American Colonization Society, a group
devoted to deporting Negroes to Africa and Central America. And
Stokely Carmichael did not begin his ideological voyage with the
slogan of Black Power; as a teen-ager he was opposed to student sit-
ins in the South. What makes a man shift from "reform" to "revolution" is, it seems to me, primarily to be explained by the intransigence
or indifference of his society: either society refuses reforms or gives
them in the form of tokens. Thus, *if* one views the Garrisons and Car-
michaels as extremists, one should at least place the blame for that
extremism where it belongs—not on their individual temperaments,
their genetic predispositions, but on a society which scorned or toyed
with their initial pleas for justice.

III

In turning to the anarchist movement, I think we can see between
it and the new turn taken by SNCC and CORE (or, more compre-
hensively still, by much of the New Left) significant affinities of style
and thought. These are largely unconscious and unexplored; I have
seen almost no overt references to them either in the movement's
official literature or in its unofficial pronouncements. Yet the affinities
seem to me important.

But first I should make clear that in speaking of anarchism as if it were a unified tradition I am necessarily oversimplifying. The anarchist movement contained a variety of contending factions, disparate personalities, and differing national patterns. Some Anarchists believed in terrorism, others insisted upon nonviolence; some aimed for a communal life based on trade union "syndicates," others refused to bind the individual by organizational ties of any kind; some wished to retain private ownership of property, others demanded its collectivization.[9]

Despite these differing perspectives, all Anarchists did share one major premise: a distrust of authority, the rejection of all forms of rule by man over man, especially that embodied in the state but also that exemplified by parent, teacher, lawyer, priest. They justified their opposition in the name of the individual; the Anarchists wished each man to develop his "specialness" without the inhibiting interference imposed by authority, be it political or economic, moral or intellectual. This does not mean that the Anarchists sanctioned the idea "each against all." On the contrary, they believed that man was a social creature—that is, that he needed the affection and assistance of his fellows—and most anarchist versions of the good life (Max Stirner would be the major exception) involved the idea of community. The Anarchists insisted, moreover, that it was not their vision of the future but rather society as presently constructed, which represented chaos; with privilege the lot of the few and misery the lot of the many, society was currently the essence of *dis*order. The Anarchists envisioned a system which would substitute mutual aid for mutual exploitation, voluntarism for force, individual decision-making for centralized dictation.

All of these emphases find echo today in SNCC and CORE. The echoes are not perfect: Black Power, after all, is essentially a call to organization, and its acceptance of politics (and therefore of "governing") would offend a true Anarchist—as would such collectivist terms as "black psyche" or "black personality." Nonetheless, the affinities of SNCC and CORE with the anarchist position are substantial.

There is, first of all, the same belief in the possibilities of "community" and the same insistence that community be the product of voluntary association. This in turn reflects a second and still more basic affinity: the distrust of centralized authority. SNCC and CORE's energies, and also those of such other New Left groups as Students for a Democratic Society (sds), are increasingly channeled into local, community organizing. On this level, it is felt, "participatory" democracy, as opposed to the authoritarianism of "representative" democracy, becomes possible. And in the Black Panther Party, where the poor and disinherited do take a direct role in decision-making, theory has become reality (as it has, on the economic side, in the Mississippi-based Poor People's Corporation, which to date has formed some fifteen cooperatives).[10]

Then, too, sncc and core, like the Anarchists, talk increasingly of the supreme importance of the individual. They do so, paradoxically, in a rhetoric strongly reminiscent of that long associated with the right. It could be Herbert Hoover (or Booker T. Washington), but in fact it is Rap Brown who now reiterates the Negro's need to stand on his own two feet, to make his own decisions, to develop self-reliance and a sense of self-worth.[11] sncc may be scornful of present-day liberals and "statism," but it seems hardly to realize that the laissez-faire rhetoric it prefers derives almost verbatim from the classic liberalism of John Stuart Mill.

A final, more intangible affinity between anarchism and the entire New Left, including the advocates of Black Power, is in the area of personal style. Both hold up similar values for highest praise and emulation: simplicity, spontaneity, "naturalness," and "primitivism." Both reject modes of dress, music, personal relations, even of intoxication, which might be associated with the dominant middle-class culture. Both, finally, tend to link the basic virtues with "the people," and especially with the poor, the downtrodden, the alienated. It is this *Lumpenproletariat*—long kept outside the "system" and thus uncorrupted by its values—who are looked to as a repository of virtue, an example of a better way. The New Left, even while demanding that the lot of the underclasses be improved, implicitly venerates that lot; the desire to cure poverty co-habits with the wish to emulate it.

IV

The anarchist movement in the United States never made much headway. A few individuals—Benjamin Tucker, Adin Ballou, Lysander Spooner, Stephen Pearl Andrews, Emma Goldman, Josiah Warren—are still faintly remembered, but more for the style of their lives than for any impact on their society.[12] It is not difficult to see what prevented them from attracting a large following. Their very distaste for organization and power precluded the traditional modes for exerting influence. More important, their philosophy ran directly counter to the national hierarchy of values, a system of beliefs, conscious and otherwise, which has always impeded the drive for rapid change in this country. And it is a system which constitutes a roadblock at least as formidable today as at any previous point in our history.

This value structure stresses, first of all, the prime virtue of "accumulation," chiefly of goods, but also of power and prestige. Any group, be it Anarchists or New Leftists, which challenges the soundness of that goal, which suggests that it interferes with the more important pursuits of self-realization and human fellowship, presents so basic a threat to our national and individual identities as to invite almost automatic rejection.

A second obstacle that our value structure places in the path of radical change is its insistence on the benevolence of history. To the average American, human history is the story of automatic progress. Every day in every way we have got better and better. *Ergo,* there is no need for a frontal assault on our ills; time alone will be sufficient to cure them. Thus it is that many whites considered the "Negro Problem" solved by the passage of civil rights legislation. They choose to ignore the fact that the daily lives of most Negroes have changed but slightly, or, as in the case of unemployment, for the worse. They ignore, too, the group of hard-core problems that have only recently emerged: maldistribution of income, urban slums, disparities in education and training, the breakdown of family structure in the ghetto, technological unemployment—problems which show no signs of yielding to time, but which will require concentrated energy and resources for solution.

Without a massive assault on these basic ills, ours will continue to be a society where the gap between rich and poor widens, where the major rewards go to the few (who are not to be confused with the best). Yet it seems highly unlikely, as of 1968, that the public pressure needed for such an assault will be forthcoming. Most Americans still prefer to believe that ours is either already the best of all possible worlds or will shortly, and without any special effort, become such. It is this deep-seated smugness, this intractable optimism, which must be reckoned with—which, indeed, will almost certainly destroy any call for substantive change.

A further obstacle facing the New Left today, Black Power advocates and otherwise, is that its anarchist style and mood run directly counter to the prevailing tendencies in our national life, especially of conformity and centralization. The conformity has been commented on too often to bear repetition, except to point out that the young radicals' unorthodox mores (sexual, social, cultural) are in themselves enough to produce uneasiness and anger in the average American. In insisting on the right of the individual to please himself and to rely on his own judgment (whether in dress, speech, music, sex, or stimulants), SNCC and SDS may be solidly within the American tradition —indeed may be its main stream—but this tradition is now more central to our rhetoric than to our behavior.

The anarchist focus in SNCC and SDS on decentralization, participatory democracy, and community organizing likewise runs counter to dominant national trends. Consolidation, not dispersion, is currently king. There are some signs that a counterdevelopment has begun—such as the pending decentralization of the New York City school system— but as yet the overwhelming pattern continues to be consolidation. Both big government and big business are getting bigger and, more ominous still, are coming into ever closer partnership. As Richard J. Barber has recently documented, the federal government is not only failing to block the growth of huge "conglomerate" firms by antitrust action but it is contributing to that growth through procurement contracts and the exchange of personnel.[13] The traditional hostility between business and government has rapidly drawn to a close. Washington is no longer interested in restraining the giant corporations, and the corporations have lost much of their fear of federal intentions. The two, in happy tandem, are moving the country still further along the road to oligopoly, militarism, economic imperialism, and greater privileges for the already-privileged. The trend is so pronounced, and there is so little effective opposition to it, that it begins to take on an irrevocable, even irreversible, quality.

In the face of these monoliths of national power, Black Power in Lowndes County is pathetic by comparison. Yet while the formation of the Black Panther Party in Lowndes brought out paroxysms of fear in the nation at large, the announcement that General Motors' 1965 sales totaled $21 billion—exceeding the gross national product of all but nine countries in the world—produced barely a tremor of apprehension. The unspoken assumption can only be something like this: It is less dangerous for a few whites to control the whole nation than for a local majority of Negroes to control their own community. The Kafkaesque dimension of life in America continues to grow.

Black Power is both a product of our society and a repudiation of it. Confronted with the continuing indifference of the majority of whites to the Negro's plight, SNCC and CORE have lost faith in conscience and time and have shifted to a position which the white majority finds infuriating. The nation as a whole—as in the case of the Abolitionists over a hundred years ago—has created the climate in which earlier tactics no longer seem relevant, in which new directions become mandatory if frustration is to be met and hope maintained. And if the new turn proves a wrong one, if Black Power forecloses rather than animates further debate on the Negro's condition, if it destroys previous alliances without opening up promising new options, it is the nation as a whole that must bear the responsibility. There seems little likelihood that the American majority will admit to that responsibility. Let us at least hope it will not fail to recognize the rage which Black Power represents, to hear the message at the movement's core:

> *Sweethearts, the script has changed . . .*
> *And with it the stage directions which advise*
> *Lowered voices, genteel asides,*
> *And the white hand slowly turning the dark page.*[14]

[1] Jeremy Larner has recently pointed out ("Initiation for Whitey: Notes on Poverty and Riot," *Dissent* [November–December, 1967]) that the young Negro in the ghetto mainly seeks the kind of knowledge which can serve as a "ready-made line, a set of hard-nosed aphorisms," and that both Malcolm X and Stokely Carmichael have understood this need. In this regard Larner quotes a speech by Carmichael to the students of Morgan State College, as transcribed in *The Movement* (June, 1967): ". . . Now then we come to the question of definitions . . . [and] it is very, very important because I believe that people who can define are masters. I want to read a quote. It is one of my favorite quotes. It comes from *Alice in Wonderland*, [by] Lewis Carroll. . . .
" 'When I use a word,' Humpty Dumpty said in a rather scornful tone, 'I mean just what I choose it to mean, neither more nor less.' 'The question is,' said Alice, 'whether you can make words mean so many different things.' 'The question is,' said Humpty Dumpty, 'who is to be master.'

"That is all. That is all. Understand that . . . the first need of a free people is to define their own terms."

As Larner comments, "Mr. Carmichael, unlike Mr. Carroll, identifies with Humpty Dumpty."

[2] "The Lair of the Black Panther," *New Republic*, August 13, 1966.

[3] I have not seen a clear assessment of the causes for this defeat. The "Newsletter" from the New York office of SNCC of November, 1966, makes two points regarding the election: according to a November report from the Southern Regional Council, 2,823 whites and 2,758 Negroes had registered in Lowndes County, though the white population was approximately 1,900; and "the influential Baptist Alliance told Negroes throughout Alabama to vote the straight Democratic ticket."

[4] On this point, see what I think are the persuasive arguments made by Pat Watters in "The Negroes Enter Southern Politics," *Dissent* (July–August, 1966), and Bayard Rustin, in "Black Power and Coalition Politics," *Commentary* (September, 1966).

[5] See David Danzig, "In Defense of 'Black Power,'" *Commentary*, September, 1966.

[6] SNCC's "position paper" was printed in the *New York Times*, August 5, 1966. It is important to point out, however, that SNCC staffers have since denied the official nature of this paper. See, for example, Elizabeth Sutherland's letter to the editors of *Liberation* (November, 1966), in which she insists that it was "not a SNCC position paper but a document prepared by a group of workers on one SNCC project." (She goes on to note that the *Times* refused to print a SNCC letter to this effect.) For other denials of the "racist" overtones in Black Power, see Stokely Carmichael, "What We Want," *New York Review of Books* (September 22, 1966), and C. E. Wilson, "Black Power and the Myth of Black Racism," *Liberation* (September, 1966). But Andrew Kopkind's report on SNCC staff conferences, "The Future of Black Power," in the *New Republic* of January 7, 1967, makes me believe that the dangers of black racism are real and not merely the invention of frightened white liberals. See also James Peck, "Black Racism," *Liberation* (October, 1966).

[7] For a discussion of "extremism" and the confused uses to which the word can be and has been put, see Howard Zinn, "Abolitionists, Freedom-Riders, and the Tactics of Agitation," *The Antislavery Vanguard*, ed. Martin Duberman (Princeton, 1965), esp. pp. 421–26.

[8] For the shifting nature of SNCC, see Howard Zinn, *SNCC: The New Abolitionists* (Boston, 1964), and Gene Roberts, "From 'Freedom High' to 'Black Power,'" *New York Times*, September 25, 1966.

[9] In recent years several excellent histories and anthologies of anarchism have been published: George Woodcock's brilliant *Anarchism* (Meridian,

1962); James Joll's *The Anarchists* (Eyre and Spottiswoode, 1964); Irving L. Horowitz's anthology *The Anarchists* (Dell, 1964), which concentrates on the "classics" of the literature; and Leonard Krimerman and Lewis Perry's collection, *Patterns of Anarchy* (Anchor, 1966), which presents a less familiar and more variegated selection of anarchist writings.

[10] See Art Goldberg, "Negro Self-Help," *New Republic*, June 10, 1967, and Abbie Hoffman, "Liberty House / Poor People's Corporation," *Liberation*, April, 1967.

[11] For more detailed discussions of the way in which the rhetoric of the New Left and the traditional right have begun to merge, see Ronald Hamowy, "Left and Right Meet," *New Republic*, March 12, 1966; Martin Duberman, "Anarchism Left and Right," *Partisan Review*, Fall, 1966; Paul Feldman, "The Pathos of 'Black Power,'" *Dissent*, January–February, 1967; and Carl Oglesby and Richard Schaull, *Containment and Change* (Macmillan, 1967). Oglesby (on p. 167) seems actually to call for a merger between the two groups, arguing that both are "in the grain of American humanist individualism and voluntaristic associational action." He confuses, it seems to me, a similarity of rhetoric and means with a similarity of goals.

[12] The only overall study of American anarchism is Eunice M. Schuster's *Native American Anarchism* (Northampton, 1932), but some useful biographies exist of individual figures in the movement; see especially, Richard Drinnon, *Rebel in Paradise: A Biography of Emma Goldman* (Chicago, 1961).

[13] "The New Partnership: Big Government and Big Business," *New Republic*, August 13, 1966. But see, too, Alexander Bickel's article in the same journal (May 20, 1967).

[14] Kay Boyle, "On Black Power," *Liberation*, January, 1967.

Black Radicalism: The Road from Montgomery

Vincent Harding

Martin Duberman compares Black Power with radical movements of the past, and Vincent Harding attempts the most difficult task of the analyst of contemporary events, the transition of a movement from one phase to the next. He writes from the vantage point of a participant in many of the events he analyzes: with SCLC and SNCC and the Mississippi Freedom Summer Project of 1964, as a member of the Newark Black Power Conference of 1967, and as a teacher at Spelman College, Atlanta, where he is Chairman of the Department of History.

Harding's training uniquely equips him for understanding the religious component in black radicalism. His doctoral thesis at the University of Chicago, under Sidney Mead and Martin Marty, was on Lyman Beecher. For four years he was the southern representative of the Mennonite Service Committee. He is a contributing editor of *The Christian Century* and *Christianity and Crisis*, and his articles also have appeared in *The Reporter*, *The New South*, *Negro Digest*, and various European journals. He is now exploring "the relationship between religious conviction and radical social thought and action among the black people of America." He has two books in progress, one on the figure of the black messiah in American history, the other (from which this essay is taken) a history of black radicalism from the days of slavery to the present.

O Americans! Americans!! I call God—I call angels—I call men, to witness that your DESTRUCTION *is at hand*, and will be speedily consummated unless you *REPENT*.

—David Walker's *Appeal*, 1829

Is white America really sorry for her crimes against the black people? Does white America have the capacity to repent—and to atone? . . . What atonement would the God of Justice demand for the robbery of the black people's labor, their lives, their true identities, their culture, their history—and even their human dignity?

—Malcolm X, *Autobiography*, 1965

America, you'd better repent and straighten up or we'll burn you down.

—H. Rap Brown, 1967

The living annals of oppressed and troubled peoples abound in wry, unanswerable comments; it is said among black people here that when Lenin was told there were black conservatives in America, he raised his eyebrows and exclaimed: "Oh! And what precisely do they have to conserve?" [1] In an age when instantaneous global communications were only beginning to be exploited, this was a natural question for an outsider to ask, and especially for a stranger who dealt in revolution. At a time when lynchings and emasculations of Negroes were public celebrations, when urban riots meant that white mobs were raging for the lives of defenseless Negroes, who could fault such a question from afar? For anyone who was close to the black communities of the United States, however, there was an answer: They had their *lives* to conserve.

Throughout most of their strange black pilgrimage in this often threatening land, the struggle to stay alive—to conserve their lives and the lives of their children—has been the dominant concern of Afro-Americans. The bravado cry of "Liberty or Death!" has sprung from their lips no more readily than from the lips of other men. Their shaping of revolutionary institutions has not been a significant activity. Neither radical words nor deeds have surged easily from black people in America. They have, instead, survived within the realities of Claude McKay's poignant lines:

> . . . I was born, far from my native clime,
> Under the white man's menace, out of time. [2]

For most of those who live as an indelibly marked minority in the heart of such a menace, conservatism—at least in public—comes as naturally as breathing. (And, like breathing, it often seems a necessary condition for staying alive.) Indeed, even the special black breed that has courageously dared to raise voices of protest in the midst of such a hostile situation has had to come to terms with their distance from "home," and their darkly obvious status as the outnumbered ones. So for those who have been at once black, angry, and wise, protest has never moved easily over into radicalism. Even when protest has made this leap, most of its actions and energies have been defensive. Black radicalism, therefore, has been focused largely on the means for realizing "the American promise" rather than on shaping new, dissenting goals.

One facet of the dilemma was described a decade ago by one of the most famous black radicals, Paul Robeson. In his autobiographical statement, *Here I Stand*, Robeson delineated what he called "a certain protective tactic of Negro life in America." Speaking from bitter experience, this politically sensitive artist said:

> Even while demonstrating that he is really an equal . . . the Negro must never appear to be challenging white superiority. Climb up if you can—but don't act "uppity." Always show that you are *grateful*. (Even if what you have gained has been wrested from unwilling powers, be sure to be grateful lest "they" take it all away.) Above all, *do nothing to give them cause to fear you*, for then the oppressing hand, which might at times ease up a little, will surely become a fist to knock you down again! [3]

Robeson's conclusions are confirmed by Lerone Bennett, another perceptive recorder of the black experience, in *The Negro Mood*. "The history of the Negro in America . . . has been a quest for a revolt that was not a revolt . . . a revolt . . . that did not seem to the white power structure to be an open revolt." [4]

If in one sense these analyses are being outstripped by the pace of current events in the nation's black communities, they nonetheless describe much that has happened up to now (and the death of Martin Luther King appeared to many persons as additional proof of their validity). Such insights, moreover, suggest a set of guidelines for understanding the nature of black radicalism in America.

At what point does black radicalism begin? Perhaps it begins when black men lose or repress their fear of the descending white fist and carry Negro protest to one of its logical conclusions, regardless of the consequences. Perhaps it begins when sensitive, restive souls lose faith in "the myth of Negro progress" within the American system.[5] Perhaps we may speak of black radicalism when men are pressed by our society to seek alternatives (even though chimerical and "unrealistic") to the American way of life for Afro-Americans. Even now, black radicalism is more a reaction than a calculated strategy, more an agonized thrust than a body of thought; and this is one of its weaknesses.

Inchoate though they may be, as one sorts out the elements of the Afro-American experience with radicalism, several themes can be identified. First of all, it becomes clear that the classic, primarily European terms of "left" and "right" or "communist" and "capitalist" usually provide insufficient contexts for a discussion of American black radicalism. Even the sometimes helpful separation into social, political, economic, and racial radicalism at last becomes a tiresome burden in probing the subject. This radicalism, which grows out of a situation as emotionally weighted and psychologically distorted as the black-white encounter in America, cannot adequately be described in terms that are largely intellectual and theoretical. For such "irrational" reasons (among others), those classic "radicals," the Communists, found American black revolutionaries a very difficult brood to cultivate.

Another thematic reality is that in every generation there has been a group of black radicals (marked with the blood that always accompanies new births and violent deaths) that has moved far beyond the acceptable or customary lines of protest and revolt. Sometimes this has been simply a personal groping with the menace; sometimes it has been organized. At various times the emphasis of the radical approach has been on armed self-defense; and occasionally it has urged armed uprisings against the status quo. In each generation the "radical edge" has reached a different point in the overall experience, but it has always been present—marked by despair, alienation, fierce anger, and sometimes even by hope.

A third continuity is found in the constantly recurring, religiously oriented themes of apocalyptic messianism and atonement. Basically this has implied the conviction that there could be no ultimate deliverance for blacks (or whites) without a black-led rebellious movement, which would involve levels of anguish and blood-letting surpassing those of the Civil War. From the first attempts to capture their slave ships to the current talk of "taking over the ghettos," the black radical impulse has been informed by a vision of blood, a vision often understood as being of divine origin.

Usually, however, the goal of black radicalism has appeared to be the simplistic, "moderate" goal of assimilation into American society; but many radicals have realized there is nothing simple or moderate about such an aim. They knew that the American nation would have to be drastically transformed before it would fully open itself to the native-yet-alien presence in its midst. This was what a black leader of the Communist Party meant when she said, in the 1930's, "It is impossible to take one step in the direction of winning for the Negro people their elementary rights that is not revolutionary." [6] Nevertheless, other radicals eventually became convinced that such a transformation is impossible. Thus black nationalism and black zionism also have sought to chart a course in the endless search. Their path, of course, has not been towards assimilation.

Against such a background it becomes clear that the transformation of black radicals from the singing, integration-directed marchers of Montgomery, Alabama, in 1955 into the avowed guerrilla fighters and alienated rebels of the late 1960's was in keeping with historical precedents.[7]

I

In 1955 Martin Luther King and the black community in Montgomery faced a situation that contained much that was new as well as much that was brutally old. Social, political, and economic injustices to Negro citizens were evident on every hand; the South was considered the major bastion of enforced second-class citizenship; and segregation in public facilities seemed the most blatant example of racial humiliation. But there was something new as well. The previous spring the Bandung Conference in Southeast Asia had reminded the world how much World War II had done to intensify the struggles of formerly colonized people in wrenching themselves free of Western domination. In New York City the United Nations was an expanding forum for the views of the formerly silent peoples of the earth. The United States was deeply engaged in ideological—and occasionally military—struggles with powers that were quick to exploit this nation's poor record as a protector of its own oppressed. Younger, better-educated black people and their families were moving from rural to urban areas and were determined to play a new role in American society.

In this context, and under the prodding of the National Association for the Advancement of Colored People, the Supreme Court in 1954 had declared that racial segregation in public schools was unconstitutional. Concern about school segregation focused on the South, for it was recognized that the decision, if firmly enforced, also could signal the end of many other institutionalized forms of segregation. Some blacks who saw this possibility now moved forward with a conviction that, for the first time, the nation's highest tribunal was on their side. At the same moment, the Court's decision was a call to fierce resistance for many white persons.[8]

It was at this point that Martin Luther King entered the scene.

The decision of a gentle black lady to retain her disputed seat on a segregated bus, then the decision of Montgomery's Negro community that her subsequent arrest be protested—these and other events helped press the twenty-six-year-old Baptist minister into the radical path.[9] Neither his somewhat sheltered middle-class Atlanta background nor his rather conventional education had prepared him for such a mission, but he accepted it. Martin Luther King's brand of radicalism can be traced to a number of sources: the lives and the teachings of Christ and Gandhi, the thinking of Thoreau, the aborted hopes of James Farmer and A. Philip Randolph,[10] the tough strategy talks of Bayard Rustin, and the exigencies of the situation. From these and other sources King shaped his old-new hope, catalyzed by his own creative impulses.

Love was the answer. Not sentimentality, but the tough and resolute love that refused bitterness and hatred but stood firmly against every shred of injustice. Few brands of black radicalism had ever required so much. Men were not only urged to stand and face the menace, they were called upon to be true to themselves and to reject the very weapons that had destroyed them for so long. They were called upon to transform American life by substituting moral and spiritual courage for its traditional dependence upon violence and coercion. This new (and untried) weapon could easily be distributed to—eventually—the overwhelming majority of ordinary black people. To the confused and often fearful white faces behind the menacing fists Dr. King addressed these words:

> We will match your capacity to inflict suffering with our capacity to endure suffering. We will meet your physical force with soul force. We will not hate you, but we cannnot . . . obey your unjust laws. Do to us what you will and we will still love you. Bomb our homes and threaten our children; send your hooded perpetrators of violence into our communities and drag us out on some wayside road, beating us and leaving us half dead, and we will still love you. But we will soon wear you down by our capacity to suffer. And in winning our freedom we will so appeal to your heart and conscience that we will win you in the process.[11]

After the victory against segregation in public buses in Montgomery (which many persons explained away in legal terms), King sought to institutionalize his vision in the Southern Christian Leadership Conference. King and the SCLC still harbored David Walker's messianic hope that black people would lead the way to a redeemed America, but they would not use Walker's method. The new radical hope (is it not always radical to think of redemption for America?) was expressed in an SCLC document:

> Creatively used, the philosophy of nonviolence can restore the broken community in America. SCLC is convinced that nonviolence is the most potent force available to an oppressed people in their struggle for freedom and dignity.[12]

In uniting the broken community King and the SCLC sought to build what they called "the beloved community," in which black and white Americans of every social and economic level would recognize their bonds of human unity.

The power of nonviolence, however, was temporarily vitiated in the attempt to apply the tactic to its immense task. SCLC could not maintain the dynamic level of Montgomery in the new challenges it faced. Perhaps this was partly because SCLC was made up not of black radicals but for the most part of Negro Baptist ministers, but, whatever the reasons, it was not until 1960 that the vision King projected was snatched up by an even younger generation of southern Negro students; and the sit-in movement was born. Black southern students had not been noted for their radicalism, but this generation had grown up as witnesses of the successful struggles of other non-white peoples for freedom. Although they had seen white resistance to legal desegregation solidify in their own section, they had less to lose than Baptist ministers.

Beginning in Greensboro, North Carolina, they went beyond the marches and sermons of Montgomery; they walked through the "white only" doors, stood and sat where blacks had never dared go before, and confronted the protectors of the status quo with their insistent black presence. In all of this the students were aided by television and other mass media, which carried their crusading image to other students and persons all over the world.

As the movement spread across the southland and even into the Deep South, and to many places in the North, it was clear that this public defiance of all the institutions of the fist was a most radical move for that place and hour. There had been scattered precedents, but never a campaign that involved thousands of persons in hundreds of cities. In a revolutionary generation, however, the radical actions of the preceding year may appear moderate or even acceptable the next year, especially in America, where the domesticating of radical impulses seems to take place with ease and rapidity. In some ways this was what happened to the nonviolent (actually un-violent) attempts to desegregate public facilities in the South.[13]

II

As the sit-ins, freedom rides, and other demonstrations moved across the South, white resistance stiffened, and some black radicals were not convinced that nonviolence was their most effective weapon. They saw little evidence of the pliable "hearts and consciences" to which King had addressed his appeal; rather, they saw mobs, heard bombs, felt the impact of heavy clubs. Thereupon they chose Denmark Vesey, David Walker, and Nat Turner as the fathers of their black radicalism. Indeed, it was in North Carolina, the state in which the mass sit-in movement was born, that the newest call to armed Negro self-defense was sounded.

In 1959 Robert F. Williams, a Marine Corps veteran, drew attention to himself and to his branch of the NAACP in Monroe, North Carolina. Williams had changed the usual middle-class makeup of the association's branches by forming a group from laborers and other persons whose thoughts and inclinations were closer to his own. He had already begun to talk of Negroes' arming themselves when, in 1959, a white man was acquitted of charges of physical assault and attempted rape of a black woman, despite the testimony of a number of Negro witnesses.

> This . . . shows [Williams said] that the Negro in the South cannot expect justice in the courts. He must convict his attackers on the spot. He must meet violence with violence, lynching with lynching.

The NAACP's national office immediately disassociated itself from Williams' statement and attempted to remove him from his position. Eventually, however, the local and state officials took care of this matter; they hounded the burly, outspoken black radical from the city and the state. But Williams was not silenced. In 1962, when nonviolence was still in its ascendancy, he maintained that

> any struggle for liberation should be a flexible struggle. We must

use non-violence as a means as long as this is feasible, but the day will come when conditions become so pronounced that non-violence will be suicidal. . . . The day is surely coming when we will see more violence on the same American scene. The day is surely coming when some of the same Negroes who have denounced our using weapons for self-defense will be arming themselves.[14]

Events made Williams a prophet; but the question that continues to rise from such thinking is whether the call to armed self-defense is a conservative or a radical move? It can be argued that Williams— and others like him—simply become part of the violent pattern of American life and promise no more than its continuation. Can a nation that is built on violence be constructively transformed by violence? On the other hand one faces the perennial, inherent ambiguity in black radicalism: in the minds of some persons nothing could have been more radical, even in the 1960's, than the decision of Negroes to arm themselves. Williams' group, in arming itself, determined to defy both the southern mob and the southern police, who seemed ready to expose them to the mob's fury. On one such occasion a "very old . . . white man . . . started screaming and crying like a baby, [while saying:]

'God damn, God damn, what is this God damn country coming to that niggers have got guns, the niggers are armed and the police can't even arrest them.' [15]

Whatever the accuracy of definitions of black radicalism from the lips of very old southern white men, Williams soon would follow a familiar black radical path as he moved from Cuba to Moscow to Peking. Later, his call for armed self-defense would be accepted by a black revolutionary liberation struggle in America, and by 1968 he would be elected Provisional President of a separatist black nation in American exile.[16]

Behind the most militant words and deepest commitments to black radicalism of all who have spoken of black revolution in America, whatever the variety, has been a battery of unresolved but realistic questions. How does an easily identifiable minority carry out such a revolution? Where does it find allies in a hostile and threatened nation? Against whom will the revolution be directed, and what are its goals? These were the questions of the early sixties, when nonviolence was counterposed against armed and militant self-defense.

After 1954 it was generally assumed that the enemy was the system of segregation in the South and that the major allies were the federal government, the liberals of the North, and the conscience of the nation. But step by step this assumption was transformed. More and more black persons began to ask whether segregation properly could be isolated in the South merely because it was supported by law only in that region. Others wondered how a "federal government" could be separate from the pervasive prejudice and discrimination black men had always found in the nation as a whole. Was the United States Congress really more liberal than the homeowners, real estate dealers, and corporations it represented? Was it not obvious that, when serious attempts were made to direct action into the North, there was a noticeable cooling of ardor among erstwhile allies, especially when issues of compensatory hiring, suburban housing, and integrated education were raised? [17]

Moreover, as the nation became more deeply enmeshed in Vietnam, who was willing to approve the scores-of-billions-of-dollars price tag for the rehabilitation of the black communities? And what kind of radicalism was needed to force a complacent nation to confront the need to rehabilitate the black community? What kind of a "revolution" depended on federal troops to protect and advance it? These were some of the vexing questions of the post-Montgomery decade. In Birmingham, Alabama, in the spring of 1963, sclc activists attempted tentative answers to some of those questions.[18] More black people than ever before were called into the streets to face the prospect of jail. Larger numbers of children and young people were involved in sclc-directed civil disobedience. At the same time, King's group raised its sights beyond the integration of public facilities: jobs for black people became part of the broader demands. But broader demands meant the willingness to launch in Birmingham a long seige of direct action, and sclc did not seem prepared for such a trial. Besides, more and more young people of the city became involved in the protest, and their susceptibility to violent radicalism was not easy to control. Therefore the city's business leaders (forever concerned with images), the federal administration, and parts of the sclc leadership seemed ready to bring the Birmingham campaign to a halt sooner than the results might have indicated. Thus the expanded agenda did not bring the predicted results, but some observers thought they saw the direction nonviolent action must take if it was to remain on the constantly moving forward edge of black radicalism.

One of the insights that emerged from the Birmingham demonstrations was the need for even larger attempts at civil disobedience, aimed at Washington, D.C., and utilizing the pent-up energies of thousands of black young people. A civil rights bill had finally been introduced in Congress, in response to Birmingham, but some SCLC staff members and others were determined to push the nation even beyond such legalities. It was proposed that A. Philip Randolph's old idea for a march on Washington be revived and that thousands of black people be brought to the capital for a massive act of nonviolent civil disobedience. The objective was to paralyze the life of the nation's capital until Congress and the country were willing to move much more meaningfully toward equality. But because of opposition within the civil rights establishment—from financial benefactors and from the highest level of the federal government—this massive nonviolent "attack" on the nation's capital became the "polite" March on Washington.[19]

America had domesticated another radical movement. The militant speeches were censored, the taverns were closed for the day. Radicalism that sought to reach the heart of the black condition in America also sought to remain on good terms with the President and the Attorney General. It had been easily seduced, but the lesson was not lost on some of the younger militants. The words that had been censored from one of the speeches had questioned whether the federal government was truly an ally of the black movement, and some of these perceptive young people soon answered this question in the negative.[20] Other radicals continued to urge that the nonviolent movement engage in massive civil disobedience or lose its relevance to the condition of black America.

At a SCLC convention soon after the Washington march, Wyatt Tee Walker, the conference's executive director, said:

> The question is, whether we want to continue local guerrilla battles against discrimination and segregation or go to all-out war. . . . has the moment come in the development of the non-violent revolution that we are forced . . . on some appointed day . . . literally [to] immobilize the nation until she acts on our pleas for justice and morality? . . . Is the day far-off that major transportation centers would be deluged with mass acts of civil disobedience; air-

ports, train stations, bus terminals, the traffic of large cities, inter-
state commerce, would be halted by the bodies of witnesses nonviolently insisting on "Freedom Now"? I suppose a nationwide work
stoppage might attract enough attention to persuade someone to do
something to get this monkey of segregation and discrimination off
our backs, once, now and forever. Will it take one or all of
these? [21]

Because Walker was known to be given to flights of rhetoric, it
was difficult to ascertain how serious he was, but he seemed to sense
the new mood. The nonviolent movement would die if it did not become more radical—to a degree that would shock most civil rights
leaders and more radical than its chief financial backers would approve. Part of the familiar frustration was symbolized by Walker's
vague reference to the need "to persuade someone to do something":
Who should they try to persuade, with even the most radical action,
and *what* should they be persuaded to do? Walker's organization did
not support him, nor was there support for a proposed large cadre of
nonviolent demonstrators who would commit themselves for at least
a year of continuous action before they returned to their homes, jobs,
or school. In the North, attempts at school boycotts, traffic disruption,
and other forms of civil disobedience met with indifferent success.
None of the major organizations was ready to move in the direction of
large-scale civil disobedience. With court-enforced desegregation de-
priving the black movement of easily articulated goals for the struggle,
momentum could not be built. Meanwhile, however, another kind of
black momentum built fiercely.

III

In the summer of 1967 the transportation, commerce, commuting,
and other schedules of more than one American city were totally disrupted by "witnessing" blacks, but not in the way that Walker had
considered four years earlier. The young people who were to have
been the core of the rejected nonviolent campaigns stormed angrily
through the cities, witnessing with bricks, Molotov cocktails, and
rifles. Much of their violence was a reaction to the callousness of
American society at large, but it was certainly aggravated by the
lack of meaningful alternatives, the result of the nonviolent movement's failure to move with the urgency the situation demanded.

What had happened between Walker's speech in 1963 and the immobilization of the cities by fear and fire in 1967? What turns black minds upon the path of alienation and armed violence? One of the crucial events was the bombing in Birmingham, less than a month after the March on Washington. The exhausted civil rights movement was mesmerized before the spectacle of the death of four black children in Birmingham, the result of a bomb that had been planted in the Sixteenth Street Baptist Church. Negro radicals saw this atrocity as a typical white American response to increasingly cautious, impotent, religiously oriented nonviolence. One of the younger black radicals wrote:

> What was needed that Sunday [of the bombing] was ol' John Brown to come riding into Birmingham as he had ridden into Lawrence, Kansas, burning every building that stood and killing every man, woman and child that ran from his onslaught. Killing, killing, killing, turning men into fountains of blood, . . . until Heaven itself drew back before the frothing red ocean.
>
> But the Liberal and his Negro sycophants would've cried, Vengeance accomplishes nothing. You are only acting like your oppressor and such an act makes you no better than him. John Brown, his hands and wrists slick with blood, would've said, oh so softly and so quietly, Mere Vengeance is folly. Purgation is necessary.[22]

Atonement by blood is a persistent motif in the minds of black radicals.

Other youths were utterly embittered by the refusal of "liberal" northern political leaders even to admit that psychological violence and destruction was wreaked daily upon the lives of black ghetto-dwellers. Nothing was getting better for the submerged black people despite all the talk of "Negro progress" and "going too fast." Their schools were progressively miseducating more black children. Their houses were still decaying. Their incomes relative to whites' were decreasing. No one—radical or otherwise—seemed to be creating meaningful programs to deal with the immense problems, to challenge the widening alienation.

Equally significant, perhaps, was the growing perception that political leaders did not intend to take chances with their white constituencies by enforcing the civil rights legislation that had been enacted in 1964. When tough choices had to be made, they still seemed to favor the whites. In this "reconstruction," as in the first, the key to basic change for Negroes seemed to be in the hands of the white North, which in the mid-1960's appeared no more committed to full equality and restitution for black men than it had been a century before. Perhaps now, as then, politicians and people intuitively recognized that the social, economic, and political changes that were necessary for the rehabilitation of black America would constitute a revolution. What majority has ever presented a minority with a legislated revolution?

Therefore, as he had predicted, Robert Williams—in Cuba—spoke for more and more black persons when he said: "What is integration when the law says yes, but the police and howling mobs say no? Our only logical and successful answer is to meet organized and massive violence with massive and organized violence. Our people must prepare to wage an urban guerrilla war of self-defense." [23] In Williams' opinion, racism had become so intrinsic a part of the nation's life that it could be exorcised only with "shock treatment." Only in this way, he said, could America be saved.

Other conclusions also were drawn from Williams' premise. By 1963 America's attention had been called to Elijah Muhammad's Nation of Islam, largely through the work of the group's outstanding spokesman, Malcolm X. The Nation, which claimed a tie to the Islamic peoples of the world, had its organizational roots in the broken black hopes of the 1930's. Focusing on the black lower classes and teaching a version of religious black nationalism, the group successfully attempted to rehabilitate some of society's most alienated black rejects, and Malcolm X was one of these. He had heard the teachings of the "messenger," Elijah Muhammad while serving a term in prison for his activities as "Detroit Red," a pimp and a narcotics pusher.[24]

Speaking for his group, Minister Malcolm said: "We don't think that it is possible for the American white man in sincerity to take the action necessary to correct the unjust conditions that 20 million black people here are made to suffer morning, noon, and night." From such a premise there followed a logical conclusion, one also derived from a long history of black radicalism. Malcolm continued,

> Because we don't have any hope or confidence or faith in the American white man's ability to bring about a change in the in-

justices that exist, instead of asking or seeking to integrate into the American society we want to face the facts of the problem the way they are, and separate ourselves. . . .

. . . This doesn't mean that we are anti-white or anti-American, or anti-anything. We feel, that if integration all these years hasn't solved the problem yet, then we want to try something new, something different and something that is in accord with the conditions as they actually exist.[25]

Elijah Muhummad's people were moved by what was surely to come, by Malcolm's conviction that "we are living at the end of time," when "the earth will become all . . . Islam," and when those who reject the Prophet's teachings will be destroyed by Allah. They were separatists, therefore, because "we don't want to be wiped out with the American white man." What other conclusions were logical for those who had lost all faith in American whites but had gained a faith in a just and all-conquering God? Except for "Allah," of course, the script had been written in America many times over since 1800.[26]

By 1964 this remarkable young radical had rejected Elijah Muhammad's version of the old script, apparently having decided against separatism, and therefore he was faced with the dilemma Frederick Douglass and others had faced before him. In a speech before an integrated group in New York that same year, Malcolm X demonstrated his ambivalence. First he predicted that

1964 will see the Negro revolt evolve and merge into the worldwide black revolution that has been taking place on this earth since 1945. The so-called revolt will become a real black revolution. . . . Revolutions are never . . . based upon . . . begging a corrupt society or a corrupt system to accept us into it. Revolutions overturn systems. And there is no system on this earth which has proved itself more corrupt, more criminal, than this system that in 1964 still colonizes 22 million . . . Afro-Americans.

But instead of describing the terrors of the coming revolution, he seemed to backtrack: "America is the only country in history in a position to bring about a revolution without violence and bloodshed by granting the suffrage to all black people." Like Douglass, however, he had to admit: "But America is not morally equipped to do so."[27] Malcolm seemed to be caught in a painful ambivalence similar to that which had dogged the earlier radicals.

In an anguished display of mixed emotions and convictions, Malcolm nevertheless predicted that blacks' use of the franchise would "sweep all of the racists and the segregationists out of office." This, in his opinion, would "wipe out the Southern segregationism that now controls America's foreign policy, as well as America's domestic policy." More and more frequently Malcolm X proclaimed that, for the Negroes, it had to be "either ballots or bullets," either a revolution of votes or guerrilla warfare. How he expected to gain the franchise in a totally corrupt system was never made clear. (This, of course, is one of the basic dilemmas for all black leaders who have tried to help their people through a reformist ballot method. Who will vote with this minority, with those who are at once powerless and most in need of the help that can come only from a transformed society? Who will vote with them when giving that help may mean the loss of a significant share of power? In light of this conundrum, what shall black radicals do if they are determined to remain loyal to the way of life that has been blessed as most truly democratic by the rest of the society?)

Struggling with the problems of tactics and strategy, Malcolm X formed his own group, the Organization of Afro-American Unity. Avowedly black nationalist, he saw no other position for those who would work for, with, and in the black ghettos. As he traveled in various parts of the world his religious commitment deepened and was transformed. He also became more convinced of the classic black nationalist vision of the need for internationalizing the struggle of American Negroes, and with this in mind he began to seek aid from African leaders in bringing the plight of Afro-Americans before the United Nations. "Our African . . . Asian . . . [and] Latin-American brothers can throw their weight on our side, and . . . 800 million Chinamen are . . . waiting to throw their weight on our side.[28] A troubled spirit, Malcolm moved through the ghettos and college campuses trying to construct a way where so many other brilliant black radicals before him had failed.

On self-defense he was positive and clear. Black men must exercise their right, he said, especially "in areas where the government has proven itself either unwilling or unable to defend the lives and the property of Negroes." On other issues he moved from guerrilla warfare to the ballot, but he never seemed to believe that the vote could be gained without the shedding of much blood, and perhaps not even then. On economic issues he took the predictable path of espousing socialism, partly because "almost every one of the countries that has gotten independence has devised some kind of socialistic system." Besides, he said, "you can't operate a capitalistic system unless you are vulturistic; you have to have someone else's blood to suck to be a capitalist. You show me a capitalist, I'll show you a bloodsucker." [29]

Up to the time of his death, however, Malcolm had had no vision of the path to final liberation. Near the end of his life, and before a predominantly black audience, he succumbed to the natural temptation to oversimplify the problem and its solution. In late 1964 he said: "What we need in this country is the same type of Mau Mau here that they had over there in Kenya. . . . If they were over here, they'd get this problem straightened up just like that." [30] But such loose words were testimony more to the desperation he felt before a host of enemies and an unfeeling nation than to the real level of his searching. His seeking was profound, burdened by all the agony that radical black integrity must carry, and it was complicated by his new vision of Islam and its commitment to an all-inclusive brotherhood of many-colored men. How could this be achieved in a country whose seeds of racism were embedded so deep? Perhaps all that one can, tentatively, say of him was compressed into the lines of Robert Hayden:

> He fell upon his face before
> Allah the raceless in whose blazing Oneness all . . . .
>
> Were one. He rose renewed, renamed, became
> much more than there was time for him to be.[31]

First among the black rebels to be cut down in the classic American style—by gunfire at a public meeting—Malcolm X had become a martyr and a saint even before his last breath escaped his body. He had helped bring modernity and a new respectability to black nationalism among the younger militants of his day. Even before he died the integrity of his life and his obvious identification with the masses among whom he had hustled and been reborn had deeply impressed the angry young men. Just before and just after his death a new flowering of militant black nationalist organizations testified to his impact on the ghettos.

IV

If one group inherited the time that had been denied Malcolm it was the Student Nonviolent Coordinating Committee, which earlier had served as the shock troops of the nonviolent movement. Organized in 1960, soon after the sit-in movement began and committed to radical nonviolent direct action, these high school and college-age young people invaded the worst hard-core racist sections of the Deep South: southwest Georgia, black belt Alabama, and Mississippi's rural areas. They had paid more of the dues of the movement than any other group. In 1962 and 1963 SNCC leaders had agreed (for complicated and fascinating reasons) to switch from conventional direct action to voter-registration campaigns. Although such campaigns would be considered a defiant form of action in many of the most resistant parts of the South, by the 1960's they could certainly not be called radical action. Nevertheless the SNCC corps seemed to founder, physically and psychologically, and became increasingly impatient with southern resistance and increasingly disillusioned by temporizing and northern evasion. They had been influenced, moreover, by Malcolm X, a man who was "up tight" and "knew what was happening." Then, in 1964, several developments drove SNCC into a more radical nationalist direction.[32]

After having decided to organize a new black-led nonsegregated Democratic party in Mississippi, SNCC and other groups sponsored the "Mississippi Summer."[33] During these months hundreds of white persons, especially college students, moved into the state to help with various kinds of community organization and voter-registration tasks among black people (few were willing to try their skills on Mississippi whites). Forthrightly, SNCC admitted that the white newcomers had been invited as hostages to a white world that did not seem to care as much about black deaths as it did about white deaths. But the young white crowd brought something more than their willing bodies. Often, despite great personal bravery and compassion, they were insensitive to the kind of development that had to take place in the black persons with whom they worked. Too often they tended to take over tasks, conversations, meetings, and publicity that should have been handled by Negroes. Sexual competition and jealousy was another divisive issue. Many of the less articulate but no less sensitive Mississippi Negroes who worked in the summer project grew restive and resentful; and by the time the summer was over it was clear that all this would force SNCC to examine its much-publicized interraciality more closely. Could black people really grow and develop under the tutelage of white allies? "Black Power" became one of the basic responses to this basic question.

The summer of 1964 also saw the failure of the Mississippi Freedom Democratic Party to win official recognition and the state's delegate votes at the Democratic National Convention. The maneuvering and attempts at political compromise that met this challenge only strengthened the conviction of young radicals that allies were not to be found in any of the traditional sources that the civil rights movement had heretofore taken for granted. Of even more significance was the increased disillusionment with the black civil rights establishment that resulted from the Atlantic City experience.[34]

Finally, 1964 was the summer in which the black ghettos exploded, after which black leaders everywhere were forced to ask what effect their programs thus far had had in the ghettos. Among the radicals, only Malcolm X seemed to have even a tenuous claim to leadership in a dissenting, explosive world. His "thing" had been blackness; and other radicals now saw that this also would have to be their "thing" if they were to learn to speak with and for the Negro masses. SNCC heard the message.

In 1965 the impulse to a new version of black radicalism was intensified when Malcolm X was cut down by bullets. Almost none of the black radicals believed the story that the Muslims were responsible. Why, they asked, had the French government refused Malcolm permission to visit that country just before his death? What did the French know of Malcolm's enemies? Had the CIA somehow been involved? It seemed to them that America had destroyed another black man who had refused to cower before the fist and who had threatened to bring its shame fully before the world. The alienation deepened; this was not a nation that listened to moral appeals, they said. In the month after Malcolm's death the last major attempt at tactical nonviolence in the South reached a cruel climax in Selma, Alabama, one of the areas in which SNCC had conducted a voter-registration campaign. State troopers, "performing" on foot and horseback before television cameras, waded into marchers and scattered broken bodies and broken hopes before them. Understandably, many persons asked if a march in support of the right to vote was worth all of that.[35]

The summer of 1965 was the summer of Watts, of burning, of a hostile, fearful response from a nation that for many generations had prepared the tinder and matches. The event was followed by the usual investigation, the usual recommendations, and the usual inaction. Meanwhile, urban school segregation went on unchecked in the North. In South Vietnam, another American war for the right of self-determination of other men was absorbing more energies, more money, and the best of the black "rejects."

So the score was in for the new breed of black radicals, grouped organizationally in SNCC and CORE but spread throughout the ghettos of America. It seemed to them that nonviolence and integration were not only failures but probably a betrayal: "The only thing non-violence proved was how savage whites were." [36] Other radicals claimed that integration meant only a constant drain of the best-trained black brains into a white-oriented world, leaving the ghettos as exploited, colonized infernos. Holding such convictions, the younger radicals turned ever more sharply from the path of Martin Luther King, not only because they could not believe in his weapon but because they no longer believed in his dream of integration. King's eloquent vision seemed irrelevant to the conditions of the black masses, who, like Malcolm X, began to assail the dream of middle-class integration as the substitute for the nightmare all around them. Like other radicals before them, they questioned the ultimate value of a way of life that permitted so much suffering and injustice in the most affluent nation in the world. They turned their backs on the respectable and secure ideology of assimilation to such a society, and they trumpeted their refusal to take up arms to fight such a society's overseas wars.

Like Malcolm X, their hero, these radicals are often tossed on uncertain waves of ideology. Sometimes they search for new weapons, new programs, new issues that might lead to black freedom; at other times they are given to despair, and occasionally to blind rage. Sometimes, in sheer frustration, they break down and weep. Almost always, they look only to the black communities.

Much of the feeling of this new generation of Afro-American rebels was gathered up by Julius Lester, a gifted writer:

> America has had chance after chance to show that it really meant that "all men are endowed with certain inalienable rights." America has had precious chances in this decade to make it come true. Now

it is over. The days of singing freedom songs and the days of com-
bating bullets and billy clubs with Love. "We Shall Overcome" (and
we have overcome our blindness) sounds old, out-dated and can
enter the pantheon of the greats along with the iww songs and the
union songs. As one sncc veteran put it after the Mississippi March,
"Man, the people are too busy getting ready to fight to bother with
singing anymore." And as for Love? That's always been better done
in bed than on the picket lines and marches. Love is fragile and
gentle and seeks a like response. They used to sing "I Love Everybody" as they ducked bricks and bottles. Now they sing

> "Too much love,
> Too much love,
> Nothing kills a nigger like
> Too much love."

They know, because they still get headaches from the beatings they
took while love, love, loving. They know, because they died on
those highways and in those jail cells, died from trying to change
the hearts of men who had none. They know, the ones who have
bleeding ulcers when they're twenty-three and the ones who have
to have the eye operations. They know that nothing kills a nigger
like too much love.[37]

Perhaps because the hopes had been so immense, rarely had a
movement of black radicalism turned so fully from its former dreams.

> At one time [Lester wrote], black people desperately wanted to be
> American, to communicate with whites, to live in the Beloved Com-
> munity. Now that is irrelevant. They know that it can't be until
> whites want it to be and it is obvious now that the whites don't
> want it.

As Lester saw it, while some black radicals would now like all
whites who so deeply disappointed them to be destroyed, he was
personally convinced that "the white man is simply to be ignored,
because the time has come for the black man to control the things
which affect his life." According to this view the black man must no
longer live his life in reaction to whites. And, Lester continues:

> Now he will live it only within the framework of his own blackness
> and his blackness links him with the Indians of Peru, the miner in
> Bolivia, the African and the freedom fighters of Vietnam. What they

fight for is what the American black man fights for—the right to govern his own life. If the white man interprets that to mean hatred, it is only a reflection of his own fears and anxieties and black people leave him to deal with it. There is too much to do to waste time and energy hating white people.[38]

v

With the new ideology fermenting, it was not long before the nation's news media sensationalized the situation through their vast image-creating (and image-destroying) techniques. At the same time, ironically, when the occasion came, one of the most articulate new voices had two of the most honored black prophets of the earlier radicalism as his foils. James Meredith, the black Mississippian who had caused a riot when he attempted to enter his state university in 1962, returned to Mississippi in June of 1966 to walk the length of the state on foot as a witness against black fear. After he was shot from ambush and hospitalized, the march was continued by leaders of what still was called the civil rights movement, among whom were Dr. King and Stokely Carmichael, the self-possessed new chairman of SNCC. In the course of the rejuvenated march there were many open as well as private debates among the leaders about the need for a renewed emphasis on "blackness" in the movement. The debates were not really settled at that time but SNCC and Carmichael were the obvious victors in the jousting for publicity from the mass media, and King's international prestige served to bring public attention to the phrase that had been germinating for a long time.[39]

"We shall overcome" already was tame enough for a Texas-born president to quote in a national address, but the young radicals had moved on. Thus the press corps and a people, both of them constantly in search of fearful sensations, found them in "Black Power" and Stokely Carmichael. Only the term, however, and the violent response of the public media and the nation, were new; its concepts were old. "Black Power" merely expressed the radicalism of Afro-Americans who had decided there was no physical escape from this land and who saw no future in an integration that demanded the giving up of blackness. "Black Power" therefore meant turning away from assimilation and emphasizing the existence and beauty of an authentic Afro-American culture. "Black Power" meant a movement of and for the masses that honored the memory of Marcus Garvey and Malcolm X and the early Adam Clayton Powell. It also meant a proud association with Africa and pan-Africanism and a connection with oppressed and colonized people all over the world. Who could not hear W. E. B. Du Bois' impeccable language paraphrased in Harlem slang?

Again it was the radicalism of those who had tried white allies and had found them wanting in the tasks of building the black community. Black power sent such allies away, some with less ceremony than others. It told them to work with the white menace and to transform it into something healthy and new. It sometimes indicated that one day there might be a meeting, after the work had been done on both sides of the wall, but only blacks could now move effectively among their teeming, disaffected masses. As in an earlier day, Black Power meant armed self-defense for many adherents, who later would advance the rhetoric and the reality of the positive benefits of violence. Its emphasis was on self-determination for black people in their communities, which included political, educational, and cultural self-determination.

As the idioms of a colonialized people began to be used, the maxims of Frantz Fanon became more clear; a century-old phrase was frequently heard: "We are a nation within a nation." [40] (How can one account for the resilience of this concept? How do we explain the fact that today it is more widely accepted among Negroes than it was in the nineteenth-century day of Martin Delany—more readily heard today than it was forty years ago, when the Third Communist International appropriated black nationality as a major organizing theme for America?) [41] The words came readily but the new programs were not yet clear, and radicals who saw Black Power as more than rhetoric attempted to fill that vacuum. To those who had no response to the new version of black radicalism save an accusation of riot instigation, Stokely Carmichael gave this answer:

> As long as people in the ghettos . . . feel that they are victims of the misuse of white power without any way to have their needs represented . . . we will continue to have riots. These are not the products of "black power" but the absence of any organization capable of giving the community the power, the black power, to deal with its problems.
>
> . . . Without the power to control their lives and their commu-

nities . . . these communities will exist in a constant state of insurrection. This is a choice that the country will have to make.[42]

The voices of black alienation and black wisdom were again, combined this time in a group whose politics clearly were counter to almost everything America considered was in its self-interest on the
international scene. Adherents of Black Power were among the earliest
black critics of the war in Vietnam, on the grounds that it was racist,
anti-revolutionary, and diverted critically needed men and money
from the ghettos.

By the end of 1966 Carmichael was suggesting that sncc change its
name to the Student Liberation Movement, thereby identifying themselves with anti-colonial national liberation movements throughout
the non-white world. Before 1967 was over, he would be in Havana—
at a conference of Latin-American revolutionaries—echoing the calls
of Robert Williams for a black guerrilla-type liberation struggle in
the ghettos of America. And later he would visit Hanoi. Thus he became the most recent leader in the long procession of black aliens
("alien" is used in its broadest sense) who have lost faith in the
promises of the American way. At the same time, however, like so
many of these aliens, he has found it almost impossible to break
completely with American myths and formulate a constructive radical
program that, in the last analysis, does not depend upon the grudging
largesse and enlightened self-interest of the white American society.[43]

VI

sncc was only the clearest manifestation of a black radicalism that
had many indigenous ghetto roots as, was shown when a National Conference on Black Power met in July, 1967, in Newark, New Jersey.
Although various radicals seriously questioned the motivation of the
conveners and would not attend, a thousand Afro-Americans came
from scores of different communities (the Newark uprising earlier
in the month was a spectacular spur to attendance).[44]

The speeches, clothing, and variety of visions and commitments
showed that every strain of black radicalism was represented at this
meeting. Indeed, there was an awesome terror in the fact that—more
than a century after the Civil War—these strains should still be so
obvious in the North and often so strong: separatism, radical black
nonviolence, armed struggle, the Harlem Mau Mau. And a telegram

was received from Robert Williams, in Peking, urging a long guerrilla struggle. The entire scene was filled with a sense of angry, outraged determination, and sometimes one could sense an air of millennarian expectation.

White members of the press corps tasted black anger at some of the four-day sessions; indeed, their bodily eviction from one of the meeting places was symptomatic of the intensity and hostility of some of the younger radicals. Members of this group urged a march through the streets, in direct confrontation with the police riot forces that patrolled the area, to protest the fact that hundreds of blacks still were in jail as a result of the recent uprising. At the highly charged plenary session where this call was issued, more than at any other time, this group resembled conventional revolutionary elements. Rap Brown and others, however, reminded the activists that violent action alone did not make radicals or revolutionaries; Brown suggested that persons who would lead unarmed men to face the guns of the frightened Newark policemen were either irresponsible fools or *agents provocateurs*. "First go and get your guns," he counseled; "then lead the march."

There was no march, partly because there were few guns, but also because black radicalism had not yet found a leader who could challenge the romanticized memory of Malcolm X and rally the forces for such a desperate move. It is much more likely, however, that there was no march because black radicalism had not yet created a program sufficiently clear and compelling to demand the rational allegiance of those who must march and perhaps die. It was obvious to many participants at Newark that such an ideology and its accompanying program would not spring from so large and disparate a group of persons and organizations.

But it was equally evident that such a gathering, if only for purposes of initial contact, could be most important. The lack of a leader and a clearly articulated framework of thought did not negate the significance of the meeting. The African costumes of explosive color, the proudly "natural" hair styles, the many persons who had adopted African and Islamic names in exchange for their "slave names," the impassioned and sometimes dangerously fiery debate—all this testified to vitality in the radical edges of the black movement.

Although the dominant idiom of the conference was the language of the ghetto, how serious was the talk of beginning a national debate on possible partition? This is yet to be seen, especially when one reflects on the fact that the delegates were housed in two of Newark's most expensive, white-owned hotels and when one recalls the black action at the New Politics convention in Chicago one month later.[45] (The luxurious housing reminded many persons of the continued dependence upon white benevolence, and the appearance in Chicago seems a strange prelude to black partition.) How significant was the constant discussion of black revolution? One of its foremost exponents, Ron Karenga, said: "We are the last revolutionaries in America. If we fail to leave a legacy of revolution for our children we have failed our mission and should be dismissed as unimportant." Although Karenga, like others, believes the cultural revolution of black consciousness is most important at the present time, he has vividly pictured the next stage:

> When the word is given we'll see how tough you are. When it's "burn," let's see how much you burn. When it's "kill," let's see how much you kill. When it's "blow up," let's see how much you blow up. And when it's "take that white girl's head too," we'll really see how tough you are.[46]

After the Newark Conference Rap Brown, SNCC's chairman, added his cry: "Straighten up America, or we'll burn you down."

Had revolt come out of hiding, no longer fearful of white men's thoughts or fists? If it had come out of hiding, what were the implications of revolution, of threats to wage war by fire? As a collective black *cri de coeur* the threats and implications were completely understandable. As radical programs, as proposals to change America by guns and flames, they were at least open to question, especially because so many of the front-line ghetto guerrillas are so young, impressionable, and desperate for a self-affirming role in life. Would the advocates of guerrilla warfare miss the point that paratroopers were brought into Detroit, some of them veterans of guerrilla struggles in Vietnam? Did they misjudge America's military capacity to crush troublesome revolutionaries, or had they overestimated their own strength? Were they responsible for the young black dead in those calls for guns? Had they felt that death was preferable to the stunted, broken lives that would be forced upon those teen-age boys? Did they deem death in Newark and Detroit more honorable than death in Vietnam? At Newark, and especially after the Detroit riot, many less publicized black radicals began to evaluate the military assets of America much more carefully and to speak less frequently of urban warfare. For some of them this coming to realistic terms with American power led (as it had often led in the past) from black radicalism to despair and total cynicism. Others felt that "liberty or death" was still a meaningful cry, regardless of paratroopers. But they knew that both liberty and meaningful struggles to the death required far more planning and discipline than had yet evolved in the black movement.

Shortly after the Newark Conference, with the sounds of Detroit's dying still hanging in the air, it became clear that the nation's resistance to basic change was pushing relatively moderate black leaders into more radical positions. This was especially true of Martin Luther King, Jr. who had already become a major critic of American foreign policy and the war in Vietnam. At the end of August, 1967, in another SCLC convention, King called for a level of central economic planning that could have been easily labelled as socialism. Of even more immediate importance for the black movement, the SCLC leader went on to announce plans for his organization's entry into the kind of radical, massive civil disobedience which had been urged by Wyatt T. Walker and others four years before.

Soon it became clear that King intended to expand the struggle of black people in America to take in other oppressed minorities in the land: Indians, Mexican-Americans, Puerto Ricans, and poor whites. He promised to mobilize these forces and move on Washington, D.C. in a "last chance" for nonviolent direct action. There was even talk of "dislocating" the city until Congress and the nation acted on the needs and demands of the poor. The obvious revolutionary potentials of such a class-oriented mobilization were not lost on the minds of many persons. In his plans for a "Poor People's Campaign," King was now going in a direction which seemed far removed from Montgomery in 1955 and Washington in 1963—but was it?

Whatever the meaning of his actions, his mood was indicated late in 1967 when he faced an Atlanta, Georgia audience, pressed his hands up to his eyes and said, "My God, the dream I once had for America seems to be turning into a nightmare." On April 4, 1968, in Memphis, Tennessee, the nightmare was momentarily extended to the world when a sniper's bullet blasted the life from Martin Luther King who was standing on a motel balcony. Another insistent black seeker after justice had been cut down in America. For countless thousands of Afro-Americans the message seemed clearer than ever before now, and it was articulated by a young speaker in Atlanta on the night of King's death: "O.K., America, Nonviolence is dead. You just killed your last chance for peaceful revolution. We won't forget." The radical black edge had been moved even further out into the bleakness of alienation, and the eventual essential failure of the Poor People's Campaign served to accelerate its motion.

VII

In light of even so cursory an historical survey it is essential to question some of the interpretations of black radicalism in America. John P. Roche, in his introduction to Wilson Record's *Race and Radicalism,* agrees with that book's thesis that

> the "radicalism" of the American Negro today is nothing more than a radical Americanism. Despite subjection to slavery and discrimination, the Negro has never massively responded to gospels of alienation but has persistently and with incredible patience fought for his rightful membership in the American community.[47]

Because these lines were published in 1964, and probably were written at the apex of the nonviolent movement, Mr. Roche might be forgiven for some of his myopia. However, if we have established the fact that radicalism is never measured by "massive" responses, we must add an insistent question mark to such an evaluation of the black radical past. Alienation has often been at its heart, and alienation was its dominant hallmark in the past decade.

In many ways a much more sensitive appreciation of black radicalism is suggested by a European radical. Victor Serge's *"Memoirs of a Revolutionary, 1901–1941"* opens with lines that are strongly reminiscent of some of the men we have met in these pages.

> Even before I emerged from childhood, I seem to have experienced, deeply at heart, that paradoxical feeling which was to dominate me all through the first part of my life: that of living in a world without any possible escape, in which there was nothing . . . but to fight for an impossible escape. I felt repugnance mingled with wrath and indignation, toward people whom I saw settled comfortably in this world. How could they not be conscious of their captivity, of their unrighteousness?

Irving Howe wrote, in response to this remarkably sensitive opening of the heart: "Few Americans could, in good faith, say as much: perhaps none but a handful of jail-hardened militants at the outer edge of the Negro movement who have chosen alienation from American society as a badge of honor." [48]

Howe is only partly right. The number of alienated black militants greatly exceeds "a handful," and they are not on the "outer edge" of the Negro movement in America; indeed, the center of the movement draws closer to them each day. And they discovered their "badge of honor" buried deep within their breasts almost as soon as they came to know themselves.

What is the future of this black radicalism that claims no desire for membership in the American community? Will sensitive, justice-starved black aliens be condemned to an endless search for "an impossible escape"? Are they damned to move, like burning, cursing wraiths, in the midst of unending darkness? Of if they find, from some now unknown source, the strength to do the task, will their most noble vocation be to "tear this building down"? [49] It may be that the growing number of radically engaged black intellectuals will avoid the pitfalls of despair, accommodation, and empty rhetoric and will, instead propose acceptable alternatives to the society they increasingly scorn. Therefore,—if theory does indeed follow practice, if ideologies are most often worked out in the midst of fiery social transformation —the whole or partial tearing down may yet come, as a beginning rather than as an end.

Are there still grounds for radical hope? Perhaps some statements of the "shining black prince" of this generation's black radicals will help illuminate the enigmatic answers to this question. In one of his most thoughtful moments Malcolm X entered into the black radical religious tradition to speak of judgment and atonement:

> I believe that God now is giving the world's so-called 'Christian' white society its last opportunity to repent and atone for the crimes of exploiting and enslaving the world's non-white peoples, but is white America really sorry for her crimes against the black people? Does white America have the capacity to repent—and to atone? Does the capacity to repent, to atone, exist in a majority, in one-half, in even one-third of American white society? Indeed, how *can* white society atone for enslaving, for raping, for unmanning, for

otherwise brutalizing *millions* of human beings, for centuries? What atonement would the God of Justice demand for the robbery of the black people's labor, their lives, their true identities, their culture, their history—and even their human dignity? [50]

The former "Detroit Red" knew the ghettos well enough to be clear on what was *not* the answer: "A desegregated cup of coffee, a theater, public toilets—the whole range of hypocritical 'integration'— these are not atonement." Malcolm X was never given a clear answer nor did he provide one, but the man who saw life in America "like it is" also knew that it must get much better or much worse. "Only such real, meaningful actions as those which are sincerely motivated from a deep sense of humanism and moral responsibility can get at the basic causes that produce the racial explosions in America today." Without such actions, "the racial explosions are only going to grow worse." [51]

This was written in 1964, a few months before the man who struggled to grow under the menace from Detroit Red to El-Hajj Malik El-Shabazz was given a personal reply to the questions he had so insistently raised. Nor was Martin King allowed to come any closer to the "Promised Land" of true freedom which he constantly spoke of. Would it really materialize in America as he desperately hoped to the end, or would there come instead some brutal fulfillment of the tragic nightmares both he and Malcolm had foreseen? Whether their deaths were an answer or only another question is not certain, but this much seems sure: Unless America becomes as different from the rest of the world as its most blind lovers already believe it is, the necessary radical social movement toward black liberation (and therefore toward the liberation of all) will not take place without the acute suffering and the shedding of blood that has long been predicted by black radicals. The hundreds of billions of dollars, the unfeigned national commitment, the transformation of priorities and energies will not be produced without stark agony, if they come at all.

There is still a minority among black radicals who view themselves not only as major architects of the new ways and seers of the new visions but also as suffering servants who must pay the price for the change. But there is a larger group, the young and rising black tide, which, despite its alienation, has been "too American" to accept (or understand) such a role. They see blood and they know it probably will be theirs. They hear the voices of police chiefs and other officials who promise to respond to their black rebellions and to riot commission reports with increased firepower. They realize that one police commissioner most likely speaks for many others when he says "We're in a war, and law enforcement is going to win." When they heard the President of the United States define "crime in the streets" as the major domestic problem, they knew he was speaking of them. These black young men see blood, but they are determined it shall not be theirs alone. Whatever they seek in life, they seek no separate death, and the words of Malcolm X are often on their lips: "It takes two to tango. If I go, you go"—a despairing invitation to the dance of death. Surely it is not an intellectual's radical program, but for black men (especially the young and cast-off) who consider themselves "under the white man's menace, out of time," it is understandable—in the absence of other programs.

Can the menace be lifted and the times set right? Or will the forces of law and order—and death—again prevail over radical black visions of justice and hope? Will every Martin Luther King have to be buried in his native land before he can really be "free at last"? Historians can deftly refer such questions to various prophets, and walk away, but it may be that the prophets of long ago who spoke of sowing and reaping will have the last, the final, word.

[1] It has not been possible to trace this comment to its source; perhaps it is only part of the black mythology.

[2] "Outcast," in *Selected Poems* (New York, 1953), p. 41.

[3] *Here I Stand* (New York, 1958), p. 28 (emphasis in original).

In my history of the development of black radicalism since 1800, *Black Radicalism in America* (Indianapolis, 1969), I deal with Robeson at some length. One of the most interesting evaluations of his role in the Negro protest movement is Harold Cruse's *The Crisis of the Negro Intellectual* (New York, 1967), pp. 285–301.

[4] Lerone Bennett, Jr., *The Negro Mood* (Chicago, 1964), p. 10.

[5] *Idem, Confrontation: Black and White* (Baltimore, 1966), p. 169: "The Myth of Negro Progress . . . is the only thing that stands between the Negro and revolt."

[6] Louise Thompson, "Southern Terror," *Crisis*, 41 (November, 1934): 328.

[7] For a brief and perhaps more philosophically oriented examination of the path from Montgomery to the ghetto explosions, see my "Where

Have All the Lovers Gone?" in Alan D. Austin, ed., *The Revolutionary Imperative* (Nashville, 1966), pp. 110–27.

[8] Few works deal adequately with the historical developments of the 1945–55 preparatory period, but two lively and valuable accounts are Bennett's *Confrontation*, pp. 169–91, and Langston Hughes' *Fight for Freedom* (New York, 1962), pp. 90–139.

[9] The story of Montgomery is covered adequately (but not critically) in Martin Luther King, Jr., *Stride toward Freedom* (New York, 1958), and Lerone Bennett, *What Manner of Man?* (Chicago, 1965), pp. 55–105.

[10] Some of the earlier ideas of Farmer and Randolph on nonviolent direct action are recorded in Bennett's *Confrontation* (pp. 145–54) and James Farmer's "Memorandum to A. J. Muste" in Francis L. Broderick and August Meier, eds., *Negro Protest Thought in the Twentieth Century* (Indianapolis, 1965), pp. 210–21.

[11] King, *Stride toward Freedom*, pp. 177–78.

[12] In "This Is SCLC," in Broderick and Meier, eds., *Negro Protest Thought*, pp. 269–70.

[13] A general treatment of the student movement up to 1963 is Howard Zinn's *SNCC, The New Abolitionists* (Boston, 1964).

[14] Robert F. Williams, *Negroes with Guns* (New York, 1962), p. 63. Harold Cruse's *Crisis of the Negro Intellectual* (esp. pp. 347–419) raises important questions about the meaning of Williams' call for armed self-defense and about the current popularity of the urban guerrilla-warfare concept among black radicals.

[15] Williams, *Negroes with Guns*, p. 46.

[16] See *idem*, "U.S.A.: The Potential of a Minority Revolution," in Broderick and Meier, eds., *Negro Protest Thought*, pp. 321–33 (published originally in *The Crusader Monthly Newsletter*, vol. 5 [May–June, 1964]).

[17] It is not possible to give proper attention to concurrent developments in the black communities of the North in this essay, but they will be discussed in the aforementioned work on *Black Radicalism*.

[18] Much of the material that follows is based on my own participation in the events in Birmingham. See also Bennett's treatment in *Confrontation*, pp. 235–44, and *The Negro Mood*, pp. 3–23. (Randolph's March on Washington Movement developed in the 1940's.)

[19] This section is based on my recollections of conversations I heard in Birmingham and elsewhere at that time.

[20] This is based on my conversation during the fall of 1963 with John Lewis, whose speech was censored. The unabridged version of the speech is available in Staughton Lynd, ed., *Nonviolence in America* (Indianapolis, 1966), pp. 482–85. See also Julius Lester, "The Angry Children of Malcolm X," *Sing Out* (November, 1966), p. 22, for his knowledgeable ac-

count of the circumstances of the March on Washington. It was from the speakers' platform in Washington that the nation first heard of the death of W. E. B. Du Bois in Ghana, announced by Roy Wilkins.

21 In Bennett, *Confrontation,* p. 244. The Poor People's Campaign of 1968 was meant to realize much of Walker's hope for massive civil disobedience. See below, pp. 41–42.

22 Lester, "The Angry Children of Malcolm X," pp. 24–25.

23 Williams, "U.S.A.," in Broderick and Meier, eds., *Negro Protest Thought,* p. 330.

24 The most fascinating account of Malcolm X's conversion to the Nation of Islam cause is in his *Autobiography* (New York, 1966), pp. 151–210. The first edition of the *Autobiography* was published in 1965.

25 In Malcolm X and James Farmer, "Separation or Integration: A Debate," in Broderick and Meier, eds., *Negro Protest Thought,* p. 363 (published originally in *Dialogue Magazine,* vol. 2 (May, 1962).

26 *Ibid.,* p. 365. Unfortunately, it is not possible for this essay to develop the ironic theme of the "Americanness"—and therefore innate conservatism—of the Nation of Islam.

27 In George Breitman, ed., *Malcolm X Speaks* (New York, 1965), pp. 49–50, 56–57.

28 *Ibid.,* p. 35. Of course Malcolm X knew that mainland China was not a member of the United Nations. Rather he was being pointedly precise when he referred to that country as "waiting" to throw its weight on the side of the black cause.

29 *Ibid.,* pp. 43, 128–29.

30 *Ibid.,* pp. 141–42.

31 Quoted in Dudley Randall and Margaret G. Burroughs, eds., *For Malcolm X* (Detroit, 1967), p. 16. Hayden's lines are part of a longer poem, "El-Hajj Malik El-Shabazz."

32 For the background of SNCC's participation in the Voter Education Project, see Pat Watters and Reese Cleghorn, *Climbing Jacob's Ladder* (New York, 1967), pp. 41–74.

33 Again, much of the material that follows is based on my experience in Mississippi and my relationships with many persons who were involved in the 1964 experiment. For an independently formulated corroboration of my views, see Alvin F. Poussaint, "How the 'White Problem' Spawned 'Black Power,' " *Ebony,* August, 1967, pp. 88–94.

34 This paragraph is based partly on my conversations with SNCC staff members who helped formulate the strategy for the MFDP challenge and who were present in Atlantic City (especially Charlie Cobb, James Foreman, and Robert Moses). See also Len Holt, *The Summer That Didn't End* (New York, 1965), pp. 149–183.

[35] The Selma episode is treated in Bennett, *Confrontation*, p. 252.

[36] In Clyde Halisi and James Mtume, eds., *The Quotable Karenga* (Los Angeles, 1967), p. 13.

[37] Lester, "The Angry Children of Malcolm X," p. 25.

[38] *Ibid.*

[39] Dr. King's account of the Mississippi discussions can be found in his *Where Do We Go from Here?* (New York, 1967), pp. 23–32.

[40] Fanon's work, *The Wretched of the Earth* (New York, 1965), has often—and rightly—been mandatory reading material for would-be revolutionaries of the non-white world.

[41] One of the most fascinating aspects of the entire situation is the fact that the American Communist Party jettisoned the self-determination theme when the hope for integration had been paramount, in 1959 and 1960. Partly as a result of this move, they often find they are ideologically outflanked in their efforts to make contact with the newest black movements. Instead they must watch—no doubt in doubled vexation—as Peking-oriented Marxists enter the black nationalist mood with what seems to be much greater ease. For the story of the American Communists' change, see Joseph C. Mouledous, "From Browderism to Peaceful Co-Existence," *Phylon*, 25, 1 (Spring, 1964): 79–90. James Farmer, the national chairman of CORE, offers a terse but intriguing comment on some of the Mao–black nationalist relationships in his *Freedom When?* (New York, 1965), pp. 102–3.

[42] "Towards Black Liberation," *Massachusetts Review* (Autumn, 1966), pp. 648–51.

[43] This problem is evidenced throughout Carmichael's book (co-authored with Charles Hamilton), *Black Power* (New York, 1967).

[44] The statements concerning the Newark Conference are based almost entirely on my own notes and reflections as a participant.

[45] The relationship of the New Politics convention to the development of black radicalism will be discussed in my aforementioned essay, on *Black Radicalism*.

[46] In Halisi and Mtume, *The Quotable Karenga*, pp. 11, 10.

[47] In Wilson Record, *Race and Radicalism: The NAACP and the Communist Party in Conflict* (Ithaca, N.Y., 1964), p. vi.

[48] In Irving Howe, ed., *Steady Work: Essays in the Politics of Democratic Radicalism, 1953–1966* (New York, 1966), pp. 258, 258–59.

[49] A nineteenth-century Afro-American spiritual constantly repeats these words: "If I had-a my way, I'd tear this building down." See one version of the song in Sterling A. Brown *et al.*, eds., *The Negro Caravan* (New York, 1941), p. 443.

[50] Malcolm X, *Autobiography*, p. 370.

[51] *Ibid.*, pp. 370, 377.

Marxism and the New Left

Howard Zinn

Howard Zinn elsewhere explored some of the differences in "style" between the Old Left of the 1930's and the New Left of the 1960's.* In this essay he focuses on the relationship of the New Left to Marxian theory. Impatient with the limitations of anti-theory on the one hand and dogmatism on the other, he writes: "If the New Left is wise, it will take from Marxism not all of the exact propositions about the world Marx and Engels lived in . . . but its approach. This approach demands a constant redefinition of theory in light of immediate reality, and an insistence on action as a way of testing and reworking theory."

Zinn's experiences as citizen and scholar bridge the philosophic worlds and the two generations he writes of. His scholarship on the thirties is represented by his monograph *La Guardia in Congress* (New York, 1959) and by his anthology *New Deal Thought* (Indianapolis, 1966), which emphasized the unfulfilled programs of the reform movement. *SNCC: The New Abolitionists* (Boston, 1964) and *The Southern Mystique* (New York, 1965) have shown him to be a leading interpreter of one of the most important New Left movements and the Southern scene it has been trying to remold. Both books draw on his experience as Chairman of the Department of History at Spelman College, Atlanta. *Vietnam: The Logic of Withdrawal* (Boston, 1967) bespeaks his commitment as a trenchant critic of American foreign policy.

Zinn's articles have appeared in a dozen or more leading journals. He is currently at work on a history of the United States since World War II. Zinn received his doctorate from Columbia and was a Fellow in East Asian studies at Harvard. He is now a member of the Department of Government at Boston University.

* "A Comparison of the Militant Left of the Thirties and Sixties" (in Morton J. Frisch and Martin Diamond, eds., *The Thirties: A Reconsideration in Light of the American Political Tradition* [DeKalb, Ill., 1968]).

Between the thirties and the sixties the American left was ground down by war, the cold war, McCarthyism, and prosperity. The New Left that has emerged shares many of the old concerns: poverty in the midst of wealth, sins committed against the Negro, limitations on free expression by congressional committees and public prosecutors, shameful behavior in foreign policy. And yet it is different: the new militant groups lack ideology to an extent that was unthinkable in the Old Left.

Alfred Kazin, in *Starting Out in the Thirties*, referred to many leftists of his time as "ideologues." [1] They were always attending classes on Marxist theory on buying or selling or arguing about works by the "Big Four" (Marx, Engels, Lenin, and Stalin—with Trotsky sometimes substituted for Stalin). They engaged in endless discussions on surplus value, dialectical materialism, the absolute impoverishment of the working class, Plekhanov's theory of the role of the individual, Stalin's views on "the national question," Engel's views on the origin of the family, and Lenin on economism, or imperialism, or social democracy, or "the woman question." This essay, then, will discuss the special qualities of the New Left—in contrast to those of the Old Left—including its relationship to Marxian theory.

To represent the New Left of today I have chosen those elements that I know best (there are of course others): the Student Nonviolent Coordinating Committee, the most aggressive of the Negro organizations; Students for a Democratic Society, which conducts a variety of activities concerned with civil rights and foreign policy, on college campuses and in depressed urban areas; and that assorted group of intellectuals, civil rights workers, and draft-card burners who have actively opposed the war in Vietnam.

The people in SNCC, by and large, know little about Marx and have no manifesto or other laid-down guide to the truth. Their discussions, rarely theoretical, deal mostly with day-to-day practical problems: a tent city in Lowndes County, Alabama, hunger in Greenville, Mississippi, the Freedom Democratic Party, how to meet their next payroll, and the like. SDS has more white, more middle-class, and more intellectual people than SNCC, and thus they have read more of Marx, but they don't seem to take him as gospel. The Old Left would have had a quotation from Lenin on the headquarters wall but, in the dilapidated SNCC offices in Atlanta I saw not long ago:

> Ever danced out on a limb?
> It doesn't always break.
> And sometimes when it does you fall
> into a grassy meadow.

This refreshing lack of pompous intellectuality, however—of quotations from the great, of a "line"—has an unfortunate side: the lack of analyses of alternative tactics, systems, and institutions. Would public corporations, or private cooperatives, or nationalized enterprises serve society best, and in what situations? Should one work inside or outside the present two-party system? What institutions can substitute for the repressive state in a new society? It nevertheless is admirable that the new generation of radicals starts with no oaths of loyalty, has no illusions about the purity of any nation or system.

It has seen Stalinism unmasked, by Khrushchev. It has seen aggression, subversion, and double-dealing on all sides, West as well as East, by the "free world" as well as the "communist world." It remembers Russia's aggression in Hungary and China's repression in Tibet, and it is very much aware of the problem of power in even the best revolution. But the new generation of radicals also knows that the American CIA overthrew a democratically elected government in Guatemala, that the United States conspired in the invasion of Cuba, that our Marines invaded the Dominican Republic in violation of the Rio Pact. The new radicals, who have grown up in a world where force and deception are ubiquitous, have developed a healthy disposition to call all shots as they see them.

The Old Left was sectarian, suspicious, exclusive; Socialists would expel Communists, Trotskyists would expel Socialists, and Communists would expel almost everyone. Although SNCC indulges in sniping at

other civil rights groups, SNCC—and SDS as well—are open organizations: they welcome anyone who will work, regardless of his affiliation
or ideology. In 1963, when Theodore White referred to "penetration"
of SNCC by "unidentified elements" (White seemed bashful about saying he meant Communists),[2] Bob Moses, leader of the Mississippi
project, replied for SNCC: "It seems to me that . . . we have to throw
what little weight we have on the side of free association."[3]

The radicals of the thirties, immersed in traditional politics, ran
their candidates and sought entry into legislative bodies: William Z.
Foster and Earl Browder were Communist candidates for President
at various times; Norman Thomas was the perennial Socialist candidate for President. Their suspicion of parliamentary democracy did
not seem very penetrating. Despite the fact that the cards are stacked
against minority candidates in the American electoral system—Socialists who had been elected to Congress and to the New York legislature were expelled during World War I and New York City abolished
the system of proportional representation when Communists succeeded
in electing party members to the city council—the Communist and the
Socialist parties retained a curious faith in the ballot box.

The militants of today, although they have worked hard in the
South to register Negroes to vote, have formed the Freedom Democratic Party in Mississippi and the Lowndes County Freedom Organization in Alabama, and have tried to replace the Mississippi congressional delegation with black Mississippians, have always had a basic
mistrust of politics.[4] The vote, these New Left people know, is only an
occasional flicker of democracy in an otherwise elitist system. The
voice of the people, therefore, must be manifested in other ways: by
day-to-day activity, by demonstrations, by a politics of constant protest rather than by the traditional politics of the ballot.

One cannot define the radicalism of the New Left in Marxian terms
without *re*definition, for the spirit of Marxism requires that one declare what something *is* by declaring what it *should be*. Marxism
assumes that everything, including an idea, takes on a new meaning
in each additional moment of time, in each unique historical situation.
It tries to avoid academic scholasticism, which dutifully pretends to
record in full, to describe accurately—forgetting that mere description
is the same as circumscription. The pretense of "passive" description
is what Herbert Marcuse calls "operationalism."[5]

It is the spirit, not the letter, of Marxism that the New Left upholds—not a fixed body of dogma to be put into big black books or little red books but a set of specific propositions about the modern world that are both tough and tentative. Also, such propositions have a vague but exhilarating vision of the future and, more fundamentally, reflect an approach to life—a particular way of thinking about thinking as well as about being. Most of all, this way of thinking is intended to promote action. If the New Left is wise, it will take from Marxism not all the exact propositions about the world that Marx and Engels lived in (a world that today is partly the same and partly different), but its approach, which demands constant redefinitions of theory in the light of immediate reality and insistence on *action* as a way of both testing and reworking theory.

One of Marx's most-quoted statements—and one most ignored in practice—is point 11 in his *Theses on Feuerbach* (written about 1845): "The philosophers have only interpreted the world in various ways; the point however is to change it." Because every body of ideas is part of the world, this suggests that one cannot merely *interpret* Marxism, and the New Left, but must *change* them in the course of the discussion. Earlier in his *Theses* Marx criticized Feuerbach's emphasis on "the theoretical attitude." "Social life is essentially practical," Marx said. "All mysteries . . . find their rational solution in human practice." [6]

In their best moments, thinking revolutionaries agree with this. In Yenan after the "Long March," Mao Tse-tung in his lecture "On Practice" talked of the primacy of experience in knowledge, of the union of perceptual knowledge with rational knowledge and of rationalism with empiricism. "The Marxist recognizes that in the absolute, total process of the development of the universe, the development of each concrete process is relative; hence in the great stream of absolute truth, man's knowledge of the concrete process at each given stage of development is only relatively true." [7] This spirit, of course, is different from the spirit one often encounters in the *Peking Review* these days, in the many articles headed "Long Live Chairman Mao." [8]

To "act out" the Marxian approach is to remind ourselves, even at this moment of writing-reading, that much of what is called "intellectual history" is the aimless dredging up of what is and was rather than a creative recollection of experience that points to the betterment of human life. We are surrounded by solemn, pretentious argument about what Marx or Machiavelli or Rousseau really meant, about who was right and who was wrong—all of which is another way the pedant has of saying "I am right and you are wrong." Too much of what passes for the critical discussion of public issues is really a personal duel for honor or privilege, with each discussant like the character in *Catch–22* who saw every event as either a feather in his cap or a black eye—and this while men were dying all around him.

This scholasticism, oddly enough, is typical not only of the Old Left but of today's academic journals, which would be horrified at being called left or right, and indeed can hardly be accused of moving in any direction. And because the New Left is a successor to the Old Left in American history, and because to a large extent it comes from the academic world (whether from the Negro colleges of the South or the Berkeleys of the North), it is always tempted by theoretical irrelevancies. Fortunately, however, the young people of today seem more nimble than their predecessors in avoiding this trap.

The valuable contributions of the Old Left—and they were considerable—came not out of its ideological fetishism but from its action. Its dynamism came not from its classroom sessions on surplus value but from the organization of the CIO, not from the analyses of Stalin's views on "the national question" but from the fight for the Scottsboro boys, not from the labored rationales for dictatorship of the proletariat but from the sacrifices of the Abraham Lincoln Battalion. I am not arguing against theoretical discussions, or against long-range principles, or the analysis of sub-surface realities, I am asserting that theory must be informed by observation and must be expressed in action. It must, in other words, be relevant.

Robert Havemann, a German Marxist and physicist whose views got him into difficulty with the East German regime, said in his Leipzig lectures "Dialectic without Dogma?":

> Dialectical materialism is not a philosophy in the sense of any earlier philosophical doctrine or system. It is a *Weltanschauung*, a fundamental spiritual attitude and a method of thought, which comprehends the world in its insuperable contradictoriness as well as in its unity. But it is not a philosophical catechism made up of principles and general definitions that are immutable, eternal, and binding . . . the dialectical-materialist philosophy is not a court that can decide questions before they have been settled scientifically.[9]

This admixture of pragmatism, empiricism, and existentialism into Marxist theory goes straight back to the *Theses on Feuerbach* and straight ahead to the spirit of the New Left.

A materialist approach should, in the Marxian sense, make suggestions rather than demands; for example, that we should know the situational circumstances behind men's behavior and thoughts if we want to affect them. A dialectical approach, in the Marxian sense, suggests that we evaluate a situation not as fixed but in motion, and that this evaluation affects that motion. Dialectical materialism asks awareness that we are creatures of limited vision, ocularly and intellectually, and therefore must not assume that we see or perceive everything—that conflicting tendencies often lie beneath the surface of events.

These are not just academic considerations; such an approach should make it easier for us to understand what is wrong when the government says to a penniless Negro in the Mississippi delta: We have passed a law, and now you are free. Such an approach should help us sense the elements of a violent insurrection as we walk past the tenements of a city that temporarily is quiet. Marx's emphasis on the tyranny of economics can't tell us *how much* economic motivation is behind a specific political act, but it can lead us to look for it. Thus the New Left might go overboard in stressing economic interests in Southeast Asia as an explanation for our escalation of the war in Vietnam—but it might be devilishly right in noting the connection between the United States' economic interests in Latin-American nations and the pro-American votes of these nations in the UN. Marxism doesn't tell us exactly what we will find beneath the surface, it suggests what we should look for; and it certainly insists that we look. A Marxist would have given Lysenko his microscope, but it was a Stalinist who told him—or created an atmosphere that told him—what he must find with it.

If someone says that this is not dialectical materialism or Marxism, that it is simply common sense, or rationalism, or pragmatism, or naturalism, the New Left is not disposed to argue. Who cares about credit? The Old Left, on the other hand, didn't like to admit relationships with any other ideology; it remained virginal and lonely.

There has been much talk about a Christian-Marxist dialogue, but if such a dialogue is to be useful perhaps it should begin with the idea that both God and Marx are dead but Yossarian lives. This is only another way of saying: Let's not spend our time arguing whether God exists or what Marx really meant, because while we argue the world moves; while we publish, others perish. The best use of our energy is in resisting those who would send us, after so many missions of murder, on still another such mission.

The new radicalism, I believe, should be anti-ideological, in the sense I have discussed, but it should also be—and has not sufficiently been—concerned with theory. It needs a vision of what it is working toward, a vision that is based on transcendental human needs and that will not be limited by the reality we are stuck with. This theory should analyze the present reality, but not through the prism of old, fixed categories—rather, with awareness of the uniqueness of the here and now, of the need to make its irrationality intelligible to those around us. Such a theory would also explore, in the midst of action, the best techniques for social change in the particular circumstances of the moment.

In the first requirement of this theory, the vision of the future, the Marxian vision is useful. (Of course it is vague, but what better guard is there against dogmatism?) I call this a Marxian vision, even though many non-Marxists have held the same type of vision, because —while it is necessary to emphasize to the left that it does not have a monopoly on compassion or insight— it is necessary to remind everyone else—Christians, Jews, Buddhists, Humanists, etc.—that they share various common aims with Marxism. Because none of these groups can revolutionize the world by itself, all must be reminded of a consensus of humanistic values that has developed in the modern world. Marxists and liberals, at their best (they have not usually been at their best), share this consensus in theory. One of the great contributions of the New Left can be to remind Marxist and liberal capitalist countries alike how far they are straying from the values they claim.

In *The Holy Family*, one of their early writings (about 1845), Marx and Engels said that man should be "not negatively free to avoid this or that event [but] positively free to express his true individuality." They said this requires arranging the empirical world around us so that "man experiences and assimilates there what is really human, that he experiences himself as man," and that, rather than punishing individuals for their crimes, we should "destroy the social conditions which engender crime, and give to each individual the scope which he needs in society in order to develop his life." [10] This speaks to the so-called socialist countries of today that imprison writers who speak their minds. It also speaks to a country like the United States, which gives its people the negative freedoms of the Bill of Rights but very unequally limits the scope in which they can develop their individuality, can exercise their freedom—so that some children can roam in little suburban mansions surrounded by gardens and others are equally free to play in rat-infested tenements. Although everyone has freedom of speech, the corporation with a million dollars to spend on television can speak to thirty million people and the individual with only a soap box can speak to thirty people.

What makes the New Left so critical of the wealthiest nation in the world is its acute consciousness that freedom means not only legal permission to occupy space but the resources with which to make the most of this freedom. The New Left has not even begun to think of a way to explain this complex problem of freedom to everyone in the United States who has been brought up on simplistic high school history books and American Legion essay contests. The new radicalism can be made really new, and really pertinent to the here and now, if (without recourse to the stale slogans about "bourgeois freedom") it can do justice to the degree of genuine freedom that exists for people in the United States—to speak, to write, to spend—while noting that freedom *is* a matter of degree, that freedom in America is like wealth, plentiful but unequally distributed.

Let me turn to another element in the Marxian vision. There is still a widespread popular belief (heavily stressed on the *Reader's Digest* level) that Marxism believes in the supremacy of the state over the individual and democracy believes the opposite. Indeed, the existence of oppressively overbearing states that call themselves Marxist reinforces this idea. A true radicalism, however, would remind people in socialist and in capitalist countries—for in both of these the state is an oppressive force—of the hope of Marx and Engels (expressed in the Manifesto) that some day "the public power will lose its political character" and "we shall have an association in which the free development of each is the condition for the free development of all." This was not just a youthful aberration (it is fashionable now to speak of the young, romantic Marx and the old, practical Marx) because twenty-five years later, in his *Critique of the Gotha Program*, Marx said: "Freedom consists in converting the state from an organ superimposed upon society into one completely subordinate to it." As for the necessity of the state's education of the people, "the state has need, on the contrary, of a very stern education by the people." And in 1884, one year after Marx's death, Engels wrote in his *Origin of the Family, Private Property and the State*:

> The society that will organize production on the basis of a free and equal association of the producers will put the whole machinery of state where it will then belong: into the museum of antiquities, by the side of the spinning wheel and the bronze ax.[11]

This attitude to the state is even more clear and specific in Marx's *The Civil War in France* and Engels' introduction to it.[12] Both men admiringly cite the Paris Commune of early 1871, which abolished conscription and the standing army, declared universal suffrage, proclaimed the right of citizens to recall their elected officials at any time, decreed that all officials, high or low, should be paid the same wages as other workers, and publicly burned the guillotine.

The New Left is similarly anti-authoritarian; it would, I expect, burn draft cards in any society. It is anarchistic not merely in the Marxist sense of the ultimate abolition of the state but in demanding its abolition as an immediate requirement. Authority and coercion, moreover, must be abolished in every sphere of existence, and, from the outset, ends must be represented in the means. Marx and Bakunin disagreed on this point,[13] but the New Left has the advantage over Marx in having had an extra century of history to study. This generation has seen how a dictatorship of the proletariat can easily become a dictatorship over the proletariat, as both Trotsky and Rosa Luxemburg warned.[14] The New Left can well remind the socialist states, as well as the capitalist states, of Marx's letter of 1853 to the *New York Tribune* in which he said he didn't know how capital punishment could be justified "in a society glorying in its civilization." [15]

In America, liberalism and radicalism alike were beguiled into cheering for state power because under F.D.R. it seemed beneficent: it enacted various economic reforms and it waged war against Hitler. The New Left, we must hope, will continue to recognize that a state cannot be trusted, as a "liberal America" could not be trusted to carry reforms far enough or to drop bombs only on Nazi invaders and not on Asian peasants in their own countries. The New Left, therefore, will create constellations of power outside the state to pressure it into humane actions, to resist its inhumane actions, and eventually to replace it by voluntary associations that seek to maintain, in small groups, individuality and cooperation (Black Power, in its best aspects, suggests such an endeavor). The New Left in America has the job of publicly demonstrating that the state, whether a proletarian dictatorship or welfare capitalism, is fundamentally an autonomous special interest and thus deserves not loyalty, but criticism and resistance intermittently, and watchfulness always.

On another important element in the Marxian vision Marx seems to speak even more directly to our present-day mass society, and therefore to the new radicals in mass society, in his *Economic and Philosophical Manuscripts* (1844). The estrangement of man that Marx described pertains not only to the classical proletariat of his own time but to all classes in every modern industrial society, and especially to the young people of the present generation in the United States. He talked of men who produce things that are alien to them, that become (so to speak) monsters that are independent of them (an anticipation, perhaps, of our automobiles, television sets, skyscrapers, and even our universities). Few people find satisfaction in their work; and Marx points to the irony that in man's specifically human functions (working, creating) he feels like an animal, but only in his animal functions (eating, sex) does he feel like a human being. Our specifically human activity is not enjoyable in itself; primarily it is no more than the means for staying alive. Activity *is* life, however, and yet in modern society it becomes only a *means* to life. Thus we become estranged from what we produce (from our own activity), from our fellow men, from nature (here Marxism must share credit with Taoism), and finally from ourselves. We find ourselves living a life that is different from the one we really want to live.[16]

The new radicals of today are conscious of this, and try desperately to escape it. Because they want to do work that is congenial to them, they go to Mississippi or they move into the ghetto, or they don't work at all rather than work at hateful or parasitic jobs. Often they try to create relationships with one another that are not warped by the rules and the demands of the world around them. The basic reason or cause for all these forms of estrangement, Marx said, is that people's activities are coerced rather than free. Thus the young people of today are trying to defy the coercive forces all around them, which is enormously difficult, but the very attempt to do this is a free act.

From all this it is quite clear that Marx valued the free man, in his individuality, his sociality, his oneness with nature. The New Left is in accord here, but it parts, I think, from Marx's claim (although some attribute it to Engels—another academic dispute!) that the vision of unalienated man springs not from a wish but from an observation— from a "scientific" plotting of a historical curve that moves inevitably in the direction of man's freedom. And surely we don't have such confidence in inevitability these days; we've had too many surprises in this century. Simone de Beauvoir, in *The Ethics of Ambiguity*, says that a proletarian uprising is not inevitable; the movement of history can go in many different directions.[17]

Today, furthermore, we are unabashed in declaring our subjective wants and desires; we do not need a "scientific" basis for them. Here again, the debate whether ethical norms are grounded in empirical science is an academic discussion that leads us nowhere (Abraham Edel finds such grounding; Hans Reichenbach says it's not required).[18] Because most people agree on the gross necessities of life—food, sex, peace, freedom, dignity, self-realization—our energy should be spent in working toward achieving them, not in discussing their metaphysical meaning.

I suggested above that the second requirement of a pertinent radical theory is an analysis of the *particulars* of today's reality; and one of Marx's great perceptions was the material basis for man's alienation and unhappiness: the scarcity of goods in society, which produces conflict, exploitation, coercion. Thus abundance is a prerequisite, though not a guarantee, of man's freedom. And thus the United States counterposes these particulars in a paradox: the state that has an enormous productive apparatus—indeed the only state in the world that has the technological base required for communism, in which a communist society would have the greatest chance of preserving the freedom of the individual (because the socialist countries are plagued by scarcity)—becomes apoplectic at the very mention of communism. It is, in short, only in the United States that the slogan "to each according to his need" can have real meaning.

The United States, for example, has enough doctors and hospitals to give adequate medical care to everybody who needs it, without "rationing" this care on the basis of wealth. We grow enough food that we do not, in effect, have to insist that people without money do with very little food. We can, if we want, build enough homes in this country to eliminate slums. And so on.

There is room for much scholarly work here. Economists could work out a specific plan for free food in America, college tuition and allowances, and the like. The New Left, accordingly, should locate and specify the resources of this country, how they are being used, and how they *could* be used.

The Marxian economic categories have long provided material for academic controversy, which the Marx of *Das Kapital* stimulated and the Marx of *Theses on Feuerbach* could only regret. Marx, who was only human, perhaps fell prey to the usual temptations of intellectuals; perhaps he was carried away by his research, curiosity, and his passion for scheme-building and scientific constructions. Was his huge second volume of *Das Kapital* on the circulation of commodities or his long exposition of absolute and differential rent essential to revolutionary theory? Does it really matter whether Böhm-Bawerk was right or wrong on the relationship between surplus value and aggregate prices of production? How relevant is even so brilliant a theory as surplus value to social action? Has the historic militancy of workingmen required such analyses to sustain it? Has such militancy ever been transformed into revolutionary consciousness by the comprehension of the distinction between the use value and exchange value of labor power?

James Bevel seems to be right when he says one can organize large numbers of people only around issues that are obvious or that can easily be made obvious. Thus the New Left, instead of discussing the falling rate of profit or the organic composition of capital, very sensibly appears to be concentrating on what is readily observable: this country has enormous resources that it shamelessly wastes and unjustly distributes. A country that can produce 750 billion dollars worth of goods and services a year (at less than full capacity) should not have ten million families that live below the $3,000-a-year level. All the Chamber of Commerce pronouncements, the fancy *Fortune* magazine charts about our economic progress, the confident State of the Union addresses are seen to be irrelevant during a walk through any major American city, especially through Harlem, or Roxbury, or Chicago's south side.

The most useful Marxian statement about capitalist society also is the most crucial: In an era when production is a social process, and requires rationality, our system is incredibly irrational—because corporate profit, not human need, governs what is produced and what is not produced. In addition, it is irrational because of our huge vested interest—economic, military, political, psychological—in the production of corpses, on which we spend seventy billion dollars a year. We spend another twenty billion dollars a year on public relations, advertising, product promotion. We build too many cars, too many highways, too many office buildings, produce too many cigarets, too much liquor, too many gadgets, and not enough homes, schools, and hospitals. If from corporate after-tax profits of forty billion dollars a year we confiscated thirty billion dollars and distributed it—in services rather than cash (in food, rent, education, health)— to the bottom fifth of our population, we could in one stroke raise them from a $3,000-a-year to a $6,000-a-year standard of living. The New Left, instead of becoming involved in theoretical discussions about economic categories, should find ways to make clear to Americans the wastefulness, irrationality, and unjustness of our economy.

Because of our vision of how men *should* live and the contrast with our knowledge of how they *do* live (although many of us need to be shown how our fellow city dwellers live), the most urgent theoretical question for the New Left (in which traditional Marxism gives least guidance) is: How do we change society? How do we redistribute power in order to redistribute wealth? How do we overcome those who enjoy power and wealth and won't give them up? How do we stop the fanaticism of civilian and military leaders who feel it is America's duty to establish its power (or its puppets) wherever possible in the world, and do not care how many people, Americans or others, they kill in the process?

The traditional Marxian idea of revolution because of a breakdown in the capitalist mechanism and its replacement by an organized class-conscious proletariat is hardly tenable today. (Socialist revolutions have been possible mostly because war had weakened or destroyed a state and created a vacuum in which organized revolutionaries could come to power.) Likewise, the traditional liberal idea of a gradual evolution toward freedom, peace, and democracy through parliamentary reform no longer is supportable. We have seen that poverty and racism can be institutionalized, and only token measures taken to assuage their worst aspects—that by creating a contented, bloated middle class and by introducing state regulatory mechanisms in the economy the status quo can be maintained. Furthermore, we have seen that the President and a small group of advisers can make foreign policy and the mass communications industry can create a nation of sheep who give assent to it.

Certainly in the United States, the traditional idea that the agent of social change will be the proletariat needs reexamination inasmuch as the best-organized workers are bribed into silence with TV and automobiles and are drugged into complacency by entertainment. Unorganized workers, perhaps—and by far most of the labor force is unorganized—may play a part in producing social change, but these consist of white-collar and domestic workers, migratory and farm laborers, and service industry workers, the groups that are the hardest to organize. Recent experience suggests that Negroes, especially those in the ghetto, may be the most powerful single force for social change in the United States. Marx saw the industrial proletariat as the revolutionary force because it was motivated by exploitation and was organized by the factory. Black people in the United States, who also are exploited, are concentrated in the ghetto. Since the protest demonstrations at Berkeley there also is evidence that students, especially as they are pushed closer toward the cannon's mouth, may become another important agent of social change.

How will this change come about? The overwhelming power of the state will permit only tactics that fall short of violent revolution, but these tactics will have to be much more energetic than those of normal parliamentary procedure. Even the mass demonstrations of the civil rights movement were not enough to get more than tokens of change, as L.B.J. recited "We shall overcome." Spontaneous uprisings in the ghetto are alarm signals but they do not produce change. Perhaps it will take systematic, persistent organizing and education, in the ghettos and in the universities. It also will take various kinds of coordinated actions that are designed to shock society out of its lethargy. The New Left's idea of parallel organizations as a way of *demonstrating* what people should do and how people should live has enormous possibilities: freedom schools, free universities, free cities (remember that these grew up in medieval times outside the feudal system)—and pockets of free people inside the traditional cities, universities, and corporations.

Guerrilla warfare arose as an answer to overwhelming centralized military power, and perhaps we are in need of a kind of political guerrilla warfare as an answer to the power of mass society. Enclaves of freedom might be created in the midst of the orthodox way of life, enclaves that would become centers of protest and examples to others. The new radicals must give much thought and direct most of their action to the techniques of organization, pressure, and change.

In this era of the giant state, when the feeling of helplessness is so widespread, we are in special need of the existentialist emphasis on our freedom of action (the Marxist-existentialist debate between determinism and freedom seems to me empty and academic). To stress our freedom, to insist on ignoring a priori restraints and the binding effect of "human nature," is not to ignore that we have a history and a limiting environment. Existentialism, aware of these pressures, also is aware of a huge element of indeterminacy in our combat with the obstacles around us. We never know the exact strength or weakness of resistance to our actions, nor exactly what effect they will have. They may lead to nothing (except in changing us); they may have a tiny cumulative effect (along with a thousand other actions); they may lead to social upheaval. This indeterminacy suggests that we should not be preoccupied with prediction or with measuring immediate success; we should act and take the risk.

We are not totally free, but our strength will be maximized if we act *as if* we are free (this is William James' "as if" merging with Sartre's "freedom").[19] Even as observers, students, theorizers, we are not totally passive; our very thoughts and our statements, speeches, and essays throw a weight into a balance that is sensitive to such acts. The existentialist emphasis on the necessity for action—based on conscience but avoiding careful weighing of what passive liberals call "the realities"—is one of the most refreshing characteristics of the New Left in America. It combines Emerson's transcendentalism, Marx's revolutionary actionism, Dewey's pragmatism, and Camus' rebelliousness. It may yet revive the waning spirit of this country.

[1] Boston, 1965, p. 8.

[2] *Life*, November 29, 1963.

[3] From my notes of a SNCC Executive Committee Meeting.

[4] See Stokely Carmichael and Charles V. Hamilton, *Black Power: The Politics of Liberation in America* (New York, 1967).

[5] *One-Dimensional Man* (Boston, 1964), chap. 4.

[6] Marx and Engels, *Selected Works*, 2 vols. (Moscow, 1958), 2: 405.

[7] *Selected Works of Mao Tse-tung*, 4 vols. (Peking, 1965), 1: 307.

[8] In six consecutive issues of the *Peking Review*, from September 29 through November 3, 1967 (an arbitrary sample), Mao is either mentioned or depicted on the cover of each issue.

[9] Quoted in Neil McInnes, "Havemann and the Dialectic," *Survey* (January, 1967).

[10] In T. B. Bottomore and Maximilien Rubel, eds., *Karl Marx: Selected Writings in Sociology and Social Philosophy* (New York, 1964), p. 243.

[11] Marx and Engels, *Selected Works*, 1: 54, 2: 35, 322.

[12] *Ibid.*, 1: 473–545.

[13] See George Woodcock, *Anarchism* (Cleveland, 1962), chap. 6.

[14] See Rosa Luxemburg, *Leninism or Marxism?* (Ann Arbor, Mich., 1961), p. 84, and Robert V. Daniels, ed., *A Documentary History of Communism* (New York, 1960), p. 31.

[15] In Lewis Feuer, ed., *Marx and Engels: Basic Writings on Politics and Philosophy* (Garden City, N.Y., 1959), p. 487.

[16] See Dirk Struik, ed., *The Economic and Philosophical Manuscripts of 1844* (New York, 1964).

[17] See the passage in George Novack, ed., *Existentialism versus Marxism* (New York, 1966).

[18] See Abraham Edel, *Ethical Judgment* (Glencoe, Ill., 1955), and Hans Reichenbach, *The Rise of Scientific Philosophy* (Berkeley, 1961).

[19] See William James, *Essays in Pragmatism* (New York, 1954), p. 37.

Index